PENGUIN BOOKS

HUMANLY POSSIBLE

Sarah Bakewell had a wandering childhood, growing up on the "hippie trail" through Asia and in Australia. She studied philosophy at the University of Essex and worked for many years as a curator of early printed books at the Wellcome Library, London, before becoming a full-time writer. Her books include *How to Live, or A Life of Montaigne in One Question and Twenty Attempts at an Answer*, which won the Duff Cooper Prize and the National Book Critics Circle Award, and *At the Existentialist Café: Freedom, Being, and Apricot Cocktails*, one of the *New York Times* Ten Best Books of 2016. Bakewell was also among the winners of the 2018 Windham-Campbell Prize. She still has a tendency to wander but is mostly to be found either in London or in Italy with her wife and their family of dogs and chickens.

Praise for *Humanly Possible*

"*Humanly Possible* is a terrific invitation to argument, to conversation, to all the fun people make together, on their own." —*The Washington Post*

"Lively . . . [Bakewell's] new book is filled with her characteristic wit and clarity; she manages to wrangle seven centuries of humanist thought into a brisk narrative, resisting the traps of windy abstraction and glib oversimplification. . . . She puts her entire self into this book, linking philosophical reflections with vibrant anecdotes. She delights in the paradoxical and the particular, reminding us that every human being contains multitudes." —Jennifer Szalai, *The New York Times*

"A book of big and bold ideas, *Humanly Possible* is humane in approach and, more important, readable and worth reading. . . . Bakewell is wide-ranging, witty, and compassionate." —*The Wall Street Journal*

"Bakewell's writing inspires immense pleasure. She is a warm, engaging, and clear explicator of dense ideas." —*The Atlantic*

"Dazzling . . . *Humanly Possible* captures the lives of dozens of people across more than a half dozen centuries. The result is a model of sprezzatura—the Italian Renaissance ideal of making the epic look easy." —*Los Angeles Review of Books*

"Bakewell exemplifies the thirst for life and learning of humanism at its best."
—*The Literary Review*

"Exhilarating." —*The Times*

"Like Bakewell's previous two books, *Humanly Possible* skillfully combines philosophy, history, and biography. She is scholarly yet accessible and portrays people and ideas with vitality and without anachronism, making them affecting and alive."
—*The Guardian*

"Witty and warmhearted." —*The Daily Telegraph*

"In this exhilarating handbook Sarah Bakewell explains that a humanist philosopher is one who puts the whole living person at the center of things. . . . Bakewell finishes this bracing book by urging us to draw inspiration from these earlier men and women as we try hard to live bravely and humanly in what sometimes seems like an aridly abstract and loveless world." —*The Sunday Times*

"Readers will feel assured that they are in the company of a gifted guide."
—*The Economist*

"An expansive tour of European humanism . . . Bakewell brings out sharply how much contrarian courage it took to stand up for secularism. . . . These dangers are not a thing of the past. . . . Humanism is not just a hard-won victory, as Sarah Bakewell documents, but a fragile one, threatened by theocracy and neofascism, by politicians for whom the point of education is entirely economic, and by movements that aspire to leave humanity behind." —*The Times Literary Supplement*

"An intimidatingly impressive work of popular history . . . packed with erudition and information. It will widen the horizons of anyone who thinks of themselves as a mere secular humanist." —*Winnipeg Free Press*

"NBCC Award winner Bakewell (*How to Live*) brilliantly tracks the development of humanism over seven centuries of intellectual history. . . . Erudite and accessible, Bakewell's survey pulls together diverse historical threads without sacrificing the up close details that give this work its spark. Even those who already consider themselves humanists will be enlightened." —*Publishers Weekly* (starred review)

"In this fascinating, well-organized journey through the evolution of humanism, Bakewell, award-winning author of *At the Existential Café* and *How to Live*, introduces us to the men and women who have resisted religious dogma and fixed ideologies to carve out a way of thinking in which individuals occupy center stage. . . . A wonderfully learned, gracefully written, and simply enjoyable intellectual history of humanism." —*Kirkus Reviews* (starred review)

"Engagingly written as well as richly informative . . . every thinker, every book, every movement is located lightly and precisely in relation to its past and its influence on the present day. I can't imagine a better history of humanism, nor one that is so vividly persuasive. Bakewell is a wonderful writer." —Philip Pullman

"I've long admired Sarah Bakewell's extraordinary talent for breathing life into philosophy, making vivid the historical circumstances that give birth to new ideas. And this book is her best yet—a fascinating, moving, funny, sometimes harrowing and ultimately uplifting account of humanity's struggle to understand and fully inhabit the state of being human." —Oliver Burkeman, author of *Four Thousand Weeks*

"Sarah Bakewell's books are always a joyous education. . . . She combines a keen intellect with a lightness of touch, and one always feels that she delights in sharing what she has learned. That delight is contagious. . . . The world looked different when I finished this book."

—Robin Ince, cohost of *The Infinite Monkey Cage* and author of
The Importance of Being Interested

ALSO BY SARAH BAKEWELL

*At the Existentialist Café: Freedom,
Being, and Apricot Cocktails*

*How to Live, or A Life of Montaigne in One
Question and Twenty Attempts at an Answer*

The English Dane

The Smart

HUMANLY POSSIBLE

*Seven Hundred Years
of Humanist Freethinking,
Inquiry, and Hope*

Sarah Bakewell

PENGUIN BOOKS

PENGUIN BOOKS
An imprint of Penguin Random House LLC
penguinrandomhouse.com

First published in the United States of America by Penguin Press,
an imprint of Penguin Random House LLC, 2023
Published in Penguin Books 2024

Illustration credits appear on pages 433–36.

ISBN 9780735223394 (paperback)

THE LIBRARY OF CONGRESS HAS CATALOGED THE
HARDCOVER EDITION AS FOLLOWS:
Names: Bakewell, Sarah, author.
Title: Humanly possible : seven hundred years of humanist
freethinking, inquiry, and hope / Sarah Bakewell.
Description: New York : Penguin Press, 2023. |
Includes bibliographical references and index.
Identifiers: LCCN 2022037286 (print) | LCCN 2022037287 (ebook) |
ISBN 9780735223370 (hardcover) | ISBN 9780735223387 (ebook)
Subjects: LCSH: Humanistic ethics—History. | Humanistic ethics. | Humanism.
Classification: LCC BJ1360 .B36 2023 (print) | LCC BJ1360 (ebook) |
DDC 171/.2—dc23/eng/20220928
LC record available at https://lccn.loc.gov/2022037286
LC ebook record available at https://lccn.loc.gov/2022037287

Printed in the United States of America
1st Printing

Designed by Amanda Dewey

CONTENTS

HUMANLY
POSSIBLE

ONLY CONNECT!
AN INTRODUCTION

W hat is humanism?" That is the question posed, in David Nobbs's 1983 comic novel *Second from Last in the Sack Race*, at the inaugural meeting of the Thurmarsh Grammar School Bisexual Humanist Society—"bisexual" because it includes both girls and boys. Chaos ensues.

One girl begins by saying that it means the Renaissance's attempt to escape from the Middle Ages. She is thinking of the literary and cultural revival conducted by energetic, free-spirited intellectuals in Italian cities such as Florence in the fourteenth and fifteenth centuries. But that's not right, says another of the society's members. Humanism means "being kind, and nice to animals and things, and having charities, and visiting old people and things."

A third member replies scathingly that this is to confuse humanism with humanitarianism. A fourth complains that they are all wasting time. The humanitarian bristles: "Do you call bandaging sick animals and looking after old people and things a waste of time?"

The scathing one now puts forward a different definition altogether. "It's a philosophy that rejects supernaturalism, regards man as a natural object and asserts the essential dignity and worth of man and his capacity to achieve self-realisation through the use of reason and the scientific method." This is well received, until someone else raises a problem: some people do believe in God, yet they call themselves humanists. The meeting ends with everyone more confused than they were at the start.

But the Thurmarsh students need not have worried: they were *all* on the right track. Each of their descriptions—and more—contributes to the fullest, richest picture of what humanism means, and of what humanists have done, studied, and believed through the centuries.

Thus, as the student who spoke about the non-supernatural vision of life knew, many modern humanists are people who prefer to live without religious beliefs and to make their moral choices based on empathy, reason, and a sense of responsibility to other living creatures. Their worldview has been summed up by the writer Kurt Vonnegut: "I am a humanist," he said, "which means, in part, that I have tried to behave decently without any expectation of rewards or punishments after I'm dead."

Yet the other Thurmarshian was also right to say that some of those considered humanists do have religious beliefs. They can still be described as humanists, insofar as their focus remains mostly on the lives and experiences of people here on Earth, rather than on institutions or doctrines, or the theology of the Beyond.

Other meanings have nothing to do with religious questions at all. A humanist philosopher, for example, is one who puts the whole living person at the center of things, rather than deconstructing that person into systems of words, signs, or abstract principles. A humanist architect designs buildings on a human scale, in ways that do not overwhelm or frustrate those who have to live in them. Similarly there can be a humanist medicine, politics, or education; we have humanism in literature, photography, and film. In each case, the individual is kept at the top of the list of concerns, not subordinated to some grander concept or ideal. This is closer to what the "humanitarian" student was getting at.

But what about those scholars of fourteenth- and fifteenth-century Italy and beyond—the ones the first Thurmarsh speaker was talking about? These were humanists of another type: they translated and edited books, taught students, corresponded with their clever friends, debated interpretations, advanced intellectual life, and generally wrote and talked a lot. In short, they were specialists in the humanities, or the *studia humanitatis*, meaning "human studies." From this Latin term, they became known in Italian as *umanisti*, and so they are humanists, too; American English usage still calls them humanists today. Many have shared the ethical interests of the other kinds of humanists, believing that learning and teaching the human studies enables a more virtuous and civilized life. Humanities teachers still often think this, in a modernized form. By introducing students to literary and cultural experiences, and to the tools of critical analysis, they hope to help them to acquire extra sensitivity to the perspectives of others, a subtler grasp of how political and historical events unfold, and a more judicious and thoughtful approach to life generally. They hope to cultivate *humanitas*, which in Latin means being human, but with added overtones of being refined, knowledgeable, articulate, generous, and well mannered.

Religious, non-religious, philosophical, practical, and humanities-teaching humanists—what do all these meanings have in common, if anything? The answer is right there in the name: they all look to the *human* dimension of life.

What is that dimension? It can be hard to pin down, but it lies somewhere in between the physical realm of matter and whatever purely spiritual or divine realm may be thought to exist. We humans are made of matter, of course, like everything else around us. At the other end of the spectrum, we may (some believe) connect in some way with the numinous realm. At the same time, however, we also occupy a field of reality that is neither entirely physical nor entirely spiritual. This is where we practice culture, thought, morality, ritual, art—activities that are (mostly, though not entirely) distinctive to our species. Here is where we invest much of our time and energy: we spend it talking, telling stories, making pictures or models, working out ethical judgments and struggling to do the right thing, negotiating social agreements, worshipping in temples or churches or sacred groves, passing on memories, teaching, playing music, telling jokes and clowning around for others' amusement, trying to reason things out, and just generally being the kinds of beings that we are. This is the realm that humanists of all kinds put at the center of their concern.

Thus, whereas scientists study the physical world, and theologians the divine one, humanities-humanists study the human world of art, history, and culture. Non-religious humanists make their moral choices based on human well-being, not divine instruction. Religious humanists focus on human well-being, too, but within the context of a faith. Philosophical and other kinds of humanists constantly measure their ideas against the experience of real living people.

The human-centered approach was conveyed in a remark made some two and a half thousand years ago by the Greek philosopher Protagoras: "Man is the measure of all things." That may sound arrogant, but there is no need to take it as meaning that the whole universe must conform to our ideas, still less that we are entitled to lord it over other life-forms. We can read it as saying that, as humans, we experience our reality in a human-shaped way. We know and care about human things; they are important to us, so let's take them seriously.

Admittedly, by this definition almost everything we do can seem a bit humanistic. Other proposed definitions have been even more all-embracing. Here is the novelist E. M. Forster—a deeply "human" writer, and a paid-up member of humanist organizations—replying to a question about what that term means to him:

Humanism could better be honoured by reciting a list of the things one has enjoyed or found interesting, of the people who have helped one, and of the people whom one has loved and tried to help. The list would not be dramatic, it would lack the sonority of a creed and the solemnity of a sanction, but it could be recited confidently, for human gratitude and human hopefulness would be speaking.

This is irresistible, but it also comes close to giving up on definitions entirely. Yet Forster's refusal to say anything abstract or dogmatic about humanism is, in itself, a typically humanist thing to do. For him, it is a personal matter—and that is the point. Humanism often *is* personal, since it is about persons.

It is personal to me, too. I am a lifelong humanist in the non-religious sense. I've become more and more of a humanist in my philosophy and politics, prizing individual lives more than the big ideas that I used to find exciting. And, after years of reading and writing about historical humanists of the "humanities" type, I have become fascinated by this foundation that they all share in the human studies.

I am lucky in that I have been able to live out my humanism without much interference. For many people, humanism is something for which they risk their lives—and it doesn't get more personal than that. And where humanism is not well understood, such risks can be exacerbated, as is shown by the recent experience of one young humanist in Britain.

Hamza bin Walayat comes from Pakistan, but in 2017 he was living in the UK and applied for permission to remain, on the grounds that his humanist beliefs and his break with Islam had brought threats against his life in his home country, notably from his own family. He feared that, if deported, he could be killed. This was a reasonable fear; humanism is outlawed as blasphemy in Pakistan (as in several other countries) and can even be punished by execution. In practice, Pakistani humanists have been killed mostly by vigilante mobs, with the authorities looking away. A notorious case occurred in that same year, 2017: the student Mashal Khan, who posted on social media as "The Humanist," was beaten to death by fellow students.

When British Home Office staff interviewed Hamza to assess his application, they asked him to justify his fear of being persecuted as a humanist by giving a definition of that word. In his reply, he mentioned the values of Enlightenment thinkers of the eighteenth century. That was an excellent answer: much Enlightenment thought was humanistic in ways fitting several of the Thurmarshian definitions. But the assessors, either because of lack of knowledge or because they were looking for excuses to catch him out, claimed to be expecting an answer containing names of ancient *Greek* philosophers, specifically Plato and Aristotle. Which is odd, because neither Plato nor Aristotle are mentioned much in books about humanism, for the good reason that they were (in most respects) not very humanistic. The Home Office concluded, however, that it was Hamza who was not a humanist, and rejected his application.

The organization Humanists UK and other sympathizers took up his case. They pointed out the wrong choice of philosophers. More generally, they argued that humanism is not the kind of belief system that relies on a canon of authorities anyway. A humanist need not know about particular thinkers in the way that, say, a Marxist might be expected to know about Marx. Humanists often reject the concept of adhering to ideological "scriptures" at all. With so much support, and a strong case, Hamza won the right to remain in May 2019. He went on to serve as a board member of Humanists UK. And, in the wake of his victory, an introduction to humanist thought was added to all subsequent Home Office assessors' training.

So: humanism is personal, and it is a semantic cloud of meanings and implications, none attachable to any particular theorist or practitioner. Also, until recent times, humanists rarely gathered into formal groups, and many did not use the term *humanist* of themselves. Even if they were happy to be *umanisti*, they did not speak of "humanism" as a general concept or practice until the nineteenth century. (There is something pleasingly humanistic about the fact that the *people* predate the concept by several centuries.) It all seems gently foggy—and yet I do believe that there is such a thing as a coherent, shared humanist tradition, and that it makes sense to consider all these people together. They are linked by multicolored but meaningful threads. Those are the threads I want to trace in this book—and in so doing, I take as my guide another great humanist line from E. M. Forster: "Only connect!"

This is the epigraph and recurring refrain of his 1910 novel *Howards End*, and Forster meant a range of things by it. He meant that we should look to the bonds that connect us, rather than to divisions; that we should try to appreciate other people's angles on the world as well as our own; and that we should avoid the inward splintering of ourselves that is caused by self-deception or hypocrisy. I agree with all of this—and take it as encouragement to tell a story of humanism in a spirit of connection more than division.

Also in the personal spirit of E. M. Forster, I will be writing about human*ists* more than *isms*. I hope that, like me, you will be intrigued and sometimes inspired by these stories of humanists' adventures, quarrels, efforts, and tribulations, as they find their way through a world that has often treated them with incomprehension or worse. True, some had good experiences, finding enviable niches in academic or courtly environments. But they could rarely count on those positions for long, and others endured entire lives of troubled outsiderhood. Through the centuries, humanists have been scholarly exiles or wanderers, living on their wits and words. In the early modern era, several fell foul of the Inquisition or other sleuths of heresy. Others sought safety by concealing what they really thought, sometimes so effectively that we still haven't a clue. Well into the nineteenth century, non-religious humanists (often called "free-thinkers") could be reviled, banned, imprisoned, and deprived of rights. In the twentieth century they were forbidden to speak openly, told they had no hope of running for public office; they were persecuted, prosecuted, and imprisoned. In the twenty-first century so far, humanists still suffer all these things.

Humanism raises strong reactions. It is all about the human factor, but that factor is a complicated one that concerns each of us intimately: to be human is a constant puzzle and challenge. With so much hanging on our ideas of ourselves, it is not surprising that those who are open about humanist views can be victimized, especially in situations where the enforcement of religious or political conformity is strong. Yet slowly, quietly, and with setbacks, many generations of these stubborn humanists have argued their points with eloquence and reason, with the result that their ideas now permeate many societies, whether recognized as such or not.

The people we will meet in this book lived during the period when humanism was taking the forms we recognize today. My story covers seven centuries in particular, from the 1300s to our own time. Most (not all) of the book's occupants lived within that period; also, most (not all) were Europeans. I have limited the story in this way partly because so many interesting things happened within that frame, and partly because it gives a certain continuity: many of these people knew and responded to each other's work, even when they could not meet. Taking this slice of history and geography helps in drawing out some of the more concentrated forms of humanist thought, and seeing how they have evolved.

But my story should always be set mentally in the context of a bigger one: the wider, longer, fuller story of humanist lives and thoughts around the world. Humanistic ways of thinking have emerged from many cultures and epochs. I feel sure they have existed in some form ever since our species first began reflecting on itself and considering its choices and responsibilities in this world.

Before starting, therefore, let us do a tour of that wider horizon and meet a few of the key humanist ideas along the way.

We can start with the first possibility mentioned by the Thurmarshians: understanding human life non-supernaturally. Of all the views that came up in that meeting, this is the one with the oldest recorded pedigree. The first discussion of materialist views (that we know of) arose in India, as part of the Cārvāka school of thought founded by the thinker Bṛhaspati sometime before the sixth century BCE. This school's followers believed that, when our bodies die, that is the end of us as well. The philosopher Ajita Kesakambalī was quoted as saying:

> This human being is composed of the four great elements, and when one dies the earth part reverts to earth, the water part to water, the fire part to fire, the air part to air, and the faculties pass away into space. . . . Fools and wise, at the breaking-up for the body, are destroyed and perish, they do not exist after death.

A century or so later, a similar thought turns up in the coastal town of Abdera, in northeastern Greece, home of the philosopher Democritus. He taught that all entities in nature are made up of atoms—indivisible particles that combine in various ways to make all the objects we have ever touched or seen. And *we* are made of these particles, too, both mentally and physically. While we live, they combine together to form our thoughts and sensory experiences. When we die, they drift apart and go to form other things. That is the end of the thoughts and experiences—and therefore we end, too.

Is this humanist? Isn't it just depressing? No; in fact, it offers cheering and comforting consequences for our lives. If nothing of me will survive

into any afterlife, there is no point in my living in fear, worrying about what the gods may do to me or what torments or adventures may await me in future. The atomic theory made Democritus so lighthearted that he was known as "the laughing philosopher": freed from cosmic dread, he was able to chuckle at human foibles rather than weep over them as others did.

Democritus passed on his ideas to others. Among those to take them up was Epicurus, who founded a community of students and like-minded friends at his school in Athens, known as the "Garden." Epicureans sought happiness mainly through enjoying their friendships, eating a modest diet of porridge-like gruel, and cultivating mental serenity. A key component of the latter, as Epicurus wrote in a letter, was avoiding "those false ideas about the gods and death which are the chief source of mental disturbances."

Then there was Protagoras, he of the "human measure," who also came from Abdera and knew Democritus personally. His talk of measuring everything by humanity was already considered disturbing in his own time, but he was even more infamous for writing a book about the gods, which reportedly started in this surprising way:

> As to the gods, I have no means of knowing either that they exist or that they do not exist. For many are the obstacles that impede knowledge, both the obscurity of the question and the shortness of human life.

Given such a beginning, it would be nice to know what he filled the rest of the book with. But the punch is already there in this opening. There may or may not be gods in existence, but *for us* they are dubious and undetectable beings. The argument that followed was probably that we need not waste our brief lives worrying about them. Our business is with our earthly lives while they last. It is, again, another way of saying that the right measure for us is the human one.

The reason we do not know what came next in the book is that nothing beyond those few lines survives—and we have a good idea as to why. The biographer Diogenes Laertius tells us that, as soon as Protagoras's work on the gods appeared, "the Athenians expelled him; and they burnt his works in the market-place, after sending round a herald to collect them from all who had copies in their possession." Nothing directly written by Democritus survives, either, or by members of the Cārvāka school, and perhaps it is for similar reasons. From Epicurus we do have a few letters, but his teachings were also turned into verse form by a later Roman, Lucretius, in the long poem *On the Nature of Things*. That was almost lost, too, but a later copy survived in a monastery, where it was found in the fifteenth century by humanistic book collectors and circulated afresh. And so, after all these fragile moments and near losses, Democritan ideas did survive into our own era—and could thus be put into beautiful words by the American author Zora Neale Hurston, in her 1942 memoir *Dust Tracks on a Road*:

Why fear? The stuff of my being is matter, ever changing, ever moving, but never lost; so what need of denominations and creeds to deny myself the comfort of all my fellow men? The wide belt of the universe has no need for finger-rings. I am one with the infinite and need no other assurance.

The tradition lives on, too, in the words of a poster campaign of 2009 in the UK, supported by the British Humanist Association (now Humanists UK). The message, displayed on the sides of buses and in other places, was a Democritan statement of mental tranquility: "There's probably no God. Now stop worrying and enjoy your life." The idea had come from Ariane Sherine, a young writer and comedian who wanted to provide an alternative, reassuring message after she saw buses carrying an advertisement from an evangelical religious organization whose website threatened sinners with eternal hellfire.

This switching of focus to the here and now remains one of the key principles of modern humanist organizations. It was even formulated as that most unhumanist-sounding thing, a "creed," or statement of core beliefs. The author of this was Robert G. Ingersoll, a nineteenth-century American freethinker (or non-religious humanist). The creed goes like this:

> Happiness is the only good.
>
> The time to be happy is now.
>
> The place to be happy is here.

And Ingersoll ends with the all-important final line:

> The way to be happy is to make others so.

That last part takes us to a second big humanist idea: the meaning of our lives is to be found in our connections and bonds with each other.

This principle of human interconnectivity was put into a neat phrase in a play by Publius Terentius Afer, known as Terence in English. The

"Afer" refers to his origin, since he was born, probably as a slave, around 190 BCE in or near Carthage in North Africa; he then found fame in Rome as a writer of comedies. One of his characters says—and I include the Latin because it is still often quoted in the original:

Homo sum, humani nihil a me alienum puto.

Or:

I am human, and consider nothing human alien to me.

Actually, the line is a comic gag. The character who says it is known for being a nosy neighbor: this is how he replies when someone asks him why he cannot mind his own business. I am sure it got a good laugh, catching the audience off guard and mocking philosophical profundities. It tickles me, too, to think that a quotation cited seriously for so many centuries started life as a piece of knockabout comedy. Yet it does in fact do a good job of summing up an essential humanist belief: that we are all tied up in each other's lives. We are sociable beings by nature, and we can all recognize something of ourselves in each other's experiences, even those of people who seem very different from us.

A similar thought comes from the other, southern end of the African continent, captured in the Nguni Bantu word *ubuntu*, along with equivalent terms in other southern African languages. These refer to the network of mutual human relations connecting individuals in a community large or small. The late Archbishop Desmond Tutu, chairing South Africa's Truth and Reconciliation Commission during the country's transition away from apartheid in the 1990s, cited *ubuntu* along with his Christian principles as inspiration for his approach. He believed that the oppressive relationships of apartheid had damaged oppressor and oppressed alike, destroying the natural bonds of humanity that should exist within and between people. His hope was to create a process that would reestablish those connections, rather than focus on avenging wrongs. He defined *ubuntu* with these words: "We belong in a bundle of life. We say, 'a person is a person through other people.'"

In yet another part of the world, shared humanity is also considered crucial: this is in the ancient Chinese tradition of Confucian philosophy. Kongzi, or Master Kong, or Confucius, as he became known to Europeans, lived slightly before Democritus and Protagoras, and passed on a wealth of improving advice to his followers. Over the years after his death in 479 BCE, those followers collected and expanded his sayings to form the *Analects*, covering matters of morality, social etiquette, political advice, and philosophical insight of all kinds. A key term running through the collection is *ren*. This can be translated into English variously as benevolence, goodness, virtue, ethical wisdom—or simply "humanity," because it is what you cultivate if you want to become more fully and deeply human. The meaning is very close to that of *humanitas*.

When disciples asked Kongzi to give a fuller explanation of *ren*, and also to come up with a single word that would be a good guide for living, he mentioned *shu*: a network of reciprocity between people. *Shu*, he said, means that you should not do to others what you would prefer they did not do to you. If this sounds familiar, it is because it is a principle found in many other religious and ethical traditions around the world, sometimes called "the Golden Rule." The Jewish theologian Hillel the Elder said, "That which is hateful to you, do not do to your fellow. That is the whole Torah; the rest is the explanation; go and learn." The Hindu *Mahābhārata* and Christian scriptures turn it around the other way: *Do* do unto others as you would be done by—although, as George Bernard Shaw perkily pointed out, this version is less reliable because "their tastes may not be the same."

These are all ways of saying that our moral lives should be rooted in the mutual connection between people. It is fellow feeling, not being watched and judged according to divine standards, that grounds our ethics. The good news is that we seem—mostly—to feel that basic spark of fellowship spontaneously, because we are highly socialized beings who have already grown up in deep connection with the people around us.

One of Kongzi's later followers, Mengzi (or Master Meng, or Mencius), made this spontaneous recognition a starting point for a whole theory of the goodness of humanity. He invites his readers to find the source of it in themselves. Imagine that you are out one day and spot a small child about to fall into a pond. What do you feel? Almost certainly you feel an impulse to jump in and save the child. No calculation or reasoning precedes it, and it requires no commandment. That is your "seed" of a moral life—although you still have to reflect on it, and develop it, for it to become a full ethics.

The need to germinate and cultivate our potential in this way is another idea that runs through the humanist tradition. Because of this, education is all-important. As children, we learn from parents and teachers; later we continue to develop through experience and further study. We can still be human without advanced education, of course, but to realize our *ren* or *humanitas* to the utmost, mentoring and the broadening of perspectives are invaluable.

Being well educated is especially important for those who will go on to run the political and administrative systems for everyone else. Kongzi and his followers were adamant that leaders and civil servants should learn their tasks through a long and studious apprenticeship. They must learn to speak well and to know the traditions of their career, and they should also immerse themselves in literature and other humanities. Having such refined people at the helm is good for all of society, said Kongzi, because virtuous leaders help to inspire everyone else to live up to similar standards.

In Greece, Protagoras was a believer in education too, as well he might be, because he made a good living (too good, some felt) as a traveling tutor, preparing young men for political or legal careers by teaching them how to speak and argue persuasively. He even claimed to be able to teach them how to be virtuous: he could help students "to acquire a good and noble character, worthy indeed of the fee which I charge and even more."

To lure in new students, Protagoras would relate a story to show why education was vital. At the dawn of humanity, he said, people had no special qualities at all—until the two Titans Prometheus and Epimetheus steal fire from the gods for them, along with the arts of farming, sewing, building, language, and even religious observance. The myth of Prometheus's theft, and his punishment for doing it, is much told, but Protagoras's version includes some twists. When Zeus sees what has happened, he adds an extra gift for free: the capacity for forming friendships and other social bonds. Now humans can cooperate. But not so fast: they still have only the *capacity* for these things. They have a seed. To develop a truly thriving and well-managed society, humans must make that seed grow, by means of learning, and teaching each other. This is something that we must take charge of ourselves. We are showered with gifts, but they are nothing unless we work out how to collaborate in using them together.

Underlying humanists' love of education is a great optimism about what it can produce for us. We may be quite good to begin with, but we can be better. Our existing achievements are there to be built on—and meanwhile we can also take pleasure in contemplating what we have done.

Accordingly, joyful recitations of human excellences became a favorite genre of humanist writing. The Roman statesman Cicero wrote a dialogue with a section praising human excellence; others followed suit. The genre reached its height in Italy with such works as *On Human Worth and Excellence*, written in the 1450s by the diplomat, historian, biographer, and translator Giannozzo Manetti. Just look, says Manetti, at the beautiful things we have created! Look at our buildings, from the pyramids to the cathedral dome recently built by Filippo Brunelleschi in Florence, and the gilded bronze baptistery doors by Lorenzo Ghiberti nearby. Or the paintings of Giotto—the poetry of Homer or Virgil—the histories by Herodotus and others; and let's not even start on the nature-investigating philosophers, or the physicians, or Archimedes, who studied the movements of the planets.

> Ours indeed are those inventions—they are human—because it is those that are seen as made by humans: all the houses, all the towns, all the cities, including all the structures on earth.... Ours are the paintings, ours the sculptures; ours are the crafts, ours the sciences and ours the knowledge ... Ours are all the kinds of different languages and various alphabets.

Manetti celebrates the physical pleasures of life, and also the finer delights that come from using our mental and spiritual capacities to the full: "What pleasure comes from our faculties of appraisal, memory and understanding!" He makes the reader's heart swell with pride—but it is our *activities* that he praises, so this implies that we should keep laboring to do better, rather than sitting back and preening ourselves. We are building a kind of second human Creation, to complement that made by God. Also, we ourselves are such a work in progress. Much remains for us to do.

Manetti, Terence, Protagoras, Kongzi—each of these helped to weave the threads of the humanist tradition, over the millennia, and in different cultures. They share an interest in what humans can do, and a hope that we can do more. They often put great value on study and knowledge. They lean toward an ethics based on relationships with others, and on worldly and mortal existence, rather than on an anticipated afterlife. And they all seek to "connect": to live well within our cultural and moral networks, and in contact with that great "bundle of life" from which we all emerge, and which is our source of purpose and meaning.

There is much more to humanist thinking than this, and we shall meet many more strands and more types of humanists in this book. But first, a companion story must be told.

All this time, along with the humanist tradition, there has run a shadow. It is equally wide and long, and we could call it the *anti-humanist* tradition.

While humanists count out the elements of human happiness and excellence, anti-humanists sit beside them just as eagerly counting our miseries and failings. They point out the many ways in which we fall short, and the inadequacy of our talents and abilities for either dealing with problems or finding meaning in life. Anti-humanists often dislike the thought of taking delight in earthly pleasures. Instead, they argue for altering our existence in some radical way, either by turning away from the material world or by dramatically restructuring our politics—or ourselves. In ethics, they consider good nature or personal bonds less important than obeying the rules of a greater authority, whether sacred or secular. And, far from praising our best achievements as a basis for future improvements, they tend to feel that what humans mainly need is to be humbled.

In Confucian thought, for example, the philosophy espoused by Mengzi found its counterweight in that of another thinker, Xunzi, who described human nature as "detestable" in its original state. For him, it could be made better only by remolding, as when a wheelwright steams wood to make it into a different shape. He and Mengzi agreed about education being useful, but Mengzi thought we needed it to make our natural seeds of virtue grow. Xunzi thought we needed it to bend us out of our spontaneous form entirely.

Christianity also offered both options. Some early Christians were extremely humanistic: for them, praising humans was also a way of praising God, since He made us this way, after all. The fourth-century theologian Nemesius of Emesa sounds a lot like Manetti when he writes, of the human being, "Who could express the advantages of this living thing? He crosses the seas, in contemplation he enters into the heavens, he recognises the motions of the stars . . . he thinks nothing of wild beasts and sea-monsters, he controls every science, craft and procedure, he converses by writing with those with whom he wishes to do so beyond the horizon." But a few years later, Nemesius's influential fellow theologian Augustine of Hippo formulated the concept of original sin, which states that we are all born fundamentally *wrong* (thanks to Adam and Eve), and that even newborn babies start out in a flawed condition from which they had better spend their lives seeking redemption.

The most devastating attack on human self-esteem was written in the 1190s by the cardinal Lotario dei Segni, before he became Pope Innocent III: a treatise called *On the Misery of Man*. (This treatise was the main target of Manetti's later work: he sought to refute it point by point.) The cardinal does indeed tell a grim story, describing the base and nasty nature of human existence from conception onward. Never forget, he warns, that you begin as lumps of slime, dust, and filthy seed, thrown together in a moment of lust. While a fetus in the womb, you feed on a bloody maternal fluid so vile it can kill grass, blight vineyards, and give dogs rabies. You are then born naked or, worse, clothed in a caul. You grow into the ridiculous shape of an upside-down tree, your hair looking like tangled roots, your torso a trunk, and your legs two branches. Do you take pride in climbing mountains, sailing the sea, cutting and polishing stone to make gems, building with iron or wood, weaving clothes from threads, or thinking deeply about life? You should not, for all this is pointless activity that you probably do out of greed or vanity. Real life consists of toil, anxiety, and suffering—until you die, after which your soul may end up burning in hell while your body goes to feed the hunger of worms. "O the vile ignobility of human existence! O the ignoble condition of human vileness!"

The purpose of this horrorfest is to shock us awake, so that we understand the need to transform ourselves. It should make us turn away from what Augustine had called the City of Man toward the City of God. What we take to be pleasures and achievements in this world are only vanities. "Do not look for satisfaction on earth, do not hope for anything from humanity," wrote the mystic and mathematician Blaise Pascal much later. "Your good is only in God." In lectures of 1901–1902, the philosopher William James analyzed how this two-step move in religion works: first we are made uneasy, feeling "that there is *something wrong about us as we naturally stand.*" Then religion provides the solution: "a sense that *we are saved from the wrongness* by making proper connection with the higher powers."

It does not occur only in religion, however. Politics can do it, too. In the twentieth century, Fascists began by saying that something was badly wrong with current society, but that it could be fixed if all personal life was subordinated to the interests of the national State. Communist regimes, too, diagnosed errors in the preexisting capitalist system and proposed fixing them with a revolution. The new society might need, for a while, to be shored up by force, but it was worth it because it would lead the population toward an ideological promised land, a state of grace in which no more inequality or suffering would exist. Both systems were officially non-theistic, but only in that they replaced God with something similarly transcendent: the nationalist State, or Marxist theory, plus a cult of personality centered on the leader. They took away ordinary human freedoms and values and offered in return the chance to be raised up into some higher level of meaning or of "true" freedom. Whenever we see leaders or ideologies overruling the conscience, liberty, and reasoning of actual human beings with the promise of something higher, anti-humanism is probably in the ascendant.

So the opposition between humanism and anti-humanism has never mapped precisely onto that between religion and doubt: just as some atheists are anti-humanist, so most religions continue to have humanist elements that take us to a very different place from the wrongness/salvation model. Often, a balancing act goes on. Even Innocent III apparently intended to write a companion treatise on human excellence, to go with the misery—although, what with persecuting heretics and launching crusades (two activities in which he particularly distinguished himself), he did not quite get around to it. We human beings have danced a long dance with ourselves: humanist and anti-humanist thoughts have worked in opposition, but in doing so they have also renewed and energized each other.

Often the two coexist within the same person. I certainly have them both within me. When things look bad in the human world, with war, tyranny, bigotry, greed, and environmental depredation seeming to run unchecked, my inner anti-humanist mutters imprecations to itself about humans just being no damn good. I lose hope. At other times, however, I hear (for example) about collaborating teams of scientists who have designed and launched a new kind of space telescope—so powerful that it can show us remote parts of the universe as they were 13.5 billion years ago, relatively soon after the Big Bang—and I think: what extraordinary animals we are to be able to do that! Or I stand looking up at the celestial-blue stained-glass windows of Chartres cathedral in France, made in the twelfth and thirteenth centuries by long-vanished craftspeople: what expertise, what devotion! Or I simply witness one of the small or large acts of kindness or heroism that people perform every day for each other. Then I become every inch an optimist and a humanist.

Having this balance in our psyches is no bad thing. Anti-humanism usefully reminds us not to be vain or complacent; it supplies a bracing realism about what is weak or nefarious in us. It reminds us not to be naive, and prepares us for the fact that, at any moment, we and our fellows are likely to do something stupid or wicked. It forces humanism to keep working to justify itself.

Meanwhile, humanism warns us against neglecting the tasks of our current world in favor of dreams of paradise, whether on this earth or elsewhere. It helps to counter the intoxicating promises of extremists, and it wards off the despair that can come from obsessing too much over our faults. Instead of a defeatism that blames all problems on God, or our own biology, or historical inevitability, it reminds us of our human responsibility for what we do with our lives and urges us to keep our attention on earthly challenges and on our shared well-being.

So balance away—but mostly I am a humanist, and I think humanism waves the better flag.

I say this with caution, since humanists are rarely flag wavers by nature anyway. But if they did stitch words on a banner, those words might denote three principles in particular: Freethinking, Inquiry, and Hope. These take different forms, depending on what kind of humanist you are—inquiring will mean one thing to a scholar of the humanities and another to a campaigner for non-religious ethics—but they appear again and again in the many humanist stories we will encounter in the pages to come.

Freethinking: because humanists of many kinds prefer to guide their lives by their own moral conscience, or by evidence, or by their social or political responsibilities to others, rather than by dogmas justified solely by reference to authority.

Inquiry: because humanists believe in study and education, and try to practice critical reasoning, which they apply to sacred texts and to any other sources set up as being beyond question.

And Hope: because humanists feel that, failings notwithstanding, it *is* humanly possible for us to achieve worthwhile things during our brief existence on Earth, whether in literature or art or historical research, or in the furthering of scientific knowledge, or in improving the well-being of ourselves and other living beings.

During the time I have been working on this book, sinister developments have taken place in the world. Nationalist and populist leaders seem to be on a roll, the war drums are also rolling, and it can be hard not to fall into despair over our human and planetary future. I remain convinced that those things should not make us give up on freethinking, inquiry, or hope. On the contrary, I think we need them more than ever. This belief has helped to drive everything you will read here.

And now—in case *we* think we have it bad—let us turn to the southern Europe of the 1300s. Amid scenes of disorder, disease, suffering, and loss, a few enthusiasts took up the fragments of a more distant past and used them to plan a fresh start. In doing so, they made something fresh out of themselves, too: they became the first of the great literary humanists.

1.

The Land of the Living

The 1300s

*Petrarch and his books—Giovanni Boccaccio, storyteller
and scholar—it's all Greek to them—the shaggy
translator Leontius Pilatus—plague—losses and
consolations—eloquence—remedies for fortune—
a vision of light.*

If you had a choice, you probably would not want to be born on the
Italian peninsula in the early fourteenth century. Life was insecure,
with regular hostilities between cities and political groupings. A long-
running conflict between the factions known as Guelfs and Ghibellines
was resolved, only for the winning Guelfs to split into "White" and "Black"
factions and start fighting each other instead. Rome, the historic center
of Christendom, was abandoned by a beleaguered pope, Clement V; he
fled his enemies and transferred the court to Avignon, an ill-prepared
small city beyond the Alps with a terrible climate. The papacy would remain there for decades, leaving a chaotic Rome literally vegetating amid
its overgrown ruins. Tuscany was stricken by bad weather and famine—
and even worse afflictions were to come.

Yet somehow this anguished part of the world produced a surge of
literary energy. Through the 1300s, new generations of writers appeared,

filled with the spirit of recovery and revival. They hoped to reach back, past the current troubles, and even past the foundation of Christianity itself, so as to link hands with the writers of the Roman world, whose works had fallen into varying degrees of forgottenness. These new writers looked to an old model of good living, based on friendship, wisdom, virtue, and the cultivation of power and eloquence in language. From these elements, they created their own literature in a range of genres. Their weapon in all of this was the *studia humanitatis*: the human studies.

Signs of a revived interest in the human studies had already appeared in earlier decades, notably from the cosmic visionary Dante Alighieri—promoter of the Tuscan language and master of the art of taking literary revenge on his enemies by inventing a vivid Hell and putting them in it. The real beginning of the new beginning, however, came in the generation after his, with two writers who, like him, came from Tuscany: Francesco Petrarca (known as Petrarch in English) and Giovanni Boccaccio. They more or less invented the way of life that would be, for the next two centuries, the humanist one—not that they used this label of themselves. Only later did people regularly use the word *umanisti*; but Petrarch and Boccaccio put together the profile, so it seems reasonable to call them by that name.

To get there, each of them began with a similar step: rebelling against the means of living that their fathers had wanted for them. In Petrarch's case it was the law; in Boccaccio's, a choice between mercantile business or the church. Separately, they both chose a new path instead: the literary life. A youthful counterculture can take many forms: in the 1300s, it could mean reading a lot of Cicero and starting a book collection.

The older of the two was Petrarch. He was born in 1304 in Arezzo. His birthplace would have been Florence, but his parents were of the White faction when the Black Guelfs took over in the city. They had to flee, amid a group of refugees that also included Dante, another White Guelf. Neither Petrarch's parents nor Dante would ever return.

Thus, Petrarch was born already in a state of exile. His early years were lived in alternating phases of flight and temporary refuge, with some pauses lasting for months or years before the family moved on. There were adventures. In his infancy, he came close to drowning during one of his journeys: a servant carrying him on horseback across a river slipped and almost dropped him. Next, the whole family was nearly ship-wrecked in dangerous waters off Marseille. They survived and made it to Avignon, where his father found work in the papal court. They settled nearby, and Petrarch grew up in and around that city—which he did not like at all, though as he grew into his teens and twenties, he sometimes enjoyed its nightlife. Years later, he wrote to his younger brother remi-niscing about how they would try on fancy, perfumed clothes and check their curled hairstyles before going out for some fun.

Petrarch's father was a notary by profession, and this made it natural for his son to train for a career in a similar law-related field. But Petrarch hated his legal education. While supposedly studying hard, in Montpellier and then in Bologna, he put much of his energy into collecting books in-stead. This was long before printing technology; the only way to get read-ing matter was to find manuscripts to buy, beg, borrow, or transcribe—all of which he did eagerly.

A setback occurred when his father threw his first modest collection into the fire, presumably in the hope that it would help the young man concentrate on law. At the last moment, however, he relented and pulled just two books from the flames. They were Cicero on rhetoric, which might be useful for a legal career anyway, and a volume of Virgil's poetry, which Petrarch was allowed to keep for recreation. Both authors always remained stars in Petrarch's sky. They would continue to be revered by later humanists: Virgil with his poetic beauty and reinvention of classical legend, Cicero with his thoughts on morality and politics, and his out-standingly elegant Latin prose.

For the moment, Petrarch kept his head down—in both the studious and the discreet sense—but when he was twenty-two and his father died,

he gave up law and returned to Avignon to start a totally different way of life: the literary one. He began a pattern that he would follow for all his career: working in the entourages of a series of powerful patrons, in exchange for financial security and often a nice house (or two) to live in. The patrons might be noblemen, or territorial princes, or officials of the church; to prepare for the latter, he took minor orders himself as a churchman. His jobs involved some diplomatic services and secretarial labor, but most important, they meant producing a stream of pleasing, flattering, stimulating, or comforting compositions. The main task was doing what Petrarch loved anyway: reading and writing.

And, boy, did he write. He poured out treatises, dialogues, and personal narratives; mini-biographies and triumphal celebrations and Latin poems and consolatory reflections and blistering invectives. To please himself as well as others, he wrote beautiful love poetry in the vernacular, developing and perfecting his own version of the sonnet form (still called the Petrarchan sonnet today). Many of these verses were in honor of an idealized woman whom he called "Laura," and whom he said he had first seen at a church in Avignon on April 6, 1327—a date he recorded in the precious pages of a Virgil manuscript. His delirious agonizing over how unattainable and elusive she was would inspire generations of poets after him.

In between his obligations to patrons in cities, Petrarch often found himself rewarded for his work with the chance to live in attractive houses in the countryside. These interludes fed his inspiration further, as he spent periods of creative leisure wandering in woods and on riverside paths, socializing with friends, or just cohabiting with his beloved books. During his mid-thirties, he had a house in the village of Vaucluse, by the clear water of the stream of the Sorgue, not far from Avignon. Later retreats included a house in the Euganean Hills near Padua, and before that, a house at Garegnano near Milan, by another river, where he could listen to "multicoloured birds in their branches sing in various modes," and also do botanical experiments by planting different varieties of laurel bushes in the garden.

Planting laurels was a choice loaded with significance, and so probably was the pseudonym of "Laura" for his great love. In the ancient world, poets had been awarded wreaths of laurel leaves to crown their achievements. The custom had recently been revived by a Paduan poet, Albertino Mussato; he celebrated by awarding it to himself. Petrarch was granted it more officially at a ceremony in Rome in 1341, after being verbally examined on his long poem *Africa* (about the Roman general Scipio Africanus) and giving an official address in praise of poetry. Flattered, delighted, and pleased with himself, he was intensely aware of the significance of the classical precedent behind the custom. It must be said that Petrarch was never a stranger to vanity, and sometimes drifted into pomposity. He always claimed to despise his own fame and to be exhausted by the many admirers who came to his door (or doors). But it is clear that he loved it, really. He grew into the full height of his role—and that was a considerable height, literally as well as metaphorically. A later description by Giannozzo Manetti, based on reports by those who knew him, described Petrarch as being tall and having a "majesty" about him.

Despite this elevated air, he also carried a lifelong psychological mark from his insecure beginning. Alongside the moments of self-satisfaction, he would have others: episodes of depression, or *accidia*, an inability to feel anything at all, even unhappiness. At times, everything seemed unknowable and uncertain to him: in his fifties, he would describe himself in a letter as "granting myself nothing, affirming nothing, doubting all but what I consider a sacrilege to doubt."

At other times he sounded more sure of himself, and this was largely because he derived a sense of purpose from his calling to the life of literature. Although the church had long employed secretarial officials, who needed to have literary skills, no one had put as much dedication into the role of man of letters as Petrarch. He seems constantly to have been aware of the highest examples of the classical past behind him: far off, but all the more powerful for their magnificent remoteness. In his mind, they set moral tasks for him.

When not thinking of the past, he wove his life and writings deeply into the lives of his contemporaries. He developed a vast circle of interesting friends: educated men, of a literary bent themselves, sometimes rich and powerful. He circulated his works among them—so his writings were read by others besides the patrons to whom they were dedicated. This circle also became Petrarch's useful network of fellow book finders. Each time his friends went anywhere, he gave them shopping lists. Sending one such list to Giovanni dell'Incisa, the prior of San Marco in Florence, Petrarch asked him to show it to everyone he knew in Tuscany: "Let them roll out the closets and chests of their church people and other men of letters in case something might emerge that might be suitable to soothe or irritate my thirst." Manuscripts, laboriously copied or precariously lent, made their way around the Italian peninsula on dangerous roads filled with robbers; if loaned, they also had to find their way back. Petrarch himself was often on the move, for his work duties as well as social calls, and wherever he went, he would halt if he saw a monastery in the distance: "Who knows if there is something I want here?" He would go in and ask to rummage. If he found a text of value, he sometimes stayed for days or weeks to make his own copy of it.

Imagine what that was like: having to copy, by hand, every word of every book you add to your collection. Even Petrarch found it exhausting. In a letter, he describes writing out a long Cicero text that a friend had lent him, and going slowly so that he could also try to memorize it as he went. His hand became stiff and sore. But just as he thought he could hardly go on, he came to a passage where Cicero himself mentioned having copied someone's orations. Petrarch felt chastened: "I blushed as though an embarrassed soldier being chided by a respected commander." If Cicero could do it, so could he.

At other times, Petrarch found comfort rather than exhaustion in the act of writing. It was almost an addiction. "Except when writing, I am always tormented and sluggish," he admitted. One friend who saw him working over-hard on an epic poem tried what we might call an "intervention." He asked Petrarch innocently for the key to his cabinet. Once he had it, he grabbed Petrarch's books and writing materials, threw them inside, turned the key, and left. The next day, Petrarch had a headache from morning to evening, and the day after that he developed a fever. The friend gave him back the key.

Often, Petrarch did more than mechanical copying. Besides trying to remember what he read, he also applied his own growing scholarship to each new discovery. He pioneered the art of sensitive editing, using fresh manuscript finds to build up fuller versions of ancient texts that had previously existed only in fragments, doing his best to fit them together correctly. His most important production of this kind was an edition of Livy, a historian of Rome whose huge work survived only in parts. (It is still incomplete, but we have more of it now than in Petrarch's time.) Having found several new sections in different manuscript forms, he assembled them in a volume together with his copies of other existing parts. The resulting book would belong to a great scholar of the next century, Lorenzo Valla (whom we will meet properly later on); Valla added more notes of his own, improving it further. This was exactly what generations of humanists would continue to love doing—enlarging knowledge, using the evidence to make texts richer and more accurate. It was Petrarch who led the way.

The writers he investigated often provided encouragement for such work, and even direct inspiration for his own writing. A particularly energizing discovery was one of his earliest: that of Cicero's oration *Pro Archia*. Delivered in Rome in the year 62 BCE, it was a defense of the poet Archias, who as an immigrant was about to be denied citizenship of the city on a technicality. Cicero's argument was that the "human and literary studies" promoted by Archias contributed such pleasure and moral benefit to Roman society that, technicality or no, he ought to be given his citizenship anyway. Petrarch found the full text of this in a monastery in Liège, while traveling through the area with friends. They all had to wait for several days while he made himself a copy to take away. It was the perfect text for someone who was embarking on a life of literature: it meant that Cicero approved of such a life.

Another work by Cicero gave him something more: a specific project to emulate. Twelve years after the Liège discovery, Petrarch was nosing around the cathedral library of Verona when he found three manuscript copies of Cicero's letters, including those written to his lifelong friend Atticus. The letters fascinated Petrarch: they showed a more personal side to Cicero, as an informal writer and friend who reflected on human dilemmas and emotions, and responded to political events as they arose. Petrarch was also intrigued by the overall idea of making such a collection: choosing and ordering letters to make a coherent literary work.

Petrarch too was a prolific letter writer, and he too used his letters as a way of writing about almost anything he was interested in. He responded to friends' thoughts and questions, raided his stock of learning for ripostes or examples, discussed research plans, and offered personal advice. Finding the Cicero letters at a point when he had just turned forty and was ready for a midlife summation, he realized that he could do the same. He could retrieve and revisit his own letters, copy them, polish them, put them in a satisfying order, and then circulate them to anyone who cared to read them—which in turn would bring more correspondents and new friends to whom he could write even more letters.

It took him four years, but eventually he got to work and produced a first, long collection known as the *Familiares*, or *Familiar Letters*. This would be followed by another: *Seniles*, or *Letters of Old Age*. Together, they make up his most wide-ranging and, frankly, enjoyable work, filled with expressions of warmth, sorrow, concern, or anger, along with occasional posturing or umbrage-taking, and sidelong illuminations of his whole world. Some of the letters tell long stories, as with one that describes a major hike with his brother up Mont Ventoux near Avignon, carrying a copy of Augustine's *Confessions* tucked in his pocket so that he could read out an apt quotation from it at the top. (The recipient of this letter was the friend who had given him the Augustine book; it was Petrarch's way of thanking him.) All in all, these letter collections are both a tribute to Cicero and a highly personal creation, filled with life and spontaneity.

Or rather, *apparent* spontaneity. They are intensively edited and polished; to this day no one is sure whether he really went up Mont Ventoux or just composed a beautiful fantasia on the concept. The letters are literary constructions, and literature is often their subject, too. Petrarch begs for manuscripts and passes on news of other people's discoveries; he shows off his erudition with classical references and intellectual in-jokes. Writing to thank a friend for hospitality, he adds details of the many other people in literary history who have been welcomed into friends' houses. Telling his own story of how he was almost lost in the river as a baby, he alludes to a story from Virgil's *Aeneid*, in which the mythical king Metabus had to cross a river with his baby daughter, Camilla, on his journey into exile; he got her over by the unlikely method of tying her to a spear and throwing her across.

Some of the letters are addressed *to* the classical authors he admired, as though they, too, were part of his circle of friends. In place of his usual signing-off phrase, he would finish these with the words "From the land of the living." And now, reading his letters, it is we who are (temporarily) in the land of the living, while Petrarch speaks to us from the other side.

He actually does direct one of his letters to us: the last one in the final collection is written "To posterity." ("Perhaps you will have heard something about me, although this too is doubtful," he begins it coyly.)

For Petrarch, books are sociable: "They speak with us, advise us and join us together with a certain living and penetrating intimacy." The ancients make just as good companions as people who consider themselves alive because, as he writes, they can still see their breath in the frosty air. The greatest authors are guests in his home; he banters with them. Once, having bruised his heel tripping over a volume of Cicero that he had left on the floor, he asks, "What's this, my Cicero? Why do you strike me?" Is it because he is offended at being put on the floor? In another letter to Cicero, Petrarch dares to criticize some of his choices in life: "Why did you choose to become involved in so many quarrels and utterly useless feuds? . . . I am filled with shame and distress at your shortcomings." These are not fan letters but thoughtful engagements with fallible human beings who had wrestled with life's problems. They had made ordinary mistakes, like any human, yet they also came from a time that appeared to Petrarch to be wiser and more cultured than the world he saw around him.

Beneath Petrarch's quips and intimacies, a strain of melancholy runs through these letters to the past. The recipients had gone, and their epoch had gone, too. Would such notable times, or such people, ever exist again? That was what Petrarch and his circle longed to know—and what they wanted to help make possible.

Of all the friends with whom Petrarch engaged in book talk in his letters, the one who shines out of the crowd is Giovanni Boccaccio.

He, too, had come to the literary life through an early rebellion. Born in 1313, nine years later than Petrarch, he was never an exile as Petrarch was: he would live most of his life fairly well settled in Florence and his nearby family home at Certaldo. Yet his path had not been easy, either. His mother may have died early on; we know nothing about her, she played no part in his upbringing, and he grew up with a stepmother. His father, generally known as Boccaccino di Chellino (the first name, rather confusingly for us, means "Little Boccaccio"), was a merchant who was keen to see his boy follow him in this line of work. He sent Boccaccio to a businessman to learn arithmetic for six years, but it did not take. When his father contemplated training him for the church instead— as "a good way to get rich," Boccaccio commented later— it turned out that he had no liking or aptitude for that, either.

DOMINVS IOHANNES BOCCACCIVS

What he did excel at was writing, especially poetry, with which he had been experimenting since he was six years old. And so, like Petrarch, Boccaccio went through a ritual transition. He rejected what his father wanted him to do, and dedicated himself instead to the literary and human studies. Also like Petrarch, he would eventually write an account of this turn toward the humanities and make a personal legend of it.

In other ways, they were different. Boccaccio was as filled with anxieties and complexities as Petrarch was, but they were different ones. On the one hand, he was often defensive and prickly, as if he felt at some constant disadvantage in relation to others. On the other, he was more generous with his praise than Petrarch. Boccaccio never hesitated to proclaim his admiration for authors old and new. He had wonderful things to say about Petrarch himself, as well as (posthumously) about Dante, who had died in 1321. In fact, he became the first serious Dante scholar, giving a series of lectures on him and writing introductions and a biography. He called Petrarch his "revered teacher, father, and master," and said that he was so illustrious that he ought to be counted more as an ancient than as a modern. Petrarch would have loved that. His name was known all over Europe, continued Boccaccio, even in "that most remote little corner of the world, England."

Yet when it came to assessing his own work, Boccaccio grumbled that he should have been more of a contender: he could have attained greater fame as an author had he received more encouragement early on. It is hard to see what he was complaining about, since he won acclaim for his work across a huge range of genres: fiction, poetry, literary dialogues, collections of myths and tales, and works of scholarship of all kinds.

The work for which he is best remembered now is *The Decameron*, a set of one hundred tales told in vernacular Tuscan. Ten narrators, over ten days, tell ten stories each—giving Boccaccio the chance to show his versatile command of style and invention. Some pieces are high-toned

and morally improving stories of love and virtue, seasoned with insight into human psychology. Others are a riot of bawdy lusts and comic comeuppances. Tricksters get the better of hapless simpletons; sly wives cuckold their husbands in ingenious ways. Some stories mock the clergy for laziness or corruption. In one, an abbess is informed in the middle of the night that one of her nuns is in bed with a lover, so she gets up to investigate—and accidentally covers her head, not with her veil, but with the breeches of the priest with whom she herself was in bed at the time. Amid such anticlerical fun, other stories risk a more serious critique of the authority of Christianity: in one, a great lord summons his three sons in turn and gives each a ring, as if to say he has chosen that one as heir. In fact, he has made two identical copies of the original ring, so no one can tell which of the three is real. It makes a good parable for the competing truth claims of Jews, Christians, and Muslims, all thinking they have the one true religion, whereas in reality the matter is undecidable.

Similarly wide-ranging and adventurous is Boccaccio's *Genealogy of the Pagan Gods*, a compilation of classical myths. Comprehensive, scholarly, and somewhat chaotic, it was assembled by talking to knowledgeable people and scouring books—all in a time before the study of mythology or history had acquired any methodological rigor. It radiates Boccaccio's love of all things ancient, but in the closing sections also includes his thoughts on modern-day literature, with the account of his own journey toward the literary life.

While writing this and other works in different genres, Boccaccio also maintained a career in Florentine public life. At various times, he held posts as city treasurer, tax collector, and ambassador, and on civic boards and with the department overseeing public works. He was more embedded in his community than Petrarch, who was the sort of person who felt at home anywhere—or, perhaps, nowhere.

It was one of these civic involvements that finally led Boccaccio to meet Petrarch in person, after years of admiring him from afar. Boccaccio was active with a campaign in Florence to try to persuade descendants of the old exiled families to move back and become proud Florentines again. In 1350, when Petrarch was passing through the area, Boccaccio took the opportunity to invite him to the city, and he put him up in his own home, while no doubt exerting all the charm and generosity at his disposal. He arranged for the city to offer Petrarch a university chair—a considerable honor. It did not work. Petrarch never did move to Florence, and continued shifting between other places, including Milan, Padua, and Venice. Boccaccio was disappointed, having gone to so much trouble. But they got over this rocky beginning and went on to become lasting friends. Sometimes Boccaccio would visit Petrarch in his various homes. More often, they kept up their relationship through letters—filled with book talk, of course, but also with expressions of affection and a certain amount of fond scolding on both sides.

Although the age difference was not great, Boccaccio looked up to Petrarch as a father figure, while Petrarch gladly reciprocated by looking down on Boccaccio as a son. He seemed to find him a more pleasing son than his real one, also called Giovanni. Being technically a churchman, Petrarch could not marry, but he had fathered two children, a boy and a girl. His daughter, Francesca, and her family went on to look after him in old age, but Giovanni seemed not to win his father's favor. At eighteen, he spent some time mooching around in the paternal home, apparently suffering from a similar *accidia* to that of his father, but not sharing any of the latter's tendency to seek comfort in books. Petrarch found him exasperating and, eventually, in a harsh and terrible letter, ordered him to leave.

Giovanni Boccaccio, on the other hand, showed boundless interest in all the right things: the passion for language, the joy in writing, the dedication to finding and reviving ancient literature—all the elements that made up the humanities scholar of the (very early) modern world. Boccaccio loved manuscripts and raided monasteries, just as Petrarch did. He, too, had made good discoveries, including more works by Cicero in the great Benedictine monastery of Montecassino. Boccaccio had no fear of the drudgery of copying.

In one strange episode, however, Boccaccio came close to abandoning it all. A monk, Pietro Petroni of Siena, warned him in 1362 that he would die imminently if he did not get rid of all the non-Christian books in his library and stop writing such books himself. This had been revealed to Pietro in a vision. Alarmed, Boccaccio sought advice from Petrarch, who talked him down from his panic. He did also add that, if Boccaccio really wanted to clear out his book chests, he might send a list: Petrarch would be happy to acquire them.

Less selfishly, he gave Boccaccio some excellent arguments for not doing this. If a person loves literature and is good at it, wrote Petrarch, how could it be seen as morally right to abandon it? Ignorance is not the path to virtue. Petrarch was devout enough, but he had no time for the idea that a Christian life must be one of unworldly contemplation, reading sacred works only, or no works at all. He was on the side of knowledge, of learning, of a healthy abundance in words and ideas. Fortunately (or unfortunately, from the point of view of Petrarch's book collection), Boccaccio soon came around, and he kept his books. In his *Genealogy*, he did not hesitate to say that nothing should be thought "improper" for a Christian in studying even the gods or stories of the ancient world. After all, Christianity had clearly beaten the old gods by now, so there was nothing to be afraid of. Petrarch, too, wrote that non-Christian teachings—so long as they did not actually contradict the Gospel—added "a considerable measure to the enjoyment of the mind and the cultivation of life."

The passion for literature was so strong in Petrarch and Boccaccio that they even treasured texts they could not read. Their Latin was perfect, but like most western Europeans at the time, they knew little or nothing of ancient Greek. Some medieval scholars had learned it, but the majority had not, and when monastic copyists came across Greek words within a Latin text, they tended to write, *Graecum est, non legitur*—"It is Greek, and cannot be read." The phrase took on a life of its own as "It's all Greek to me," via Shakespeare's *Julius Caesar*, where Casca reports that he has heard Cicero saying something in Greek but has no idea what it was. In the fourteenth century, Greek speakers could be reliably found only in Constantinople, or the lands of modern Greece, or parts of southern Italy where there was a native-speaker community. Elsewhere, swaths of philosophy, science, cosmology, and literature remained inaccessible.

Among the authors tantalizingly unreachable for Petrarch and Boccaccio was Homer, since no Latin or vernacular translations yet existed. But Petrarch was the proud owner of a copy of the *Iliad*, given to him by a Greek friend in Constantinople. Writing to thank him, he said how much he wished the friend could come to Italy himself to teach the language; otherwise, Petrarch wrote, Homer must remain silent for him— or "rather I am deaf to him. Still I take pleasure in his mere presence and with many sighs I embrace him, saying, 'O great man, how willingly would I listen to you!'" (This may sound like a way of saying "Thank you for your useless present," but I think we can assume that Petrarch's desire to unlock Greek literature was real.)

Boccaccio also had Greek books, and he came up with a way of tackling the problem. Again courting the authorities in Florence, as he had fruitlessly done in trying to procure Petrarch a job, he persuaded them to create western Europe's first professorship of Greek in 1360, and also recruited a Calabrian Greek speaker to take it up: Leontius Pilatus. This was a brave choice. Leontius was impulsive and unreliable, and something of a wild man in appearance, with a long beard and ugly face—"for ever lost in thought, rough in manners and behaviour," as Boccaccio admitted. Petrarch had already met him, and did not like him much. Boccaccio had a reason to be more tolerant: Leontius was a font of Greek mythological and historical stories, and therefore a great source for Boccaccio's own *Genealogy of the Pagan Gods*. He let Leontius live with him in his Florence house and commissioned him to produce a word-for-word Latin version of both the *Iliad* and the *Odyssey*, ready for Boccaccio to polish for readability. Petrarch watched from afar, begging Boccaccio to send new installments as soon as they were ready, so he could make copies and send back the originals—the usual anxiety-provoking mail runs of the time.

Luckily nothing went missing, but the project was long and Leontius became ever more wayward. In 1363, after about three years of living in Boccaccio's house, but with the translations not finished, he announced that he was tired of Florence and wanted to move to Constantinople. Boccaccio accompanied him in that direction as far as Petrarch's home in Venice, and left him there; apparently Petrarch was hoping that Leontius would be sufficiently calmed by the change of scene to get back to work. This did not happen. Eventually, after voicing many complaints and insults against Italy, Leontius sailed away. Petrarch gave him a copy of Terence's comedies as a parting gift: he had noticed that Leontius enjoyed reading them, although Petrarch did wonder "what that gloomy Greek could have in common with this joyful African." (Petrarch himself, so often impatient with other people's foibles, was not *quite* in perfect tune with Terence's line, "Nothing human is alien to me.")

Once in Constantinople, Leontius changed his mind and longed for Italy again. He wrote to Petrarch—a letter "shaggier and longer than his beard and hair," said its recipient—asking for help in organizing and funding his return. By now Petrarch had become more involved in Leontius's life than Boccaccio was—but he was in his stern-father mood and commented to Boccaccio: "Where he haughtily emigrated, let him live sadly."

In truth, Petrarch admitted, he was afraid of Leontius's instability. This is understandable, of course. But one can also see why Leontius had come to be so troubled and aggrieved: he was treated as an outsider wherever he went, and goaded by these two Tuscans who kept on about his wild hairdo and spoke of him as if he were a barbarian. Yet *he* had the ancient and literary language they craved; a language that, incidentally, had come up with the word *barbarian* in the first place.

Amazingly, Petrarch resisted even when Leontius promised to bring him more manuscripts by Greek authors, a proposal that surely should have been the way to his heart. In the end Leontius managed to organize the journey himself and embarked on a ship in 1366. But it ended very badly for him. The ship, after sailing up the Adriatic and almost arriving at its destination, ran into a storm. As it rolled and plunged, Leontius clung to a mast, while the others on board seem to have found safer refuges beneath. A bolt of lightning hit the mast, and he was killed—the only one to die.

Petrarch seems to have felt some remorse. "The unhappy man, whatever he was, loved us," he wrote to Boccaccio. He died "without having seen, I believe, one serene day." One final question occurred to Petrarch (and we don't know the answer to it). He asked: did the sailors, by any chance, happen to rescue any Greek books that Leontius might have been bringing back for him?

Petrarch had his failings of humanity; Boccaccio could be huffy and difficult. Yet what comes through from all these stories of their book collecting, translating, editing, and letter writing is their total dedication to their work and to an elusive goal: the reviving of the long-ago human studies, which they hoped to see reborn from the deep and given new life for the future.

The path to that future was not, however, always easy.

Back in 1347, a few years before Petrarch and Boccaccio first met, a disease had begun quietly circulating in northern Italy and southern France; it had also appeared in parts of Asia and Africa, and would later reach more areas of Europe. The cause was a bacterium, *Yersinia pestis*, spread via fleas and other vectors, but of course no one knew that yet. Other outbreaks had occurred in Europe before, but too far in the past for anyone to be able to recognize the symptoms.

A lawyer living in Piacenza, Gabriele de' Mussi, described them. First, a person felt a "chilly stiffness" and a tingling sensation, as if "being pricked by the points of arrows." Then discolored buboes, or boils, appeared in the armpits or groin (from the enlarged lymph nodes underneath), and a fever started. Some people vomited blood. Some fell unconscious. A few recovered; the majority died. Because of the buboes, the disease became known as bubonic plague, or the Black Death.

As it spread, it initially took communities by surprise, but soon, and more frighteningly, people heard news of it advancing toward them from town to town. They tried everything they could think of to stop it. One tactic was to avoid others, isolating oneself as far as possible, as it was known that it could somehow be transmitted via the sick. This was not easy to do if it was your husband or child who (as Gabriele de' Mussi wrote) called plaintively to you: "Come here. I'm thirsty, bring me a drink of water. I'm still alive. Don't be frightened. Perhaps I won't die. Please hold me tight, hug my wasted body. You ought to be holding me in your arms."

People made efforts to remain calm and optimistic, believing that fear would make them more vulnerable—and what a psychological hall of mirrors that must have been to navigate! Meanwhile, thoughts often turned to God, who seemed to be in one of his punitive moods and in need of human penitential display. Processions were organized, with participants flagellating themselves. Sometimes these events became pogroms, as Jewish people were suspected of causing the disease. Other theories suggested that it was caused by bad air rising from the ground, or "superfluities" that built up in the body from heavy food. Some doctors cut open their patients' buboes so that bad humors could escape. One of those who favored this treatment was Guy de Chauliac, physician to the current pope in Avignon, Clement VI. Fortunately, Clement himself was not subjected to it because he never caught the disease, although he did stay on bravely in the city for a long time, while others fled. He also tried to stop anti-Semitic violence and to introduce order into the penitential processions. When cemeteries and mass graves in fields filled up, he consecrated the Rhône so that those whose bodies were thrown in the river could get to heaven.

In Florence the situation was even more extreme. It is estimated that, by the end of this initial outbreak, two-thirds of the population of 100,000 Florentines were dead. The most vivid sense of what it must have been like in the city comes from Boccaccio: although he was probably not there himself through that time, he knew people who were, and

included a short but horrifying account of it in his prelude to *The Decameron*. It sets the scene, since the ten storytellers are ten well-off young nobles who flee the city to wait out the danger in their comfortable country houses. Boccaccio describes exactly what they were running from—and apologizes to readers for reminding them of horrors that were still recent in their minds and that they would probably rather forget.

As he tells us, the city fell to pieces. People became afraid to help their relatives; even parents would not touch their own children. With few servants around, aristocratic ladies gave up their usual decorum and allowed male staff to attend them, an unheard-of breach of modesty. Bodies piled up in houses and streets; funeral rituals became more and more rudimentary until they ceased entirely. Corpses were carted away on boards, to be buried in trenches several tiers deep.

In normal times, cities closed their gates at night against external threats, but now many passed through those gates to seek safety in the countryside, as with Boccaccio's ten young people. Unlike them, most people found what was far from a pastoral idyll. The plague had often arrived before them, and the country folk had abandoned their fields and domestic animals, leaving dogs and chickens to fend for themselves. Seeds and agricultural tools, essential for future crops, had been thrown aside because no one expected ever to come back to use them.

All these details given by Boccaccio amount to a terrible reversal of ancient ideals of dignified and excellent humanity, with everyone enjoying well-regulated lives, prosperous fields, and productive crafts, and looking confidently to what they could leave for posterity. Confronted with the plague, human arts and technical inventions seemed useless. Medicine, that great improver of the human condition, could do almost nothing. The civilized arts of government and administration did not keep the plague at bay, either. As Boccaccio wrote, "All the wisdom and ingenuity of man were unavailing." The disease challenged both the Christian vision of God's order and the classical vision of a society of gifted, capable people benefiting from their sciences and arts.

Long before Boccaccio, the ancient Greek historian Thucydides had told a similar story of moral collapse caused by an epidemic (possibly of typhoid fever or typhus, though there are other theories) that hit Athens in 430 BCE, in the middle of its long war with Sparta. It was bad timing, not that there is ever a good time for such things. Thucydides, who caught the disease himself but survived, described how Athenian society disintegrated when no one believed in the future. People blew their money on instant pleasures; they broke laws, since they did not expect to live long enough to be prosecuted. "As for the gods, it seemed to be the same thing whether one worshipped them or not, when one saw the good and the bad dying indiscriminately." Boccaccio's story was similar: faced with disaster, people abandoned civilized habits because they thought that the days of civilization were over.

The true situation was probably more complex. Total collapse, like total war, makes a compelling story, but when it looms, people will also do their utmost to ward it off or mitigate the damage. Thus, in the midst of the emergency, individuals did sometimes stick at their posts and make heroic efforts to hold things together. Boccaccio acknowledges this, as well he might, because one of those who kept working to minimize suffering in Florence was apparently his own father. As a minister of trade in the city, Boccaccino stayed on at great personal risk and worked to distribute food supplies. He may have caught the disease; certainly he died shortly afterward, of unknown causes. Elsewhere, others tried to devise new medical treatments (admittedly without success) or to reduce contagion, or to continue the necessary task of disposing of corpses as effectively as possible. When it was over, they worked to start life going again.

Thus, the story—as with everything involving human culture and behavior—was morally complicated, resisting conversion to a neat fable. As the nineteenth-century novelist Alessandro Manzoni observed in relation to a 1630 plague outbreak in Milan: "In any public misfortune, in any long disturbance of whatever may be the normal order of things, we always find a growth, a heightening of human virtue; but unfortunately it is always accompanied by an increase in human wickedness." One can also put that the other way around: along with panic or selfishness, one finds feats of courage—as well as many gradations between the extremes.

The fact that Manzoni's narrative was set in an outbreak of 1630 shows how long it would take the disease to recede from Europe. Petrarch and Boccaccio lived through further outbreaks. This first one in the late 1340s—the worst—came to an end, but more followed during the rest of that century and beyond. The whole era that we think of as the "Renaissance" in Europe, with its ongoing revival of classical wisdom and knowledge, its explosions of artistic brilliance, its development of better medicine and more productive modes of inquiry—all of this happened while people were dying at regular intervals from a disease that no one understood. The last European outbreak was in in Marseille in 1720; the plague then went on causing misery and death in other parts of the world, notably in China and India in the mid-nineteenth century. It can still kill, although now there are more effective treatments.

When this first wave declined, having destroyed at least a third of the population of western Europe (and much more in particular places, such as Florence), it left a changed human landscape on the continent. It also left post-traumatic effects of depression, grief, and anxiety, all expressed in powerful terms by Boccaccio and especially by Petrarch.

Petrarch was working in Parma when the plague began, and he stayed there throughout. He did not catch it, but friends did. He lost his current patron and good friend, Cardinal Giovanni Colonna, and he also (much later) heard of the death of his "Laura" back in Avignon. After the news reached him, he took out the volume of Virgil where he had recorded their first meeting and added more lines to record her death, which he dated April 6, 1348—exactly twenty-one years after their first encounter. He continued writing love poems, but they became darker and more melancholy. He also wrote a despairing Latin verse addressed "To himself," lamenting the dying everywhere, the losses, the many graves.

A letter to his old friend Ludwig van Kempen, whom he always called "my Socrates," asks, "What shall I say? Where shall I begin? Where shall I turn? Everywhere we see sorrow, on all sides we see terror." Where, he asks, are our sweet friends? "What thunderbolt destroyed all those things, what earthquake overturned them, what storm overcame them, what abyss absorbed them?" Humanity itself was almost wiped out— why? To teach us humility? Perhaps we are meant to learn that "man is too frail and proud an animal, he builds too securely on fragile foundations," or perhaps we are meant to long for the next world instead, because everything in this world can be lost.

More losses would come with the later recurrences of the disease. One of these, in 1361, killed Petrarch's son Giovanni, now reconciled with his father after their quarrel. He was only twenty-three at the time of his death.

The same outbreak also took Petrarch's "Socrates." He wrote of this death to another beloved epistolary friend, Francesco Nelli—but then Nelli died, too, soon afterward. Another friend of thirty-four years' standing, Angelo di Pietro di Stefano dei Tosetti, was also lost. Petrarch learned of this when a messenger brought him back one of his own letters to Angelo and silently handed it over, still unopened. Writing to Boccaccio about both deaths, Petrarch said he was now too numbed even to feel grief. He invited Boccaccio to come and stay in his new home in a beautiful location by the harbor in Venice; when Boccaccio did not immediately reply, Petrarch was stricken with "a terrible fear" for him. Fortunately, all was well, but that feeling of cold dread was never far away from any friendship in those times.

As always, Petrarch's way of getting himself through each of these crises was with literature. In 1349, after the first outbreak, he started work on the delayed project of collecting his letters. He also resumed a personal piece he had recently begun writing, the *Secretum*, or *Secret Book*. This takes the form of a dialogue between himself ("Francesco") and Augustine of Hippo, who plays the wise old mentor. Francesco admits to him that he feels a "hatred and contempt for the human condition, which so weigh upon me that I cannot be other than utterly miserable." Augustine advises him to turn to classical works of consolation by authors such as Seneca and Cicero, and to take careful notes as he goes so that he will remember their advice.

That consolatory genre—popular in both Christian and classical tradition—was one that Petrarch loved to read and emulate. A consolation would often take the form of a letter addressed to a friend or patron who had suffered bereavement, illness, or some other disaster; it could be circulated for the benefit of others, too. It would be filled with morally encouraging thoughts and would also be elegantly written, because beautiful writing in itself could lift the spirits.

This was why Petrarch paid attention to questions of literary technique even in the midst of offering comfort, or while he seemed sunk in his own misery. Thus, writing to his Socrates about their losses, he begins with an inarticulate cry, "Oh brother, brother, brother," only to stop immediately to add that he knows this is an unorthodox way to open a letter, but that after all it is not *so* unorthodox: Cicero himself once did something similar. It can be disorienting for a modern reader to see Petrarch combining a heartfelt cry with reflections on Ciceronian form. How sincere can he be if he can still think about such things? And how can he care about balancing his phrases so artfully—what thunderbolt, what earthquake, what storm, what abyss?

But it would never have occurred to Petrarch and his contemporaries that writing with precision and grace, in imitation of the greatest Latin speakers and writers, took anything *away* from the impact of what they wanted to say. Their belief was that Latin eloquence could, among other benefits, help a modern person to take heart and to be morally stronger.

And no author provided a better model for this than Cicero, who had refined the art of conveying what he thought in persuasive, emotionally irresistible language, both in his oratory and in his writings. He used particular kinds of syntactical architecture: an example is the distinctive "periodic sentence," which delays a punch line by letting the sentence go on in long, leisurely loops before it snaps shut, with the most important words at the end. Latin lends itself to this better than English because it allows for variation of word order, but English can do it, too. Here it is in a short sentence from the eighteenth-century writer Edward Gibbon, relating how he came to write six volumes of Roman history: "Unprovided with original learning, unformed in the habits of thinking, unskilled in the arts of composition, I resolved—to write a book."

A much longer example with devastating emotional power comes from Martin Luther King Jr.'s 1963 "Letter from Birmingham Jail," in which he writes of forever being told to "wait" for equality and social change:

But when you have seen vicious mobs lynch your mothers and fathers at will and drown your sisters and brothers at whim; when you have seen hate filled policemen curse, kick and even kill your black brothers and sisters; when you see the vast majority of your twenty million Negro brothers smothering in an airtight cage of poverty in the midst of an affluent society; when you suddenly find your tongue twisted and your speech stammering as you seek to explain to your six year old daughter why she can't go to the public amusement park that has just been advertised on television, and see tears welling up in her eyes when she is told that Funtown is closed to colored children, and see ominous clouds of inferiority beginning to form in her little mental sky, and see her beginning to distort her personality by developing an unconscious bitterness toward white people; when you have to concoct an answer for a five year old son who is asking: "Daddy, why do white people treat colored people so mean?" . . .

And so it continues, making us *wait* for the final clause, which, when it comes, is:

then you will understand why we find it difficult to wait.

The structure here mirrors the meaning: this is Ciceronian technique in the hands of a master writer and speaker—and used in the service of one of the most important human arguments ever advanced.

That human dimension was always important. Rhetorical skill was useless, or even damaging, if it did not go with virtue and moral purpose: all must be done in the service of good. Cicero drew a distinction between virtuous eloquence and the mayhem created by demagogues. Another rhetorician who wrote an influential manual, Quintilian, emphasized that a speaker who uses such powerful forms *must* be a good person, for philosophical reasons. After all, language is "the gift that distinguishes us from other living things," and Nature would hardly have given humans such a gift if it served only to "lend arms to crime." Quintilian also suggests that people with bad intentions would be so tormented by anxiety that they could not concentrate on achieving literary excellence anyway. "You might as well look for fruit in land that is choked with thorns and brambles."

Thus, to use language well is about more than adding decorative twiddles; it is about moving other people to emotion and recognition. It is a moral activity, because being able to communicate well is at the heart of *humanitas*—of being human in the fullest way.

Nowhere was this idea more evident than in the consolation letter, that most human of genres. The humanity is especially apparent when both writer and recipient have shared similar experiences, which bind them together *ubuntu*-style. The most moving—and most characteristic— example in Petrarch's letters occurs in 1368, when he writes to a friend who has recently lost his son. He supplies many pages of examples of grief and loss drawn from classical literature but also speaks of the fact that his own grandson has just died, leaving him devastated. ("The love for that little one so filled my breast that it is not easy to say whether I ever loved anyone else so much.") He sends Boccaccio's condolences as well: "We beg you, imagine us always to be one at your right, and the other at your left." The message coming from the erudite and personal parts of this letter alike is "You are not alone."

Other literary forms provided opportunities for similar comfort. Through the 1350s, the decade between the two worst outbreaks, Petrarch worked on a book called *Remedies for Fortune Fair and Foul*. He wrote it for his friend and former patron Azzo da Correggio, a once-powerful nobleman of Parma who had fallen into a threefold misfortune that had nothing to do with the plague: his wife and children were taken captive by enemies, he had to go into exile, and he suffered a paralyzing illness that meant he needed servants to help him walk or mount his horse. He needed all the calming, improving thoughts he could get.

Petrarch's book takes the form of two contrasting conversations, in which the personified figure of Reason responds to those of Sorrow and of Joy, in turn. Reason's task is to cheer Sorrow with happy thoughts, and to dampen Joy with reminders not to get carried away.

> **JOY:** The appearance of my body is admired by everybody.
>
> **REASON:** And yet, within a very short time, this comeliness and glow of your face will change. These blond locks shall fall out . . . and rotten decay shall consume and wear away the radiant white ivory of your teeth . . . [and so on].

Some causes for celebration are more easily squashed than others:

> **JOY:** I have elephants.
>
> **REASON:** May I ask for what purpose?

(No answer is recorded.)

In the other half of the book, Sorrow has her say:

> **SORROW:** I have been ordered into exile.
>
> **REASON:** Go willingly, and it will be a journey, not exile.
>
> **SORROW:** I dread the plague.
>
> **REASON:** Why shudder at the name of the plague, since it may even be some sort of comfort to die in the company of so many?

Not all sources of misery are overt ones, and inner sufferings are harder to manage: despite the rudder of our reason, we lose our way in turbulent seas. But if our suffering is deep, so too is the pleasure offered by the best parts of life. Reason reminds Sorrow of the many gifts God has bestowed on us, from the natural beauties of the world (those burbling streams and twittering songbirds) to our own excellent achievements. Able to invent and make things, we can even repair ourselves, crafting "wooden legs, iron hands, and wax noses," as well as that relatively new invention, spectacles to see through. We ourselves are beautiful in our hu-

manity, with eyes that
show our souls and "a
forehead to be aglow
with the secrets of the
mind." As with Ma-
netti later, Petrarch is
singing the "excellence
of man" tune here. In
fact, when a friend
wrote to him around

this time asking if he would like to compose something by way of an answer to Innocent III's treatise *On the Misery of Man*, he replied saying he
was currently at work on just that—referring to the positive half of the
Remedies. As a whole, it is a work not so much of positivity as of balance,
weighing each side against the other, and reminding us that the human
story is neither all good nor all bad, but that we can use each side to tem-
per the other.

To do this, we must deploy our best skills of reasoning and wisdom.
It is never any use trusting good fortune to get us through life, says Petrarch's figure of Reason; fortune will always let us down. A better plan
is to turn to the comforts of study, reflection, and friendship—all of
which are mutually enhancing. Reason quotes the ancient philosopher
Theophrastus: "Alone of all mankind, the scholar is no stranger in foreign lands; after losing kinsmen and intimates he still finds friends; he is
a citizen in every state, and fearlessly despises the awkward chances of
fortune."

Petrarch's whole oeuvre stands as a defiance of (and defense against)
fortune's vagaries, with which he had been familiar since his unsettled
childhood. He wrote against *loss*. By finding manuscripts and collecting
his own letters, as well as writing his consolations and other works, he
shored up barriers against the ruination of things—both of friends and
of books.

Boccaccio, too, felt that wasteland of loss behind him. In the preface to his *Genealogy of the Pagan Gods*, he looked back on past centuries as a welter of destruction and misfortune. Just think, he told his readers, how little of the work of the past has survived, and how many enemies it has had: fires, floods, the wearing-away of time. He reserved a special mention for another factor: the deliberate actions of early Christians who considered it their duty to wipe out all trace of religions that had come before them.

He and Petrarch set themselves to retrieve what they could of that past, and to rework it, reimagine it, use it to strengthen themselves and their friends against grief—and to pass it on to future generations, in the hope that they, too, would use it for a rebirth. Back in 1341, when Petrarch was submitting his poem *Africa* as part of the process for being awarded the poet's laurel, he addressed his own work as if it were a child going into that future world:

> My fate is to live amid varied and confusing storms. But for you perhaps, if as I hope and wish you will live long after me, there will follow a better age. This sleep of forgetfulness will not last for ever. When the darkness has been dispersed, our descendants can come again in the former pure radiance.

Such talk of darkness and radiance would continue throughout the next century. It formed a new way of visualizing European history. Behind him, and still around him, Petrarch feels that darkness as a devouring void, into which books and humanity alike have fallen. In a long-ago time, he believes, the ancients lit up their world with their eloquence and wisdom. In some new period of time to come, future generations may illuminate their world afresh. The hope is to bridge this gap, by preserving what can be found or copied, by creating new variations on the old forms, and by keeping it all in precarious existence, long enough for the lamps to be relit.

2.

Raising Ships

79 CE onward, but mostly the 1400s

New generations—losses and finds—Renaissances of the twelfth and other centuries—Coluccio Salutati, Niccolò Niccoli, Poggio Bracciolini, and their humanist hands—Roman ruins and the Nemi ships—prisons and wrecks—women: yes, there were some—education— Urbino, Castiglione, and sprezzatura—more and better copies—printers, especially Aldus Manutius.

Petrarch and Boccaccio had set the task for their successors: digging out the traces of wisdom and excellence, studying them, disseminating them, using them to illuminate moral and political questions, and creating new works of similar wisdom and excellence on old models.

Now, as the fourteenth century ended and the fifteenth began, the task was indeed taken up with enthusiasm by fresh generations of what we can now confidently call Italian "humanists"—a description that was beginning to catch on, although it never referred to any formal or organized grouping. This chapter is about a few of these people. I say a few, but they form quite a large cast: they were manuscript hunters, shipwreck raisers, explorers, teachers, copyists, printers, courtiers, collectors, writers, and more. Almost all were men, although a handful of women excelled in these humanistic activities, too; we shall meet them later in the chapter.

But first: Were Petrarch and Boccaccio even right about the darkness and destruction? And were there really no other luminous rescuers before them? Before taking up the main story, let us detour backward in time for a few pages to consider that larger context for their image of themselves.

As often happens with long-accepted ideas of history, the humanists' vision of a joyless, lightless Dark Age invites equal responses of "Let's face it, they've got a point" and "But wait, it's not that simple."

First: Let's face it, Petrarch and Boccaccio had a point. Much knowledge, technology, and literary culture had been lost in Europe, some of it a very long time before. The works of Democritus and Epicurus had already vanished in antiquity, for example. But the process of loss accelerated after the disintegration of the Western Roman Empire in the fifth century. Along with literary culture, many other things languished: techniques for designing public buildings, good roads, sewage systems, and other life-improving urban facilities all went unexercised until no one still alive knew how they were done anymore. Further damage was caused by what might otherwise seem an admirable spirit of make-do-and-mend recycling: stones were reused from tumbledown buildings, which thus tumbled down even more and became rubble. Old texts written on papyrus faded or cracked naturally; newer ones were written on parchment, which was stronger, but making it required a stack of skins from sheep, goats, or calves. Rather than do this, it was easier to scrape off writing from older, little-read books and use the surface again. Goodbye, older, little-read books.

And in such cases, Boccaccio was partly right to blame early Christians for the loss of some ancient works. When parchment had to be cleaned for use, minor religious works were one option, but it often seemed more pious to choose a non-Christian text. When it came to buildings, the need for recycled materials could harmonize directly with the desire to crush old enemies. The latter seems to have been a factor when Benedict, the sixth-century founder of the monastic order that would bear his name, wanted a mountaintop location for a chapel. He chose a site containing a temple of Apollo, with its sacred grove of trees, flattened both temple and trees, and built what would eventually develop into the monastery of Montecassino. In the same century, incidentally, at Bamiyan in what is now Afghanistan, two beautiful giant Buddhas were being carved into the mountainside. They would survive until 2001, when the Muslim Taliban blew them to a shattered hollow. No single religion, and no single century, has a monopoly on destroying beautiful things. Religion itself has no such monopoly: secularists after the eighteenth-century French Revolution would destroy church treasures in the name of Enlightenment and Progress.

Celebrating light and progress by destroying things: that was not a new idea, either. In 384 CE, a debate had taken place over a decision to remove pre-Christian statues from the Roman Senate building. Some conservation-minded people begged the emperor Valentinian II to save them, but the theologian Ambrose of Milan wrote urging Valentinian to resist such calls. After all, everything had been getting better and better since Creation, when the Earth was separated from the sea and "rescued from dripping darkness"; likewise, each of us progresses from childhood to adulthood—so why preserve the remains of an inferior, pre-Christian past?

So far, so dark, and Petrarch and Boccaccio had a point, including about the Christian effect. But wait, it's not that simple.

Monastic libraries did sometimes clean off classical works to make room for religious ones, but it was also largely thanks to them that so many classical works remained in existence at all. They often looked after their non-Christian works well—and one of the outstanding libraries for such works was Benedict's Montecassino. The original physical books of the ancient world had little chance of surviving any other way. Besides being written on friable papyrus, they were often rolled into scrolls, and thus easily damaged every time they were read. Very few works have come to us directly in such a form, although occasionally some do surface, even today. When Vesuvius erupted in 79 CE and covered Herculaneum in ash, a villa full of scrolls was buried. The scrolls were found in the eighteenth century but were mostly too compressed and damaged to be readable at the time. New technologies have now made it possible to decipher more of them, including a whole work previously thought lost: Seneca the Elder's *Histories*.

In most cases, however, we have classical texts only because of copying done in those long "dark" and medieval periods—because, as became even more apparent after printing came along, nothing is better for keeping books alive than making many copies. Such copying happened particularly in certain times and places. From the sixth to eighth centuries, it was done most effectively in the remotest Irish and British monastic communities. From the eighth century on, it was the Arabic world that translated and preserved a wealth of material, including many Greek texts on mathematics, medicine, philosophy, and more. In Baghdad, the Abbāsid caliphate and private patrons filled a library with teams of translators, supervised at one point in the ninth century by the fascinating al-Kindi, who also wrote his own studies of everything from earthquakes to ethics. Al-Kindi has every claim to be considered a humanist, specifically of the "Only connect!" kind who seeks to build bridges between traditions. He hoped to reconcile philosophy with theology, and Greek ideas with Islamic ones. That was dangerous work, however. Whether because his ideas had upset people or just because rivals were jealous of his achievements, he was locked out from his own library and physically assaulted. Most of his writings have disappeared.

During the same period, in northwestern Europe, the emperor Charlemagne ordered monks in his territory to work hard in their libraries, and thus to recover knowledge that, he said, had been "almost forgotten by the negligence of our ancestors"—a line that could have been spoken by any of the later book-hunting humanists. Charlemagne's interest in books is all the more surprising because, although he could read, he could not write. His contemporary biographer Einhard mentioned his putting wax tablets and notebooks under his pillow at night, so that he could practice if he woke, but the effort came too late in life; he had to continue relying on scribes.

That did not hold him back. Charlemagne founded boys' schools and, unusually, insisted on education for his own daughters. He kept nagging his monks: having received nice letters from monasteries offering prayers for him, he pointed out their errors of grammar and expression and arranged for the writers to have better training. To look after collections, he recruited a librarian and teacher from the British Isles, Alcuin of York. Monks in Charlemagne's territories developed a new, more legible script for their copying: the Carolingian or Caroline minuscule. A breakthrough in allowing better, clearer, more accessible reading, it became a direct influence on the handwriting of later humanists and so provided the basis of most of the printing fonts we use today.

Monastic scriptoria could be miserable places, or they could be lively and productive ones. Benedictine monks were each issued a book a year for private study, and they listened to readings as they ate—although the Rule of Benedict decreed that "no one should venture to ask any questions about the reading or anything else, in case this encourages talking." The Rule also warned against telling jokes, grumbling about shortages of wine, or taking pride in one's personal skills in any craft. This last item would have ruled out most later humanists, who loved to vaunt their brilliance.

Then again, so did some monks. The grammarian Gunzo of Novara recalled a visit in the year 960 to St. Gall—another monastery with a fine book collection, in what is now Switzerland. Talking after dinner, he accidentally used an accusative instead of an ablative case, partly because that was the norm in his Italian homeland. The monks pounced on the aberration, and much gleeful teasing ensued. "One young monk . . .

suggested that such a crime against Latin grammar deserved the rod, and another composed a verse on the spot to mark the occasion!" writes the literary historian Anna A. Grotans. It's hard, reading this, to view those clever and high-spirited monks as being lost in solemn fanaticism.

By the 1100s, so much copying, studying, and sharing of knowledge was going on that historians speak of a "twelfth-century Renaissance." It helped that new paper technology had now arrived in Europe, from China via the Arabic world and Spain, so that more could be written without defacing old parchment. Paper was made from cloth rags, and according to a splendid theory put forward recently by Marco Mostert, there were more rags around now because people were moving from the countryside to towns, and in towns it was fashionable to wear undergarments. These wore out faster than tough upper clothing and were often discarded, so rags were easier to source. Thus, from knickers came literature.

Other centers of learning flourished in Europe, too: universities, inspired by the scholarly institutes of the Arabic world, and cathedrals with libraries and schools attached, such as those of Chartres and Orléans in France. Built with innovations such as flying buttresses and covered

Basel Cathedral apostles

with statues and stained-glass windows, these were showcases for artistic and architectural skills, as well as for the life of the mind. Chartres in particular was adorned with tall, carved, serene human figures of great beauty; similar figures adorned other cathedrals. Visiting the cathedral of Basel a few years ago, I was struck by a beautiful early twelfth-century stone panel of six apostles: instead of showing the signs of their martyrdom, as was usual, they hold bound volumes and scrolls and look thoughtful and urbane, as if caught in the middle of a discussion of their reading.

The cathedrals provided a base for scholars such as John of Salisbury, who studied at Chartres as a young man and later became its bishop, and bequeathed it his personal library. He made at least six trips to Italy and collected manuscripts while there. Like Petrarch later, he was a great correspondent, filling his epistles to colleagues and friends with talk of Cicero, Virgil, Horace, and Ovid. Classical references also abounded in his treatises, which tackled highly humanistic subjects: *Policraticus* was about the behavior of courtiers and clerks, and *Metalogicon* discussed education and other topics.

Had John of Salisbury and Petrarch been able to meet, instead of being separated by two hundred years, they would have had a great time sharing stories of their travels and their brushes with power. (John, who had known Thomas à Becket at Canterbury Cathedral and narrowly missed being there when he was slashed to death by assassins, knew a thing or two about politics and about sudden turns of fortune in life.) They would have had no problem communicating in Latin, which enabled educated men in Europe to transcend place and time.

The fact that one can so easily imagine John and Petrarch talking casts doubt on the simple story of the coming of the light. Much did change in the fourteenth and fifteenth centuries, but perhaps the most dramatic aspect of that change was in how Petrarch and his successors *thought* of themselves: their sense of drawing on a lost, distant past to create a path out of the dark.

One thing is for sure: nothing would have united John and Petrarch more than their shared hunger for books, just as it united Petrarch and Boccaccio with each other—and also with the younger generations, whose story we will now resume.

One burden that goes along with forming an important book collection is worrying about how to leave it to posterity. Petrarch, at one stage, had made an agreement to bequeath his books to the government of Venice, to form the basis for a library accessible to the public. But when he died, the day before his seventieth birthday in 1374, the books stayed in the possession of his family, suggesting that something had gone wrong with the agreement. They were later dispersed and went through multiple owners, so that they ended up in libraries around western Europe, including in London and Paris as well as in Italian cities.

Petrarch did leave an affectionate gift to Boccaccio in his will: "fifty Florentine gold florins for a winter garment to be worn by him while he is studying and working during the night hours." But Boccaccio had little time to benefit from snuggling into this, because he died as well, the following year, aged sixty-two. His library went to a friar he knew, and after the friar's death to the monastery of Santo Spirito in Florence, where the books were stored in chests and hardly used, despite a proviso in his will that they should be made available to anyone who wanted to see them.

Now that the "three crowns of Florence" (as Dante, Petrarch, and Boccaccio became known in a nice piece of Florentine marketing) were all gone, their successors applied themselves to the task of commemorating them and distributing their works. The most energetic character behind this was Florence's chancellor Coluccio Salutati, who had a network of friends and correspondents as large as Petrarch's own. Coluccio put them to work trying to locate any missing or unfinished texts left by Petrarch, particularly the notebooks in which his laurel-winning poem *Africa* was written. Coluccio also felt inspired to improve upon the excessively modest epitaph that Boccaccio himself had written for his own tomb in

Certaldo. The original was just a few lines long. Coluccio added twelve more verses, including the admonition "Distinguished poet, why speak of yourself so humbly, / As though in passing?" Had Boccaccio seen these additions, he would surely have been touched, having so often felt undervalued in life, even while being generous himself in his praise of others.

Coluccio was also a great collector, with a library of some eight hundred books, enhanced by his own marginal notes and amendments. He lent them to interested readers, and eventually they went to the monastery of San Marco in Florence. He also advanced the study of Greek in Florence, by inviting the scholar Manuel Chrysoloras from Constantinople to teach it—beginning a great flourishing of Greek studies in Italy and putting Petrarch's and Boccaccio's struggles with the language firmly in the past.

Another collector with a fine library, also of about eight hundred books, was Niccolò Niccoli. A generation younger than Coluccio, and still a child when Petrarch and Boccaccio died, Niccolò grew up to become the librarian to Cosimo de' Medici—whose family, having made a fortune by banking and trade, used part of that wealth to support scholars and artists. One of Niccolò's executive decisions was to dig out the books of Boccaccio from their neglectful storage in Santo Spirito and make them more available. He also left his own books to the Medici collections, on condition that they be accessible to anyone who wanted to see or even borrow them. The Medici books became the foundation of Florence's two main libraries today, the Biblioteca Medicea Laurenziana and the Biblioteca Nazionale Centrale.

Like Boccaccio, Niccolò was the son of a merchant and had gone through the same life-changing process of rejecting that line of work in favor of a literary and scholarly career. He delighted in both pleasures and treasures, and lived surrounded by his hoard of sculptures, mosaics, and pottery, as well as manuscripts. He did not marry and lived alone except for servants, but in company he was scintillating, according to the memoirs of book dealer Vespasiano da Bisticci, a valuable source on many humanists of the time. "Whenever he joined a discussion of learned men, which he often did for relaxation, his funny stories and mordant raillery (for he naturally overflowed with comic jests) would make all his listeners laugh continuously," wrote Vespasiano. Giannozzo Manetti wrote a biography, too, and noted how Niccolò "enhanced his natural good looks with fine, plum-colored garments." He encouraged groups of young scholars to come to his house to read his books, and then to put the books down and discuss whatever they had learned from them.

And so the tradition continued of combining friendship with bibliomania. Niccolò maintained a devoted correspondence with his younger friend Poggio Bracciolini, whose lively personality sometimes crossed the line into "strong invective" (Vespasiano again) and downright bombast. At least one of his quarrels came to the point of a physical punch-up. But Poggio was more amiable with Niccolò, and their letters are filled with happy book talk and badinage. To Niccolò's satisfaction, Poggio traveled widely in search of manuscripts and often sent them to him.

The most notable find came while Poggio was with the papal court at the Council of Constance, which ran from 1414 to 1418 in what is now Germany. The council's purpose was to try to heal an appalling mess in the church known as the Great Schism, which broke out after rival conclaves elected one pope in Rome and another in Avignon (the same replacement papal city that had been used in the previous century). Each newly elected pope promptly excommunicated the other. Cardinals met in Livorno to tackle the situation, but they did this by electing yet a third pope, who also met with no approval elsewhere. The Council of Constance had more success. Deposing all three, it suggested a fourth, who managed to establish himself as Martin V. From the point of view of the new humanistic scholars, it was a good choice: Martin liked these eloquent and knowledgeable writers and gave many of them secretarial and administrative jobs.

While working for the Roman contingent during that time, Poggio and his friends explored monasteries in a large area around Constance. Petrarch would have envied them their finds. At Cluny Abbey, they came upon more Cicero speeches. At St. Gall, they found several works, including a good text of Vitruvius's treatise on architecture, and something especially desirable: the first complete text of Quintilian's *Institutes of Oratory*—that bible of rhetorical technique, with its argument that to be an orator one must be a virtuous person. Then, probably in Fulda, Poggio and his

friend Bartolomeo da Montepulciano found Lucretius's *On the Nature of Things*, the long poem transmitting the Epicurean and Democritan theory of atoms and skepticism about the gods. Fragments had been mentioned by other authors, so it was known to exist, but it was assumed to be lost in its full form. Poggio sent it to Niccolò, who was so entranced by it that his usual openness failed him. He kept it to himself for ten years before letting anyone else, even Poggio, spend time with it.

Usually, they were more generous with each other. In 1423, while working in Rome as a papal secretary, Poggio invited Niccolò to join him to live in his comfortable apartment. "We shall talk together; day and night we shall live together; we shall root out every trace of ancient times." It must have been an entertaining household, what with Niccolò's plum-clad festivities and Poggio's ribald sense of humor. It was during this time in Rome that Poggio wrote a book of quips and anecdotes, *Facetiae*: a highly humanistic amusement full of double entendres, as in the story of the messenger who asks a woman if she wishes to send a note to her husband, who is away from home. "How can I write," she replies, "when my husband has taken his pen away with him, and left my inkwell empty?" The book circulated widely and was printed long after Poggio's death in many editions—the first published joke book.

In their copying and writing, Coluccio, Niccolò, Poggio, and others developed a new style of handwriting to reflect their new spirit. Known as the "humanistic hand," it was based on writing that they thought was from antiquity, though in fact it was none other than the minuscule first developed by Charlemagne's scribes. Simple and easier to read than the usual medieval hand, it was perfect for readers who could set their own pace and get through many books, rather than having to recite texts aloud, with slow care, at a lectern. The humanists dismissed the more elaborate style as "Gothic," an insult implying "barbarian"—as in the hordes of Goths and Vandals who had brought Rome to its earlier downfall. Their own rival style said everything about how they saw themselves: reviving old simplicity, sweeping away clutter, and ushering knowledge into the light.

Speaking of clutter, they could hardly fail to notice the ancient riches that surrounded them in Rome, albeit in a state of grim disarray. The Colosseum was then lying in a fallen heap. Many old buildings had been raided for their materials. The city's arches were broken and half buried

Poggio's humanistic hand

in plants grazed by sheep. It all intrigued the humanists greatly. Petrarch, during several visits, had done his best to match what he saw to the written accounts he had read in classical history, myth, or poetry. He and his friend and patron Giovanni Colonna, during a stay there together, made a game of working out locations. They would look around and say, "Here the circus games and the rape of the Sabines, there the marsh of Capri and the place where Romulus vanished." At sunset each day, they would climb to the roof of the baths of Diocletian to gaze at the view and compare their knowledge: Petrarch was more expert on ancient history, Colonna on early Christian times. They still made mistakes, partly because they were (mis)guided by a standard work dating to the twelfth or early thirteenth century: Magister Gregorius's *The Marvels of Rome*.

Poggio and his friend Antonio Loschi did more research, and could congratulate themselves on setting Petrarch right. Where Petrarch thought he had found the tomb of Remus, for example, Antonio realized it was that of Cestius. (Matthew Kneale comments: "Not such a hard discovery, seeing as the name Cestius was written on its side in huge letters.")

Poggio wrote his own description of the ruins of Rome, mapping presumed sites of ancient buildings and streets onto the scene that remained; he incorporated it very appropriately into a 1448 work about the vagaries of fortune. He applied similar archaeological skills to the wider countryside around the city, poring over tombs or climbing up arches to transcribe their inscriptions.

Others also studied Roman ruins, but they did so in order to learn from their building techniques, and even to work out improvements. Two youths who lived semi-wild while exploring the area in the early 1400s were assumed by locals to be destitute treasure hunters. In fact, their names were Filippo Brunelleschi and Donato di Niccolò di Betto Bardi, later known as Donatello, and they were doing research. Their own innovations, a few years later, would transform the architecture of Florence. A few travelers took their inquiries farther: Cyriac of Ancona toured Greece and Turkey recording inscriptions. Historians such as Flavio

Biondo (alternatively called Biondo Flavio, and in any case the two words both mean the same thing—"blond") became more adept at combining such physical investigations with documentary sources to create extended studies with titles such as *Decades of History*, *Rome Restored*, *Italy Illuminated*, and *Rome in Triumph*. Medieval travelers had been interested in the relics of the past, too, but these more modern ones approached them through a truly historical inquiry: *How* did each of these ruins come to be there? Who built the structures, and who destroyed them?

Also interested in Roman origins was the architect Leon Battista Alberti, who compiled a *Description of the City of Rome* in the 1440s, after lengthy surveying. In the same decade, he became involved in a dramatic project just outside Rome: trying, with Flavio Biondo and others, to raise two huge ancient ships from the bottom of nearby Lake Nemi.

People had wondered about those ships for a long time. They could be seen on clear days, as images wavering below the surface. Local fishermen sometimes found nails and wood fragments sticking in their nets. Alberti devised a method that, he hoped, would make it possible to lift the whole vessels and inspect them. Teams of divers, brought in from the port of Genoa—"more fish than men," as Biondo wrote—swam down to one of the ships and attached ropes, the other ends of which were fixed to winches on the surface, held up by floating barrels. The first stages went well. But when the winches were turned and the ship began to lift, the ropes quickly cheese-wired through its rotting timbers, and it subsided to the bottom again. A few pieces did emerge for Biondo and Alberti to inspect. They made guesses at their age, but not accurate ones. In fact, the ships were luxury barges dating from the reign of the emperor Caligula. The larger one was seventy meters long, absurdly big for use in a modest lake. They were fitted out with plumbing, mosaics, and luxuries of all kinds, signs of Roman practical achievement at its most resplendent.

Other partial attempts would be made over the years. A mosaic was detached from one of the decks in 1895 and, after various adventures, turned up converted to a coffee table in the home of a New York antiques

dealer, who was unaware of its origin. It has since been returned to the
Nemi museum, whose director has observed, "If you look at it from an
angle, you can still see traces of a ring from a cup bottom."

The full raising of the ships was finally achieved during the era of
Mussolini—a time when the grandeur of Rome was very much in fashion. Incredibly, it was done by draining a great deal of the lake, a feat that
took almost five years, between 1928 and 1932, and that suffered a literal
hiccup when the decreasing weight of water set off an eruption of mud
from the lake floor. It worked, however, and the retrieved ships were put
on display in the museum. Unfortunately, they had only a few years out
in the air. During U.S. bombing on the night of May 31, 1944, the whole
museum caught fire, including the ships. Some artifacts did survive, including the mosaic before its mysterious journey to New York. The museum is now alive and well again.

In the fifteenth century, the idea of raising barely visible wrecked
ships from the depths happened to make the perfect metaphor for the
whole humanistic project of salvaging wrecked or sunken knowledge in
all its forms. Flavio Biondo used it in his *Italy Illuminated* to describe his

vision of the historian's task. Do not complain, he wrote, if I fail to reconstruct events in their entirety, as if rescuing a whole ship. Instead, please thank me for the fragmentary reconstructions that *can* be done—"for having hauled ashore some planks from so vast a shipwreck, planks which were floating on the surface of the water or nearly lost to view."

Humanist hunters of books and ruins alike were fond of such metaphors. When not speaking of wrecks or fires or darkness, they wrote of their work as a freeing of prisoners from dungeons. Poggio described the Quintilian manuscript he found in St. Gall as sitting in a foul, dark cell at the foot of a tower, like a criminal, with a dirty beard and mud-caked hair. "He seemed to stretch out his hands and beg for the loyalty of the Roman people, to demand that he be saved from an unjust sentence." (The image is slightly spoiled by the fact that Poggio had to leave the manuscript there. But he did make his copy of it, thus liberating Quintilian in the sense that mattered.) Poggio's friend Cinzio, or Cincius, of Rome lent the books they found some eloquent imaginary lines to speak: "You men who love the Latin tongue, let me not be utterly destroyed by this woeful neglect. Snatch me from this prison in whose gloom even the bright light of the books within cannot be seen."

The play of light and darkness continued. The bookseller and biographer Vespasiano contrasted the "great darkness" in which ignorant people live with the enlightenment or illumination that writers bring to the world. Echoing the remarks Petrarch had once made to Boccaccio, he added that ignorance is sometimes considered holy, but as a virtue it is overrated. It may even be the source of worldly evil, he suggested.

As the writers and collectors went on with their humanitarian rescues of the ancients, raising them from the deep and springing them from dungeons, the ancients repaid the effort by offering a regenerative moral light to the modern world. Francesco Barbaro, a Venetian scholar, wrote to Poggio after the latter's discovery of Quintilian and other works, saying how wonderful it was to hear "of so much effort for the good of all mankind, of so many benefits that will last forever"—since "culture and mental training, which are adapted to a good and blessed life and fair speech" can bring great advantages not just to individuals but to cities, nations, and the whole world.

It was heady work: saving modern humanity, while also indulging one's own lust for acquisition, piling up the books and other artifacts for blissful gloating. "I have a room full of marble heads," wrote Poggio, and he dreamed of finding a bigger place in the country so he could fill it with even more treasures. Some collectors did have such resources: Cardinal Prospero Colonna, who had largely funded the Nemi ships project, created a garden for sculptures on the Quirinal Hill. As a bonus, while this site was being dug, still more antiquities emerged from the earth. No wonder Poggio chose the cardinal as the dedicatee of his work *On Avarice*, which argued for an ancient idea: that great wealth was not sinful but virtuous, because life-enhancing things could be done with it.

The amassing of finds continued, most notably with the Medici in Florence. Far away to the north, another collection was created by Isabella d'Este, the *marchesa* of Mantua. She turned one tower of the palace into her private study and gallery, and filled it with ancient objects, as well as paintings freshly commissioned from contemporary artists. She was a rare case of a great patron and collector who was also a woman.

Women: if only there were more of them at this stage of the story! In 1984, the historian Joan Kelly-Gadol wrote a famous paper posing the question "Did Women Have a Renaissance?" You can probably guess her conclusion. She argued that medieval Europe had offered more scope for achievement, at least for some women. They might manage large properties, especially if their husbands went off crusading. Or they might flourish in monastic communities, as in the case of the tenth-century poet, playwright, and historian Hrotswitha of Gandersheim, whose plays were found and published amid much excitement in the humanist era; or the twelfth-century composer, philosopher, physician, mystic, and inventor of an artificial language Hildegard of Bingen.

The world of the fifteenth-century humanists, by contrast, was more urban and less monastic. Humanist men worked as tutors or secretaries in private clerical or princely households, or as officials or diplomats in the public realm. In all these roles, the *studia humanitatis* were important—classically consisting of five subjects: grammar, rhetoric, poetry, history, and moral philosophy. Learning to speak and write well, and to understand historical examples and moral philosophy, formed the perfect foundation for a life dedicated to public speaking, writing, politics, and wise judgments. But that was the problem. Few parents would ever dream of their girls having a life of that sort. Well-born women were expected to stay at home, in modest seclusion, absent from the public realm entirely. They would never give addresses or write elegant letters; they had no need of Latin, and there was no point in studying the art of making wise choices, because they were unlikely to be able to make many choices at all. Lacking such training, they were excluded from most of what counted as *humanitas*. Instead, they had the virtues of chastity and modesty to look forward to, and for those one did not need much education. Some of the most vibrant humanist cities, notably Florence, were also the ones where the most pressure was put on women to be invisible.

And yet some humanist women did make their mark. An outstanding early example was the first known female professional writer, Christine de Pizan. Born in Venice in 1364, she spent most of her life in France, apparently acquiring from her physician father a reasonable education in Italian and French, and possibly also Latin. She married at fifteen and had three children. The course of her life changed when both her husband and her father died, leaving her with the responsibility of supporting herself, her children, and her mother. To do this, she turned to writing, producing works for the king and others in exchange for financial patronage. Her versatility was impressive: in addition to works on ethics, education, politics, and war—all considered masculine subjects—she wrote love poetry and some verses recounting episodes of her own life, illustrating one of Petrarch's favorite themes: *The Mutability of Fortune*. In 1405, she wrote *The Book of the City of Ladies*, a collection of stories drawing on a work by Boccaccio about women in myth and history, but adding a rousing defense of women's general skills and moral excellence. Much of the defense is spoken by the voice of Reason, who, as in the positive half of Petrarch's *Remedies for Fortune Fair and Foul*, provides cheering thoughts to offset gloom. When the narrator becomes depressed by reading the many misogynistic things men have written about women, Reason cheers her. She suggests asking the question: Have these men never been wrong about anything? Clearly they have, since they so often contradict or correct one another and cannot all have been right. "Let me tell you," she says, "that those who speak ill of women do more harm to themselves than they do to the women they actually slander." She advises the narrator to build a "City of Ladies" in her mind and fill it with all the examples she can discover of scholarly, brave, and inspiring women. This is a different sort of rescue task: deploying forgotten figures to cheer the living.

Other women found success later in that century, too: women such as Laura Cereta, who wrote poetry as well as a collection of her own letters, which she—like Petrarch—distributed as a work of literature. Among her correspondents were many notable humanistic men; she filled the letters with details about her life and with thoughts on why women should have better access to education and more independence in marriage. Another letter writer, Cassandra Fedele, collected her epistles, along with an oration in Latin, and sent the work to Angelo Ambrogini, known as Poliziano, an eminent tutor to the Medici family. He responded with a letter of elegant and condescending praise: how wonderful, he said, to encounter a woman who wielded a pen nib instead of a needle, and who painted ink on paper instead of makeup on her skin. At least this was better than being ignored, which was what happened to her for a long time after that. One of her letters provides a wry twist on Cicero's great paean to the pleasures

The City of Ladies

and benefits of the "human studies" in his *Archias* speech. She wrote: "Even though the study of letters promises and offers no reward for women and no dignity, every woman ought to seek and embrace these studies for that pleasure and delight alone that [comes] from them." After many years of poverty following her husband's death, she finally achieved an appointment as prioress of a Venice orphanage, at the age of eighty-two; at ninety, she had the honor of being asked to write and deliver an elegant Latin speech of welcome when the queen of Poland visited the city.

That was in 1556, and by that time the idea of a scholarly female perhaps seemed *very* slightly less bizarre than before, and women had a *very* slightly better chance of getting an education. The poet Vittoria Colonna benefited from access to the excellent library of another woman, Costanza d'Avalos, the aunt of the boy Vittoria had been betrothed to marry from the age of three. In far-off England, the humanist Thomas More chose to educate his daughters. So did Henry VIII: Mary was taught by the Spanish humanist Juan Luis Vives, and Elizabeth by Roger Ascham, who gushed sycophantic amazement at her precocious intellect and language skills. But these were the privileged few, educated because they did

in fact have the expectation of playing a political role and carrying moral responsibility, and so it made sense for them to learn how to do it well.

Of course, just because the boys had a finer and fuller moral education does not mean that they always came out as paragons of virtue and wisdom. The humanistic education of the time has even been described as mainly a technique for turning out cocky, fluent public figures with no genuine intellectual curiosity or serious thought in their heads at all. There is some justice in this, and I have noticed in early twenty-first-century Britain that an ability to sling around Latin quotations while behaving like a cad can still take you a long way.

Still, the ideal was certainly an admirable one, directly absorbed from such revered models as Cicero and Quintilian: to govern well, one should be able to speak well, reason well, practice moderation and balance, and be suffused with "humanity" in all its senses—including knowing something of how real human stories had played out in the past.

Good teachers should be able to impart all this to their students, and not only in a theoretical way. They should also be rounded, cultivated, excellent human beings themselves, in order to set a good example. Humanistic tutors liked to contrast themselves with old-style medieval university professors, visualized as eccentric, pedantic, and fixated on syllogisms and pointless paradoxes such as: "Ham makes us drink; drinking quenches thirst; therefore ham quenches thirst." Princess Mary's teacher, Juan Luis Vives, mocked pedants of this type, who thought themselves so clever and philosophical but fell into stammering awkwardness as soon as they were taken out of their little worlds. They knew nothing of the more valuable skills of life: "moral philosophy, which teaches us about the mind and human life, and lends grace to minds and manners; or history, which is the mother of learning and experience; or oratory, which both teaches and governs life and common sense; or the science of politics or economics, by which public and domestic affairs are regulated." These three humanistic pillars—moral philosophy, historical understanding, and good communication—were all best practiced in the world, even if that world was the rarefied one of a royal entourage. Vives thanked God for freeing him from pedantry, and for allowing him thus to discover "the true disciplines that are worthy of man, and for that reason often called the humanities."

Along with those disciplines came pleasant environments in which to study them. In Mantua, the Gonzaga family hosted a school beautifully set amid meadows, run by Vittorino da Feltre and known as La Giocosa or La Gioiosa: the Playful, or Joyful, School. In Ferrara, Guarino da Verona and his son Battista Guarini taught the Este family and their friends in an equally beautiful setting. To one pupil, Leonello d'Este, Guarino wrote in praise of the pleasures of reading books outdoors, perhaps in a boat on the river. He described gliding, book open on his knees, past vineyards and fields full of singing farmers. But reading in an indoor library could be almost as delightful. A dialogue by another author features a scene of Guarino advising Leonello on how to decorate such a library: besides books, one could add roses, sprigs of rosemary, a sundial, a lyre, and pictures of gods and scholars. Best not to include kittens or caged birds, however; their antics are too distracting.

Imagining this ideal library brings to mind another such setting: the magnificent palace of Urbino, a little farther down the Italian peninsula. The duke there, Federico da Montefeltro, began as one of Vittorino's pupils in Mantua. He then made his fortune as a *condottiere*, or mercenary soldier, and from 1454 put that fortune into building a dream palace, high on a hill, with perfectly proportioned architecture and an internal decor that sang of the humanities and humanity. In his private study were beautiful images, in colored woods, of admired writers (Homer, Virgil, Cicero, Seneca, Tacitus), and of musical instruments, classical temples, parrots, and his pet squirrel—not too distracting, since in wooden form they couldn't leap around. His full library filled two halls, adorned with frescoes of the Arts and Sciences and a Latin inscription saying, of his book collection: "In this house you have wealth, golden bowls, abundance of money, crowds of servants, sparkling gems, rich jewels, precious chains and girdles. But here is a treasure that far outshines all these splendours." The supplier of most of the contents was Vespasiano da Bisticci, who reportedly kept thirty-four copyists permanently busy just making manuscripts for the duke of Urbino. All, of course, were written in the clear humanist hand.

The Urbino court was known for its social life, and here women *were* part of the scene, both in the original duke's time (the duchess and her friends loved a party) and afterward. The atmosphere of a slightly later generation was captured by Count Baldassare Castiglione, a soldier and diplomat also from near Mantua, who spent a lot of time at the Urbino court during the first decades of the sixteenth century, studying in the library and having a simply marvelous time with the fashionable set. His dialogue *The Book of the Courtier* evokes that life, with its clever conversations, witty sallies, and debates on love or eloquence or political virtue, all taking place against the backdrop of spectacular scenery. Think of the mood of Boccaccio's *Decameron*, with its gatherings and games; but instead of telling bawdy stories, they posed such questions as: "If I had to be openly mad, what kind of folly would I be thought likely to display?"

One of these challenges was to describe the qualities of an ideal courtier. The group discusses which sports he should excel in. Tennis is good; tightrope walking is optional. Above all, they agree that he should be brave, well educated, and eloquent, and should behave with *sprezzatura*. This meant a relaxed, dismissive nonchalance: doing difficult things as if by nature, making no visible effort. The word, to me, brings to mind someone carelessly flinging a cloak around the shoulders in such a way that it is left hanging perfectly, without needing to be pinned in place or rearranged.

Sprezzatura was also the ideal in literary activity. Castiglione claims that he wrote his own book this way, tossing it together like a light salad and never intending to produce a proper edition, since that required effort. He tells us that his friend Vittoria Colonna, the poet, secretly circulated it among friends, until it had been so widely read anyway that he realized he might as well publish it. The truth was different: he took pains over his work, as most authors do, and revised *The Book of the Courtier* many times before its appearance, to high acclaim, in 1528.

Such surreptitious groundwork went into the achievements of many of these scholars, authors, and tutors. Although they liked to appear to the manner born, many came from much more modest backgrounds than their aristocratic students. Like Petrarch and Boccaccio before them, some had gone through the painful ritual of rejecting parental expectations and choosing the humanist path instead. Finding and maintaining their niches of employment or patronage surely required more toil and ingenuity than they revealed, including in the work of keeping up nonchalant appearances.

Nor did they always succeed in weeding out all traces of the mad-professor tendency. One admired scholar and tutor at the court of Forlì, Antonio Urceo, known as Codro, was given an apartment in the palace to live and work in. One day he went out, leaving a candle burning on his desk. A pile of papers caught fire; the flames spread, and when he returned, it was to find almost everything destroyed, including his current work in progress.

Forgetting all his humanistic polish and *sprezzatura*, Codro ran pell-mell out of the city into the countryside, screaming damnation against both God and the Virgin Mary, and calling on the Devil to take his soul. His cries faded as he vanished into the wilderness. By the time he was calm enough to return, the city's gates had been closed for the night. He had to sleep outside, and in the morning a kind carpenter took him in and let him stay in his house. Codro remained there for six months, not returning to the palace and not touching a book—until, at last, his equilibrium was restored and he was able to resume work.

Castiglione's book was able to become a fashionable success partly because it was not circulated only in manuscript to limited numbers of readers, as happened with earlier writers. It was printed.

Printing, both with and without movable type, had been pioneered long before in China and Korea: it was useful for the Buddhist practice of reproducing prayers in large quantities to gain merit. When the technology arrived in Europe, it would quickly be put to a similar use churning out papal indulgences—that is, tickets reducing the amount of punishment to be expected in the afterlife. Up to ten thousand such indulgences were printed by Johannes Gutenberg, who would be better remembered for producing the first major European printed book: his great 1455 Bible.

Like most inventions that improve human life, the printing press met with skepticism and resistance. The duke of Urbino wanted nothing to do with such books. A German Benedictine abbot, Johannes Trithemius, wrote *In Praise of Scribes*, arguing that manuscripts were better than printed books and that scribing was too useful a spiritual exercise for monks to give up. Then, in order to reach as wide an audience as possible, he had the book printed.

The abbot also argued that parchment was a more durable substance than paper, and this was true—although knicker-based paper has survived beautifully compared with wood-pulp paperbacks of the 1970s. Nonetheless, for making literary works survive, printing surely beats manuscript-copying, since so many copies can be made and distributed. One just has to think of Boccaccio sending the precious pages of the Homer translation back and forth to Petrarch, or Poggio being unable to get Lucretius back from Niccolò for ten years. True, many printed books have been lost from the world, too, but on the whole, books have a better chance than manuscripts. Early printing is a prime example of technical ingenuity working in harmony with cultural knowledge to produce something of lasting value. As Edward Gibbon wrote, from this group of German mechanical workers came "an art which derides the havock of time and barbarism."

Trithemius's work praised the beauties of manuscripts, but printing developed its own beauty, too, and never more so than when it was designed to be plain, clean, and readable. The German printers used a heavy "blackletter" font, which continued to be widely preferred in other places for sacred works. Because of its northern origins, it was known as "Gothic." But demand also arose for lighter fonts, to go with the light-filled qualities of rediscovered classical literature. The first (surviving) book to be printed in Italy, a 1465 edition of Cicero's *De oratore*, was done in such a font, although the printers were the Germans Arnold Pannartz and Conrad Sweynheym. They based it on the "humanist hand," which in turn was based on the Carolingian minuscule—still thought to be ancient Roman. The best use of such designs, however, had to await the Italian who would eventually publish Castiglione's *Courtier*, Aldus Manutius of Venice, along with his brilliant typecutter, Francesco Griffo.

Aldus Manutius had had a humanistic education from Battista Guarini in Ferrara, and at first he contemplated a scholarly career. But then, aged forty, he found himself in Venice and discovered printing. That city had become the great Italian center for this technology: by Aldus's time, it had about 150 presses at work and was filled with bookstalls. Aldus worked for other printers to learn the trade, then started his own business. When one of the era's regular bouts of the plague struck in 1498, he fell ill and made a vow to God: if he was spared death, he would give up printing and enter the church. He was spared death but thought better of the vow, and asked the pope himself for special dispensation to break it on the grounds that he depended financially on the business—as if priests were not able to make a perfectly good living. Fortunately for printing history, the pope, Alexander VI, himself no stranger to creative interpretations of rules, obliged him.

Aldus became a virtuoso of printing styles. At one extreme, he could do extravaganzas for vanity authors. The outstanding example, in 1499, was *Hypnerotomachia Poliphili*—or, translated in a fuller version, *Poliphilo's Hypnerotomachia Where He Teaches That All Things Human Are No More Than a Dream*. The author, a monk then in his late sixties, was in theory anonymous, but he left a massive clue in the form of an acrostic running through the first letters of all the chapters: it spelled out a sentence that included his name, Francesco Colonna. His story tells, in a hybrid Latinized Italian, of the hero Poliphilo, who wanders among ancient ruins and meadows in search of his lost love, Polia. Just like Aldus, she promised during a plague episode that she would withdraw from the world if she survived—in her case to become a chaste maiden of the goddess Diana's temple. Unlike Aldus, she has gone through with it. But the chastity part proves difficult when one day Poliphilo comes into the temple and faints handsomely at the altar: she revives him with a kiss. The high priestess sees them and drives them out of the temple. Poliphilo is happy, but when he tries to embrace Polia, she vanishes from his grasp. And so it ends—for it *was* all a dream.

As the book historian E. P. Goldschmidt put it, the book expresses "the frenzied raptures of a pedant." He also remarked, "Like some other great books it is written by a lunatic." But these are *humanistic* raptures and lunacies, filled with a sense of joy in language and in visual beauty. Thanks to Aldus, the story is printed in a clear font with plenty of surrounding space, lucid in typography if not in content. It comes with woodcuts, possibly by the artist Benedetto Bordone, which depict ruins, processions, and tombs, with lots of detailed lettering to please the inscription collectors in the audience.

Other Aldine productions were more delicate and restrained in content. He issued both modern and classical works in a portable format, perfect for reading while drifting downstream in a boat. Small books were not new: as far back as the first century CE, the Latin poet Martial had recommended that readers who wanted to take his book on a journey should buy the ones "that parchment compresses in small pages." But such books now came into their own as affordable companions for mobile humanists. To go with Aldus's clean designs, Griffo also designed a new, easy-reading font, the "italic." It made an appearance in 1500, for a few words in a frontispiece, before being used more fully for an edition of Virgil's poetry in April 1501.

Virgil was an apt choice, since he was widely adored and imitated by humanists. One of the new authors who had been emulating his pastoral sensibility was Pietro Bembo, a friend of Castiglione who had also spent time at the Urbino court and, before that, the Este court in Ferrara. He brought Aldus his first book, *De Aetna*—a beguiling example of humanistic writing and printing at its best.

The book is not printed in the italic; it appeared in February 1496 and that invention was still a few years away. But the letters are clean and clear, and include an excellent innovation: an attractive, chubby semicolon, used for the first time to indicate a break or pause. In general, the pages look fresh, expressing the humanists' ideal of light and liberation. The appearance is matched by the cheerful elegance of the story. We meet the author strolling by a river with his father, Bernardo, at their fine villa near Padua, and telling him about his recent trip to Sicily. As part of this, he and a friend had climbed the volcano, Etna, pausing along the way to contemplate ruins, Greek coins, and varieties of trees. Pietro reflects on things he had read about Etna in the ancient authors, including the geographer Strabo, who said that snow would be found at the top only in winter. It was a surprise, says Pietro, to find that this was not true: even in summer, and amid the sulfurous gas clouds and the occasional flying stone, the

PETRI BEMBI DE AETNA AD ANGELVM CHABRIELEM LIBER.
Factum a nobis pueris est , et quidem sedulo Angele; quod meminisse te certo scio;ut fructus studiorum nostrorum, quos ferebat illa aetas nó tam maturos, q̃ uberes, semper tibi aliquos promeremus: nam siue dolebas aliquid, siue gaudebas;

snow was still frozen. Could it be that the old authors sometimes got things wrong? And how do volcanoes work, anyway? Do they breathe like human lungs, inhaling vapors and then expelling them?

Showing off its author's inquiring mind, along with his immersion in classical sources and literary technique, *De Aetna* is also a perfect quiet marriage of printed format to content. It amounts to a demonstration of something remarked upon by the twentieth-century literary historian Ernst Robert Curtius: that the true humanistic temperament "delights simultaneously in the world and in the book."

Through subsequent centuries, printing would serve both world and book: both science and the humanities. It would attract masters of eloquence such as Pietro Bembo, but also more pragmatic spirits wanting to spread news of their discoveries as fast and far as possible. Aldus's printshop was already hospitable to all this. It attracted the cream of the era's scholarly community, working on the whole sequence of writing, editing, translating, and designing prints and layouts. They lived almost as a commune, often crowding into Aldus's house as guests or workers, or both. Among the many who joined in was the northern writer and scholar Desiderius Erasmus of Rotterdam, who lived with Aldus for about eight months in 1507 and worked on his own projects while there. In his *Adages*, he describes sitting in a corner writing and handing sheets to the print compositors as he finished each one—too busy to scratch his ears, as he put it.

Aldus had friends delve through their manuscript collections, or those of wealthy patrons, to find more texts to publish, or better versions to use in editing. He began printing classic works in Greek, for which a wealth of experts could now be found in Italy. Many Greek scholars had moved to Italian cities to teach, including one particular influx following an event that shocked Christians everywhere: the Turkish conquest of Constantinople in 1453. Refugees fled, but often had time to grab their book collections, filled with Greek works on philosophy, mathematics, engineering, and more. All this enhanced Italy's cultural, intellectual, and technical range and fed the circle around Aldus. He knew Greek himself, printed books in Greek, and hosted meetups with rules stating that anyone accidentally slipping up and forgetting to speak Greek must put a coin into a pot. Each time it filled up, Aldus used the money to throw a party.

As his circle of collaborators grew, so did his range of readers. Erasmus said of Aldus that he was creating a library without boundaries, the only limits of which would be those of the world itself. Perhaps even that was no limit. Beyond the real planet, Aldus's books turn up on the imaginary island of Utopia, as described by Erasmus's friend Thomas More: *Utopia*'s narrator brings the island's residents copies of Greek texts in portable Aldine editions, which they devour.

Aldus rightly congratulated himself on his achievements. In a preface to his 1509 edition of Plutarch's *Moralia*, he included Latin verses written by the humanist Jacopo Antiquari of Perugia, full of exuberance: Here comes Aldus, with Greeks in one hand and Latins in the other. Aldus is our honey, our salt, our milk! Strew flowers around the city, youths! Aldus is here!

That was how other humanists imagined themselves, too: bringing fresh air and flowers into the scholarly world while bringing the scholarly world out into real life. They also continued to enjoy their other favorite metaphors for what they were doing: raising wrecks, lighting up the darkness, saving prisoners. In one of Aldus's prefaces, to his edition of Thucydides's *Histories*, he spoke of how he was "publishing—or rather liberating good books from their harsh and gloomy prisons." He freed the authors from confinement, and freed readers from the problems they had previously had in getting hold of good books.

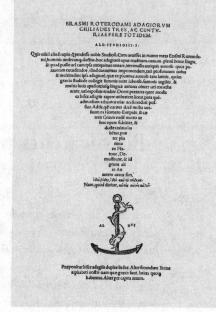

He and his editors also did their best to free texts from their errors. Weeding out mistakes by earlier copyists, endlessly consulting variants, they began to settle on an agreed standard text for most of the important classical works available. They worked as detectives, judges, and historians, developing ever better techniques for collecting and assessing evidence. Erasmus compared editorial work to weighing up statements from different witnesses: you keep on at them, comparing copies, until at last a single most plausible reading emerges.

But if you spend so much time working out the signs that texts have gone wrong or become garbled, or if you identify some of them as downright fakes, or if you just seem to be enjoying yourself too much while doing all this, then you risk upsetting some powerful people. Rather than seeming a harmless literary potterer, you might start looking like a dangerous heretic, or a provocative "pagan." And that would make you one of the subjects of the next chapter: scholarly humanists, still in Italy, still from much the same period, but driven by more rebellious purposes. Or so, at least, their enemies suspected.

Provocateurs and Pagans

Mostly 1440–1550

*Lorenzo Valla questions everything—Cicerolatry,
paganism, and Rome—Pomponio Leto and Bartolomeo
Platina, who annoyed a pope—Tuscany, especially
Florence—Pico della Mirandola and the human
chameleon—Leon Battista Alberti and the universal
man—the human measure again—Vitruvians—
Girolamo Savonarola burns the vanities—Sack of
Rome—portraits—everything in question.*

When the emperor Constantine the Great fell ill with leprosy sometime around 315 CE, he was all set to treat himself with the conventional remedy of bathing in children's blood, but a dream told him to seek help from Pope Sylvester I instead. He obeyed; the pope blessed him, and his leprosy disappeared. Constantine showed his gratitude by granting the pope and his successors dominion over all the western territory of Europe, including the Italian peninsula. The emperor had the gift recorded in a document known as the Donation of Constantine. The scene of the signing was immortalized later in a Vatican fresco painted by pupils of Raphael in the 1520s: you can stand in front of it and see with your own eyes how it happened.

Except that it didn't—a fact that was already well known at the time the fresco was done. The leprosy story was just a story, and the document was a forgery, apparently produced in the eighth century and used later to strengthen the papacy's land claims while also justifying German emperors' desire to call themselves Holy Roman Emperors. The Donation document had drawn skeptical attention for a while. But the most thorough debunking was done by a fifteenth-century literary humanist,

who brought all his century's intellectual effervescence to the task.

His name was Lorenzo Valla, and his 1440 treatise *On the Donation of Constantine* is one of the great humanist achievements. It combines a precise scholarly assault with the high rhetorical techniques learned from the ancients, served up with a sauce of hot chutzpah. All these assets were necessary to Valla, because he was daring to attack one of the church's central modern claims: its justification for having complete power over all of western Europe. It could be a short step from that to questioning its other claims to authority, too, including the authority it held over people's minds.

Valla seems to have been a man who had no fear and could never be persuaded to keep quiet. He traveled all over Italy, working for a series of patrons and supporters—at this point he was living in Naples—but he made enemies everywhere as well. The poet Maffeo Vegio had already warned him to seek advice before writing things that would hurt people's feelings, and generally to restrain his "intellectual violence." This he could or would not do. Valla's energies burst out of his body: another scholar, Bartolomeo Facio, summed him up by saying that he held his head high, he never stopped talking, he gesticulated with his hands, and he walked excitedly. (In Facio's beautifully concise Latin, this can be said in just eight words: "*Arrecta cervix, lingua loquax, gesticulatrix manus, gressus concitatior.*") Valla acknowledged his own bumptious character: in a letter, he admitted that he took on the *Donation* task partly for the sheer fun of displaying his abilities: "to show that I alone knew what no one else knew."

His attack begins in that sort of tone. He addresses the pope directly: I will show, he says, that this document is illegitimate and that claims based on it are false. He throws in jaunty insults against anyone else who has been fooled by the deception: "You blockhead, you dolt!" ("*O caudex, o stipes!*"). In fact, this way of opening the argument is also a well-calculated rhetorical strategy, grabbing the reader's attention. Having done this, he goes on to more focused arguments. First he uses the methods of a historian, inquiring into plausibility and evidence. Is it *likely*, he asks, that a ruler such as Constantine would have given away so much territory from his empire? And: Has anyone ever seen supporting documentation of Pope Sylvester's having accepted such a gift? In both cases, the answer is no.

Following these blows from rhetoric and historical reasoning, the third and last weapon in the strategic sequence is the killer one: philology, or the analysis of language. Valla shows that the document's Latin is not correct for the fourth century. He lists anachronistic blunders, as in one passage featuring the phrase "together with all our satraps" ("*cum omnibus satrapis nostris*"). Roman officials were not referred to as "satraps" until the eighth century. Another passage uses *banna* for "flag," but a pre-medieval writer would have said *vexillum*. The term *clericare*, with the meaning "to ordain," is not of the fourth century. He also points out such absurdities as a reference to *udones*, which for Romans were "felt socks," yet the text describes them as made of white linen. Felt is nothing like linen, says Valla, and it is not white. He rests his case.

Valla knew he was on firm ground as an expert Latinist (and a Hellenist, too: he later translated works by Homer, Thucydides, and Herodotus). The most influential of his works would be a style manual of good Latin, *Elegances of the Latin Language*, on which generations of later students came to rely in their compositions. "How brilliant Valla is!" gushed one of the many who learned from it. "He has raised up Latin to glory from the bondage of the barbarians. May the earth lie lightly on him and the spring shine ever round his urn!"

The *Elegances* took on the task of scraping off the medieval barnacles that had grown on the ancient language and starting again with truer, more original models instead. That notion also drove the *Donation* project, only in that case the whole thing was a barnacle. An alternative image for such a process might be digging out weeds, which was how Valla had presented a work written shortly before his *Donation*: the strikingly named *Repastinatio dialecticae et philosophiae*. The title means something like a hoeing or redigging of dialectic and philosophy. It made the case for turning over the medieval clods to get down to a more fertile field where truth might grow, even if this entailed upending such peacefully sleeping authorities as Aristotle, who had been much revered in previous centuries. Valla also redug the texts that were more revered by fellow humanists of his own time, as with the series of *Amendments* he produced to surviving books of Livy—of which he had Petrarch's personally edited copy to hand. He did the same even to the Bible. In his *Annotations to the New Testament*, he identified defects in the standard Latin translation of the Greek New Testament made in the fourth century by Jerome. Again, using his ability to think historically about processes and origins, Valla went beyond just pointing out errors to speculating about *how* they might have crept in, for example, by confusion arising from similar-looking Greek letters.

Risking enmity from old-style Aristotelian scholars, or from modern humanists, or from church authorities: none of it seemed to deter Valla. Of these opponents, the last was the most dangerous one to rouse. Sure enough, in 1444 he would become the target for an investigation by the Inquisition of Naples. Its main problem was not with his *Donation* but with some of his other unorthodox views on the Christian Trinity and on the question of free will—and on the ancient, very un-Christian philosophy of Epicureanism, which recommended living wisely and well in the present life rather than worrying about the beyond.

Valla had written the work that flirted with danger on this topic back in 1431: a dialogue called *De voluptate* (*On Pleasure*). This featured three speakers giving their views on that subject in turn. First, a Stoic says that all is misery and there can be no pleasure for human beings at all. "Oh, if only we had been born animals instead of men. If only we had not been born at all!"

Then an Epicurean puts the opposite case. Life is full of pleasurable and beautiful experiences, he says, such as listening to the voice of a woman speaking sweetly or tasting good wine. (I myself, he digresses, have cellars filled with the best vintages.) There are deeper pleasures, too, such as those that come from having a family, holding public office, and lovemaking. (He has a lot to say about this last one.) Even better is the self-satisfied glow that comes from knowing how virtuous one is: that is just another kind of pleasure.

A third speaker argues for the Christian view: pleasure *is* nice, but it is better to seek heavenly pleasures instead of worldly ones. The Christian is allowed to keep the last word and win the case, but it is hard not to notice the sympathetic treatment the Epicurean receives along the way, especially at one moment when the character of Lorenzo (that is, the author) is shown whispering to him, "My soul inclines silently in your direction."

Indeed, this was noticed. When the first version of the work attracted controversy, Valla adjusted it slightly, renaming characters, moving the scene from Rome to Pavia, and changing its title from *On Pleasure* to the more spiritually uplifting *De vero bono*—*On the True Good*. He sent the Christian final part to Pope Eugenius IV as a gift, but with a typically cheeky cover letter: "What in Heaven's name could afford you more pleasure than this book?" The letter goes on to ask for money.

So there were plenty of reasons in 1444 for the Naples Inquisition to want to Inquire into Valla. He was saved almost immediately, however, because his patron and protector, King Alfonso of Naples, intervened to stop the process. The king owed him: Valla had been part of his court entourage for some time and always lent his eloquence to helping the king's interests. As an itinerant humanist, of course, Valla had to please his current protector, just as Petrarch had. That was one of the main reasons—besides philological purism—for writing his *Donation*: at the time, Alfonso had been trying to defend his territory against attempts by Pope Eugenius in Rome to encroach on its borders. By undermining all such territorial claims from Rome in general, Valla was aiding that objective. I don't think this takes anything significant away from the achievement: Valla still loved cleaning up texts as a matter of principle. By bringing his fearless, scholarly questioning of authority to bear on the bogus Donation, and pleasing his patron, Valla also managed to save himself from the consequences of all the other fearless and scholarly questioning he had done.

The post in Naples did not last forever; humanists' positions rarely did. In the end, Valla found a substitute in the last place you might expect: in Rome, with a new pope. Succeeding Eugenius in 1447, Nicholas V was much more sympathetic to humanistic ideas and activities than his predecessor. Valla now secured a berth in the Curia (the papal court) as an apostolic scriptor, or scribe. This allowed him to live in Rome; he would also be appointed a professor of rhetoric at its university and go on to be a secretary to the next pope, Calixtus III, who also gave him a canonry at the papal basilica of St. John Lateran. You could hardly ask for a more typical array of humanist positions: royal court, church, and university, all smoothly woven into the life of a man who still managed to keep himself mostly devoted to free, bold investigations on his own terms.

But his life never became entirely relaxed or easy, and neither did his earthly afterlife. When he died in 1457 at the age of fifty, his mother—who survived him—arranged for a fine tombstone to be created in the basilica, with an inscription praising his eloquence. At some point, probably in the mid-sixteenth century, when the Reformation made the church extra-sensitive to anyone who had criticized it, the tomb was removed and placed out of sight somewhere. From there, it descended to further indignities. The German historian Barthold Georg Niebuhr, visiting Rome in 1823, was astonished to see Valla's memorial stone in the street being used as a paving slab—the same fate that had met so many other insufficiently Christian hunks of stone. It was rescued shortly afterward and moved to a safer place back inside the basilica, where it still is.

Valla's real monument was his works, but, like the memorial stone, they were also repurposed in unpredictable ways. His commentary on the New Testament seemed to be forgotten, until Erasmus found a manuscript copy in an abbey library and edited it for publication in 1505—a book-discovery story in the Petrarchan tradition, but this time of a modern work that had served its "prison" sentence for only a few decades. That discovery helped inspire Erasmus to do his own new translation of the New Testament. Like Valla, he preferred to work from old, clean sources, partly because of general pride in good scholarship and partly because he also believed that Christianity was a better thing before it became so preoccupied with its own institutional power.

Neither Erasmus nor Valla would have pursued that argument as far as did a new breed in Erasmus's time: the Protestants. In their rejection of church authority, they seized on Valla's treatise as a support. That at least was the motive of the German Ulrich von Hutten when, in 1517, he issued a new, printed version with an overtly antipapal purpose. No wonder Pope Julius II felt the need to commission the Vatican fresco at that time: it was a way of hammering home the Constantine story, while simply ignoring the fact that it had already fallen victim to the humanist harpoon.

Later still, with religious conflicts becoming less prominent, other generations of intellectuals were drawn to Valla just because they admired his methods and his goals. For them, he came to represent freethinking in the most general sense of that word—that is, the insistence on trusting expertise rather than authority and on exploring *how* texts and claims came to be the way they were. They would follow him in investigating suspicious documents and analyzing their origins and validity. Later still, non-religious humanists (thus, "freethinkers" in a more specific sense) would also recognize something of themselves in Valla's outspoken attitude and his apparent sympathy for Epicurean ideas.

Even his wild and bellicose manner has had a certain appeal, especially because he made a kind of philosophy of it. In a letter, he laid out his vision of universal contrarianism, asking, "Who has ever written on any field of learning or science without criticizing his predecessors?" Aristotle, for example, was criticized by his student and nephew Theophrastus. "Indeed, as far as I recall from my extensive reading, I can hardly find an author who does *not* at some point refute or at least reproach Aristotle." By doing that, they are following no less a model than Aristotle himself, who also took issue with his own former teacher, Plato—"Yes, Plato, the prince of philosophers!" Turning to Christian writers: Augustine criticized Jerome, and Jerome attacked older church authorities, saying that their interpretations themselves required interpretation. Physicians criticize each other and give different diagnoses. Sailors, when a storm looms, can never agree on how best to steer the ship. As for philosophers: "What Stoic can resist challenging nearly everything an Epicurean says, only to suffer the same from him in return?" Dispute and contradiction, not veneration and obedience, are the essence of intellectual life. And, crucially, Valla did not merely tell people they were wrong; he gave them the *reasons* why they were wrong.

As he concluded this letter: sometimes fighting with the dead is one's duty, because it benefits those who will follow. And that is a matter of duty, too: one must train the young and also, where possible, "restore the others to their senses."

The young did flock to Valla in search of his instruction. Poggio Bracciolini, who was among his enemies, complained that Valla was setting students a bad example by his constant picking of holes in even the most revered works, such as the classical rhetoric manual *Rhetorica ad Herennium*. Valla seemed to fancy himself "superior to any ancient writer," complained Poggio. He added violently that one would need "not words but cudgels, and Hercules' club, to beat down this monster and his pupils."

One reason Poggio had such respect for the *Rhetorica ad Herennium* was that it was thought to be by Cicero, although in fact this was the wrong attribution. (The real author is unknown.) And Poggio was one of a series of humanists who considered Cicero so eminent and perfect as to be beyond attack by any mere mortal. He thus took the opposite side from Valla in a long-running battle of many minds, concerning a question that sounds ridiculous now but seemed of great importance then. Should Cicero be the *only* guide to Latin style worth following, or might one emulate other classical authors, too? A few humanists were so dedicated to the first alternative that they swore—perhaps partly in jest—to use no word in their own writing that could not be found in their hero's works. If it wasn't in Cicero, it wasn't Latin.

Behind this lay a whole tradition of humanist Cicerolatry. Petrarch, who was less uncritical in his admiration, amused himself at the expense of a friend who was so deeply pained by hearing attacks on the great orator that he exclaimed, "Gently, please, gently with my Cicero!" The friend then admitted that, for him, Cicero was a god. That's a funny thing for a Christian to say, remarked Petrarch. The friend hurriedly explained that he meant only "a god of eloquence," not an actual divine being. Ah! said Petrarch, then if Cicero was only human, he could have flaws—and did. The friend shuddered and turned away.

That was part of the problem: treating Cicero as superhuman implied setting him on a level comparable to that of Jesus Christ himself. If that sounds like overstretching the case, consider a dream reported by the biblical translator Jerome a millennium earlier. While living in a hermit's retreat near Antioch, feverish from starvation and determined to give up classical authors and all other worldly pleasures, Jerome dreamed that he was summoned before Jesus, sitting as judge.

"What condition of man are you?" asked Jesus.

"I am a Christian," replied Jerome.

"You lie," replied Jesus. "You are not a Christian but a Ciceronian." He had him whipped for it, and when Jerome woke up, he swore never again to own or read a non-Christian book.

In reality, Jerome did continue referring to such books in his work. Commenting on this, Lorenzo Valla generously suggested that it was okay, because Christ had banned him only from using Cicero's philosophy, not from citing or imitating him as literature. Valla himself had no aversion to reading Cicero. It was merely that he thought other literary models were just as good, and maybe better—especially Quintilian, whom he greatly admired.

All these people loved their classics, but this long series of Ciceronian quarrels shows a rift appearing between two types of humanists: those who adored and imitated certain long-lost authors unquestioningly, and those who considered nothing beyond question, not even Cicero (or, indeed, the pope). It is no surprise to find Valla on the latter side. Besides his general spirit of inquiry, he had a good reason for approaching writers historically rather than seeing them as timeless models. If everyone really did start writing like Cicero, it would be impossible for those such as Valla ever to date a piece of writing by internal evidence again. All texts would sound the same, and philologists would be finished.

Fortunately, there will always be slipups that give imitators away. One of the most extreme Ciceronians was Christophorus Longolius, born Christophe de Longueil in the Low Countries in 1490. But he betrayed his difference from Cicero every time he used his own first name, whether in Latin or vernacular form, since Christophorus means "Christ-bearer," a word that Cicero, who died in 43 BCE and knew nothing of Christ, could not have used.

Longolius's problem was pointed out in a satirical dialogue by Erasmus, *The Ciceronian*, published in 1528. Two friends are trying to talk a third out of joining the fad, so they run through a list of all the writers who have tried it and failed. For a moment they think they have found one successful case in Longolius, until it dawns on them that his name makes it impossible. Erasmus is having fun at the expense of fanatics here, but he also makes a serious point. If Ciceronians cannot allow themselves to speak of any Christian subject, what does that imply about their belief system? Ciceronianism might be a sign of a secret, subversive "paganism" in the heart of the modern Christian world.

This word *pagan*, originally meaning "peasant" or "country bumpkin," was used by Christians to describe all pre-Christian religion, but especially that attached to the old Roman gods. Relations between the two traditions had always been strained, hence the eagerness of early Christians to literally stamp the Roman temples and statues out of the landscape. The relationship mellowed with time, however. It became clear that pagan traditions were so interwoven with Christian ones in European culture that they could not be fully untangled again. The very stones of Rome were pagan in origin, and Roman and Greek mythology was so full of good stories that artists, in particular, could never resist it—especially when it featured love goddesses emerging from seashells wearing floaty, translucent clothes. Perhaps, rather than trying to wipe out the pagan tradition, it was better to try to assimilate and Christianize it.

That process necessitated some mental athletics. Petrarch reassured himself that Cicero, if only he had had the chance, *would* have been a good Christian. Others tried to reinterpret classical works as prophecies of the coming religion. Virgil lent himself well to this. His Fourth *Eclogue* mentions a new age on its way and the birth of a special boy: could that be Jesus? And Aeneas's round trip to the Underworld of death, in the *Aeneid*: was that not an allegory of the Resurrection? Back in the fourth century, the poet Faltonia Betitia Proba, herself from a prominent family of pagan-to-Christian converts, had managed to assemble enough bits of Virgil to form a whole narrative telling the story of the Creation, Fall, and Flood, as well as Jesus's life and death. In the end, though, Virgil himself still had the misfortune of having been born too early to be saved. This is why Dante, despite relying on him as his guide through Hell and Purgatory in the *Comedy*, cannot let him continue as far as Paradise. He tells us that Virgil's usual home is in Limbo, a not *too* unpleasant first circle of Hell where other good pagans live, unlike such bad pagans as Epicurus (and all his followers), deep inside the sixth circle.

Ciceronians tried similar merging of pagan and Christian terms to get around their problem, such as referring to the Virgin Mary as the goddess Diana. But suspicion continued to hang over them. As Erasmus had one of his characters ask another: Have you ever seen a crucifix displayed in any of these classicists' precious private museums of antiquities? The speaker answers himself: "No, everything is full of the monuments of paganism." Given a chance, he says, they would probably bring it all back—"the flamens and vestals, . . . the supplications, the temples and shrines, the feasts of couches, the religious rites, the gods and goddesses, the Capitol and the sacred fire."

The thing is, Erasmus was clearly right, at least about some of the earlier Ciceronians. During the 1460s, several men in Rome had begun meeting up in what came to be called an "Academy," an allusion to Plato's ancient "Academy," or school, in Athens. In the Ciceronians' case, their interests were less focused on Greece than on the pre-Christian world of their own city. There was some serious history involved: the group included eminent scholars with university jobs, and they delivered lectures and gave tours of Rome's ruins. Petrarch would have loved to join such a tour. Perhaps Erasmus would have gone along, too, but he and Petrarch alike would have been shocked by some of the group's wilder evening events. They met amid the ruins, dressed up and put laurel wreaths on their brows, and enacted ancient festivities. They also recited their own

Latin poems, including love poetry addressed to each other or to younger men. They put on comedies by Plautus or Terence—a daring venture, as Christianity had disapproved of non-devotional theatrical performances ever since Justinian closed the theaters in the sixth century. The prime mover behind many of these spectacles was one Giulio Pomponio Leto, or Julius Pomponius Laetus, a professor of rhetoric originally from Naples. "Laetus" was a name of his own choice; it means "happy."

Happy professors cavorting by moonlight, declaiming love poems to one another, putting on theatrical extravaganzas: was it all . . . quite . . . Christian? Well, most of the Academy's members were employed or otherwise involved in various ways with the papal court, sometimes in combination with their other posts, so one would think so. But many intellectuals in the city held a paid role in the church, and it did not necessarily mean much. A report sent home by a Milanese ambassador alleged that their true beliefs were very different: "The humanists denied God's existence and thought that the soul died with the body," he wrote, adding that they considered Christ to be a false prophet.

With their adulation of the Rome of the Republic—of Cicero's time—they could also look seditious in other ways. Some onlookers suspected that they wanted to restore the republican political system, perhaps through an uprising or revolution. This was plausible: such a feat had previously been tried by an acquaintance of Petrarch's, Cola di Rienzo, another enthusiast for the city's ruins and inscriptions. After early failed attempts, he successfully overthrew the city's ruling barons and set himself up as a consul in the old Roman style, with a certain amount of public support—though that was short-lived, as was he. In 1353, the mood shifted, and a crowd assembled outside his palace, chanting, "Death to the traitor Cola di Rienzo!" He escaped the building in disguise and mingled with them, trying to blend in by shouting the same thing, but he was recognized, stabbed, and taken away to be hanged. Some people now wondered whether the Academicians had it in mind to see if a similar coup could have more success a second time around.

Hostility began to gather around them. At first, they remained safe in their various secretarial and clerical posts in the Curia, because the pope of the time, Pius II, was himself a humanistic and studious man who appreciated their interest in antiquity. Things changed in 1464, when the next pope succeeded him: Paul II. He had no understanding of the things humanists cared about and no respect for their studies or skills. Above all, he disliked any whiff of paganism, despite the fact that he also had a taste for lavish processions that merged classical and Christian imagery. A deeper interest in the ancients was less to his taste. It was better to be devoutly ignorant, he said, than to fill young heads with heresy and tales of sexual immorality. "Before boys have reached the age of ten and gone to school, they know a thousand immodesties; think of the thousand other vices they will learn when they read Juvenal, Terence, Plautus, and Ovid." (In truth, you didn't need classical literature to learn vices: according to a dialogue on hypocrisy by Poggio, one preacher often provided so much detail in his sermons against lust that the congregation rushed home afterward to try out the practices for themselves.)

Disliking the humanists, and wanting to save on their cost, Paul II abolished their secretarial and other jobs at the Vatican. But people who had such posts had usually paid a sum to get them in the first place, so the humanists complained about being swindled. Now that they were protesting, they sounded more like rebels than ever. One of them, named Bartolomeo Sacchi but known as "Platina" after his hometown of Piadena, was arrested for his outspokenness and spent four months in the papal prison in the Castel Sant'Angelo. He was released, but in February 1468, the pope ordered about twenty Academy members to be rounded up, including Platina again. They were charged with conspiracy, heresy, sodomy, and other crimes and put through the castle's torture chambers. Platina suffered permanent damage to his shoulder from the strappado, a hideous procedure which raised victims off the ground by their wrists tied behind their back, sometimes with the addition of sudden drops and other torments.

Pomponio Leto was not initially among the group arrested, as he was teaching in Venice at the time, but he soon joined them. He was arrested in Venice on an accusation of sodomy, because he had been writing erotic poetry to his male students; the Venetian authorities then extradited him to Rome, where the charges were altered. Like the others, he was accused of heresy.

They all now had a long ordeal, confined in their cells, uncertain how it would end. Their one consolation came from a sympathetic prison warden, Rodrigo Sánchez de Arévalo, who delivered their letters, wrote his own works of consolation for them, and allowed them to resume meeting one another. Pomponio wrote, thanking him: "Captivity is nothing amid the conversations of friends." Rodrigo expressed amazement that, in such a dismal situation, they still managed not only to write but to do it with their usual beauties of style. But as we saw with Petrarch's letters, humanists found nothing strange in expressing their sufferings in as elegant a way as possible. The cult of inarticulate or mystical silence—like the cult of ignorance—had no appeal for them. To exercise their eloquence was to affirm the values for which they were being persecuted.

Some of them were freed later that same year, but again Platina had the worst of it: he was kept inside until March 1469. None of the charges could be proved against any of them; nor did any evidence of real seditious activity ever subsequently emerge. A few years after these events, their situation became much better with another change of pope, to Sixtus IV. He allowed them to resume their jobs for the Curia. Platina would also later be taken on as the librarian of the Vatican Library. Meanwhile, he was able to resume his literary activities. He published a recipe book he had been working on for a while, with the very Epicurean title *On Right Pleasure and Good Health*; one of its dishes, grilled eel *à l'orange*, was so appealing that Leonardo da Vinci made it part of the fare in his fresco of the Last Supper. Platina also wrote a long history of all the popes, culminating in a scathing account of his former persecutor, Paul II.

The group eventually resumed its meetings and activities, though a

Platina and Pope Sixtus IV with the Vatican Library collection

little more discreetly than before. It was relaunched in 1477 as a lay
Christian fraternity, which gave it a more respectable air. All the same, its
members continued to meet sometimes in the ruins, for a discreet cavort.

While Roman humanists tended to remain bound, for better or
worse, to the affairs of the church, those farther up the peninsula in Tuscany had a different set of obligations, and different kinds of
masters to please. (Typically inclined to wandering, of course, some humanists had interludes or obligations in both places.) The Tuscan humanists were more likely to work either in purely private posts as tutors and
secretaries or to have civic, diplomatic, or political appointments in the
great Tuscan cities. These cities tended to present themselves as beacons
of freedom, openness, and harmony. Their ideal image had been given
visual form in frescoes by Ambrogio Lorenzetti in the late 1330s for the
city of Siena, bringing out a contrast between good and bad government.
One scene shows a city full of dancing merrymakers and happy traders,
surrounded by fertile fields and well-fed peasants. This is the result of
good government. Its opposite shows empty fields, desolate except for

armies advancing on one another, and a grim and ruined city: bad government at work. To prefer good government to bad is to prefer order to chaos, peace to war, prosperity to starvation, and wisdom to stupidity.

That Florence was, out of all the Tuscan cities, the epitome of the "good" option was the argument of the city's humanistic chancellor Leonardo Bruni. In his *Praise of the City of Florence*, written around 1403, he had characterized his community in terms of its freedom and its ability to harmonize sweetly with itself, like the strings of a harp. "There is nothing in it that is out of order, nothing that is ill proportioned, nothing that is out of tune, nothing that is uncertain." Its citizens surpass others in every achievement. They are "industrious, generous, elegant, pleasant, affable, and above all, urbane." And, as he wrote elsewhere, the humanistic studies—that is to say, "the best and most distinguished branches of learning and the most appropriate to humankind"—naturally flourish here:

> Who can name any poet, of this or an earlier age, who was not a Florentine? Who but our citizens brought back to light and into practice this art of public speaking which had been completely lost? Who, if not our city, recognized the value of Latin letters, which had been lying abject, prostrate, and almost dead, and saw to it that they were resurrected and restored?

He reserves a special mention for the way "even the knowledge of Greek letters, which had become obsolete in Italy for more than seven hundred years, has been brought back by our city so that we may contemplate the great philosophers and admirable orators."

Bruni himself had a lot to do with that, being a Greek expert and translator. He was especially interested in the historian Thucydides— who, among much other material, had provided a version of a famous speech given by the Athenian leader Pericles in 430 BCE. Amid an ongoing war with Sparta, Pericles addressed the citizens to commemorate fallen soldiers and praised Athens in terms that would be almost directly copied by Bruni in his praise of Florence. According to Thucydides, Pericles begins by asking, in effect, Why are we so much more wonderful than our enemies? Answer: Unlike the Spartans, obsessed with military drills and discipline, we have built Athens on a basis of freedom and harmony. Spartans shut themselves off, but we trade openly with the world. They brutalize their children to make them tough, but we educate ours for liberty. They are hierarchical, but in Athens everyone takes part freely and equally in the city's affairs. What Pericles does not think to mention is that "everyone" here excludes women and slaves. His only mention of women comes in the final words, where he reminds any war widows in the audience that none of this applies to them, since a woman's only virtue is not to be talked about by men, whether in praise or criticism.

Florence, too, had women and slaves who neither spoke in public nor were officially talked about. In general, the reality of both cities was not quite as described. Far from being harmonious, Athens experienced public disorder, plague, and uprisings, and it eventually lost that war with the Spartans. Florence, too, was a welter of dynastic conflicts, plots, regime changes, and general insecurity. Yet in both cases the humanistic ideal was central to their identities—and there is no question that Florence did become an energetic, artistic, intellectually active place through the fifteenth century, filled with larger-than-life characters and generally friendly to the activities of humanists.

The most eminent of these formed a circle associated with the Medici during the time when that family was effectively in control of the city. Several members of the circle, like their Roman counterparts, took up the Platonic name of "Academy," and got together for meetings in a semiformal group. They were particularly encouraged and supported in this by Lorenzo de' Medici, "the Magnificent," who was himself a humanistic poet, collector, and connoisseur, as well as a businessman, man of action, and political leader.

A central figure in the group was Marsilio Ficino, who translated Plato's works using manuscripts in the Medici family's collection, and also wrote his own study, *Platonic Theology*, advancing a philosophy that merged Christianity with Platonism. Plato was another of those "pagans" who had the bad luck to be born before Christ, but he did speak of the harmony of the cosmos and of an ideal "Good" in ways that some Christians had long seen as prefiguring their own theology. Although far from the first to explore this, Ficino brought a new style of scholarship to the task. Also, he was prepared to make bold claims about the role of humans in the universe. Highlighting human achievements in literature, creativity, scholarship, and political self-governance, he asked, "Who could deny that man possesses as it were almost the same genius as the Author of the heavens? And who could deny that man could somehow also make the heavens, could he only obtain the instruments, and the heavenly material . . . ?" That was quite a claim: if only we had the right tools and raw materials (admittedly, a tall order in both cases), we might rival God himself as Creator.

Similar speculations came from another member of the Academy circle in Florence: the dashing young aristocrat and book collector Giovanni Pico della Mirandola. He read widely, both within the Christian tradition and outside it, delving into esoteric and mystical ideas of all kinds. Having assembled material on such themes, he went to Rome in 1486 with the intention of organizing a giant conference, at which attendees could debate nine hundred theses or propositions supplied by himself. The event did not happen: the church did not like the sound of it and squelched it. Pico fled back to Florence for fear that he might be squelched, too. But the theses remained, and he had also written an introductory oration for them that would later acquire a resounding title: *Oration on the Dignity of Man*. For centuries, this would be held up as a kind of manifesto for the Florentine humanistic worldview, embodying a moment when the humanities research of the literary scholars became something grander: a philosophical vision of unfettered, universal humanity, proudly facing the cosmos on equal terms.

Recent Pico scholars have tried to tone down this view of him, argu-

ing that he was really more interested in arcane mysticism, and reminding readers that the "dignity of man" part of the title was not his, anyway.
This restoring of Pico's *Oration* to its original context has been a valuable
corrective to overexcitement. Still, there is no denying the emotional impact of its first few pages, where Pico, like Ficino, communicates an ambitious view of human capacities. He does it—as Protagoras had long
before him—by telling a story about human origins.

In the beginning, goes Pico's version, God created all beings. He set
each kind on its own fixed shelf, as it were, allotting places according to
whether they were plants, animals, or angelic creatures. But he also made
humans, and for them he imposed no predefined level. God told Adam:
instead of giving you a single place or nature, I will give you the seeds of
any way of being. It is up to you to choose which kinds to cultivate. If you
choose your lower seeds, you will become as an animal, or even a plant. If
you choose the higher ones, you may rise to the height of the angels. And
if you choose intermediate ones, you will fulfill your own variable,
human nature. Thus, says God: "We have made you neither of heaven
nor of earth, neither mortal nor immortal, so that you may, as the free
and extraordinary shaper of yourself, fashion yourself in whatever form
you prefer." Pico comments, "Who will not wonder at this chameleon of
ours?" And: "Who will admire any other being more?"

This passage was by far the most memorable in Pico's work, and no
wonder: this shimmering, shapeshifting chameleon presents a thrilling
image of ourselves. It seems considerably more exciting than the work of
the patient literary scholars, copying manuscripts and fussing over their
Ciceronian Latin. Yet in reality Pico was not that remote from them. He,
too, was trying to produce an erudite, cross-disciplinary work of scholarship, mixing materials from a wealth of philosophical and theological traditions. Just as humans in general can be anything they choose, he implies,
so should scholars be able to take the wisdom and knowledge they need
from any source, whether Christian or not. One can see why the church
thought his conference in Rome would be too much to tolerate.

Meanwhile, one also has to ask: Could such a multisided, self-determining, free, harmonious marvel ever actually exist? How many human chameleons were walking around Florence?

Certainly, if you hoped to find one, Florence was a good place to look. Candidates for models of all-capable humanity who might often be found there included Leonardo da Vinci, the versatile artistic and scientific genius, and the architect Leon Battista Alberti. Those were in fact the two names chosen by the nineteenth-century historian Jacob Burckhardt when he was looking for exemplars of what he considered the era's distinctive figure: the *uomo universale*, or "universal man," who could take on any form and achieve almost anything in a fluid, constantly changing society.

The choice of Leonardo makes some sense, given the astonishing range of his interests. (We will come back to him in a moment.) Leon Battista Alberti seems an apt choice, too, especially if we read a glowing contemporary account of his achievements written by an anonymous author who—we are now fairly certain—was none other than Alberti himself. It portrays him, not without justification, as a man of innumerable facets, capable in every field of life, excelling in every quality except modesty.

He did have a lot to be immodest about. Besides designing buildings and producing pictures, he wrote important treatises on the arts of painting, building, and sculpture. He was an expert surveyor and devised new techniques to produce a study of Rome's ruins. He wrote Latin poems, a theatrical comedy about Greek gods, and a book titled *Mathematical Games*. Each of his fields of expertise enhanced the others, as when he used his mathematical talents to work out rules for creating the illusion of perspective in visual art.

Those achievements are well documented, but the biography goes further. Alberti wrestled, he sang, he pole-vaulted, he climbed mountains. In youth, he was strong enough to throw an apple over the top of a church and to jump over a man's back from a standing start. He was so resistant to pain that, when he wounded his foot at the age of fifteen, he could calmly help a surgeon to stitch it closed.

He cultivated subtler abilities, too. By going bareheaded on horseback (an unusual thing to do), he trained himself to endure chills on his head, even in the fierce winds of winter. Applying the same principle to the cold winds of social life, he "deliberately exposed himself to shameless impudence just to teach himself patience." He loved talking to everyone he could find, seeking new knowledge. He would invite friends over so that they could talk about literature and philosophy, "and to these friends he would also dictate little works while he painted their portrait or made a wax model of one of them." In every situation, he sought to behave virtuously; "he wanted everything in his life, every gesture and every word, to be, as well as to seem to be, the expression of one who merits the good will of good men." At the same time, he valued *sprezzatura*, "adding art to art to make the result seem free of artifice," especially when it came to three important activities: "how one walks in the street, how one rides, and how one speaks; in these things one should make every effort to be intensely pleasing to all." Throughout all of this, he "kept a cheerful manner and even, insofar as dignity permitted, an air of gaiety."

Alberti was thus the very model of the splendid, accomplished, free human being in the full sunlight of his days. True, he *was* exceptionally able. But what is being conjured up here is more than that; it is an ideal figure of the human in general. All the qualities highlighted are those of *humanitas*: intellectual and artistic excellence, moral virtue and fortitude, sociability, good speaking, *sprezzatura*, being courteously "pleasing to all." Along with this comes his excellent physical condition: the mental abilities were reflected in his physical proportions. Reading his description, one pictures another figure of the time: that of "Vitruvian Man."

Vitruvian Man was a perfectly proportioned, steady-gazing, well-formed male figure, whose origin is purely mathematical. He illustrates the ratios of distance that were supposed to exist between parts of the

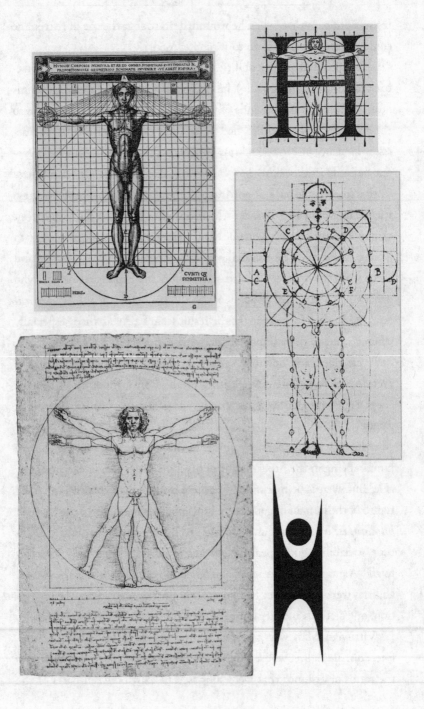

human body: the chin to the roots of the hair, the wrist to the tip of the middle finger, the chest to the crown of the head, and so on. Calculating these ratios in the first century BCE, Vitruvius was interested not so much in anatomical design as in architecture: these proportions of the male body seemed to him the best basis for the shape of a temple. Thus, the human being—as Protagoras would have said—should literally be taken as the *measure*, or criterion. Vitruvius gave the method for deriving the data. If a man lies on his back with hands and feet spread, and you draw a circle with his navel as the center, the circumference will touch his fingers and toes. You can also create a square based on the span of his arms and the length of his body, when he brings his feet together.

Artists of the fifteenth and sixteenth centuries did their best to make this Vitruvian ideal come true. Even designers of printing fonts modeled their letters on the Vitruvian body. Michelangelo Buonarroti followed the temple theme by designing a facade for the San Lorenzo church in Florence based on such dimensions—although he never built it, because he could not source the marble he wanted.

Most celebrated was the drawing made around 1490 by Leonardo da Vinci, showing a man in the two positions simultaneously, along with his measures in delicate box shapes. The man is positioned inside a circle centering on his navel, as well as a square. His expression is frowning but serene; he has a fine head of hair, and turns one foot sideways to show how its dimensions fit with the whole. He is perfect—apart from having too many arms and legs.

Leonardo's original drawing sits well guarded in the Gallerie dell'Accademia in Venice, but the disembodied image has traversed a huge sweep of history and geography, representing human confidence, beauty, harmony, and strength. It has become an instant icon for the idea of the "Renaissance," and of "universal man"; a visual companion to Pico's dignified chameleon. Even the international symbol for the modern humanist movement echoes it: the "Happy Human" image, designed by Dennis Barrington in 1965, shows a human shape with arms flung up in a similar way, full of confidence, openness, and well-being. (Interestingly, Humanists UK has now moved away from this toward a more fluid symbol resembling a dancing piece of string—chosen because it is a figure following its own motion instead of standing before us to be measured. You can see this symbol at the end of the last chapter of this book.)

In fact, what distinguishes the Leonardo image from other Vitruvian ones is that it does *not* submit to symmetrical measurements; its shapes are not concentric. Leonardo achieved the figure's visual beauty and plausibility by displacing the square downward. The circle centers on the navel, but the square centers somewhere around the base of the man's penis. Also, the upper tips of the square poke through the circle's radius. The proportions had to be tweaked, because even "ideal" humans are not a precise set of boxes and circles. Many correspondences do exist: the finger-to-finger span of a broad-shouldered man is likely to be more or less the same as his height. But without adjustment, a real Vitruvian man would look mighty weird, as is clear from some other examples, such as the one in a 1521 Italian translation of Vitruvius illustrated by Cesare Cesariano.

The message here is that real human beings, even those who match the dominant template of muscular masculinity, are characterized by something less than perfect harmony. They are subtly off-center. An ideal, harmonious human cannot be found any more than an ideal, harmonious city can (or even a harmonious chameleon). Immanuel Kant was surely closer to the truth when he wrote, three centuries later: "Out of such crooked wood as the human being is made, nothing entirely straight can be fabricated."

Another young man, from farther north in Italy, had also started his intellectual career by studying Platonic philosophy, along with medicine: Girolamo Savonarola. Born in Ferrara in 1452 to a family of physicians, he was all set to follow the same profession. As part of his studies, he wrote poetry in the Petrarchan vein and essays on Plato's dialogues. But then he heard the voice of God, quit medical school, and tore up his work on Plato.

What God said to him, in effect, was: Destroy these vanities! This appetite for knowledge, this poetry, this reading of pagan philosophers—it is all so much futility, egotism, and distraction from piety, and it must be rooted out. No earthly matter is as important as preparing for death and heaven. While in this world, as Savonarola said later, we should be "like the courier who arrives at the inn and, without removing his spurs or anything, eats a mouthful, and . . . says, 'Up, up quickly, let's get going!'"

"Up" he did. Savonarola left his family without a word and walked the fifty kilometers or so from Ferrara to Bologna. There he presented himself at the city's Dominican monastery. They took him in, and afterward he wrote to his father to tell him what he had done. To explain his reasons, he referred his father to a tract he had written on the need for contemptuous rejection of all worldly things.

Having taken his monastic vows, Savonarola found that he had a rather worldly talent, after all: he was brilliant at inspiring people with his preaching. He tried to develop this skill further by seeking lessons in humanistic eloquence and oratory—arts of pagan origin, but ones that promised to be useful. The teacher he approached for lessons, Giovanni Garzoni, gave him a rude brush-off, which would not have improved Savonarola's attitude toward the whole humanist enterprise. He started whipping himself regularly and acquired a haunted look, with frowning brow and piercing eyes, which went well with his huge nose and gave extra impact to his words. In 1482, he moved to the Convent of San Marco in Florence, where he taught novices; then he spent some years on the road preaching in other cities before being called back to Florence by no less a personage than Lorenzo de' Medici.

Lorenzo at that time was ill with an arthritic condition, perhaps

HIERONIMVS SAVONAROLA FLORENTIN

Dum fera flamma tuos, Hieronyme, pascitur artus.
Religio sanctas dilaniata comas,
Fleuit & o, dixit, crudeles parcite flamma.
Parcite, sunt isto viscere nostra rogo.

ankylosing spondylitis; he would soon die. Being in extremis might help explain his seeking someone as extreme as Savonarola to guide him spiritually through to the end. Yet many of the other humanists in his circle became fascinated by Savonarola too, including both Pico and Ficino. They were drawn to his talk of cleansing Christianity of the corruption that had crept into it; as we saw with Valla, humanists were often interested in clearing out corruption, of texts as well as of morals. There was also Savonarola's charismatic intensity, which seemed to hypnotize everyone; the humanists fell for it without thinking that they, and everything they held dear, might easily join his other targets. The possibility became clearer only when he proposed making more funds available to the poor—by removing such funds from the university. Not all the humanists were connected with that institution, but it represented principles of learning and scholarship generally. One thinks of the way some twentieth-century Western intellectuals fell in love with totalitarian communism, never considering what such a regime would be likely to do to them.

Savonarola's appeal to the poor was easier to understand, with his condemnation of elitism and of the greed of clergymen. He built up a huge audience for his sermons at San Marco, and at the Florence cathedral—where ten thousand people at a time could hear him under the beautiful cupola designed earlier that century by Filippo Brunelleschi.

As he acquired more followers, they took to processing through the streets chanting and lamenting, and became known as his *piagnoni*: big weepers, or wailers. Gangs of children, *fanciulli*, were organized to march behind banners and collect money. They assaulted passersby, especially women considered immodestly dressed, and went from house to house demanding "vanities." As a witness wrote, describing the scenes of February 16, 1496:

> So great was the grace poured out on their lips that all were moved to tears, and even those who were their enemies would give them everything, weeping, men as well as women, diligently searching out everything such as cards, tables, chessboards, harps, lutes, citterns, cymbals, bagpipes, dulcimers, wigs, veils (which at the time were very lascivious ornaments for women's heads), disgraceful and lascivious paintings and sculptures, mirrors, powder and other cosmetics and lascivious perfumes, hats, masks, poetry books in the vernacular as well as Latin, and every other disgraceful reading material, and books of music. These children inspired fear in any place where they were seen, and when they came down one street, the wicked fled down another.

In following years, the processions culminated in bonfires. A huge eight-sided wooden pyramid would be built in advance, stocked with logs inside for fuel; then the vanities collected by children could be balanced

or hung on tiers on each side. There they went—mirrors, perfume bottles, paintings, musical instruments—all arranged "in a varied and distinctive way in order to appear delectable to the eye," as one witness said. (The burners of vanities were not lacking in aesthetic sense themselves.)

Savonarola was not the first to devise such a spectacle. Fra Bernardino da Siena and Fra Bernardino da Feltre had burned books and other items a decade earlier in Florence, the latter while declaiming catchy phrases such as "Each time we read the ribald Ovid we crucify Christ!" Savonarola's bonfires featured modern authors together with the classical ones. And if the books were beautifully written and bound, so much the better: among the items in his 1498 fire was a Petrarch collection "adorned with illustrations in gold and silver."

He would also have liked to do the same thing to certain kinds of people. He called for hideous penalties for "sodomites"—homosexuality being officially illegal in Florence at the time, but seldom actually punished. Instead, he thought the law should be administered "without pity, so that such persons are stoned and burned." He did succeed in persuading the city's legislators to some extent: mild incidents previously punishable by a fine were now deemed to require an escalating series of atrocities for repeat offenders: the pillory, then branding, and finally burning alive. When officials proved sluggish about imposing such horrors (the fines had been more lucrative, after all), Savonarola raged: "I'd like to see you build a nice fire of these sodomites in the piazza, two or three, male and female, because there are also women who practice that damnable vice." They must be made "a sacrifice to God."

In the end, Savonarola himself suffered the fate he was so keen to see others suffer. He fell foul of the church, not directly for the bonfires or processions but because he claimed to be led by visions, particularly one in which the Virgin Mary told him that Florentines must repent of their ways. Personal visions, especially when combined with anticlericalism, amounted to a challenge to the church's right to mediate all religious experience. The pope called Savonarola to Rome to explain himself in

1497 and, when he refused to go, excommunicated him. The Florentine authorities did not want to fight with the Roman ones, so they arrested Savonarola and tortured him with the strappado until he signed a confession saying that he had only pretended to have real visions. After a series of further inquisitions and trials, he was sentenced to death. On May 23, 1498, he was hanged with two other men, then burned on the scaffold. The ashes were taken away on wagons and thrown into the river, so that no relics would remain. Even La Piagnona, the bell at San Marco that had called his followers to his sermons, was put on a cart and whipped through the streets, then exiled from the city. But Savonarola did live on in human memories, which were harder to obliterate. The city's two greatest historians of the next generation were both affected by their experiences of this time: one, Francesco Guicciardini, was the son of a *piagnone* and may have been a *fanciullo* himself. The other, Niccolò Machiavelli, had heard Savonarola preach. Machiavelli tried to work out why someone so able to tap into popular feeling had ended so badly, and concluded that the main problem was that Savonarola had failed to enforce continuation of that feeling by keeping a private army.

One might feel a certain sympathy for Savonarola, precisely because his story did end so ignominiously, and because of his salutary critique of church corruption and his championing of the interests of the poor. He gave eloquent voice to real grievances. Like Valla, he was unafraid to challenge a huge institution whose claim to authority rested on dubious foundations. And to be *really* generous to him: he wanted to help Florentines by pulling them back from the risk of damnation after death.

But he was a man of violence, whose desire to kill sodomites was murderous, and who used his oratorical skills to raise a storm of angry self-righteousness in his listeners. He sent out his followers to gather everything that showed a love of the human body or mind, everything that was refulgent and decorative and exquisitely wrought, every game that was fun to play, every book that was delightful to read, every flirtatious trinket, every symbol of worldly joy. He assembled these things with the dedication of the great humanist collectors—and burned them. All those productions of human skill and beauty were converted to carbon dioxide and ashen sludge.

As for his overall philosophy, Thomas Paine would sum it up centuries later when he wrote that some people seem to think it an expression of humility to call "the fertile earth a dunghill, and all the blessings of life by the thankless name of vanities." Instead, in Paine's opinion, it looks more like ingratitude.

Violence against art and people alike swept through other parts of the Italian peninsula at the end of that century, with invasions by French forces, who seized the territory of Naples, so ably defended by Valla and his philology, and took it over without a battle in 1495. Their advance through the rest of the peninsula left much trauma in its wake. The worst shock for Rome came a few decades later, in 1527, when unpaid, mutinous former soldiers of the emperor Charles V broke through its defenses and sacked the city. Many of the soldiers were followers of Martin Luther, leader of the Protestant Reformation: a rather more successful rebel against church authority than Savonarola could ever have been. Having been deprived of their own pay, they grabbed any money or treasures they could find, and smashed things they could not use. They moved through the streets attacking locals unfortunate enough to meet them, and hauled out relics from churches. Among graffiti on the walls inside the Vatican, one can still see the single word "Luther" scratched into the plaster under a Raphael fresco.

Many books were destroyed in the city, too, both from the Vatican Library and from private collections. After the humanist Jacopo Sadoleto's library was wrecked, he wrote to Erasmus, "It is unbelievable, all the tragedy and loss that the ruin of this city has brought upon mankind. Despite its vices, it was virtue that occupied the greater place. A haven of humanity, hospitality, and wisdom is what Rome has always been."

Among others who lost a personal library was Paolo Giovio, physician to Pope Clement VII. He helped Clement to escape, lending him his own cloak to cover the distinctive white papal gown as they scurried along a secret passageway out of the Vatican to the Castel Sant'Angelo: the very place where the church had tortured Platina and the other Academy members six decades earlier.

Later, Giovio left the city and spent some time getting over it all on the island of Ischia, where Vittoria Colonna hosted a retreat for her friends, with the old humanist entertainments to soothe them. They spent their days telling stories, like those refugee nobles of *The Decameron* again, and elegantly debating topics, just as Castiglione's courtiers did in Urbino. Giovio would publish their discussions in a work called *Notable Men and Women of Our Time*.

In the real world, much had changed, for humanists and for others. Rome's sufferings in 1527 shocked all of Catholic Europe. It was one thing for a humanist to mock and goad Roman authority, but this was food for thought: If even this ancient and august city could be attacked in such a way, how could anyone feel safe anywhere? The rest of the 1500s bore out such fears, as religious war and chaos raged through Europe.

Out of such experiences, as well as other challenges to Europeans' understanding of life—notably their encounter with a "new" world across the Atlantic and an explosion in the amount of printed information available—sixteenth-century humanists would become ever less naively adoring of the past and ever more interested in social complexity, human fallibility, and the effects of large-scale events on individual lives. The spirit of questioning, pioneered by Valla and other humanistic scholars who refused to limit themselves to approved sources, gained further ground. The interest in the changeable human chameleon shown by a Pico or Ficino remained but became less theological and more pragmatic. For example, the historians Niccolò Machiavelli and Francesco Guicciardini developed a tough, investigative attitude; they reflected on the causes of historical changes and on the reasons *why* people behave as they do.

A similar interest in human complexity brought a revival of another human-centered genre: biography, with its questioning of causes and consequences in individual lives. Paolo Giovio was among the new biographers, though his work was gentler than the historians'. He returned north to his home region near Lake Como and built himself a villa, as you do when you want to get away from mayhem and discord. He based the design on descriptions of ancient villas once owned in the area by the local uncle-and-nephew team, Pliny the Elder and Pliny the Younger. The latter had even written of having a bedroom window so close to the lake that he could fish from it: a beautiful thought. Giovio did not manage that, but he did turn his villa into an even more extraordinary window on life. He used it to house a museum, open to visitors and filled with portraits of people who he hoped would inspire viewers to emulation. He also published a book of these pictures, writing a potted text to go with each woodcut. The original villa collection does not survive, but copies of the portraits were painted for Cosimo I de' Medici by Cristofano dell'Altissimo. These works now run high on the walls down the whole First (or East) Corridor of Florence's Uffizi Galleries, occupying such an honored position that many people, hurrying toward their Botticellis, don't quite notice that they are there.

One evening at a dinner party, Giovio mentioned that he would like to devote a volume to the modern artists of the day. Sitting near him was the painter Giorgio Vasari, who knew absolutely *everyone* in the art world. Splendid idea, he said. But why not bring in a real expert to advise on it? Others at the table chimed in: *You* should do it, Giorgio!

So he did, and Vasari's *Lives of the Great Painters, Sculptors, and Architects* was published in 1550. It was a treasure house of gossip and of reputation-making praise, as well as an assessment of techniques written by a working professional. (Vasari's work included gigantic, somewhat blowsy frescoes, but he also did smaller paintings, one of which is a chronologically fanciful group portrait of six Tuscan poets, dominated at the center by Dante and Petrarch with Boccaccio peeking between their shoulders.) In the *Lives*, Vasari did more than anyone else to advance the idea that a "renaissance," or "rebirth," had taken place since the times of those poets: thus, he suggested the fulfillment of Petrarch's dream, albeit in the visual rather than literary arts. But Vasari saw a rebirth in the world of scholarship, too: he compared his own project to the achievements of the new, subtle historians "who realize that history is truly the mirror of human life—not merely the dry narration of events . . . but a means of pointing out the judgments, counsels, decisions, and plans of human beings, as well as the reason for their successful or unsuccessful actions; this is the true spirit of history."

The actions of humans, the difficulty of making good judgments, the uncertainty of all things—these themes would continue to fascinate sixteenth-century writers. They would have to face the religious split in western Europe, and the revelation that the world was much bigger and more diverse than the ancients had expected. This would bring some of them to a subtle understanding of uncertainty and complexity. A few would also realize that nothing was more complex or self-divided than an individual human being.

We shall see where these ideas took them. But first, let's talk about bodies.

4.

Marvelous Network

Mostly 1492–1559

*Books and bodies—Girolamo Fracastoro and his
beautiful poem on a terrible disease—Niccolò
Leoniceno: bad texts kill people—botanists and
anatomists—death delights in helping life—Andreas
Vesalius and his humanistic masterpiece—although
he did overlook something—all is in flux.*

Just as a mighty city like Rome could be invaded and turned into a scarred, depleted mess, so could a human being be invaded and ruined by disease. This was the starting point for a poetic journey through a not very glamorous topic: *Syphilis, or The French Disease*, published by the humanist physician Girolamo Fracastoro in 1530, though written earlier and influenced by the general disasters suffered throughout the peninsula. He addresses Italy: Look, he says, how you were once so happy and peaceful—loved by the gods, fertile, wealthy—and yet now your land has been plundered, your holy sites defiled, and your relics stolen. This calls to mind the likely fate of a good-looking young man if syphilis were to attack his face and body, and wreck his mind and spirit.

As he says all this, Fracastoro's poem is achieving the opposite: turning an ugly subject into beautiful Virgilian verse. Like Boccaccio in his plague prelude to *The Decameron*, Fracastoro piles on the miseries at the beginning, but soon goes on to the pleasures of storytelling. He gives us magical rivers of mercury flowing underground, beaches sparkling with gold dust, air filled with brightly colored birds, and the tribulations of a naive shepherd—all doubling as ways of presenting possible syphilis cures. Applying the best medical expertise of the era, he explores a series of approaches culminating in the medicament he thinks most likely to succeed: the bark of guaiacum, or guaiac wood, which comes from a flowering shrub found in the New World.

What I love about Fracastoro's poem is its blend, characteristic of its time, of genuine inquiry into the world with literary elegance reveled in for its own sake. It resembles Pietro Bembo's dialogue *De Aetna*—and lo, Bembo is its dedicatee. There are two good English translations through which non-Latin readers can appreciate Fracastoro's imagery. I have a fondness for the 1984 one by Geoffrey Eatough, which, although in prose, really goes to town with Fracastoro's voluptuous love of words. Here is dietary advice for the syphilitic:

> Shun tender chitterlings, the belly of a pig curving with fat, and, alas, the chine of pig; don't feed on boar's loin, however often you have slain boars out hunting. Moreover, don't let cucumber, hard to digest, nor truffles entice you, nor satisfy your hunger with artichokes or lecherous onions.

And here is his final paean to guaiacum:

> Hail great tree sown from a sacred seed by the hand of the Gods, with beautiful tresses, esteemed for your new virtues: hope of mankind, pride and new glory from a foreign world; most happy tree ... you will also be sung under our heavens, wherever through our song the Muses can make you travel by the lips of men.

HIERONYMVS   FRACASTORIVS
De Larmessin fecit

Besides giving rein to his literary skills, Fracastoro was a working physician who genuinely wanted to help people recover. Sadly, guaiacum, which induces sweating, is of little use against syphilis. (It does have another application today, however: by reacting chemically with hemoglobin, it can flag the presence of blood in urine or feces.) But Fracastoro could draw only on the materials of his time. Like any researcher or practitioner today, he studied the literature, tried to excel in his field, and worked toward the goal of all medicine: reducing suffering and improving human lives. He just did it in hexameters.

Mitigating the suffering of one's fellows is a humanistic goal in the broadest sense, and in general the practice of medicine straddles the worlds of science and of humanistic study. It uses quantifiable research (far more so now than in Fracastoro's day) but also patients' personal accounts of what they feel; a working doctor must know how to listen and talk well with those patients. Medicine deals in observable and experienced phenomena. But it also relies on books: knowledge is passed from practitioner to practitioner through education and the sharing of professional experience. Like other sciences, it explicitly deploys the humanities, especially history, so as to reflect on its own past and to refine its approach. Far more than other sciences, it draws on contemporary prevailing ideas of who and what we are as humans, and generally as living beings. In return, medicine helps to *change* what we are, as we become (hopefully) more knowledgeable about our own systems and ultimately able to meddle a little with our own basic chemistry and processes.

This is why, in his 1979 book *Humanism and the Physician*, Edmund D. Pellegrino wrote that medicine "stands at the confluence of all the humanities." And the nineteenth-century scientist and educationalist T. H. Huxley (who will reappear in a later chapter) recommended the study of human physiology as the best foundation for education of *any* kind:

> There is no side of the intellect which it does not call into play, no region of human knowledge into which either its roots, or its branches, do not extend; like the Atlantic between the Old and the New Worlds, its waves wash the shores of the two worlds of matter and of mind.

Humanism and medicine mingle: this chapter is a case study in how humanistic skills intertwined themselves with early modern attempts at the study of actual people. It could be read as an interlude, but it is also a turning point in our story, as European humanists become less subservient to the ancients, look more closely at the real world, and inquire into physical and mental life, asking, What sort of creatures are we, and what does it mean to have a human body?

I said that the aim of medicine is to reduce suffering, but unfortunately for much of history it failed to achieve this, and even inadvertently made things worse. Some practices were needlessly invasive, as with cutting to release blood in the belief that it had become toxic or needed reducing. Ingesting substances such as dung or "mummy" (fragments of human remains, sometimes blended with bitumen) was thought to be good for you precisely because it was disgusting. The luckiest patients received treatments that were merely useless instead of life-threatening. Ideas of regimen were also variable: shunning chitterlings might be helpful at times, but Petrarch was advised by doctors to avoid all vegetables, fruit, and fresh water—not considered healthy advice for most situations today. No wonder Petrarch had nothing but invective for doctors, even though he counted several among his best friends. He reserved special scorn for those who showed off their humanistic learning most: "All are learned and courteous, able to converse extraordinarily well, to argue vigorously, to make quite powerful and sweet-sounding speeches, but in the long run capable of killing quite artistically."

Some thirty years after these remarks by Petrarch, Geoffrey Chaucer included a physician in his *Canterbury Tales* who thought gold was the best remedy for the plague—if administered to himself in the form of a coin. "Gold in phisik is a cordial. / Therfore he lovede gold in special." Chaucer prefaces that remark by listing the authorities the physician has studied: Hippocrates, Dioscorides, Galen, Rhazes, Avicenna. This amounts to a good summary of the canon of early medicine. The first two were Greek pioneers; the last two were the great Persian scholars al-Rāzī and Ibn Sīna. The most influential authority on the list was the middle one: Galen, physician to the emperor of Rome in the second century CE and writer on almost every area of medical practice, ranging from anatomy and pathology to diet and psychology.

All these authors were intelligent, judicious, and full of good advice, but they all had failings. Also, as happened in other fields, their texts had become fragmentary and corrupted by repeated copying. With Greek having been unreadable to most western Europeans for so many centuries, the Greek authors tended to come into Latin via Arabic, doubling the potential for mistranslation. In the 1400s and 1500s, new generations of humanists applied their philological skills to translating the authors afresh, using the most accurate sources they could find. They promoted their work with the usual jailbreak images: one physician rejoiced in his preface at how, thanks to himself, Hippocrates and Galen had both been "rescued from darkness perpetual and silent night."

More than with other subject areas, medical humanists had an urgent sense of the need for such work. No one is likely to die because a line of Homer has been misread. If a fake legal or political document is allowed to pass, as with the Donation of Constantine, it can have major consequences but is not directly lethal. But when a medical text is garbled, people can die.

The first to make this point forcefully was Niccolò Leoniceno, in his *On the Errors of Pliny and Other Medical Writers*, first published in 1492. Pliny the Elder's *Natural History* was a first-century compilation of secondhand information about herbs and health, among other topics, and it was often relied upon too much, even though Pliny himself made no claims to quality control. Humanists loved him just as much as their medieval predecessors did. Petrarch filled his Pliny manuscript with notes, and a copy now in Oxford's Bodleian Library glories in notes by Coluccio Salutati, Niccolò Niccoli, *and* Bartolomeo Platina. For humanists, Pliny's appetite for miscellaneous information was congenial, and if they noticed errors, they politely blamed them on copyists, not on him. Leoniceno, however, squarely blamed the author. He said he could fill a whole book with Pliny's blunders, especially when it came to identifying medicinal plants. The question is not just one of words, he wrote, but of things. And people's health and lives depend on getting medical language right.

Like Lorenzo Valla before him, Leoniceno was not afraid to attack an ancient authority when he felt the truth was important. Also like Valla, he preferred to lead readers away from bad versions and back to earlier, more authentic sources. In his case, that could include looking at the actual plants. He ended his treatise:

> Why did nature grant us eyes and other senses, if not that we might see and investigate the truth with our own resources? We should not deprive ourselves and, following always in others' steps, notice nothing for ourselves: this would be to see with others' eyes, hear with others' ears, smell with others' noses, understand with others' minds, and decree that we are nothing more than stones, if

we commit everything to the judgment of others and decide on nothing ourselves.

Even with this defense of what now sounds like a modern empirical approach, Leoniceno was still a humanist. He expresses himself with the usual gestures of elegance; he sees no conflict between being a good philologist and being a good investigator of the real world—in fact, they go well together. After all, Lorenzo Valla, too, had looked into questions of real-life plausibility and veracity, as well as purely linguistic considerations. What neither of them believed in was excessive veneration of authorities just because they were authorities.

Leoniceno collected manuscripts himself, and he was that other very humanist thing: a courtier, working in the ambit of rich patrons. He developed his career while working as physician to the Este dukes in Ferrara, the intellectually lively court now presided over by Alfonso I and his wife, Lucrezia Borgia—who was a great friend to humanists. Leoniceno dedicated his little treatise *On the Dipsas and Various Other Snakes* to Lucrezia, perhaps *very* delicately implying that she had a special interest in the venom of the species described in ancient literature as dipsas. (The snakes now called that are not venomous at all.) He also published a work on syphilis in 1497, thirty-three years before Fracastoro, no doubt another subject that had a certain relevance at court. Like good popular science writers today, Leoniceno could communicate well with a nonexpert audience while also pursuing specialist work. His combined editing and scientific career was crowned when, at the age of eighty-six, he produced his own edition of selected Galen works with a commentary, published by the French humanist printer Henri Estienne in 1514.

By that time, checking books against plants was becoming easier, thanks to the creation of botanical gardens in courts and university towns around Italy. These gardens positively bloomed with humanists. In Ferrara, the court physician Antonio Musa Brasavola simultaneously gathered plants from the surrounding countryside and multilingual synonyms for their names from books. In Bologna, Ulisse Aldrovandi assembled huge volumes of natural history based on his personal museum of specimens and also wrote commentaries on ancient texts.

While the philologist-botanists were comparing plants and words, other critical thinkers were applying a similar principle elsewhere. They began comparing anatomical books to the human bodies those books claimed to describe.

It had long been recognized that looking inside bodies was a good idea, when possible. Galen was all in favor. But in practice it was hard to achieve, because religious and political authorities in the early Roman, Christian, and Islamic worlds alike outlawed it. Galen had to use non-human species such as sheep or the Barbary macaque for his dissections. Later, a long shadow was cast by Augustine's view in the early fifth century that anatomical dissection was wrong because it ignored the holistic harmony of the living body—never mind the fact that better anatomical knowledge might help stop that harmonious living body from dropping dead. As the nineteenth-century pro-anatomy campaigner Thomas Southwood Smith would later say, "The question is, whether the surgeon shall be allowed to gain knowledge by operating on the bodies of the dead, or driven to obtain it by practising on the bodies of the living."

By the late thirteenth century, some had begun to defy the dissecting ban, notably in Bologna, where Mondino dei Liuzzi used corpses of executed criminals to demonstrate anatomy to students. Others followed him. Eventually, the rules were relaxed and anatomy teachers were permitted a small number of human bodies per year. Since opportunities were so limited, it was important that everyone have a good view, so purpose-built theaters were designed. One from the 1590s survives at the University of Padua: an unnervingly small room with six narrow oval galleries rising steeply around the central table. The students leaned forward against the balustrades; there was no room to sit. What with the heat and smoke from the illuminating torches, and the smell of the open cadaver slowly rotting as it went through dissection by stages, it was

not unusual for members of the class to faint. The balustrades and the shoulders of their fellow students prevented them from falling headfirst into the scene below.

Even today, nice and clean and empty, the theater in Padua calls to mind Dante's circles of Hell. Unlike Dante's version, however, this was not a place that needed a sign telling anyone to abandon hope upon entering. On the contrary, hope was what it was about. The words inscribed at the entrance of the Padua theater were *Mors ubi gaudet succurrere vitae*: "Where death delights in helping life."

In the early stages of this new educational method, the corpse, however formidably real and uncompromising in appearance, was still expected to defer to the book. A lowly barber or surgeon would do the cutting, an "ostensor" would point out each part, and somewhere above it all the professor would stand at a lectern reciting from (usually) Galen.

But, awkward: the body sometimes refused to cooperate. For example, Galen had described an organ at the base of the brain known as the

rete mirabile, or "marvelous network." In life, it was supposed to infuse "vital spirits" into the blood, to be further distributed by nerves; the process left a phlegmy residue to be excreted via the brain and down the nostrils. (We can probably all recognize this substance; its familiarity perhaps made the theory sound more credible.) But ostensors blushed for their inability to point to the *rete mirabile* when it was called for. The Parisian professor Jacobus Sylvius desperately wondered whether it had existed in Galen's time but then degenerated out of existence in modern humans.

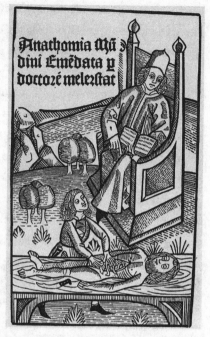

The real reason is simply that humans don't have it. Dogs do. Dolphins do. Giraffes do, to protect them from blood pressure surges when they lower their heads to drink. But in humans it is just not there. Galen had probably seen it while dissecting sheep. Some commentators began suggesting this, notably Giacomo Berengario da Carpi, a Bologna professor who wrote, "I have worked hard to discover this *rete* and its location; I have dissected more than a hundred heads almost solely for the sake of this *rete* and even now I don't understand it."

The final blow came from a brilliant former student of Sylvius: Andreas Vesalius, born Andries van Wesel in Brussels in 1514. Besides being an anatomist, Vesalius was an innovative educationalist, a writer, an editor of classical texts, and the creator of one of the outstanding works in printing history—in short, a perfect humanist, but of the kind who subjected ancient authorities to scrutiny and testing.

He began his investigations as a young student in Louvain, where he and a friend would sneak outside the city walls at night to collect easily detachable parts from rotting victims of execution who were displayed at the roadside as a warning. He and his friend used them for a different kind of edification. While still at Louvain, Vesalius also wrote a commentary on al-Rāzī, correcting errors of terminology that had crept in from previous translations and trying to identify the substances referred to: a project in the spirit of Leoniceno.

He went on to study in Paris and then in Padua, where he was so precocious that he was taken on to teach surgery and anatomy the very day after he graduated. He immediately set to devising better ways of preparing bodies for educational demonstration, and, unlike others, he insisted on doing the cutting himself as he lectured. Surviving notes made by a student show how he proceeded through the parts of the body over several days, racing against time and decay as dissectors always had to.

To help with this problem and provide more leisurely aids to study, he began working up large printed illustrations. First came a set of six tables, big enough to show the body parts clearly. It did still include the *rete mirabile*; later Vesalius confessed that he had used a non-human animal as the source, since he was embarrassed to admit not having found it.

That feeling would change as his confidence grew. A couple of years later, he was carrying out dissections in Bologna with his colleague Matteo Corti. Unusually, Vesalius played the role of humble cutter and ostensor while Corti read out the texts. Vesalius became annoyed with Corti's loyalty to the standard sources, so

Vesalius's copy of works on respiration by Galen

he kept interrupting to point out where the body differed, until the two anatomists were arguing openly over the body in front of the onlookers. (I see them throwing kidneys and clavicles at each other, but that's just me.)

At last, in 1543, Vesalius produced his masterwork: *De humani corporis fabrica*, or *Of the Structure of the Human Body*, in which he repudiated the notion of a human *rete* for once and for all. He blamed both himself and other anatomists for having been too Galen-reliant: "I shall say nothing more about these others; instead I shall marvel more at my own stupidity and blind faith in the writings of Galen and other anatomists." He ends the section by urging students to rely on their own careful examinations, taking no one's word for anything, not even his own.

This was a good warning, since Vesalius himself did not get everything right. One error was that he failed to identify the clitoris correctly, misdescribing it as part of the labia. It took another Padua anatomist, Realdo Colombo, to correct him. Realdo even knew what it was for, which implies that he had noticed it in contexts other than the dissection table. He named it *"amor Veneris, vel dulcedo"* ("love of Venus, or thing of pleasure"), gave details of its role in women's sexual experiences, and remarked, "It cannot be said how astonished I am that so many famous anatomists had not even an inkling of such a lovely thing, perfected with such art for the sake of such utility."

With a few such exceptions, Vesalius's *Fabrica* is distinguished by its detail, its description of methods of preparing the bodies, and its judicious assessment of errors in the classical authorities. And, with all this, it is also a superb work of humanistic book-production and visual art. It is printed in a clear, easy-to-read font, and features eighty-three plates of images, drawn under Vesalius's guidance by Jan van Calcar and engraved by various hands. The engravings were made in Italy on blocks of pear-tree wood, which were then transported by a mercantile firm across the Alps to Vesalius's publisher of choice in Basel, Joannes Oporinus. The author followed behind, ready to attend every phase of the operation. He constitutes an equally personal presence in the book itself, which includes a portrait of him, with a rather solemn and challenging-looking expression as he demonstrates the muscles in an arm, and a scene on the engraved title page showing him dissecting a body in a packed lecture theater. Balustrades notwithstanding, students and eminent officials—as well as Galen, Hippocrates, Aristotle, and a dog—almost tumble around him in their eagerness to see. The whole work is filled with such stylish touches: cherubs fly around in the capitals, a skeletal figure leans on a tomb contemplating a skull, a muscular man flings back his head in anguish. Many of the figures are shown against natural backgrounds or the scenes of half-ruined classical buildings that so many humanists loved. Their poses are those of heroes, especially when they are displaying the structure of muscles.

It is poignant to see these dignified human beings and to reflect that their models were likely to have been executed as criminals, or else were destitute people who had died in poverty and had no say in the fate of their bodies. They almost certainly never chose to end up on the page like this: right through to the nineteenth century, many people resisted the prospect of being dissected. One reason was that they believed in physical resurrection in the afterlife; no one wants to rise into heaven as an empty torso or a flapping curtain of shredded nerves and muscles. The prospect of helping anatomical students to learn—far from being

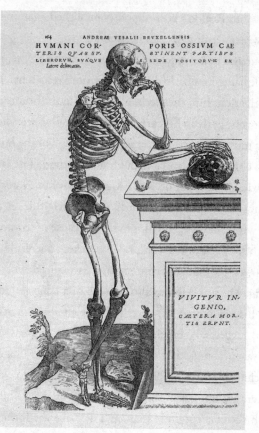

something to "delight" in, as the Padua motto had it—was considered a powerful deterrent to crime, almost more so than execution itself.

Yet these unfortunate nameless people have indeed made it possible for others to live. And here they are, in one of the most magnificent books in history, in their full dignity, after all: forthright, muscular, and beautiful. They look, many of them, as if they had been sculpted by Michelangelo.

There is a good reason for this similarity: fascinated by musculature and sheer physical heft, as well as by human dignity, Michelangelo made a close study of anatomy in order to improve his art. He was friends with Realdo Colombo, and they planned to produce a book together. This did not happen, but Realdo's posthumously published anatomy book probably does owe something to their collaboration.

Other artists had conducted anatomical study before, the outstanding example being Leonardo da Vinci. A serious researcher, he undertook deep investigations into the mechanics as well as the beauty and harmony of bodily forms. Early in his career, he drew detailed sections of a human skull and a muscular leg. Later, studying each end of the human span, he dissected a child of two and a man of one hundred. The latter, a pauper in the charitable hospital of Santa Maria Nuova in Florence, told Leonardo almost with his dying words that he felt fine, if a little weak. Leonardo wrote: "I dissected him to see the cause of so sweet a death."

As with so much of his work, Leonardo kept his results to himself in his notebooks, so that few contemporaries realized what a pioneer of many sciences he was. He was also rather better educated in classical culture than his oft-quoted self-description as an *omo sanza lettere* (unlettered man) suggests: he brushed up his Latin to compensate for learning it poorly when young, and was the owner of a reasonable number of books (including a copy of Pliny). Leonardo intended to write a full treatise on anatomy, but got no further than an outline: "This work should begin with the conception of man, and describe the form of the womb, and how the child lives in it. . . . Then you will describe which parts grow more than others after the infant is born, and give the measurements of a child of one year. Then describe the grown man and woman, and their measurements . . ." and so on, presumably through to the centenarian stage.

As an anatomical textbook, this would have been extraordinary in also being a *narrative* account of human bodily life. Artists and anatomists alike knew very well that we do not hold to one unchanging form throughout our lives. Contrary to the image in Vitruvian Man, there is no single, static model for how to be a human being. We are born, we develop, we decline. As Lucretius had said, both spirit and body have "a birthday and a funeral." Along the path between these events, all is in flux. The mind certainly is. For all our exalted sense of ourselves as spiritual beings, our conscious selves are prone to being befuddled by alcohol or enfeebled by disease. Even the wisest sage can lose her reason in a flash if a stone falls on her head. Lucretius and his ultimate source, Democritus, observed how mind and body alike are affected by the senses and events throughout life; they reminded us that, one day, each of us will come to an end in the gentle, silent dissolution of our atoms. Writers through the sixteenth and seventeenth centuries continued to reflect on these thoughts; a new sensibility was formed around them. Ultimately, as it turns out, neither books nor bodies are completely reliable.

5.

Human Stuff

Mainly the 1500s

Over the Alps, with the northern humanists—Conrad Celtis—Rodolphus Agricola—Desiderius Erasmus, who promoted civilized living and friendship among many—Michel de Montaigne, who turned humanism in a different direction—novelists.

Vesalius and his pear woodblocks were almost in danger of running into a traffic jam on their journey over the Alps, so numerous were artistic, medical, and literary travelers on that route. The exchange of visitors between north and south had been the norm for a long time. Italians went north out of curiosity or in search of new patrons to flatter and entertain. Northerners went south to acquire those desirable Italian things: a book collection, the finest university experiences available, the latest scholarly methods, and an extra level of humanistic polish in manners and language. Armed with these attainments, they returned to their own lands eager to share their findings with others, and to apply the methods to their own history and culture.

An early example of how this worked—and we are backtracking a little in time here—can be found by dipping into the life of Conrad Celtis, or Celtes, born in 1459 as Konrad Pickel. (Like many humanists, he switched to a Latinized version of his name.) He ran away from his tiny Bavarian hometown of Wipfeld by hopping on a timber raft headed down the river Main, then went on to study in the universities of Cologne and Heidelberg before spending two years traveling around Italy. While there, he hung out with the humanists of Venice, Padua, Ferrara, Bologna, Florence, and Rome—especially with members of the Academies of the latter two cities. He then went north again and had an illustrious career teaching in a series of universities, setting up his own Academies in several places. He tried to bestow the benefit of his experience on his compatriots, by scolding students for their drunkenness and advising his fellow professors to learn to speak properly instead of "honking like geese."

Yet Celtis also took much interest and pride in Germanic literature. It was he who discovered the manuscript plays by the tenth-century nun Hrotswitha in the monastery of Saint Emmeram in Regensburg and spread the word about them. He helped Hartmann Schedel make revisions to his massive historical and geographical survey, the *Nuremberg Chronicle*. And he edited for publication a recently discovered work by the Roman historian Tacitus, *Germania*, which expressed admiration for the simple, honest, and rather sexily savage ways of the German peoples.

This was all typical Italianate humanist activity, applied to the materials of a different territory. But Celtis also advocated other forms of study. He urged everyone he knew to improve their intellectual level, not only in literary pursuits but also in fields that we would now think of as scientific:

> Find out the nature of formless Chaos. . . . Find out with soaring mind the causes of individual things: investigate the blowing of the winds and the tides of the raging sea. . . . Find out why dark hollows of the earth produce sulphur and veins of fair metals, and why hot springs restore the bodies of the sick. . . . Learn something of the various peoples of the world and their different languages and customs.

A similar appetite for varied forms of knowledge emerged in advice given by a northerner from the Low Countries, Rudolf or Rodolphus Agricola, born Roelof Huysman. (Both forms of the surname meant "farmer.") Writing to a fellow teacher, he recommended having students investigate "the geography and nature of lands, seas, mountains and rivers; the customs, borders and circumstances of nations that live on earth; ... the medicinal properties of trees and herbs," and so on. They should, of course, study literary and moral subjects, because these will help them to live well. But learning about "things themselves" is worthwhile just because they are so *interesting*.

The voracious eagerness of such lists invited mockery, and sure enough, in 1532 they attracted the wicked wit of the French satirist François Rabelais. He had his fictional giant, Gargantua, present his son, Pantagruel, with a similar syllabus to take off to university with him. Learn Greek, then Latin, then Hebrew, and also Chaldean and Arabic. Study history, arithmetic, music; learn "all of the beautiful texts of Civil Law by heart and compare them to moral philosophy." Study nature; "let there be no sea, river or stream the fishes of which you do not know. Know all the birds of the air, all the trees, bushes and shrubs of the forests, all the herbs in the soil, all the metals hidden deep in the womb of the Earth." Study medicine, and "by frequent dissections acquire a perfect knowledge of that other world which is Man. . . . In short, let me see you an abyss of erudition." He added, "I see even today's brigands, hangmen, mercenaries and stable-lads better taught than the teachers and preachers of my day. Even the very women and children have aspired to such praise and to the heavenly manna of sound learning."

In fact, Rabelais had mastered a fair range of these topics himself, being a former monk, polyglot, trained lawyer, and practicing physician: he produced scholarly editions of Galen and Hippocrates and had some involvement in at least one public dissection. And Agricola had a similarly formidable array of accomplishments. Agricola sounds like another Leon Battista Alberti in the scope of his excellences and the charm of

his manner. For ten years
Agricola traveled in Italy,
where he not only taught students rhetoric but also played
the church organ; much of
his time there was spent in
the entourage of the duke of
Este. His musical ear probably helped him in learning
languages; those who knew
him commented on how good
his accent was. He spoke
French, Italian, High German and Low German, the
Frisian of his homeland, and

of course Latin and Greek. Toward the end of his life he added some
study of Hebrew. His other talents included drawing: he would secretly
observe people's faces in church (while playing organ at the same time, I
wonder?) and afterward reproduce them perfectly in charcoal. He was
good-looking, with Vitruvian proportions, according to admiring descriptions by friends: "His frame was big and strong and he was taller
than most, with wide shoulders and chest, to which the other parts of his
body from head to foot harmoniously corresponded, so that as regards
his whole body, he was striking to behold." Everyone loved him, and his
influence on others was greater than is implied by his relatively sparse,
not terribly exciting publications.

We know in particular that he made an impression on one boy of
about fourteen, a pupil at a school in Deventer in the Netherlands that
Agricola visited in 1480. Agricola probably went there to address the students. We do not know what he said; it may have been along the lines of
his advice in the letter I just quoted. He may even have gone on to add, as
he said in that letter, that a student should not put too much reliance on

what he learns at school. It is far more important to study history, poetry, and philosophy from the original sources, as well as religious texts, and above all to learn the ultimate skill: how to live well.

Whatever Agricola said that day, that teenage boy took it to heart. His name was Desiderius Erasmus—and, so far as we know, he actually *was* given this name at birth, rather than adopting it later. He grew up to be the most eminent northern humanist of his century. He is one of our two main subjects in this chapter, the other being the French writer Michel de Montaigne, another product of the transalpine influence. Montaigne belonged to a younger generation, and this made a difference to his sensibility. Erasmus's Europe was that of the late 1400s and early 1500s—a time of dramatic social transformation to which he was an often-horrified witness. Montaigne, instead, would find himself in that transformed world from the start; its instability was a constant for him. This difference aside, the two men had similar temperaments, characterized by tolerance and a great love for the life of the mind; I am sure they would have liked each other had they been able to meet.

Erasmus and Agricola could have had a fine friendship, too, had they reencountered each other as adults and equals. Unfortunately, Agricola died too soon. It was a sudden death of the sort that was then common, and that could have been avoided in an era of better medicine. While traveling home from another Italian trip to his residence in Heidelberg, he developed a kidney infection and a fever. No effective treatment was available for such infections, and it killed him. He was only forty-two; Erasmus was then about nineteen and trying to decide what to do with his life.

Desiderius Erasmus is remembered as one of the most many-faceted of humanists, author of translations, dialogues, diatribes, theological tracts, writing manuals, study guides, proverb collections, amusing diversions, and astonishing quantities of letters. He developed a circle of

correspondents and friends to rival Petrarch's. By comparison with Petrarch, he had the benefit of almost two hundred years' worth of extra scholarship to draw on, as well as an ever more well-connected continent to explore. He was no questioner of Christian faith, being very devout—but he did add his own deep belief in the importance of living wisely and well in *this* world. An advocate of principles of peace and friendship, he was also much concerned with manners and civilized behavior. He believed completely in the benefits of education and in the ways in which literature and study could help people to flourish in disturbing and complicated times.

None of that long list of cultural contributions would have seemed especially likely when he was born, in Rotterdam, probably in 1466. He was illegitimate: his parents, though living in domestic contentment, could not marry because his father was a priest. They took care to give Erasmus and his older brother the best schooling they could, however.

This meant a series of monastic institutions culminating in the one in Deventer, run by a community called the Brethren of the Common Life.

The Deventer monks were highly respected, and the community had long been known for its excellent manuscript copying. But Erasmus came to view this and his previous schools with loathing. One reason was the air of violence. In that era it was considered normal, and even essential, to beat pupils, but Erasmus had been traumatized at his earlier school by being hit merely as a test of how good he was at bearing it, rather than because he had done anything wrong. As he wrote, "This incident destroyed all love of study within me and flung my young mind into such a deep depression that I nearly wasted away with heart-break." The Deventer monks were probably less arbitrary, but they, too, seemed to Erasmus to want to knock the spirit out of the boys, all the better to prepare them for following the monastic life themselves.

Instead, the effect on Erasmus was to implant in him a lifelong aversion to cruelty or intimidation of any kind. He would have agreed with a remark made centuries later by E. M. Forster in describing the miseries of his own public-school education: "The worst trick it ever played me was to pretend that it was the world in miniature. For it hindered me from discovering how lovely and delightful and kind the world can be, and how much of it is intelligible."

That was another reason Erasmus took a poor view of his schooling: the unworldliness and irrelevance to real life of the monks' attitudes. It was a common humanist complaint to say that such institutions were old-fashioned, pedantic, and out of touch with reality. For Erasmus, as for Agricola, and later for Forster, a young mind needs to be liberated from meaningless, useless systems of knowledge as taught by unenlightened masters of an outmoded stamp who themselves have no idea how to live.

Erasmus came to this view slowly. At first, he did follow the expected path, and took orders himself in another monastery. He even wrote a treatise in praise of monastic existence: *On Contempt for the World*. But he wrote another one at around the same time, boldly called *Anti-Barbarians*, which attacked ill-educated monks and their tendency to ignore the humanistic subjects of moral philosophy, history, and good Latin. Erasmus was apparently trying his hand at different arguments, and showing his literary versatility. It was his writing skill that earned him his escape when the bishop of Cambrai took him on as a secretary to accompany him on his travels. After that departure, Erasmus never went back to the monastery. The bishop also arranged for him to be allowed to go to Paris and study at the university of the Sorbonne.

That was unsatisfactory, too, and for similar reasons. The Sorbonne was another bastion of medieval scholasticism, at a time when other European universities were slowly becoming more hospitable to humanist ideas of learning. Not in Paris: there, the professors still seemed to be socially inept oddballs, preoccupied with paradoxes and syllogisms. Also, Erasmus's lodgings were squalid, and he was very poor. A lack of civilized living conditions formed another aspect of the attitude of "contempt for the world" that Erasmus was now rejecting. Instead, he felt that education should train a person to be at *home* in the world, in tune with fellow humans, able to make friends, act wisely, and share the light of knowledge while treating all people with courtesy. That is, it should encourage the development of *humanitas*.

So he left Paris, too, and adopted the pattern of life that he would continue to follow for the rest of his days: that of a traveling humanist. He would earn his way as a scholar, a writer, a publisher's assistant, a teacher, and a sort of general humanist consultant in institutions all over Europe. It was not easy: he had no truly settled home, and, like so many other humanists, remained dependent on pleasing those who supported him. But intellectually, for the most part, it was a life of freedom.

His sojourns in various countries included several in England. During one of these, from 1509 to 1514, he taught at both Oxford and Cambridge—universities that were now relaxing their medieval syllabus slightly to allow in a little of the humanistic light. Erasmus contributed to that process. He also worked with the English humanist John Colet to design a curriculum for Colet's newly opened school at St. Paul's Cathedral. Another Englishman who became a great friend during this time was Thomas More, the lawyer and statesman who later entangled himself fatally with King Henry VIII. You can feel the exuberance of his and Erasmus's friendship by reading the two books they wrote in each other's honor. Erasmus's *In Praise of Folly—Moriae encomium*, a pun on More's name—is a flight of mischievous fancy, including some daring ideas but putting them into the mouth of "Folly," which means they can be safely disowned. More's political satire *Utopia* tells of travels to an imaginary island society that has a tolerant, almost Epicurean approach to religion, alongside some eccentric ideas about the sharing of jobs and houses. Erasmus did much to help him compose and publish it.

On the basis of his experiences in developing educational programs in England, Erasmus produced a series of treatises on the subject of training the young in humanistic life and techniques of study. Like Celtis and others, he thought it was vital for students to acquire good manners—which is to say, ways of expressing fellow feeling and consideration for others. His 1530 work *De civilitate morum puerilium*, or *On Good Manners for Boys*, summed up the dos and don'ts of civilized behavior. Don't wipe your nose on your sleeve, but blow it with a handkerchief—not too loudly, because trumpeting is for elephants. If you must sneeze, turn away from others, and when people bless you (or when you assume they have, since while sneezing you won't hear them), raise your cap in acknowledgment. When you spit, aim it so you don't spray people. Look after your teeth, although there is no need to whiten them with powder. "To brush them with urine is a custom of the Spaniards." Don't toss your hair like a frolicsome horse. To deal with intestinal gas, opinions differ: some say you should clench your buttocks to block its exit, yet "it is no part of good manners to bring illness upon yourself," so just be considerate and step away from others, or at least cover the sound with a cough. While doing all this, maintain an easy, relaxed look. "The brow also should be cheerful and smooth, indicating a good conscience and an open mind: not lined with wrinkles, a sign of old age; not irresolute like a hedgehog's; not menacing like a bull's."

The aim is something like Castiglione's ideal of casual poise, but it is not done mainly with the intention of showing off one's own cool. The aim is, rather, to make life nicer for others. It is a method for *not* separating oneself from the world, like those awkward Sorbonne teachers or bad-tempered monks. It means knowing how to put companions at ease and to take your place in a generally pleasant society, living with humanity in every sense. It even makes you human. "Manners maketh man," as the motto of Winchester College and New College, Oxford, still maintains—a line dating from a couple of centuries earlier, in fact.

Of course, there is more to education and *humanitas* than looking relaxed and farting quietly. Erasmus also taught the habits needed for a fulfilling *intellectual* life, and here the key thing is to have a richly stocked mind with as large a frame of reference as possible. This will bring better judgment and an ability to express yourself with understanding as well as elegance. He recommends reading good books and following a popular technique of the time: keeping notes grouped by subject, so you can remember what you read and combine it with other ideas in useful ways. If no paper is to hand, you can paint notes on a wall, or even scratch them into window glass. The important thing is to build up a treasure house—the literal meaning of "thesaurus"—in your mind, so it is always there as a resource.

He gave ample materials for such a treasure house himself in his work *On the Abundant Style*, or, in Latin, *De copia*, which evokes both copying and abundance. (The "abundant" implication is also there in the English word *copious*.) This treatise lists ways of varying and expanding what you want to say, according to a principle quoted from the rhetorician Quintilian: "Nature above all delights in variety." For example, you might develop an account of an event by looking into its causes or consequences, or by expanding vivid details connected with it. Erasmus gives an example from Plutarch, who really pushed the boat out in finding ways of describing Cleopatra's famously luxurious barge. Most of Erasmus's text consists of lists of phrases and variations for conveying concepts such as "customary," "doubt," or "wheedling." Number 195 could come in useful if your parrot dies:

> *mortem obiit*: he met his end.
>
> *vita defunctus est*: he has done with life.
>
> *vixit*: his life is over.
>
> *in vivis esse desiit*: he has ceased to be numbered with the living. . . .
>
> *concessit in fata*: he passed to his fated end.
>
> *vitae peregit fabulam*: he has played his last scene in life.

Erasmus certainly brought copious abundance to his own work. His expanding, burgeoning method appears most strikingly in a collection of *Adages*, which gives commentaries on well-worn quotations and phrases such as "to leave no stone unturned" or "to be in the same boat." From a first version with 818 adages, this grew to a final edition with 4,251 of them. Some of the commentaries themselves became so long that they appeared as separate books, often including more personal reflections alongside the erudite glosses of literature. Having started as a literary exercise, the *Adages* evolved into something like a portrait of Erasmus's own voluminous mind. They are suffused with his personality: wry, learned, generous with his knowledge, and informed by his years of traveling, reading, and friendship.

Those were the three great themes of his life, and each of them fed the others. Traveling brought endless new friends; friends brought new projects, appointments, and ideas for further study; and these in turn prompted further travels. And so it went on. He followed where these opportunities led, sometimes staying for long periods, sometimes only briefly passing through. As he once said: "My home is wherever I keep my library."

One of Erasmus's longest sojourns was in the Swiss city of Basel. This was a great city for humanists, having an excellent university and many publishers—which was why Vesalius would choose it for his *Fabrica* edition in 1543. During the slightly earlier period when Erasmus was there, the city's leading humanist printer was Johannes Froben, himself very scholarly and, like Aldus Manutius in Venice, the host of a bookish community. Erasmus moved into Froben's house and wrote excitedly to a friend, "They all know Latin, they all know Greek, most of them know Hebrew too; one is an expert historian, another an experienced theologian; one is skilled in the mathematics, one a keen antiquary, another a jurist. . . . I certainly have before never had the luck to live in such a gifted company. And to say nothing of that, how open-hearted they are, how gay, how well they get on together!" He admired Froben for his joyful dedication to the literary life: "It was delightful to see him with the first pages of some new book in his hands, some author of whom he approved. His face was radiant with pleasure."

Erasmus brought his own works in progress with him, including the latest *Adages* expansion, and also started on an important project for Froben: producing a new Latin translation of the New Testament, breaking away from the standard fourth-century one by Jerome. Such work was in line with Erasmus's other intellectual endeavors: he sought not only to improve the general education of Europeans but also to improve the moral excellence and quality of their spiritual lives, by going back to the original sources. It was just as important for Christians to have a good version of Scripture based on the latest research as it was for classicists to have good texts of their ancient authors. New scholarship, he thought, would invigorate people's belief—rather than undermining it, as some apparently feared.

The possibility of retranslating the biblical text itself was partly inspired by our old friend Lorenzo Valla, who had picked holes in Jerome in his *Annotations on the New Testament*, implying that some of what the church considered unalterable truth might be the result of human errors. Erasmus knew Valla's ideas well. In his youth, he had even written an abridgment of Valla's style manual the *Elegances*, an unobjectionable work—vanilla Valla. The *Annotations* were more controversial, but Erasmus had found a copy of them in an abbey near Louvain and arranged for them to be published in 1505. Now he picked up on Valla's implications and went back to the Greek testament himself, to create his new, dual-language Greek and Latin edition. It came out from Froben in 1516, and as was his wont, Erasmus kept adding revisions at regular intervals after that—because of course he was as prone to error as other humans. He vented his annoyance at those who objected that he should not have done any of it in the first place, exclaiming, "How much more truly Christian it would be to have done with quarrelling and for each man cheerfully to offer what he can to the common stock and to accept with good will what is offered!"

Alas, the cheerful putting aside of quarrels was just what was *not* happening in Europe at that time. After Martin Luther's posting of his ninety-five anticlerical theses in Wittenberg in 1517 and his subsequent break with Rome, the pope excommunicated him, and so western Europe was set on its long path of religious conflict. Centuries of intermittent, bloody wars, complicated by political struggles, would shatter communities and bring suffering, most of it to people who would not normally expect to have their lives affected greatly by theology at all. Erasmus, and his later admirers and followers, spoke up against such destruction where they could, but usually found they could do little to prevent it from happening.

In the early stages, Erasmus showed a certain sympathy for Luther's position, feeling that the church ought to have dealt more wisely and sensitively with such challenges to its authority. What is to be gained, he asked in 1519, from people's being quick to cry "heresy" at such times?

Whatever is not pleasing, whatever they do not understand is a heresy. To know Greek is a heresy. To speak in a polished manner is a heresy. Whatever they themselves do not do is a heresy. . . . Who does not see what these men stand for and in what direction they are heading? Once the restraints on their evil passions are relaxed, they will begin to rage indiscriminately against every good man.

On the other hand, he also became repelled by the aggression of Luther, who was a born contrarian and fighter. Erasmus was not of that type, and he thought that it would make more sense "to mitigate through courteous treatment an issue sharp by its very nature than to add ill will to ill will." Courtesy, of course, was everything to him: more than just a social veneer, it was the very basis for all mutual respect and concord. He and Luther had theological disagreements, too, notably on the question of human free will. (Erasmus, remaining consistent with the church's position, believed that humans could freely choose their own path, for good or ill; Luther thought we had no such freedom and that our only route to salvation lay through God's grace.)

Erasmus's increasing aversion to Luther's approach caused difficult moments with Froben, who was working on a set of Luther's works—a good publishing proposition at a moment when Luther's rebellion was *the* subject much of Europe was talking about. Feeling uncomfortable in an increasingly pro-Reformist Basel, Erasmus moved again, to Freiburg im Breisgau: another university town but one that remained calmly Catholic. He made no secret of the fact that he preferred tranquility. "When popes and emperors make the right decisions I follow, which is godly; if they decide wrongly I tolerate them, which is safe." Erasmus did have courage, but it was of a different sort: he preferred to be discreet but to advance arguments for peace quietly and persistently.

What he hated above all was war. Already before the Reformation, he had used his *In Praise of Folly* to describe war as a monster, a wild beast, and a plague. In his 1515 *Adages*, he included a long entry discussing a saying by Vegetius: *Dulce bellum inexpertis*—three neat Latin words that come out more laboriously in English as "War is sweet to those who have not experienced it." Here and in his 1517 *Complaint of Peace*, Erasmus set out reasons to avoid war. The most fundamental one is that, in his view, it contradicts our *true* humanity, which we should be striving to develop and fulfill.

Like Protagoras and Pico before him, he communicates his view of human nature through a flight of narrative fancy. Imagine, he says, Nature coming to the human world and seeing a battlefield full of soldiers. She exclaims in horror: "Where did you get that threatening crest on your head? that glittering helmet? those horns of iron? those winged elbow-cops? that scaly cuirass? those brazen teeth? that plate armour? those death-dealing darts? that more than savage voice? that more than bestial face?" These are not the proper features of human beings. "I made you a creature near divine," says Nature. What got into you, to change yourselves into such beasts?

Erasmus takes us on a tour of the body and mind, pointing out each of the features that obviously suit us better to a life of mutual assistance and kindness, rather than one of fighting. A bull has horns and a crocodile has armor, but we have soft skin, embracing arms, and "friendly eyes, revealing the soul." We laugh and cry, revealing our sensitivity. We have

speech and reason, with which to communicate. We even have a natural attraction to the love of learning, which "has the greatest power of knitting up friendships."

Of course, being free, we can choose to ignore these affinities in ourselves. But if only we followed the promptings of our natural humanity, we would do far better. Erasmus evokes a scene reminiscent of that in Lorenzetti's Sienese fresco *The Allegory of Good Government*: well-tilled fields, grazing flocks, workers putting up new buildings or renovating old ones, all the arts flourishing, the young studying, the elderly enjoying their leisure. This is a life of peace, and he defines it beautifully as "friendship among many."

Instead of such a life, however, we keep unleashing the furor of war and its ugly consequences: rape, the sacking of churches, "the trampled crops, the burnt-out farms, the villages set on fire, the cattle driven away." That is not friendship but murder among many.

So why do we do it? Erasmus's explanation is the same as that suggested by the Siena frescoes: bad government. Wars start because rulers are foolish or irresponsible, whipping up the worst of human emotions. Lawyers and theologians, who ought to be looking for peaceful solutions, instead make things worse. The situation escalates, and it becomes too late to stop it. War is a blunder: a failure to be human. In Protagoras's story, Zeus had given humans the skills for a happy society, but it is up to us to develop and refine those skills, or they will be of no use. Erasmus agreed with this notion. We have what we need in our nature already, yet we must still learn to manage our relationships, society, and politics. This learning is acquired from each other, and we in turn should always pass it on. This is a key reason why education, especially in the arts of civics and civility, is so central to the humanist view of the world.

Later commentators observed, with sadness, that Erasmus seemed to underestimate the real depth of human attraction to violence, unreason, and fanaticism—probably because of his own cordial personality. Immune to the thrill of battle and the intoxication of radical ideas himself, he simply could not understand why others found them so powerful. He was no Machiavelli in his reading of the psychological (or political, or economic) machinery that can lead to war. Other humanists have had a similar blind spot, in other times, and many are thus left helplessly wondering again and again why everyone around them seems to have gone mad. But then, they are not always wrong: sometimes the Erasmian spirit does return, at least for a while, and when it does, it is often a reaction against the episodes of suffering caused by its opposite.

Like many generally peaceful people, meanwhile, Erasmus could also be stubborn, and his friends would commemorate this aspect of him. In 1536, approaching his seventieth birthday and in fragile health, he was on the point of taking up an offer from Queen Mary of Hungary, regent of the Netherlands, to return—after his lifetime of wandering—to live near his birthplace, in Brabant. First, however, he went to spend a little time in Basel again. While there, that July, he had a sudden bout of dysentery and died. His Basel friends arranged for him to be buried in the city's minster; they created a memorial plaque featuring the emblem and motto of Terminus, Roman god of boundaries and limits. The motto was one Erasmus had long adopted as his own: *Concedo nulli*, or "I yield to no one."

As with other humanists in our story, his real memorial and afterlife are found in the legacy of his ideas: on education (where Erasmian advice and principles remained hugely influential), on religion (his theological tracts as well as translations remained standard for a long time), and on the movement for peace and international cooperation.

One of the most admirable examples of the latter is found in a program inaugurated in 1987 and administered by the European Union. It enables students to travel and study in each other's countries and to have their resulting qualifications recognized as equally valid everywhere in the union. The program was a long time in the making and required plenty of stubbornness from its supporters, notably the Italian educationalist Sofia Corradi, who came up with the idea in 1969 and campaigned for it for eighteen years. At the time I am writing, over ten million people have participated, gaining immensely from the opportunity to live in different countries, learn languages, and make friends and professional contacts that can last a lifetime.

Officially, the name of this program is European Region Action Scheme for the Mobility of University Students (now with an added "+"

on the end). What a lucky coincidence that this just happens to spell out ERASMUS+. It thus honors the legacy of Europe's great pioneer of peace, mutual understanding, educational innovation, the sharing of knowledge and experience, free movement, and especially "friendship among many."

As Erasmus was dying, a three-year-old boy in southwestern France was receiving an unusual education at the hands of a father who had been completely won over by the new humanistic approach. The son's name was Michel Eyquem de Montaigne; he would go on to take that humanistic education, excel in it, turn it around, deconstruct it, and send it off in a completely new direction.

It all began with that father. Pierre Eyquem had never been very humanistically polished himself. But he had been to Italy, admittedly as a soldier in the French wars of invasion, which was perhaps not the most Erasmian way to get to know the place. He must have absorbed some of the Italian spirit, however—and of Erasmianism, too—because, when his eldest son, Michel, was born, he decided to give him a perfect Latinized start in life. He set out to make the boy something that had not been seen for a thousand years: a *native* Latin speaker. The method was to bring in a German-born tutor who knew Latin but no French, and to forbid anyone else, even the servants, to use anything but Latin in the boy's hearing. Even the most extreme Ciceronians hadn't dreamed of doing this.

The result of these early years was that Montaigne grew up to write a vast, erudite, wide-ranging work of humanistic literature—in French. He explained that he made this choice because French was a fleeting, changeable modern language that might disappear entirely from the world, rather than the supposedly eternal language of the ancients. Since he, too, was fleeting and changeable and would definitely disappear from the world in a few years, the choice seemed appropriate.

A similar taste for instability and endless movement inspired the book itself: *Essais* (a word he coined, meaning "tryouts" or "attempts"), first published in 1580 and enlarged later. The words flow, take unexpected changes of direction, and contradict each other; they tumble into digressions, some of which become many pages long. They trace the changes in Montaigne's own mind as he comes up with new thoughts. The book also records the vagaries of his physical existence: one day he feels exuberant because the sunshine feels good; the next day he has a corn on his toe and is bad-tempered. One piece, recalling a day when he nearly died after being thrown from his horse, explores what it feels like to drift near death in a state of semiconsciousness. Others give excruciating amounts of detail about his diet, illnesses, sexual habits, and aging process.

Montaigne's interests in both physicality and change make you wonder if he has been reading Epicurean philosophy, and, sure enough, he has. His copy of Lucretius's *On the Nature of Things* survives, and is filled with his notes and marginal marks, so we know he read it closely. But he would also have absorbed a sense of the transitory and unpredictable nature of human life from the general state of affairs around him. He lived in a time of political and religious upheaval—the long-term consequences of the first stirrings Erasmus had seen earlier in the century. In Montaigne's case, it lasted his whole adult life: France suffered one wave after another of civil war, driven by religion and the maneuvering of various political factions for power. The split between Catholic and Protestant carved through communities and families, including his own: he was on the Catholic side, but he had siblings who became Protestants.

Had Erasmus lived to see any of this, he would have come close to losing hope. The belligerent spirit of a Luther, or of a John Calvin (the even more uncompromising theologian based in Geneva, and influential in Protestant France),

seemed to have won. These were times of the kind when fanatics are admired for the intensity of their commitment, while those who prefer tolerance or compromise are vilified. Montaigne, like Erasmus before him, was fanatically nonfanatical. He had no time for the idea that "we gratify heaven and nature by committing massacre and homicide, a belief universally embraced in all religions." He, too, respected the god of limits, looking for middle paths in everything, and he generally sought to practice the methods of openness and reconciliation.

Montaigne's dislike of violence made him abhor the prevailing tendency to burn heretics, witches, and anyone else thought to be in league with the Devil. As he said, it was "putting a very high price on one's conjectures to have a man roasted alive because of them." Yet he had no intention of putting a high price on his own thoughts, either—or *paying* a high price for them. Like Erasmus, he preferred to follow the path of discretion, and would have liked to keep himself aloof from political divisions. This was not easy, since he held posts as a magistrate and later as the mayor of Bordeaux, and he was a friend of the future king Henri IV.

He also had many practical obligations to fulfill on his own wine-growing estate, which he had inherited on the death of his father. Still, in between such worrisome duties, Montaigne would slip away to his little stone tower, at one corner of the estate, and write.

Politics proved difficult to evade, but what of religion? Here he had a very different attitude to that of Erasmus. The earlier humanist had been deeply engaged in religious thought and scholarship. Montaigne seemed to think very little about it at all. He showed no interest in close reading or editing or retranslating of Scripture, or in revitalizing Christianity to raise the moral standards of Europe. Having been born a Catholic, he declared himself happy to believe whatever the church told him to believe. This, he explained, had helped him to remain safe and undisturbed during the wars.

His real religion, if that is what it is, seems best captured by a line near the end of the last essay in the book:

> I love life and cultivate it just as God has been pleased to grant it to us. . . . I accept with all my heart and with gratitude what nature has done for me, and I am pleased with myself and proud of myself that I do. We wrong that great and all-powerful Giver by refusing his gift, nullifying it, and disfiguring it.

And if this statement summarizes Montaigne's theology, then another in the same essay expresses his philosophy:

> There is nothing so beautiful and legitimate as to play the man well and properly, no knowledge so hard to acquire as the knowledge of how to live this life well and naturally; and the most barbarous of our maladies is to despise our being.

These thoughts, combined with the whole skeptical, literary, and civilized spirit of the *Essays*, make Montaigne one of the great humanists of history. But he was no ordinary humanist.

For one thing, the passages I just quoted have an odd ring to them, coming at the end of a book in which Montaigne has spent hundreds of pages debunking all human claims to rationality or excellence. "Is it possible to imagine anything so ridiculous as that this miserable and puny creature, who is not even master of himself, exposed to the attacks of all things, should call himself master and emperor of the universe, the least part of which it is not in his power to know, much less to command?" Montaigne even strikes a blow against Protagoras, saying that he must have been having a laugh by making "man the measure of all things," when, like all of us, he could not even have achieved any definite measure of himself.

Also, for a humanist, his relationship with books is different from what we have come to expect from Petrarch onward. Montaigne did know his classics intimately, and his love for his favorite authors was profound. He built up his own book collection and housed them on shelves built to fit the round interior of his tower. He also had that tower's ceiling beams painted with quotations, so that he could look up and see them at any time—as if taking Erasmus at his word about carving notes into the fixtures and fittings. In pride of place was Terence's *Homo sum, humani nihil a me alienum puto*: "I am human, and consider nothing human alien to me." The *Essays* themselves are studded with pungent classical quotations like cloves in an orange. It could not be a more bookish book, or one more immersed in humanist culture.

Yet Montaigne trashes all the humanistic pieties on the subject of reading. As soon as he gets bored with a book, he says, he flings it aside. The books that bore him most are the most revered ones: he comes right out with it and calls Cicero "nothing but wind." One can almost hear the gasps from the humanists behind us in earlier chapters. Virgil is all right, says Montaigne, but he wonders if the poet might have done more to brush up certain passages in the *Aeneid*. He also had little patience with the subjects of rhetoric and eloquence. It is a fine thing to speak well, "but it is not as fine as they make it out; and I am vexed that we keep busy all our life at that."

Instead, he likes books when they enhance *life* and when they expand his understanding of the many people who have lived in the past. Biographies and histories are good, because they show the human being "more alive and entire than in any other place—the diversity and truth of his inner qualities in the mass and in detail, the variety of the ways he is put together, and the accidents that threaten him." Terence's plays also represent "to the life the movements of the soul and the state of our characters; at every moment our actions throw me back to him." Montaigne was not the only humanist to look for such personal connections in books, but he is exceptional in his insistence that the books *in themselves* have no appeal to him. (He just happens to read an enormous number of them, build shelves for them, and have hundreds of quotes at his fingertips as well as literally hanging over his head.)

Montaigne was certainly a humanist: the *Essays* return constantly to the classic humanist themes of moral judgment, courtesy, education, virtue, politics, elegant writing, rhetoric, the beauties of books and texts, and the question of whether we are excellent or despicable. But, pondering each of these themes with a skeptical and questioning eye, he dismantles them. Once they are lying around him in pieces, he reassembles them in a more interesting, more disconcerting, and more thought-provoking spirit than before.

Thus, he writes as a moralist, but a moralist who acknowledges fallibility and slips out from underneath every consistent moral rule. He is political, but expresses his views through evasiveness, insistence on privacy, and refusal to conform. He has an educational theory, but it is one that has no time for schools or rhetorical exercises or compulsion of any kind. When it comes to etiquette, style, virtue, or almost anything else, he constantly adds remarks along the lines of "But I don't know" or "Then again" before switching to some unexpected new angle.

Those angles often derive from his respect for diversity and variety. "I believe in and conceive a thousand contrary ways of life," he writes. This belief makes him an advocate of travel as the best means of encountering some of those varied ways. His own commitments at home meant that he could not move around as much as Erasmus did. (Also, he would have hated to be beholden to employers and patrons as Erasmus and many other humanists were; Montaigne was lucky in having the independence brought by inheriting an estate.) Still, he did manage one major eighteen-month tour of German, Swiss, and Italian territories in the early 1580s: his ERASMUS experience. He used it to immerse himself in the atmosphere of each place and to meet as many people as he could. In order to learn something of cultures from farther afield, he filled his library with travelers' tales. He even managed to talk briefly with some Tupinambá people from Brazil, who had crossed the Atlantic on a French ship. He asked them, through a translator, what they thought about France; they replied, among other things, that they were shocked to see rich people gorging themselves at banquets while their poorer "other halves" starved beside them. That could never happen in their own society, they said disapprovingly. Montaigne relished the reminder that European assumptions of superiority over other cultures were not beyond question; they could always be viewed in reverse. (Not that he stopped attending or hosting banquets himself.) So great was his love of diverse perspectives that he chose the word *diversité* to close the first edition of his *Essays*: "And there were never in the world two opinions alike, any more than two hairs or two grains. Their most universal quality is diversity."

Yet the whole project of the *Essays* also relies on a belief that all people share an essential, common humanity. Montaigne writes that each of us is a bearer of the human condition in its "entire form." This is why we can recognize ourselves in the experiences and characters of others, however much we diverge from them in cultural attitudes or background. This forms part of his justification for writing so much about himself: he is an ordinary example of a human being, and one he happens to know intimately. "You can tie up all moral philosophy with a common and private life just as well as with a life of richer stuff."

It is this writing-out of his essential humanity that makes his book such an advance in humanistic writing. It is a *human* book, both in the traditional sense of a work of gentlemanly scholarship and in a revolutionary new way, at once philosophical and personal. Its humanness brings another benefit. Writing a book of this sort, Montaigne knows he need not have compunctions about ignoring theological questions. "I set forth notions that are human and my own, simply as human notions considered in themselves," he writes. He goes on to say that he has heard of other writers being criticized for being too "human," in that they omit any considerations of the divine realm. Good for them: he intends to do the same. Let us leave divine writing to its own rank, he says, just as royalty sets itself apart from commoners. We are then free to write as human beings, about human things. It was as close as he came to writing a manifesto for himself and for the countless essayists and novelists who would follow him.

Montaigne founded no formal school of thought; he strove for no philosophical rigor, and promoted no dogma. Yet his impact on literature was enormous. The century after his own, the seventeenth, saw an explosion of personal essays written on his model: reflective, skeptical, witty, self-indulgent, sometimes mercilessly critical, and generally dedicated to the spirit of freethinking in the widest sense. The modern world is still filled with such writing. Every time we enjoy reading someone's spontaneous-looking airing of feelings or thoughts, online or off, characterized by greater or lesser degrees of erudition or profundity, we are reaping a little of the afterlife of Montaigne.

The same digressive, exploratory, personal spirit also permeated other genres, producing what the nineteenth-century critic Walter Pater would call "the *Montaignesque* element in literature." In particular, it found its way into a very successful form: the novel. You can see Montaigne himself as a kind of novelist, albeit one who features just one central character—himself—along with walk-on roles for others encountered in his life or reading. He pioneered the stream-of-consciousness narration that would be a feature of modern novels long before consciously modernist experiments in that line came along in the twentieth century. The great psychological and social novels of the eighteenth and nineteenth centuries are positive waterfalls of streaming consciousness. They allow us to hitch a ride inside each of several characters in turn, occupying their perspectives as they reflect on events or interact with each other, and as they change through experience. A spirit of Montaignesque abundance often prevails: the rich texture of human existence is seen as it plays out through time. Henry Fielding's *Tom Jones*, of 1749, opens the story by promising the reader that the "provision" (as in a restaurant's bill of fare) offered to them is nothing less than "HUMAN NATURE." It is just one dish, it is true—but do not fear that it will be monotonous: "Here collected under one general name, is such a prodigious variety, that a cook will have sooner gone through all the several species of animal and vegetable food in the world, than an author will be able to exhaust so extensive a subject."

Later novels delved ever more deeply into characters' minds, reaching virtuoso level in Tolstoy's *War and Peace* or *Anna Karenina*, or in George Eliot's *Middlemarch*. The latter novel—humanistic in several senses, intellectually sophisticated, and constantly surfing between characters—was described by the psychologist William James as "fuller of human stuff than any novel that was ever written." This makes a good description of Montaigne's *Essays*, too: a book all about *human stuff*.

George Eliot believed that reading imaginative fiction brought real moral benefits, because of the way it enlarged the circle of our sympathy, or what we would now call "empathy." In an essay, she wrote, "The greatest benefit we owe to the artist, whether painter, poet, or novelist, is the extension of our sympathies. . . . A picture of human life such as a great artist can give, surprises even the trivial and the selfish into that attention to what is apart from themselves, which may be called the raw material of moral sentiment."

In recent times, some research has supported this argument, suggesting that reading fiction does lead us to be more empathetic and make more morally generous choices. Other commentators disagree, and some even wonder whether heightening empathy is a good thing, since reason may at times be a better guide to action. The whole question, for the moment, remains in a Montaignesque state of complexity and undecidability.

There is another factor, too. Merely understanding and sympathizing with the sufferings of others gets us only so far. Much better would be to prevent such sufferings from happening at all. George Eliot believed this, and so did a number of writers who lived between Montaigne's time and hers: thinkers who are sometimes referred to under the label "Enlightenment." It is time for them to join our story.

6.

Perpetual Miracles

1682–1819

The Enlighteners—Whatever is: is it right?—Voltaire,
Denis Diderot, and others—atheists and deists—fellow
feeling and moral taste—the Earl of Shaftesbury—
Pierre Bayle—prisons and manuscript adventures—
Malesherbes, the censor who saved books—Thomas
Paine and the Age of Reason—David Hume, the
merciless and amiable.

In Lisbon, at about half past nine on the morning of November 1, 1755, the English merchant Thomas Chase felt everything begin to shake. He went up to roof level to see what was going on outside. The buildings stood very close to each other; as he reached out to steady himself against his neighbor's wall, it slid away from his hand. It was not the neighbor's house that was falling, but his own. He plummeted the whole height with it and found himself on the ground, astonished to be still alive.

Others were less fortunate. Three quakes struck in succession that morning, and by the end of it, some thirty to forty thousand people were dead, along with another ten thousand in surrounding areas. Boats in the harbor had been washed away by tidal waves. Fires broke out everywhere.

Tremors had been felt as far away as France and Italy; even in Scotland and Scandinavia the water reportedly rose and fell in lakes.

The event also produced a psychological shock around Europe. Eighteenth-century Lisbon was a prosperous, cosmopolitan, and confident city, a hub for international traders. As in the case of New York after the World Trade Center attacks in September 2001, many found it hard to believe that such a lucky place could be so badly damaged, so fast.

Those hearing the news tried to make sense of it—including Johann Wolfgang von Goethe in Frankfurt, just six years old, who felt scared and disoriented when he heard adults discussing it. The event would later merge in his memory with a more local intrusion of natural forces the following summer, when a hailstorm broke the windows at the back of his family's house, and "all the house servants frantically pulled us out with them into a dark passageway where, kneeling, they set up a terrible howling and crying in an attempt to appease the angry deity."

But why *did* that deity inflict such things? Just as with the plague in the fourteenth century, theologians and preachers had their explanations for Lisbon ready. The Jesuit Gabriel Malagrida said that the earthquake was a punishment for those who indulged in music or attended the theater and bullfights. Speaking for the Jansenists—sworn enemies and rivals to the Jesuit order—Laurent-Étienne Rondet instead argued that it was God's punishment for . . . the Jesuits. It showed his disapproval of their having engineered the destruction of the Jansenist abbey of Port-Royal-des-Champs fifty years earlier—never mind the long time gap, and the fact that the abbey was nowhere near Lisbon.

Philosophers considered another possibility. Even if the disaster was not specifically ordained by God, it could still be explained as part of his overall plan or balancing act for the universe. They drew on a tradition of "theodicy": the attempt to explain and justify God's actions, especially when those actions were so obviously unpleasant for humans. Augustine had urged his readers to rise above personal feelings in order to see "the whole design, in which these small parts, which are to us so disagreeable, fit together to make a scheme of ordered beauty." In 1710, this had been made into a formal argument by Gottfried Wilhelm Leibniz: God could have given us a world without such things, but he didn't, so presumably he knew that those other possible worlds would have been less good in the long run. And if this is the best world feasible, then whatever happens in it must be for the best, even if does not feel that way. This was presented as a philosophy of optimism: *Everything's fine.* A similar idea was concisely phrased by the poet Alexander Pope a couple of decades later in his poem *An Essay on Man*: "Whatever is, is RIGHT."

Despite the philosophers, human beings going through traumatic experiences kept insisting on their own personal perspectives. Chaucer had told the story of Dorigen, a Breton woman whose sailor husband is out in a stormy sea. Watching the waves crashing on the rocks offshore, she acknowledges that scholars may argue that "al is for the beste." If it were up to her, however, she would send every one of those rocks to Hell to keep her husband safe. This is a very human response: who would deny her right to cry out in anguish against all the theodicy in the world?

In the wake of the Lisbon earthquake, this right to protest was championed by a different kind of philosopher: the French poet, playwright, encyclopedist, polemicist, historian, satirist, and activist François-Marie

Arouet, better known as Voltaire.

When he heard about the earthquake, he felt as others did: thrown into doubts and anxieties. He tried to imagine what it must have been like to be there, crushed like an ant or dying slowly in the rubble afterward. His fellow feeling and sense of reason rebelled against any attempt to explain such miseries away. Being a poet, his natural impulse was to write a poem, "On the Disaster of Lisbon," asking why people should accept or even justify such things. Is it not more natural to reject them as vehemently as we can? The problem arose again later in his *Philosophical Dictionary*, in an entry headed "Good, all is." It is very fine, he wrote, to observe a beautiful kidney stone growing in my body, and to marvel as it resists surgeons' attempts to remove it, turns toxic, and finally kills me in agony. That is, it may be fine in the abstract. But don't ask me to love the kidney stone or interpret it as meaning "all is good." At least let me shake my puny fist against suffering. In other words: the human measure is as valid as the divine one.

Voltaire's most eloquent response to Lisbon took the form of a philosophical novella of 1759: *Candide, or Optimism*. Candide is a naive young hero whose tutor Pangloss has instilled in him the motto that all is for the best in this best of possible worlds. But then everything that could conceivably go wrong does go wrong, for him and Pangloss and everyone else. Pangloss suffers the most: first he is caught in the earthquake, then he is almost hanged (and dissected) for heresy. He escapes but is caught and confined as a galley slave on a Turkish ship. Through it all, he maintains, at first brightly, then with more and more difficulty, that all is for the best.

Meanwhile Candide goes through separate misadventures of his own and comes to doubt the theory entirely. This "mania for insisting that all is well when things are going badly" is not as optimistic as it is cracked up to be, he realizes. It is more like a philosophy of despair, because (as Voltaire explained elsewhere, in a letter) it suggests that there is no room for improvement. A real optimist would hope for things to get better and might even look for ways in which we could make them better ourselves. We cannot stop earthquakes from happening, but we can study them and build safer buildings that don't collapse so easily. Later generations would extend such achievements: seismologists have now learned to predict the patterns of earthquakes and tsunamis with ever greater accuracy. Experts in other fields can also break up kidney stones with lithotripsy, and design antibiotics to prevent infections, and put sonar on ships, and track weather patterns to see storms coming and get ships into harbor before they strike.

Voltaire ended *Candide* by having all his characters move in together, with a plot of land. Instead of continuing to look for cosmic justifications, Candide says only, "We must cultivate our garden." This may sound as though Candide wants to retire from the world and potter in seclusion, but Voltaire surely meant something more like: Let each of us work to make things better on whichever patch of the Earth we occupy.

Long after Voltaire, E. M. Forster distinguished between the two kinds of response to disaster in his novel *The Longest Journey.* A child has died after being hit by a train, because the warning system on a level crossing failed to work. A group of people, discussing the fate of the child's soul, challenge a young philosopher to say something profound about the meaning of such a shocking death. (It is the usual question asked of philosophers: What's it all about, then, eh?) He replies: It means that the civic authorities ought to build a proper, well-constructed bridge across the track and get rid of the inadequate crossing. "Then the child's soul, as you call it—well, nothing would have happened to the child at all."

This, in a word, was the philosophy of Voltaire and his intellectual circle—and that word could be "progress," "improvement," "reason," or "enlightenment," depending on where you prefer the emphasis. The principle of "light," embedded in the last of these, became the source of names later used to designate such thinkers and their views in several European languages: *les lumières* in French, *Aufklärung* in German, *illuminismo* in Italian, the *Enlightenment* in English. Few of the thinkers used these labels of themselves, but they did tend to use a language of light and darkness—a language reminiscent of that favored by earlier humanists, the ones who delved into monastery storerooms to find books. Those humanists had thought of themselves as rescuers who brought literature into the brightly lit world of printing and free reading; the new Enlighteners saw themselves as helping to bring *people* into the light. They hoped, by means of better reasoning, more effective science and technology, and more beneficial political systems, to help their fellow humans to emerge into the sun and air and live more bravely and happily.

Their philosophy of pragmatic, rational improvement could also be described by another term, although it was invented only later: "meliorism," based on the Latin for "better." It began appearing in English in the mid-nineteenth century. One early adopter was George Eliot, who, in a letter of 1877, mentioned having used it before. It certainly matched her own worldview. Discussing Eliot's meliorism, her biographer Rosemary Ashton defined it as "the belief that the world is neither the best nor the worst of all possible worlds, but that it may be improved up to a point, and suffering alleviated, at least in part, by human effort." Or, as Voltaire's biographer Theodore Besterman wrote of his subject: Voltaire "asserted that the human condition can become better, and invited mankind to do something about it."

This attitude and an inclination to value the human measure more highly than mystical submission to fate are two features that unite the Enlightenment spirit to the humanist one. Not all Enlighteners are humanists, and vice versa: differences of emphasis exist between the two sets of ideas, and in any case individuals in both categories vary greatly among themselves. Still, generally, Enlightenment and humanist thinkers share a tendency to look to this world more than to the next, and to humanity more than to divinity. Both consider the use of our reason and scientific understanding, as well as improvement of our technology and politics, to be our best path toward an improved life.

These beliefs lay behind the most renowned Enlightenment production: the multivolume, luxuriously illustrated *Encyclopédie*, which Denis Diderot and Jean le Rond d'Alembert launched together in 1751. In later stages it was edited mostly alone by the indefatigable Diderot, who also wrote some seven thousand of its entries. (Even so, he was not the most prolific contributor: that was Louis de Jaucourt, who wrote around seventeen thousand entries, or 28 percent of the whole. Many of his contributions were about medicine, apparently because he had been just about to put the final touches to a fuller medical dictionary of his own when he lost the manuscript of it at sea.)

Contributors to the *Encyclopédie* wrote on philosophy, religion, literature, and many other humanistic subjects, as well as on machines, crafts, tools, engineering systems, and devices of all kinds. D'Alembert was a mathematician and physicist; Diderot had grown up as the son of a master cutler; they both considered practical invention beneficial to human life. Diderot also took a philosophical view of the project. In his entry under "Encyclopedia," setting out the guiding ideas, he wrote that the overall aim was to write about the world—that great circle of reality— but always to keep "man" at the center of the circle of topics, since as conscious beings we are the ones who bring them together in our minds. Humans are the hub; revolving around us is the wheel of knowledge, available for all—or at least all who could afford to buy the book.

Some Enlightenment thinkers had an even more exalted vision of where technology could take us. Nicolas de Condorcet was a statistician and political theorist who applied his mathematical expertise to every life-enhancing project he could think of, from the analysis of democratic voting to canal design and the measurement of tonnage of ships. He thought that increasing knowledge would lead to ever better social and political conditions, and that those in turn would eventually produce a world of complete, rational happiness and of equality between sexes, races, and classes. Superstition and priesthood would vanish as education improved and society became more enlightened in every way—until "tyrants and slaves, priests and their stupid or hypocritical instruments" could be found only in history books (and in some educational plays, to be performed as a reminder of how good it was to have escaped such a past).

Voltaire was less carried away by future visions: his attitude was that we should get on with cultivating our garden and see what happens. Yet he shared the overall humanistic hope: that humans could take more control of their own destiny and arrange their lives more rationally and tolerantly, in ways more conducive to well-being. In short, people could be happier. And in some cases, they could be more alive, having not been killed by diseases, bad engineering, earthquakes, or the violence of fanatics.

One of the main routes to improvement, it seemed to some Enlightenment authors, could be found in thinking differently about religion.

Some of them went a long way in this direction, believing that religious beliefs were wrong about how the universe worked and also did human beings more psychological harm than good. One outright materialist and atheist, a close friend of Diderot's, was Paul-Henri Thiry, Baron d'Holbach. He wrote in his 1770 work *The System of Nature* that people should be encouraged to escape from the "mists of darkness" in which religion had been keeping them—there is that contrast between light and dark again. He had come to this view partly because of a personal experience. While his wife was dying, a priest had come to her bedside and lectured her on the dangers of hell. Holbach witnessed her terror as she listened to him. It convinced him that, just as Epicurus and Lucretius

had said long ago, beliefs about gods and the afterlife made people scared
and miserable. As Holbach wrote, "Far from holding forth consolation
to mortals, far from cultivating man's reason, far from teaching him to
yield under the hands of necessity religion strives to render death still
more bitter to him, to make its yoke sit heavy, to fill up its retinue with a
multitude of hideous phantoms, and to render its approach terrible."
Moreover: "It has at length persuaded man that his actual existence is
only a journey by which he will arrive at a more important life." But we
can liberate ourselves by learning to understand the world better—that
is, by learning to see it as essentially material.

Holbach himself seemed a good example of this liberating effect: he
was an irrepressible enthusiast who kept a large collection of natural history specimens for his daytime studies and an equally large collection of
fine wines and foods for his evening salon, at which he entertained fellow
lumières twice weekly. Among the whole group, he and Diderot were
known as the two greatest atheists, although Diderot was more cautious
about going fully public.

Other Enlightenment thinkers were not atheists at all, and some ad-
hered to formal religions, yet they almost all ended up on the wrong side
of theological and political authorities at times. The philosopher and historian Pierre Bayle, for example, was a Protestant—although his version
of his religion is best captured in an answer he allegedly gave when asked
about it: "I am a good Protestant and in the full sense of the term, for,
from the bottom of my soul, I protest against everything that is said, and
everything that is done."

Some departed from institutional religious beliefs without becoming
entirely atheistic; this was the case with Voltaire. He campaigned against
the damage caused by religious fanaticism, especially in his efforts to re-
habilitate the memory of a Protestant, Jean Calas, who had been tortured and executed on a trumped-up charge of having murdered his son
to stop him from converting to Catholicism. The campaign was a success; it came too late to save Calas but helped his family and provided a

focus for the cause of tolerance in general. One could say that tolerance *was* Voltaire's religion. What he mostly was, however, was a *deist*.

Deism, widespread among European intellectuals from the late seventeenth century on, began with the belief that the universe is sufficiently huge and complex that it must have had some equally huge and capable Creator. But that does not mean that the Supreme Being takes any further interest in the day-to-day details of planetary management or human affairs. Some deists also return that favor by taking no great interest in the Supreme Being.

Thus, we can protest against kidney stones and shipwrecks, because it is natural for us to do so, but there is no point in expecting such a Being to care, or even notice our prayers and complaints. If we find elaborate ways of justifying disasters, it will not notice that, either. It will not lay on special miracles to help convert us. It will not—and this is a crucial divergence with Christian orthodoxy—send its only begotten Son to save us. That is a purely human myth. On the other hand, and this is some comfort, it will not send earthquakes or diseases to demonstrate its petty disapproval of musical shows or of the actions of Jesuits, either.

And if we still want miracles, what greater miracle could there be than this beautifully ordered, varied world all round us? As Voltaire wrote: "A miracle, in the full meaning of the word, is an admirable thing. In this sense everything is miraculous. The prodigious order of nature, the rotation of 100 million globes around a million suns, the activity of light, the life of animals are perpetual miracles."

Meanwhile, if we want to reduce human suffering and improve our lot, we must get to work on that ourselves. (In fact, this *is* what people have usually done, whatever their beliefs. To quote the nineteenth-century humanist Robert Ingersoll, "In all ages man has prayed for help, and then helped himself.")

Deism was so upsetting to all church authorities that it may as well have been atheism. It allowed no room for the Christian message of personal redemption and sacrifice, it said nothing about the afterlife, and it contradicted or ignored almost every story told in the Bible after the first page. The authorities suppressed it accordingly, believing it dangerous. They also suppressed other variant theologies of a similar tendency, such as those derived from the thought of the seventeenth-century philosopher Baruch Spinoza. He had described God as so universally infused into everything around us that we can *almost* regard him as identical to Nature. It takes a very fine scalpel indeed to distinguish between that and the assertion that Nature is all that exists. Spinoza had already been excommunicated from his own Jewish community in Amsterdam before he had even published anything—a devastating punishment, as his friends and family were forbidden to talk to him or help him in any way. His works were later also banned by both the Protestant and the Catholic authorities.

The humanistic thrust of these ideas had less to do with their theoretical content than with the consequences for ourselves. If prayer and ritual do not matter, and if nothing happens outside the general order of nature, then our lives are entirely human concerns. What we lose in personal attention and miracles, we gain in the benefits of being responsible for our world, and able to improve things if we want to without any comment from above.

The results for ethics are dramatic. If we want to live in a well-regulated, peaceful society, then we must create one and maintain it. Instead of referring moral questions to divine commandments, we must also work out our own system of good, generous, mutually beneficial ethics. We can try to generate our own rules—such as "do as you would be done by," or "treat all human beings as an end in themselves, not a means to something else," or "choose the action that brings the greatest happiness to the greatest number." These are handy tools for moral thinking, but they are not the same as a set of orders literally set in stone tablets by God. Our moral lives remain complex and personal—and human.

Humanists and Enlighteners were thus drawn to an old idea: that the best foundation for this human, moral world lies in our spontaneous tendency to respond to one another with fellow feeling: "sympathy," or empathy, or the sense of interrelatedness expressed by *ren* or *ubuntu*. It is what Condorcet called "a delicate and generous sensibility which nature has implanted in the hearts of all and whose flowering waits only upon the favourable influence of enlightenment and freedom."

Earlier humanists had written about this moral fellow feeling; Michel de Montaigne observed it as being particularly strong in himself, and not only in relation to humans. He could not bear to watch a chicken having its neck wrung for dinner, and he deduced that "there is a certain respect, and a general duty of humanity, that attaches us not only to animals, who have life and feeling, but even to trees and plants." If he saw someone weeping, or even a picture of such a person, it would bring tears to his own eyes. Above all, he felt anguished when he witnessed the judicial tortures and executions that were normal at the time, and that he sometimes had to attend as part of his official duties. It was as if he were permeable, absorbing others' feelings and merging them with his.

Incidentally, given that humans do seem inclined to such responses, it is hard to comprehend why one is supposed to rejoice at the thought of others suffering in hell. Yet this was apparently no problem for such early theologians as Tertullian, who wrote that watching anti-Christian persecutors burn would be more fun for Christians than the circus, theater, and racecourse rolled into one. Admittedly, he was writing at a time when Christians had suffered so much persecution themselves that their thirst for revenge seems understandable. But in the twelfth century we can still find the monk Bernard of Cluny promising, "As it pleases you now to observe fishes sport in the ocean, so you will not groan over your own offspring seen in Hell." It seems that some major psychological operation would have to be performed on compassionate and virtuous Christians after death to enable them to watch their daughters and sons being tortured without a flicker of response. By the nineteenth century, this had become one of the features most likely to drive people away from Christianity. Charles Darwin said that he lost his religious belief partly because he could not see how anyone could even *want* the story of Hell to be true, and the philosopher John Stuart Mill said, "I will call no being good, who is not what I mean when I apply that epithet to my fellow-creatures; and if such a being can sentence me to hell for not so calling him, to hell I will go." For him, the humanistic version of goodness was so all-embracing a principle that even God had better conform to it.

The basics of an ethical system founded on fellow feeling and a kind of moral "good taste" were put together in 1699 by the English philosopher Anthony Ashley Cooper, the Third Earl of Shaftesbury. He was a deist, too, with a vision of the universe as a generally benign and harmonious place (to the point that Voltaire mocked him for this in his dictionary entry on "Good, all is"). For Shaftesbury, all things are interconnected, including humans, and this underlies our ability to respond sympathetically to one another. That response, in turn, is the seed from which we can cultivate a fully developed moral life. Crucially, this moral cultivation does not require any particular belief system, since it emerges from our nature. We need only improve our ethical good taste, much as we can develop good taste in the arts. The process relies on pleasure more than anything else: when we do something nice for others, they like and approve of us—and that is a pleasurable feeling, so we do more nice things. Eventually one may become what the French were calling an *honnête homme*, literally an "honest man": cultivated, humane, well balanced, at ease in the world—a person with *humanitas*.

Shaftesbury's *Inquiry Concerning Virtue and Merit*, where he put forward these arguments, impressed French readers, especially Diderot, who did a translation so free and creative that it was as much his own work as Shaftesbury's. Diderot published it, although he had to be careful of the French censors, so it came out without either his name or Shaftesbury's on the title page, and with the place of publication falsely stated to be Amsterdam.

These precautions were necessary because presenting an argument for a human source of moral feeling was risky in the Catholic, politically authoritarian France of the day. Human-based morality implied that we needed no external authority to guide our ethical choices. This worried the political establishment, as well as the religious one, because it suggested a state of moral anarchy in which people could follow their own ideas. That would not do: for a coherent state, there must be unity, not pluralism; conformity, not independence; hierarchy, not individuality. Besides, the very word *atheist* was still considered synonymous with "a person devoid of morals." If a society tolerated such people, breakdown would ensue. (Thus, the English philosopher John Locke argued for religious toleration in many cases, but not for atheists, because promises and oaths could have no hold on them: "For the taking away of God, even only in thought, dissolves all.")

The rebels thought, however, that it need not be that way. Pierre Bayle wrote a book in 1682 with the deceptively mild title *Various Thoughts on the Occasion of a Comet.* He was referring to the comet first seen late in 1680, which many people took as a sign of divine intervention in human affairs. Bayle argued against that belief and went on to consider ways in which humans might be able to live well without any such intervention. Some people might still be morally good without recognizing religious authority—and what is more, he said, even a whole society composed of such people might be a morally good one. Perhaps that human ability to live by our own moral values and social connections

was really all that was needed, with each person guided by an innate desire to be liked and well thought of by others.

Bayle knew that he could not put out such a book in France, and also that, as a Protestant known to have unorthodox views, it might be wiser not to stay there himself. He sought refuge in the Low Countries and published the book there, anonymously and with a false Cologne imprint for further protection. He settled into a well-established community of other refugees; friends helped to find him a teaching post.

But the French authorities had another way of communicating their belief that morality, church, and state must be defended. Unable to get Pierre, they arrested his brother Jacob instead. He was incarcerated in terrible conditions, until, after five months, he died. When Pierre heard what had happened, he had a complete psychological breakdown.

Such elaborate threats of prison, harassment, exile, book burning, and worse were constant companions for the French Enlightenment authors. Voltaire spent periods of time in prison and went into self-exile in England early in life after unwisely provoking a French nobleman to threats of violence. The exile worked out well for him, as it brought him into contact with English scientists and moral philosophers. Among other things, it converted him to the practice of inoculation against smallpox—newly fashionable in England, and a good example of meliorism in action. The whole experience gave him material for a successful book, *Letters on England*. But that book contained unacceptable material, including passages in which he criticized the French system of censorship. Annoyance concerning this accusation about suppressing free speech was expressed by burning *Letters* on the steps of the Palais de Justice in Paris. A few years later, his *Philosophical Dictionary* was also burned, both in Catholic Paris and in the Calvinist city-state of Geneva, which was just as repressive in its policies. Voltaire took the precaution of living close to the border between France and Geneva, so he could nip from one to the other, depending on which one was persecuting him most at the time.

Diderot also served time, in his case in the fortress prison of Vincennes in 1749. He wrote letters humbly begging for his freedom and promising to stop publishing the wrong sorts of books; it still took several months before he was released. Both he and Voltaire were determined to avoid such ordeals again if possible. Neither stopped writing, but they— and other writers of their ilk—adopted a range of deflecting devices and tricks to evade trouble. They had their works printed outside France and smuggled into the country, often in very small numbers, carried by travelers with false-bottomed suitcases and the like. They used misleading titles, anonymity, and false names. They sometimes circulated works in manuscript only—thus leading to a revival of the old, pre-printing techniques of manuscript copying and distribution, with all the risks of loss and damage that entailed.

In the Netherlands, too, Spinoza had resorted to manuscript circulation in the previous century. A few of his works did come out in his lifetime, but his great opus, *Ethics*, was passed around among his friends in handwritten form only. On his deathbed, he asked those friends to send a chest full of such papers by barge to Amsterdam, where more copies and translations could be made, hopefully leading to a posthumous printed edition. This was done while both Dutch Protestant and Catholic authorities, having heard rumors about what was happening, followed in hot pursuit. The Catholics even recruited an Amsterdam rabbi to try to find out where the manuscripts were. Three sets of religious hounds were thus set on the trail, but all three failed to pin down the manuscripts in time to thwart publication.

The one good thing you could say about suppression—to set against the misery and loss it caused—is that it fostered ingenuity. The Baron d'Holbach published *The System of Nature* by having the manuscript sent to his secretary's brother, who made a new copy and destroyed the original so that the handwriting could not be traced. Then the brother wrapped and sealed the new manuscript and sent it to a friend in Liège. The friend passed it to an Amsterdam publisher, Marc-Michel Rey, who brought it out with the author named as a different, deceased French writer, Jean-Baptiste de Mirabaud.

Voltaire also covered his writings with mystery: *Candide* appeared pseudonymously under the name of a "Mr. le Docteur Ralph," masquerading as a translation from the German. He then had fun writing to friends asking if they could get him a copy of this infamous book he kept hearing about. In other cases, he printed his work abroad, although on occasion it was then intercepted while being smuggled in. He complained, "These days, no book can enter France by post without being seized by the officials, who for some time have been building up a rather fine library and who will soon become in every sense men of letters."

As it happened, one of the key figures in charge of censorship during this period *was* a man of letters, and a man of Enlightenment, too: Guillaume-Chrétien de Lamoignon de Malesherbes. What he really wanted to do with his life was pursue his love of plant collecting and ponder questions of botanical classification. Instead, he found himself in frontline positions, advising Louis XV on policy and taking up a role as director of publications. This entailed his being censor in chief, managing more than a hundred people who inspected books and pamphlets all day, looking for anything suspicious. But some of the authors of such books were among Malesherbes's friends, and he respected their reasons for writing them. In a treatise on press freedom in 1788, he pointed out a problem with too much censorship: it is often the more extreme authors who defy it, whereas many writers with more moderate and socially beneficial views are put off expressing them, to the detriment of a well-informed, well-balanced public discourse.

When called on to censor or block his friends' works, Malesherbes obeyed, but he found ways of helping them at the same time. This happened with the *Encyclopédie*, which, after just two volumes had appeared, was banned by royal order on the grounds that they contained material tending to undermine both morals and royal authority and to raise a spirit of independence, revolt, and unbelief. All further work in progress was to be seized. Malesherbes had the task of raiding Diderot's house, which might have exposed even more dangerous material, but he

LAMOIGNON DE MALESHERBES;
Ministre d'Etat en 1776 et en 1788 Défenseur de Louis XVI en 1793

secretly met Diderot the evening before and offered to hide such material in his own house: the one place no one would think of looking. He also later negotiated a new censorship arrangement, whereby later *Encyclopédie* volumes could go through an approval process in advance: not ideal, but better than being banned after the event. The king even recovered his tolerance for the work, encouraged by the fact that his former lover and favorite, Madame de Pompadour, championed it: she said that she wanted to be able to look up information on where the silk in her clothes came from. The fourth volume of the *Encyclopédie* appears, along with books by Voltaire and others, as a prop in a fine portrait of her by Maurice-Quentin de La Tour.

As to the other manuscripts by Diderot that could not have made it through any pre-censorship process, he mostly refrained from even trying to publish them. Among works that did not appear until well after his death were *The Skeptic's Walk* (a set of discussions between an atheist, a deist, and a pantheist), *The Nun* (an exposé of enforced monastic life), and *Rameau's Nephew* (a dialogue covering matters from music to morality to pleasure). The last-named work would not come out in French until 1821, in a version badly retranslated from a German translation made in 1805 by Goethe—which itself was based on a copy made from the original. Only much later, in 1891, did that original turn up, found on a secondhand book stall. It is an irony that Diderot, who praised printing among other modern technology in the *Encyclopédie*, was obliged to confine himself to the methods of medieval monks for so much of his own work.

He had another distressing experience: when the publication of the *Encyclopédie* resumed, he learned that his publisher had begun secretly bowdlerizing all the entries, removing anything he thought troublesome—and then destroying the manuscripts so the lost bits could not be restored. After that shock, Diderot never fully recovered his enthusiasm for the project.

Yet he and Voltaire did at least get through their lives without too much further personal risk. Malesherbes did not, but it was not the church or the monarchy that killed him. It was a new set of repressive authorities: the officials of the Terror, following the French Revolution.

Malesherbes had retired by that time—pursuing his botany at last—but in December 1792, aged seventy-one, he made a surprise return to his legal calling in order to present the defense and plea of mercy for the captured king, Louis XVI. This was a brave thing to do, and it had no effect since the king was guillotined all the same. Malesherbes withdrew to his country estate, but refused to flee France. A year later—the Terror now fully under way—he was arrested with almost his whole family on a charge of conspiring to help émigrés. They were imprisoned for several months, then guillotined one by one. The first to die was Malesherbes's son-in-law. Then, on April 22, 1794, his daughter, *her* daughter Aline, and Aline's husband were all guillotined while Malesherbes himself had to watch. After that, his neck, too, went under the blade. The same thing happened to his sister later, and to his two secretaries; only his valet was spared.

Other Enlightenment thinkers had also met their doom for opposing the king's execution. Among them was a feminist and anti-slavery activist, Olympe de Gouges, who had addressed a Declaration of the Rights of Woman and of the Female Citizen to the French Assembly in 1791, urging them to give the much-trumpeted new human rights to women as well as men. They ignored her arguments, and beheaded her on November 3, 1793. One of the ideologues responsible, Pierre-Gaspard Chaumette, explained where she had erred: "Forgetfulness of the virtues of her sex led her to the scaffold." (He himself died on the scaffold a few months later.)

Another victim, though he was not actually guillotined, was that believer in human progress through better mathematics and fellow feeling: Condorcet. He, too, argued that full citizenship rights should be extended to women, and he, too, got nowhere with it. He wrote his main work presenting his theory of progress, *Sketch for a Historical Picture of the Progress of the Human Mind*, in haste while fearing arrest, or worse, and hiding out with a friend. He had been in favor of the Revolution itself, but did not agree with the level of violence and especially the killing of the king, so he was also placed on the hit list. In March 1794, he became worried that he was putting his hostess in danger, so he left the hideout and tried to disappear into the countryside by dressing as a peasant. He was intercepted and thrown into a local prison, where he was found dead the next day, although whether by suicide or murder has never been certain. It is a strange experience to read the posthumously published *Sketch* today, with its radiant vision of a perfectly rational future without oppression, inequality, violence, or political stupidity of any kind, and reflect on the circumstances under which it was written. But of course, that was the point. How consoling it is, he wrote there, for an afflicted philosopher to meditate on the thought of future humanity "advancing with a firm and sure step along the path of truth, virtue and happiness!" Also: "Such contemplation is for him a refuge where the memory of his persecutors cannot pursue him; there he lives in thought, with man restored to his natural rights and dignity, and forgets how man can be tormented and corrupted by greed, fear, or envy."

One final author who was imprisoned (but not executed) for his advocacy of mercy for the king was Thomas Paine, a friend of Condorcet's, known for his pro-revolutionary works in America as well as in France.

Although English by origin, he had American citizenship, and this saved him. After his arrest in December 1793 and ten months spent in prison worrying that he might be executed at any moment, he was freed: a new American representative to France, James Monroe, had been able to secure his release.

On the day he was bundled off to prison, Paine had just been finishing off part one of a work titled *The Age of Reason*, putting forth arguments for an enlightened and tolerant deism, and against conventional religion. He managed to pass the manuscript to a friend as he was taken away. Now, staying safely with Monroe, he was able to resume work and finish the second part of the book.

It is the first, hastily written part that is the more persuasive and eloquent, however. (The second mostly consists of biblical references that support his argument.) How astonishing it is, Paine wrote, to think that the church persecuted Galileo for studying the sky—those very heavens that, in their beauty and order, testified so vividly to the power of their Creator. It seemed unbelievable "that anything should exist under the name of a *religion* that held it to be *irreligious* to study and contemplate the structure of the universe that God had made." Paine's reflections were typically deist ones, and so was his rejection of the notion that Jesus was sent down to Earth to offer personal redemption to humans. The scriptures describing the crucifixion, in particular, Paine considered cruel stories, "better suited to the gloomy genius of a monk in a cell, by whom it is not impossible they were written," than to anyone "breathing the open air of the creation." And the church institutions created later to promote such stories were even worse: they were "human inventions set up to terrify and enslave mankind, and monopolize power and profit."

Instead, Paine's preferred principles were humanist ones: be grateful for life, do not make a cult of suffering, be tolerant toward others, and try to deal with problems as rationally as possible. He summed up his Enlightenment humanist credo:

I believe in the equality of man, and I believe that religious duties
consist in doing justice, loving mercy, and endeavouring to make
our fellow-creatures happy.

The Age of Reason, with its message of fellow feeling, equality, happiness, and the enlightened celebration of a magnificent cosmos, brought
Paine some far-from-happy experiences. A stagecoach driver, having read
scurrilous reports of the book in the newspapers, refused to let the author
aboard his coach from Washington to New York in 1802. On Christmas
Eve of the same year, an unknown person tried to shoot Paine in the head
at his home in New Rochelle, New York, and narrowly missed. When
Paine did die (of natural causes), his stated wish to be buried in a Quaker
graveyard—he was of Quaker origin himself—was not fulfilled, because
the community rejected him. He was buried in the grounds of his own
home instead. An odd sequel occurred: The English political journalist
William Cobbett disinterred Paine's remains in 1819 and took them to
England, wanting to give him a more fitting memorial there. But something went wrong with the plan and Cobbett kept the remains until
his own death, at which point they went missing. They have never been
found.

The Age of Reason continued to gather readers in America and Britain alike—although it has always tended to be ignored, at best, by the
Establishment. At worst, it was banned. Britain deemed it blasphemous;
publishing it was illegal. So was publishing Paine's other works. Even
when not blasphemous, they were thought politically seditious. A few publishers persisted anyway, and even produced cheap editions for working-
class readers—a further point of concern, since these seemed likely to
inspire actual uprisings rather than a more safe, more gentlemanly kind
of unorthodoxy.

The great champion of Paine in Britain was Richard Carlile, who was
both a socialist and a deist. He spent about ten years in prison in total for

his productions, which included affordable sets of Paine's works. In 1819, Carlile was tried for publishing both his own experiences of the Peterloo Massacre (a lethal cavalry attack on protesters at Manchester's St. Peter's Fields) and Paine's *Age of Reason*. To defy the rules on the latter, Carlile tried a clever courtroom trick. He recited the work in its entirety in court as part of his defense, on the basis that it was important for understanding the principles of the case. The plan was that, afterward, everything said at the trial could be legally published as a transcript—the full text of *The Age of Reason* included. Had that succeeded, it would have gone down in humanist history as one of the best feats of censorship beating ever, but sadly, it did not; no transcript ever appeared.

Richard Carlile was found guilty, and he served two years in Dorchester Prison. At first his wife, Jane, kept the printing press going in his absence. Then she was convicted for this, too, and was sent to Dorchester to join him. His sister Mary Ann Carlile took up the printing responsibilities—and thus eventually was sent there, too. The three of them shared the same cell. Richard spent the time writing works which he either smuggled out or saved for later. One of his productions of this time was *An Address to Men of Science*, which argued that education should treat sciences such as astronomy and chemistry rather than religion or the classics as its foundation, thus introducing children early on to the idea that we are physical beings and part of nature.

And so the battle of wits went on: as prison cells kept filling up with unorthodox thinkers, those thinkers kept coming up with new and more elaborate evasions and feats of ingenuity and misdirection, especially by using the old humanists' copying skills.

But this situation also forced them into a life of disturbing dishonesty. They could not speak plainly; it was hard for any of them to be an *honnête homme* or *femme*. They often had to write "esoterically," combining an apparent meaning for outsiders with a hidden real one for initiates. They became elusive and allusive by necessity, not choice. As Shaftesbury observed in 1714, people who are not allowed to speak forthrightly will do it through irony: "It is the persecuting spirit that has raised the bantering one."

In doing this, they lost some of their integrity, and put themselves and others in danger. Having to pretend that one believes what one does not, wrote Paine, is much worse than outright disbelief: it is "mental lying," and that comes at a cost. Atheists and freethinkers were accused of lacking morals—but in fact their morals were being compromised on a regular basis because of the persecution they suffered. If most of them managed to keep some *honnêteté* intact through it all, it was—one might say—nothing short of a miracle.

For anyone who thought that an irreligious person could not be a good person, one example was particularly confounding: the Scottish Enlightenment philosopher David Hume. He was just so *nice*.

This is confounding in another way, because Hume was also the

most intellectually merciless thinker of his time. His *Treatise of Human Nature*, published between 1739 and 1740, destroyed almost every scrap of reliability or certainty that a human being might feel about life, or experience, or the world. He tells us that we cannot be sure that any cause will lead to any effect, or that the sun will rise tomorrow, or that we have any consistent personal identity. We *feel* that there are real, coherent causes and identities, but those are just feelings, born of habit and association of ideas. The twentieth-century philosopher and broadcaster Bryan Magee summed him up well by saying, "What Hume characteristically tells you when you go to him with a problem is: 'It's worse than you think.'"

Then there were his assaults on conventional belief. We are told stories of miracles, he says—the paralyzed who stand up and walk, personal appearances by saints, prayers being answered. But stop and think. Which is more likely to be true? Has something really happened that contradicts every other experience you have ever had of how nature works? Or has someone made a mistake, lied, made it up, garbled the account, or said something that listeners misunderstood? He suggests applying a basic principle: that "no testimony is sufficient to establish a miracle, unless the testimony be of such a kind, that its falsehood would be more miraculous, than the fact, which it endeavours to establish." (The later science communicator Carl Sagan put it more neatly: "Extraordinary claims require extraordinary evidence.")

Imagine, continues Hume, that someone speaks of having seen a dead man come back to life. This is a thing normally never occurring, so it conflicts with everything else we have experienced about dead bodies. If you apply the test, you have to ask which is more likely, that such a bizarre thing happened, or that something has gone awry with the report. In writing to an audience of Christians whose faith rested in large part on the Resurrection story, this was quite an example to choose.

That fact clearly struck the first person on whom Hume tried out the argument, and no wonder, since he was a Jesuit. Hume was then staying at La Flèche in France, because it was a cheap place to live while writing the *Treatise*, and he got on well with the Jesuits from the college there; they let him use their library. On this occasion, one of them had been telling him about a miraculous event said to have occurred in their community. On hearing this, the test principle popped into Hume's head, and he aired it. The Jesuit thought for a moment and said that it could not be right, because, if it was, it could be used against the stories in the New Testament as well as modern miracles. It is pretty clear that Hume had considered this possibility and was fine with it.

At first he intended to include the miracles argument in the *Treatise* itself, but he lost his nerve. It would appear only in his later reworking of the *Treatise*'s philosophy, *An Enquiry Concerning Human Understanding*. He kept some of his other writings to himself for even longer, including essays on the moral question of suicide, and on the immortality of the soul. He wrote *The Natural History of Religion*, but delayed publication for several years, and completely withheld a set of *Dialogues Concerning Natural Religion*, in which the participants compare their different points of view on the subject. One of the issues they discuss is whether atheists can be expected to behave well. One speaker says (as Voltaire also apparently thought) that it might be useful if people believed in the afterlife, because it gave them motivation to be good. Another speaker disagrees. If that is true, he asks, why then is history so full of stories of persecution, oppression, and religious civil wars? "If the religious spirit be ever mentioned in any historical narration, we are sure to meet afterwards with a detail of the miseries, which attend it. And no period of time can be happier or more prosperous, than those in which it is never regarded or heard of."

Despite Hume's precautions, everyone in his hometown of Edinburgh, as well as the *lumières* in France, seemed to know that he was, at the very least, an extremely skeptical freethinker. His nicknames included "the Atheist" and "the Great Infidel." Because of the infamy this brought him, opponents blocked him from university posts in both Edinburgh and Glasgow, and he was also maneuvered out of a job as the librarian of Edinburgh's Faculty of Advocates. It could have been worse: not many decades had passed since a twenty-year-old student in the same city, Thomas Aikenhead, had been executed for blasphemy because he had talked dismissively about Bible stories and said that "God, the world, and nature, are but one thing."

And yet, contrary to his alarming reputation, Hume amazed almost everyone who met him by his good nature and sheer likability. His other nickname was *le bon David*—the good David. A fellow Scot, James Boswell, wrote: "Were it not for his infidel writings, every body would love him." Once, when the architect Robert Adam wanted to invite Hume to dinner at his family's home in Edinburgh, Adam's mother balked: "I shall be glad to see any of your companions to dinner, but I hope you will never bring the Atheist here to disturb my peace." Shortly afterward, at another dinner, Adam brought Hume anyway, without revealing who he was. After the guests left, his mother said that everyone had been agreeable, "but the large jolly man who sat next me is the most agreeable of them all." Said Adam: That was the Atheist! "Well," she said, "you may bring him here as much as you please." David Hume was living, laughing proof of the point made by his spokesman in his own *Dialogues*: "The smallest grain of natural honesty and benevolence has more effect on men's conduct, than the most pompous views, suggested by theological theories and systems."

He had become so easygoing—and had also become that "large jolly man"—after having put himself through a sort of therapy to counter too much futile battling with philosophy in his youth. Having cudgeled his brains with unresolvable philosophical puzzles, he fell into a wan state and wrote to a doctor asking for advice. The doctor suggested dropping the philosophy and drinking a pint of claret a day, combined with some gentle horse riding. Hume tried it and soon became, as he wrote, "the most sturdy, robust, healthful-like fellow you have seen, with a ruddy complexion and a cheerful countenance."

This robust state continued even when he resumed reading philosophy, not least because he now approached it in a more constructive way, by starting from "human nature" instead of trying to build up theories from abstract foundations. Like Montaigne, he began with the human measure: observing himself and others, and taking such experiences and behavior as material for questioning.

Hume resembled Montaigne in other respects, too, notably in his striking combination of the toughest intellectual skepticism with tolerant good humor. One can hear Montaigne's voice, for example, when Hume tells us, at the end of the devastating first book of the *Treatise*, that its contents have taken him to such a strange place that he now feels like a monster ("Where am I, or what? From what causes do I derive my existence, and to what condition shall I return? Whose favour shall I court, and whose anger must I dread? What beings surround me?")—only to then conclude that there is no cause for concern. Reason may not be able to help him, but Nature promptly cures him of his "melancholy and delirium" by distracting him with the everyday enjoyments of life. "I dine, I play a game of back-gammon, I converse, and am merry with my friends."

Restored, he does return to his speculations, and the remaining sections of the *Treatise* explore questions of emotion and of morality. Like Montaigne and Shaftesbury—and like his friend Adam Smith, who also wrote on this subject—Hume locates the basis of morality in "sympathy," or fellow feeling. When someone feels an emotion, it may show in that person's face or voice. Seeing or hearing this, I feel a kind of replay of the emotion myself, based on my own, similar experiences of feeling that way in the past. Our minds work as "mirrors to one another," he says: a very Montaignesque way of putting it. Hume also seems to be anticipating something like our modern understanding of "mirror neurons" here. But he is drawing on a tradition that was now well established in moral psychology. Like others before him, he followed the idea through to produce a theory of ethics. Because of our mirroring of emotions, he explained, we usually feel happier when we think of other people also feeling happy, and this inclines us to approve of whatever promotes a general flourishing among our fellow humans.

Something else Hume shared with Montaigne (and with Erasmus) was a tendency to be audacious in his thought yet cautious in his behavior. He was not one of life's Lorenzo Vallas; he was not even a Voltaire.

He enjoyed an existence based around friendships and intellectual pursuits, rather than scandal and conflict. He wrote to a friend once, "I could cover the Floor of a large Room with Books and Pamphlets wrote against me, to none of which I ever made the least Reply, not from Disdain (for the Authors of some of them, I respect) but from my Desire of Ease and Tranquility."

He therefore continued to hold back the writings that would have been most likely to shatter that tranquility. From the outset, when he decided to keep the miracles argument out of the *Treatise*, he admitted, "This is a piece of Cowardice, for which I blame myself." Later, in 1757, he published a set of *Four Dissertations* on various topics but removed two pieces at the last minute: the ones on suicide and the immortality of the soul. They were physically cut out of copies and replaced with a different essay. In bibliographical terminology, they were "canceled"—a term that has recently acquired a wider cultural meaning to describe what happens to a person or work considered unacceptable to public sensibilities and forced into silence or withdrawal. Hume canceled his own work but did not destroy it, and he did not stop writing it.

In other ways, he was extraordinarily fearless. James Boswell was struck by Hume's ability not to worry about having no personal expectation of a heavenly afterlife. Boswell decided to grill him, as was his wont with famous people: he followed his friend Samuel Johnson around, noting down everything he said, including remarks on religion. Boswell also visited Voltaire and put him on the spot: "I demanded of him an honest confession of his real sentiments." When Voltaire said that his real sentiments were love for the Supreme Being and the desire to be good, in order to emulate the "Author of Goodness," Boswell admitted, "I was moved; I was sorry. I doubted his sincerity. I called to him with emotion, 'Are you sincere? Are you really sincere?'" He answered that he was.

One day, then, while listening in church to a sermon about the consolations of faith, Boswell made a mental note: Must ask Hume how he manages to remain in such good spirits as an unbeliever. It might be useful to know, just in case Boswell's own faith ever failed him. It would be only "humane" for Hume to equip him with any advice he might need.

By the time the chance for such a conversation came, in 1776, the circumstances were worse than Boswell could have expected. Hume had just been diagnosed with a lethal tumor in his abdomen, large enough to feel through the skin, and he knew that he was going to die of it. Boswell wanted more than ever to find out how he could bear his lack of futurity.

Calling on the philosopher, Boswell found him in his front room, looking thin and ill, without his previous plumpness. But Hume was cheerful and confirmed matter-of-factly that he was close to death. Boswell asked about his faith. Hume said that he had lost it long ago. "He then said flatly that the morality of every religion was bad, and, I really thought, was not jocular when he said that when he heard a man was religious, he concluded he was a rascal." Boswell was amazed that Hume could speak in such a way when death was before his eyes.

Boswell asked Hume (and I am paraphrasing his own paraphrase of what was said): Is it not possible that there is some future life, after all?

It is possible that a piece of coal put on the fire might not burn, replied Hume, alluding to his own philosophical arguments about causation and miracles; but it is not likely.

Yes, but does the thought of annihilation not make you uneasy all the same? asked Boswell.

Not in the least, said Hume.

These responses, on the one hand, cheered Boswell: "Mr. Hume's pleasantry was such that there was no solemnity in the scene; and death for the time did not seem dismal." At the same time, he was unnerved: "I left him with impressions which disturbed me for some time." If a man facing death could speak in this way, how could any of the prevailing views on atheists be true—that they were bad; that they always returned to religion in the end because they could not live without it; that they were incapable of heroism or nobility?

In fact, when Boswell told Samuel Johnson about Hume later, Johnson flatly refused to believe it. "He lied," said Johnson. "He had a vanity in being thought easy. It is more probable that he lied than that so very improbable a thing should be as a man not afraid of death." Thus Johnson wittily turned Hume's own miracles argument back upon him. But Boswell was more astute in perceiving Johnson's real reasons for speaking so brusquely: being particularly prone to anxieties about death, and about the firmness of his own faith, he had to work hard to maintain his feeling of certainty.

Meanwhile, in Edinburgh, Hume's friend Adam Smith stayed close by him as his illness worsened, and later published a short account of his last weeks. Hume also wrote a brief memoir, *My Own Life*, later published by Smith, and he kept working at revisions of his other works. He had many visits from friends and played his new favorite game of whist with them. Often he seemed so normal that the friends could hardly believe he was really dying. It is true, said Hume. "I am dying as fast as my enemies, if I have any, could wish, and as easily and cheerfully as my best friends could desire." He joked about looking for excuses to persuade the boatman Charon to delay ferrying him across to the land of the dead (according to another mythology in which, of course, he did not believe). "Good Charon, I have been correcting my works for a new edition. Allow me a little time, that I may see how the Public receives the alterations."

Among the works he brushed up were his long-secret texts on religion and doubt. He tried his best to make arrangements for them to be published posthumously. First he asked Smith if he would take on the task, but Smith seemed nervous, so Hume let him off. He changed his will to leave the request to his usual publisher, William Strahan, asking him to bring out the *Dialogues* within two years, and the canceled essays "Of Suicide" and "Of the Immortality of the Soul" at his discretion. As with many other humanists, these matters of publishing and readership on Earth *were* the form of immortality that mattered to Hume.

Strahan never did produce those works, however. The *Dialogues Concerning Natural Religion* would come out in 1779, but anonymously and in a publication arranged by Hume's nephew, not by Strahan. The suicide and immortality essays trickled out in anonymous and unauthorized editions, too, but proper publication with Hume's name attached had to wait until the nineteenth century.

Charon also failed to comply with Hume's wishes. He could not wait forever—Hume would just keep adding more and more edits and would never be done. So come, said Charon, "please step into the boat." Hume died on August 25, 1776, showing, according to his doctor, nothing but "happy composure of mind" to the last. A crowd gathered outside his home four days later to see the coffin conveyed to the cemetery, in heavy rain. Boswell went along, watching from afar but paying his respects. Someone in the crowd was heard to say, "Ah, he was an Atheist." To this, someone else responded: "No matter, he was an *honest* man."

Smith agreed, and concluded his account of Hume's death by writing, "I have always considered him, both in his lifetime and since his death, as approaching as nearly to the idea of a perfectly wise and virtuous man, as perhaps the nature of human frailty will permit."

Prudent and heroic in equal measure, loved for his friendliness but formidable in his assault on bad reasoning, fond of distraction but set on improving the intellectual and moral tools available to the human mind: *le bon David* was the perfect example of a *lumière*—and a man of *humanitas*.

7.

Sphere for All Human Beings

1405–1971

*Universality, diversity, critical reasoning, moral
connection: four ideas that shaped humanism and were
shaped by it—Mary Wollstonecraft, Harriet Taylor
Mill, and the largest and highest—Jeremy Bentham,
Oscar Wilde, and being made for exceptions—Frederick
Douglass and eternal wakefulness—E. M. Forster
again—connecting up the fragments.*

aving said that, *perfect* is not the right word for Hume (or indeed for anyone else).

Almost all the humanists in this book so far had a severe limitation: they applied their ideas of humanity or *humanitas* almost exclusively to white, able-bodied, gender-conforming males—that is, to people who looked more or less like Leonardo's Vitruvian figure. Only this subset of the species could aspire to be "universal man." Any other type was treated as a deficiency and a falling-off, perhaps falling below the level of the human altogether.

Humanistic thinkers were far from alone in these assumptions, which were shared by most European intellectuals in history. Some of the Enlightenment-era humanists had a particular tendency, however, to speak of such matters with a specious air of scientific confidence. Hume was among them: in a footnote that has become notorious, he asserted that non-white people were "naturally inferior," producing nothing culturally comparable to European creations. "No ingenious manufactures amongst them, no arts, no sciences." In the wake of a critique by James Beattie, accusing him and other philosophers of thinking that "every practice and sentiment is barbarous which is not according to the usages of modern Europe," Hume later revised the insult to apply it only to those of African origin—which is no improvement.

Several Enlightenment authors had similar failures of insight, including one from whom we might have expected better: Condorcet. In general terms, he strongly condemned colonialism, racism, and sexism, and had a vision of all humanity sharing an enlightened future. Yet he did not think of all humans as *starting* at an equal level on that progressive ladder, and he wondered if some cultures might not make it to the top, after all; they might simply fade away, without their loss affecting the overall picture of progress.

Then there was the subject of women. One of that era's most radical political thinkers was Jean-Jacques Rousseau—until he wrote about the subject of girls' education, at which point he turned into the stuffiest of old conservatives. In his pedagogical treatise *Émile*, he wrote that girls need not study philosophy or science because all they would ever need to know was how to please a husband. (And he was not being ironic.) Voltaire did think women made good scientists: he shared his studies of Newtonian physics and other matters with his friend and lover, the mathematician and translator Émilie du Châtelet. Still, when she died, he considered it a compliment to write, "I have lost one who was my friend for twenty-five years, a great man, whose only defect was being a woman."

On the whole, these Enlightenment authors were just carrying on an older tradition of mixing brilliance about some matters with daftness about others. In ancient Greece, for example, Plato approved of female education, yet also thought that women were the reincarnations of men who had been cowardly or immoral in a previous life. (It could have been worse: more serious failures were reborn as shellfish.) Aristotle wrote Europe's greatest foundational works of ethics and politics, but only in the context of free Greek males: everyone else was of a lesser nature. This meant women, of course, but also those he categorized as naturally born for enslavement. The way to identify such a person, according to Aristotle, was this: "Someone is . . . a slave by nature if he is capable of becoming the property of another (and for this reason does actually become another's property) and if he participates in reason to the extent of apprehending it in another, though destitute of it himself." This last clause was mainly to distinguish enslaved people from non-human animals, who could not even recognize reason when they saw it. With that proviso, the main point here was that you could spot those who were meant to be enslaved from the fact that they were currently enslaved. For them, clearly, "the condition of slavery is both beneficial and just." Aristotle further clarified the situation by comparing enslavement to the equally natural dominance of men over women.

Aristotle's "slave nature" theory was used to justify centuries of later exploitation. The philosopher Juan Ginés de Sepúlveda applied its principles in the sixteenth century to defend Spanish abuse of Caribbean and Central American people, saying that they were the products of a separate Creation and could therefore be treated as domestic animals. In a speech of 1844, the Alabama surgeon Josiah Clark Nott justified North American slavery by referring to this theory of separate origins, and added a final flourish—taken not from Aristotle but from Alexander Pope. It was that endlessly convenient line from the *Essay on Man*, with the addition of even more emphatic typography: "'One truth is clear, WHATEVER *IS*, IS RIGHT.'" In effect, that is what most of Aristotle's argument also boiled down to—except that Nott is purportedly writing as a Christian.

Actually, on the humanity question, some Christian institutions had a better record than secular philosophers. Augustine had influentially stated in his *City of God* that all human beings, however varied, had the same origins—although as examples he chose old stories of races with dog heads or a single giant foot that could be used as an umbrella. Even those people must have a human soul; therefore, they can be saved, if only they are introduced to the doctrines of Christianity. Two things follow: slavery is bad, and missionary activity is good. This theology was confirmed in 1537, when the pope issued a bull ruling that enslaving people in the Americas was wrong. The debate did not die, however. Christians continued looking for ways of defending the practice, often by denying that different peoples *did* have a common origin. But several denominations came over to the abolitionist side, by stages. Quakers were the pioneers; then came movements run by Evangelical Anglicans and others, all emphasizing the principle of universally shared humanity. It was conveyed with most impact in a medal made by Josiah Wedgwood in 1787 for the Society for Effecting the Abolition of the Slave Trade: it shows a Black man in chains, on his knees, asking, "Am I not a man and a brother?"

When it came to women's claims to humanity and freedom, Christianity leaned more toward the "Whatever is, is right" route. Men looked at the women they knew, especially genteel ones in polite society, and could detect no sign of educational achievement or sophistication: women's interests seemed frivolous, and their behavior was modest and submissive. It followed that it was eternally "beneficial and just" for them to continue as they were: that is, to grow up with a frivolous, minimal education, and to have any act of immodest self-assertion suppressed.

It seems surprising that Enlightenment-era humanists did not break out of such reasonings more often than they did. After all, they prided themselves on critical questioning of received ideas, and many also valued "sympathy" and fellow feeling as a basis for morality. In most situations, they were with Terence: "I am human, and consider nothing human alien to me." Yet they often seemed willing to append exceptions to the end of that sentence.

This was not true of all of them, however, and some did widen their perspective. Several key humanist voices spoke up for the idea of everyone sharing an essential humanity, and for reasons to do with life in *this* world, not prospects of salvation in the next. It was thanks to humanistic beliefs in reason and meliorism that Voltaire argued for tolerance of different religions, Condorcet and Olympe de Gouges argued for including women and non-European races in the French Revolutionary idea of human liberation, and their fellow Enlightenment thinker Jeremy Bentham argued for what would now be called LGBTQ+ rights.

These pioneers, and others after them, advanced arguments based on four big humanistic ideas in particular. The first of these is the one just mentioned: that we are all united in our humanity, so that "nothing human is alien."

A second idea, conversely, stresses not universality but diversity. Yes, we are all human, but we also experience life differently depending on culture, political situation, and other factors—and such differences should be respected and celebrated.

The third principle is the valuing of critical thinking and inquiry. For a humanist of any kind, nothing about human life should ever be taken as self-evident or accepted on grounds of authority and tradition. What IS may NOT be right, and should be questioned.

Fourth is the general belief that our moral lives, which are central to our humanity, are best served by looking for ways of connecting and communicating between ourselves.

Universality, diversity, critical thinking, moral connection: these have all become widely held values in our day, although still less so than a humanist might wish. Each of them draws on parts of humanistic tradition that we have already encountered: from Protagoras's human measure to Montaigne's *diversité* to Valla's critical thinking to the empathy-based ethics of a Shaftesbury or Hume.

Meanwhile, the influence has also run the other way: as humanists advanced such ideas and explored a new and more open way of thinking about humanity, that new way of thinking helped reshape what it meant to be a humanist. Humanists became less elitist, and more hospitable to cultural differences. Some tried to question their own assumptions more. They continued applying the old skills of critical investigation and eloquence, but to new fields of inquiry.

Let us visit each of those four ideas in turn—leaping around in time through this chapter—and see what kind of changes humanists of different eras were prepared to contemplate.

Just for a person to lay claim to that first element, equal humanity, could sound like a big challenge—especially if it came from the wrong sort of person.

In 1900, the classical scholar Jane Harrison wrote an essay with the title "*Homo sum*," the opening words of Terence's line. It was provocative, because *homo* was invariably translated as "man" (even though in Latin it does mean "human"; a male adult is *vir*). Yet here was a woman applying it to herself! Her point, of course, was that she had as much right as men to use it and to access the full range of possibilities in life that came with it. The Dante translator and novelist Dorothy L. Sayers reprised the argument in her even more strikingly titled 1938 talk "Are Women Human?" She elucidated by giving examples. People ask: Should women wear trousers? Some think not, on the grounds that trousers are thought to suit women less well than they do men. But Sayers finds trousers more comfortable. "I want to enjoy myself as a human being, and why not?" (If it seems strange to make so much of this example, think of the jeering that greeted Amelia Bloomer's eponymous pantaloons in the previous century, liberating women from garments so cumbrous that they could barely sit down comfortably, never mind take proper exercise.) Here is another question discussed by Sayers: Should women go to university? Some say no, because apparently women in general don't want to study

Aristotle. But the point is that *Sayers* wants to study Aristotle.

Of course, for university to be accessible to any particular woman, some collective struggle has to take place. And it did: much campaigning was needed before the first universities accepted female students, beginning with nine admitted to the forward-looking University of London in 1868. Others followed, but it took even more activism to convince them that female students should actually receive degrees for their studies. Sayers herself was awarded none when she finished her undergraduate work at Oxford in 1915; she had to wait until 1920, when Oxford relented and

AMELIA BLOOMER, ORIGINATOR OF THE NEW DRESS.—FROM A DAGUERREOTYPE BY T. W. BROWN.—(SEE PRECEDING PAGE.)

she was able to collect it along with her master's degree. At the time of her talk in 1938, Cambridge was still holding out, and it continued to do so for another ten years.

But her argument was not that women should not bother to fight together. It was that the *reason* for the fight remains an individual one: it is so that each person can do what she personally wants to do in life. Men keep asking, "What on earth do women want?" The answers: "As human beings they want, my good men, exactly what you want yourselves: interesting occupation, reasonable freedom for their pleasures, and a sufficient emotional outlet." They want the same great open sky of possibilities above their heads as men do, not some smaller dome for ladies.

This thought had been given eloquent expression earlier, in an 1851 article by the feminist Harriet Taylor. People, she wrote, speak of women as having their own "proper sphere." But:

We deny the right of any portion of the species to decide for another portion, or any individual for another individual, what is and what is not their "proper sphere." The proper sphere for all human beings is the largest and highest which they are able to attain to. What this is, cannot be ascertained, without complete liberty of choice.

Confinement to a limited sphere is what happens every time people are assigned to a particular range of activities from birth, especially for any reason to do with social class, caste, ethnic group, or other factors. If, like Plato, you believe in reincarnation and the transmigration of souls, well, at least you can console yourself with the hope of getting better status in the next life. But if, like most humanists, you think that *this* is the life that matters, then it is unacceptable to lose the "largest and highest" options in that life because of typecasting. To refuse such limitation is implicitly to make a philosophical claim: that universal humanity belongs to each of us. This was what Montaigne had said—we each bear the entire form of the human condition—although his readiness to apply that principle to the situation of women was variable. (Everything in Montaigne is variable.)

After the claim to humanity, another claim follows: that we should all have the full range of human virtues to aspire to, not a set of virtues particular to our group. Such a claim matters greatly to humanists, because they are so absorbed in questions of virtue generally: they want to know what it is to be a good human being. You may remember an earlier mention of Pericles telling Athenian free men in 430 BCE that they are excellent because they are harmonious, responsible, and politically active—only to add that this does not apply to women, whose only virtue is never to be mentioned by anyone at all. That continued to be the norm for millennia: instead of the mainstream of human excellence, women were offered a rivulet of negative side virtues: modesty, silence, placidity, innocence, chastity. Each of these is characterized by the *absence* of some positive quality (confidence, eloquence, active responsibility, experience, and—

well, I'll leave it to you to decide what the virtuous opposite of chastity is, but whatever we call it, it is surely more fun). Those negativities are the "virtues of her sex" that Olympe de Gouges was accused of forgetting, and that were said to have led her to the scaffold during the Terror.

The virtue question was tackled by Olympe de Gouges's fellow feminist of the revolutionary Enlightenment, the Englishwoman Mary Wollstonecraft. Her *Vindication of the Rights of Women* of 1792 began by stating: "I shall first consider women in the grand light of human creatures, who, in common with men, are placed on this earth to unfold their faculties." Then she points out that women can do this unfolding only if they have access to the full set of human qualities. True, different duties may sometimes fall to women, especially when it comes to motherhood (and she soon found out what that entailed, becoming a single mother of a daughter by the rascally Gilbert Imlay a little after this). But, she argues, however different such duties are, they still form part of overall "*human* duties."

To be fully humanized in matters of virtue, women must also share in a fully humanizing education. Wollstonecraft had scathing things to say about the female education of her own day, especially among the supposedly privileged classes. They were taught deportment, a few domestic accomplishments, and many flirtatious ways to attract a husband: thus, they often emerged as very limited beings. "Confined then in cages like the feathered race, they have nothing to do but to plume themselves, and stalk with mock majesty from perch to perch." Instead, she hoped to see an education that would enable women to grow up as adults and to take adult responsibility for their lives. As she wrote, "I wish to see my sex become more like moral agents."

The key ingredient in achieving this was freedom—as was more explicitly asserted in *The Subjection of Women*, a book published in 1869 by John Stuart Mill, Harriet's second husband and a great feminist himself. There, he invited male readers to remember that exhilarating moment of their lives when they legally came of age and suddenly had the right to determine their own paths as adults. Did you not feel "twice as much alive, twice as much a human being, as before?" he asks. But that is something that women can never feel throughout their entire lives. That is not so far from saying that they can, after all, never be fully human.

So the whole sphere, and Montaigne's whole condition, should be opened to all without being limited by one's particular characteristics. But then, particularity mattered to humanists, too.

That might sound like a contradiction. But that first idea—universality—and this second idea of diversity or particularity were never really at cross-purposes. In fact, they work best in combination. Universality without diversity would be an empty abstraction; there would even be something inhuman about it. Diversity without an idea of universal humanity would leave us all isolated, with few avenues of contact. Each enhances the other. And when these principles go missing in an oppressive society, they often go missing together. Regimes that disrespect human differences also tend to fail to recognize those universal "mirrors" in human lives through which we can see ourselves *and* the other.

Think, for example, of the experiences someone might have living as a person with a disability. If you live in a society where universal humanity is recognized, you might hope that everything possible would be done to support your capacity to enjoy and "unfold" your humanity in the fullest way possible—at its most basic level, by making sure that if you use a wheelchair, you can easily get into buildings. Underlying this is that mirror recognition of a fellow human's experience: obviously, like everyone else, you want to be able to go places, do stuff, follow your interests, and engage fully in the world.

But a society that respects the principle of diversity might also respond to your experience by seeking to enlarge its notion of what a full human life *is*. Dan Goodley has argued this in his 2021 book *Disability and Other Human Questions*: societies that are ableist also have a tendency to set up a "self-congratulatory kind of self-sufficient humanness" as their general ideal. (One thinks of muscly Vitruvian Man again, standing alone.) Such a society might make less provision for differing needs in other areas of life and perhaps incline toward a harsher economic model based on "self-reliance" for everyone. A society that questioned its ableism, on the other hand, might learn to put more emphasis on collaboration and community and be more aware in general of "the perilous, precarious, diverse and unstable nature of humanity."

Sexuality is another area where a single, exclusive model of what is "natural" does more harm than good. This was investigated in the early nineteenth century by the Enlightenment philosopher and political theorist Jeremy Bentham. He is best known for devising an ethical system that offers an alternative to basing moral choices on either divine laws or on such bogus notions as "repugnancy to Nature." For Bentham, Nature does

not find things repugnant; people do. And just because some people do not like the sound of something, or do not want to do it themselves, that does not mean that it is wrong.

Instead, Bentham proposes a test: If I do something, will it (so far as I can tell) make everyone involved happier, or will it make them more miserable? This is the "felicific calculus," or calculation of happiness, and it is the central move in the ethical system known as utilitarianism. The process of applying it is

JEREMY BENTHAM.

invariably complicated, of course, by such questions as who makes the decision, how exactly the mathematics can be done, and what constitutes misery or happiness. As a tool, it is fallible, but when it works, it is not only effective but humanistic, because it puts people, not laws, at the center of things. And not only people. Bentham extended the principle to animal welfare, writing: "The question is not, Can they *reason*? nor, Can they *talk*? but, Can they *suffer*?"

In a treatise, "Of Sexual Irregularities," and other brief works, he applied the calculus to minority consensual practices such as (although he does not spell this out) homosexuality. For Bentham, the only questions that need asking in such cases are: Does this harm anyone? Does it cause suffering? If it does not—if it makes those involved happy and hurts no one else (except through a self-inflicted "repugnance")—then where is the problem? All that matters is that it is adding to the amount of happiness in the world instead of subtracting from it. Utilitarianism has sometimes been regarded as a cold thing, yet this strikes me as a generous and rather beautiful principle for living.

Bentham was never afraid to go his own way, being a renowned eccentric in his dress and thinking. (Eccentricity is another good test case for the happiness calculus: in his case it seems to have made him happy, and it hurt no one else.) In his will, he left his body partly to be dissected for medical science, and partly to be made into an effigy, or "auto-icon," to inspire and delight friends, followers, and future generations—clearly a happiness gain, although I am not sure whether he took into account the disappointed worms in the graveyard.

Yet even this indomitable man did not feel, having written "Of Sexual Irregularities" in 1814, that he could publish it. Thus—like so many other humanist works—his writings on this subject languished as manuscripts until they finally saw print two hundred years later, in 2014.

His caution was understandable. Homosexual acts between men were still illegal, and the negative effect of such laws on human felicity became even more apparent at the end of that century, when the playwright, wit, and aesthete Oscar Wilde was imprisoned for two years from 1895 for exactly the "repugnancy to Nature" that Bentham wished to debunk. Besides losing his liberty, Wilde lost almost all of his possessions to pay the imposed legal costs. At a chaotic auction on the street outside his house, his book collection, fine china, furniture, and other treasures—all things of the type that Savonarola would have called "vanities"—were sold or in some cases looted. Wilde himself was put to hard labor in Pentonville, working the treadmill and picking oakum: a deliberately punitive finger-shredding job, teasing apart old tarry ropes to be recycled as a fibrous sealant. Later he was moved to slightly better conditions at Reading Gaol, via a humiliating train journey during which he, waiting with his guards to change trains at Clapham Junction, was recognized and mocked by the crowd. The experience of having lost so much—his collection, his dignity, his freedom—changed his personality forever, leaving him gloomier, with his flamboyance muted.

But perhaps not entirely. When at last he was released, he reversed the journey through Clapham Junction, not in handcuffs but still accompanied by prison officials. This time, while they were waiting, Wilde saw plants in bloom near the platform; he opened his arms toward them, exclaiming, "Oh beautiful world! Oh beautiful world!" The warder said, "Now, Mr. Wilde, you mustn't give yourself away like that. You're the only man in England who would talk like that in a railway station."

Indeed he was. But as he had written in his *De Profundis* a few months earlier, while still inside: "I am one of those who are made for exceptions, not for laws."

A long with the entwined braid of universality and diversity, our humanists also value a third quality: they do their best to reason critically, rather than accepting situations just because they have always been that way. They ask *how* those situations developed, and wonder whether, sometimes, what IS might NOT BE RIGHT, AFTER ALL.

A few humanists long ago raised this question about women. Compiling lists of notable female figures from history or mythology became a fashionable game, with the earliest great list being Boccaccio's *On Famous Women*, written in the early 1360s. Paolo Giovio's 1527 dialogue *Notable Men and Women of Our Time* quoted the humanist statesman Giovanni Antonio Muscettola saying that women could be as clever as men, if only they were taught "the best arts and extraordinary virtues." Their bodies are made of the same blood and marrow, he says, and they have "the same longing for life"; why would their minds be different? Montaigne, in his better moments, made similar observations about women behaving in certain ways, not by nature, but because of social expectations and roles.

All these opinions came from men, but women had also been advancing such arguments themselves for just as long. Christine de Pizan, the pioneering humanist we met earlier, set them at the heart of her *Book of the City of Ladies* in 1405. Her figure of Reason asks, "Do you know why it is that women know less than men?" and answers herself, "It's because they are less exposed to a wide variety of experiences since they have to stay at home all day to look after the household." She goes on to compare women to villagers from remote mountain communities: they may appear naive and dull-witted, but only because they have seen so little of the world.

Later, this became the basis of Mary Wollstonecraft's critique of women's education, and twentieth-century feminists tested it out with thought experiments. Virginia Woolf imagined what life might have held in store for a sister of William Shakespeare, born with the same talents but thwarted and excluded at every turn. Simone de Beauvoir, in her 1949 work *The Second Sex*, traced a woman's life from girlhood through adolescence to maturity and old age, showing how her confidence and sense of self are affected at each stage by social expectations and pressures. In a neat formulation, she writes, "One is not born, but rather becomes, a woman."

All of these are examples of genealogical and critical thinking: look-ing for origins and causes. John Stuart Mill, in *The Subjection of Women*, wrote that we simply cannot know what either sex is "really" like, because there has never been a society in which women were not influenced by male domination. This distorts women, like hothouse plants made to grow into a particular shape or size. (It distorts men, too.) Meanwhile "men, with that inability to recognize their own work which distin-guishes the unanalytic mind, indolently believe that the tree grows of it-self in the way they have made it grow."

But part of the humanist tradition is to try not to "indolently believe" anything at all without analyzing it. A humanist asks questions, as Lo-renzo Valla did in inspecting the documents before him: Where did this come from? What is the source of the evidence being put forward for it? Whose interest has it served? Mill praised his own mentor Bentham for making such inquiries in all matters: he called Bentham "the great ques-tioner of things established" and "the great *subversive*, or, in the language of continental philosophers, the great *critical*, thinker of his age and country." Similar things could be said about Mill himself, in most re-spects. He made connections—for example, between the reasons given to justify slavery and the reasons given to justify women's oppression. In both cases, many people apparently failed to see the underlying point about human beings in general: that people are affected by their experi-ence and education. That failure of insight was, for Mill, the greatest im-pediment that existed to social progress.

Yet the amount of thinking required should not be that demanding. The great abolitionist and autobiographer Frederick Douglass put the point with memorable force and clarity in a Fourth of July oration of 1852, saying: "There is not a man beneath the canopy of heaven, that does not know that slavery is wrong *for him*." That single line destroys whole volumes of faulty argument—beginning with Aristotle.

Behind the apparent simplicity of the remark lies a deep critical analysis—and much personal experience. Frederick Douglass had lived out the effects of such fallacies, in his own body and mind. He knew what enslavement and dehumanizing treatment did to people, because it had been done to him.

Born in Maryland in 1817 or 1818 to an enslaved mother, Harriet Bailey, and an unknown white father (probably an overseer, or perhaps the "master" himself), Douglass was never acknowledged by that father and was separated from his mother when he was very young, as she was sent to another property twelve miles away. He saw her only four or five times after that, on the rare nights when she secretly walked that great distance in the dark, spent a few hours with him, and then walked back in order to be in the fields for the next day's work at sunrise. Had she been a moment late, she would have suffered the torture of whipping. Douglass himself was later sent to an even more brutal household. Children went barefoot, with little bedding or clothing; they ate cornmeal mush from a trough, like pigs, and had no education.

On growing up, Douglass made several attempts to escape to the North and was caught each time, until at last he succeeded. Having freed himself, he went on to write and speak about his experience with devastating eloquence and power. He wrote three autobiographical works, of which the 1845 *Narrative of the Life of Frederick Douglass, an American Slave* has remained an American classic. It is also a classic of humanist literature, in several senses. It is a story about an education; it is a story of freethinking in matters of religion (Douglass was a Christian but hated the hypocrisy of southern preachers who defended slavery). And it is a story of a human being emerging from an attempt to dehumanize him.

Among Douglass's other works was an open letter to his (second) ex-master, Thomas Auld, written on the tenth anniversary of his escape. It includes an attempt to get Auld to think with at least rudimentary critical skills about what he has done: to imagine what it would be like if their roles were reversed, and to reflect on causes and consequences. Douglass reminds Auld of the intensity of the abuses, especially recalling an occasion when he was recaptured and dragged fifteen miles at gun-point to be sold, "like a beast in the market," with his hands bound together—"this right hand, with which I am now penning this letter, . . . closely tied to my left." How would Auld feel, he asks, if such pain and humiliation were inflicted on, say, Auld's daughter Amanda—kidnapped at night, carried off, tortured, her name written into a ledger as being property? Would he find a way of justifying it, as being natural?

As Douglass puts it elsewhere, in *My Bondage and My Freedom*, nothing in the human world is the way it is by necessity or by nature. He applies this even to brutal slaveholders, who, he suggests, could have been humane and respectable had their lives had a different context. On a moral and human level, the institution of slavery had destroyed them, too: "The slaveholder, as well as the slave, is the victim of the slave sys-tem." As we saw earlier, Archbishop Desmond Tutu would later say something similar about South African apartheid, and James Baldwin said it, too, in 1960: "It is a terrible, an inexorable, law that one cannot deny the humanity of another without diminishing one's own." In gen-eral, wrote Douglass, "a man's character greatly takes its hue and shape from the form and color of things about him."

We are shaped by our surroundings. On the other hand, we do still have an essential freedom—which means that we can also work to *change* those formative forces. That was just what Douglass dedicated his life to doing, continuing to travel, write, and campaign tirelessly for the aboli-tionist movement. As a speaker, he had a considerable impact, and not only because of his words themselves. (As Cicero and Quintilian knew, oratory is never just about the words.) Douglass had a compelling voice, and such a talent for imitating the voices of slaveholders and other ene-mies that the audience would roll around with laughter. But then he could switch from humor to melodrama in an instant. His appearance helped: he was tall, with striking good looks, and he deliberately made use of this factor, especially through photography. That new art interested him greatly; he gave four lectures on the subject, and also sat for at least 160

different portraits of himself, becoming one of the most photographed Americans of his day.

Along with all this, he had a fine command of rhetorical technique— an authority that owed much to a rare stroke of luck he had when he was about seven or eight years old. In what he came to consider the great turning point in his life, he was sent to live for a while with members of the Auld family in Baltimore. A city environment offered slightly better opportunities to learn, and the mistress of the house, Sophia Auld, taught him the basics of reading, until her husband put a stop to it, saying that teaching an enslaved boy to read only made him more discontented. Sure enough, it did; when he heard that remark, Douglass felt an instant enlightenment: "I understood the pathway from slavery to freedom." The lessons stopped, but he continued to practice reading and writing by seeking out help from white boys on the streets around the area.

In the process, he came across a book that changed his life: *The Columbian Orator: Containing a Variety of Original and Selected Pieces; Together*

*with Rules; Calculated to Improve Youth and Others in the Ornamental
and Useful Art of Eloquence*, by Caleb Bingham. This was filled with examples of eloquent language for study and imitation, many of them
aimed at advancing ideas about abolition and general social justice. One
dialogue featured a discussion of the slavery question between the slaveholder and an enslaved man who had been recaptured after running away
three times. The latter argued his case so well that the slaveholder was at
last convinced to set him free voluntarily. This rather over-optimistic tale
convinced the young Douglass of the value of both speaking well and of
being on the side of truth. His soul was roused "to eternal wakefulness."

As an adult, Douglass crafted his speeches and writings using skills of
eloquence drawn from many sources—including, but not limited to, the
Greek and Roman models that had been promoted in *The Columbian
Orator*. He favored Ciceronian constructions, such as the long periodic
sentence with its delayed finale, and the device known as "chiasmus," in
which two parts of a sentence reverse each other, as in: "You have seen
how a man was made a slave; you shall see how a slave was made a man."
In his autobiography, Douglass really fills his rhetorical sails with this
apostrophe addressed to the ships he can see far away in Chesapeake Bay:

> You are loosed from your moorings, and are free; I am fast in my
> chains, and am a slave! You move merrily before the gentle gale,
> and I sadly before the bloody whip! You are freedom's swift-winged
> angels, that fly round the world; I am confined in bands of iron!

He does not hold back on vivid effects. Here he is again, laying into
those southern churches: "We have men-stealers for ministers, women-
whippers for missionaries, and cradle-plunderers for church members.
The man who wields the blood-clotted cowskin during the week fills the
pulpit on Sunday. . . . The slave auctioneer's bell and the church-going
bell chime in with each other."

Eloquence—as the humanists of earlier centuries, and orators in
every culture, had always known—is of essential importance to human

beings. Language in general is our very element: the basis of our social and moral lives. It enables us to work out our intellectual critiques of the existing world in detail, to apply our best reasonings to it, and to imagine in words how things might be different—and then to persuade others of these imaginings and reasonings.

Language also plays a big part in binding us into what Archbishop Desmond Tutu called the "bundle of humanity." We communicate and *connect* with each other. And that is the fourth of the ideas that has helped humanists to expand their field of concern.

While anti-humanists were busy saying "Whatever is, is right," a good choice as a rival slogan for humanists would be the one we met earlier in this book: E. M. Forster's "Only connect!"

The phrase features in his 1910 novel *Howards End*, in which a complicated story unfolds between two bourgeois families, the Schlegels and the Wilcoxes, and the working-class Bast couple whose lives become entangled with theirs. The head of the Wilcoxes, Henry, is a judgmental and hypocritical bully. Looking on from the Schlegel perspective, Margaret Schlegel reflects that he does not *notice* things. He is oblivious to "the lights and shades that exist in the grayest conversation, the fingerposts, the milestones, the collisions, the illimitable views." He does not see what connects those things, or the people whose lives are affected by them. He therefore makes no link from his own failings (an affair he has had with Mrs. Bast and some catastrophic business advice he gave to her husband) to their consequences for others—or to the things others have done in response. And so, concludes Margaret in her musings: "Only connect! . . . Live in fragments no longer." Later she confronts him directly: "You shall see the connection if it kills you, Henry! . . . A man who ruins a woman for his pleasure . . . And gives bad financial advice, and then says he is not responsible. These men are you."

This was what Frederick Douglass was saying to Thomas Auld when he urged him to compare the sufferings of enslaved Black people with his own family's pampered life, or when he contrasted the fine thoughts of Sunday preachers with the tortures administered on other days. In his own campaigning, Douglass always tried to see such parallels—which was why he, unlike many others, was in favor of the abolitionist movement endorsing women's battle for the right to vote.

Forster also tried his best to apply the principle of integrity to his own life. He wrote to a friend in 1915, "My defence at any Last Judgement would be 'I was trying to connect up and use all the fragments I was born with.'" But it was not easy, and particularly when it came to the difficulty of being honest about being gay—the context for his remark. Homosexual acts were still illegal in Britain; Forster, having written a novel called *Maurice*, about a gay man very much like himself, was facing up to the reality that he could not risk publishing it.

The idea for the book had come to him two years earlier when he visited the author Edward Carpenter, who—amazingly—lived openly with his partner, George Merrill. Sharing a home in an idyllic forest setting, they were countercultural vegetarians who chopped their own wood and, in Carpenter's case, wrote books. These books presented the case for women's rights, better education in matters of sexuality, and more acceptance of sexual diversity. In *Love's Coming-of-Age*, published in 1896 (thus, while Oscar Wilde was still in prison), Carpenter argued for a richer, less *fragmented* understanding of human life, which would integrate the sexual part of our existence with the rest, rather than treating it as something never to be mentioned. For Carpenter, that exclusion impoverished life. It entailed a "*thinning out* of human nature." It would be much better if sexuality were a subject taught in schools, not just to give information on physical basics, but especially to discuss the more important "*human* element in love."

Carpenter and Merrill welcomed visitors to their happy forest glade, although with exceptions. One door-to-door missionary who asked if they did not want to get to heaven was banished by Merrill with

the answer "Can't you see that *we're in heaven here*—and we don't *want* any better than this, so go away!"

Forster was more warmly received. Later he said that the idea for *Maurice* had popped fully formed into his head when Merrill, in a flirtatious moment, slapped him playfully on his behind. It converted Forster—not to homosexuality itself (he was already well aware of that), but to the idea that one could live joyously and openly, acknowledging all the parts of one's life instead of leaving some in shameful obscurity. He set to work almost immediately on the novel, which tells the story of its hero's gradual realization of his sexuality, from his student years until at last he finds love with a working-class man, Alec Scudder (perhaps inspired by Merrill, who was also working class).

This class aspect is important in the book. Making connections again, Forster explores the relationship between class and sexuality, at a time when more-well-off gay men always had to be wary of being blackmailed. Maurice and Alec have to work out how to move beyond the effects of such fears. Meanwhile, Maurice also moves past his earlier unquestioning acceptance of privilege, which had led him to say idly that the poor "haven't our feelings. They don't suffer as we should in their place." He learns that other humans do have their own inner lives, just as he does. He connects.

Forster had been through similar awakenings. He had no experience of poverty or class prejudice himself, but he did develop a strong sense of the damage they cause. He explored it (rather awkwardly, some feel) in

Howards End, as the aspirational Leonard Bast finds himself shut out from the cultural landscape that others consider their birthright.

When it came to women, Forster's connective ability had to compete with more difficult feelings. In a late notebook, he wrote that he was happy to support political rights for women just so long as he personally could get away from them. This shrinking from women's company no doubt owed much to his having been denied the male company *he* wanted for himself. He also wearied of always having to center novels on heterosexual love affairs, which bored him. It may have been one reason why, eventually, he gave up writing novels altogether.

Despite this, Forster actually wrote female characters very well, and he was alive to that desire for the fullest "sphere" that Harriet Taylor Mill had described. His 1908 novel *A Room with a View* shows his protagonist Lucy Honeychurch longing for freedom and the chance to live as a human individual, rather than in the elevated and empty manner of a lady in a medieval romance, waiting for a knight:

> She too is enamoured of heavy winds, and vast panoramas, and green expanses of the sea. She has marked the kingdom of this world, how full it is of wealth, and beauty, and war—a radiant crust, built around the central fires, spinning towards the receding heavens. Men, declaring that she inspires them to it, move joyfully over the surface, having the most delightful meetings with other men, happy, not because they are masculine, but because they are alive. Before the show breaks up she would like to drop the august title of the Eternal Woman, and go there as her transitory self.

What Forster never forgot, amid all this connection and universality, was that class, race, and sexuality *matter* more than most of his peers admitted. In a talk to an international writers' congress in Paris in 1935, inspired by the suppression of another (much grimmer) gay-themed novel, James Hanley's *Boy*, Forster remarked that the English sense of freedom was at once powerful and limited. "It is race-bound and it's class-bound. It means freedom for the Englishman, but not for the subject-races of his Empire." Within England, it means freedom for the well-off but not for the poor. And it is highly limited when it comes to sexuality.

So limited was it that, having written *Maurice* in his rush of openness and honesty, Forster drew back from publishing it. It became another of those manuscripts we have met throughout our story: hidden, copied out in different versions, almost vanishing. He did have it typed up, but as a precaution he gave separate segments to two different typists, so that (he thought) they would not grasp the book's full meaning. Talk about fragmentation and lack of connection!

The work remained in Forster's desk for six decades; occasionally he took it out to make additions or revisions. Only after his death in 1970—three years after homosexuality was decriminalized in England and Wales for men aged over twenty-one—did *Maurice* finally go to the publishers, and it appeared the following year.

Connections, communications, moral and intellectual links of all kinds, as well as the recognition of difference and the questioning of arbitrary rules: these all go to form the web of humanity. They enable each of us to live a fulfilling life on Earth, in whichever cultural context we are at home, and also to try to understand each other the best we can. They are more likely to encourage an ethics of worldly flourishing, in contrast with belief systems that picture each frustrated soul waiting hopefully for a correction of fortunes in the afterlife. The modern humanist will always prefer to say, with Robert G. Ingersoll, that the place to be happy is *here*, in this world, and the way to be happy is to try to make others so.

The old Golden Rule, associated with several religions as well as with secular morality, has much to offer here: "Do as you would be done by." Or, in the more modest, reversed form that is more hospitable to diversity: *Don't* do something to others if you wouldn't like it yourself.

It is not perfect, but a good rule of the humanist thumb is to say that, if you don't like being told to stay silent and invisible, or being enslaved and abused, or being unable to get into buildings because no one thought to install a ramp, or being considered less than human, then the chances are that other people are not fond of it, either.

Or, as Kongzi said: "The Master's way consists of doing one's best to fulfill one's humanity and treating others with an awareness that they, too, are alive with humanity."

8.

Unfolding Humanity

Mostly 1800s

*Bear cubs and seedlings—Three great liberal humanists
on education, freedom, and flourishing—Wilhelm von
Humboldt, who wanted to be fully human—John
Stuart Mill, who wanted to be free and happy—
Matthew Arnold, who wanted sweetness and light.*

When Simone de Beauvoir wrote, "One is not born, but rather becomes, a woman," she was putting a new spin on older thoughts by educationalists such as Erasmus, who said that "man certainly is not born, but made man." Erasmus cited an old legend taken from Pliny: that baby bears were born as formless lumps, and then licked into a proper bear shape by their mothers. Perhaps humans needed to be formed into a human shape, too, at least mentally if not physically.

It was a nice thought for teachers to contemplate, since it made them sound very important. They actually *made* human beings! But some preferred to say that humans—while needing the guidance of good educators and influences—came out best if they developed their own natural "seeds" of humanity from within. The two aspects of development were not contradictory: the student still needed a good teacher to nurture that growth and ward off bad influences. Even if teachers were there mainly to nudge and guide, rather than to create a shape, they still had reason to feel pride in their work. One could even see them as guiding the whole future development of humanity. If each generation had a better education than the one before, and then produced new teachers in their turn, the result was that great Enlightenment goal: progress. The Prussian philosopher Immanuel Kant promoted this idea in a series of lectures on education in the late eighteenth century: by helping individuals to reach their highest capacity, the teacher also helps generally to "unfold humanity from its seeds." It would be hard to top that on the importance scale.

Similar visions of education as an unfolding of humanity would live on throughout the nineteenth century, initially in Prussia and other German-speaking lands, then elsewhere as other countries picked up on these (literally) progressive ideas. The approach can be summed up in two German words. One is *Bildung*, which means "education," but with an added implication of making or forming an image, since it comes from the root *Bild*, meaning "picture." *Bildung* suggests the making or forming of a person, usually a young man. Life experiences and the influence of mentors help him to develop his complete humanity as he grows, until he is ready to take up his place as a well-rounded personage in adult society.

The other word was *Humanismus*. Surprisingly, it was not until nineteenth-century German usage that this emerges as a noun describing a whole field of activity or philosophy of life. There had been *umanisti* aplenty in Italy in earlier centuries, but what they did was not yet summed up as *umanesimo*. Initially, the German term meant mainly an educational approach based heavily on Greek and Roman classics: that was the context for its first recorded use, by the pedagogue Friedrich Immanuel Niethammer in 1808. It later expanded to denote the whole area of history, language, the arts, and moral thinking, as well as education. By the mid-nineteenth century, German historians were also applying it retrospectively to the Italians of the earlier era: it features prominently in the Leipzig professor Georg Voigt's 1859 book *The Revival of Classical*

Antiquity, or The First Century of Humanism—a huge survey starting with a long chapter on Petrarch, casting him as the embodiment of "*humanitas*, all that was uniquely human in the spirit and soul of man." It also comes up as a theme in the Swiss historian Jacob Burckhardt's *Civilization of the Renaissance in Italy* the following year, although Burckhardt was less keen on the book collectors and philologists. He was more excited by figures such as Leonardo da Vinci, the multidimensional, versatile "universal man" of his time. Now the educators of the north wondered if they could produce such figures, or fairly good approximations to them, by means of a new education system. It should be an education aimed at many-sidedness, or complete human harmony, rather than on the narrow business of inculcating skills.

The first person to have a chance actually to put this into practice on a large scale was Wilhelm von Humboldt, the man to whom the Prussian government entrusted the job in 1809 of redesigning their entire educational system for a new era. Prussian education would acquire a reputation for being strict and regimented, yet the man who invented it was startlingly unconventional in many ways, driven by a great personal love of freedom and of humanistic culture. His ideas—those he was able to promote in his lifetime, as well as those he had to keep unpublished for a while—would inspire other educators and thinkers around Europe, including in Britain. They would influence two English writers in particular, and we will come back to them later in the chapter.

But first, Wilhelm von Humboldt. Besides his educational work, he was an art collector, a serious linguist, and a decidedly kinky character in his sex life. Curious to find out what kind of art he collected and which languages he studied? Read on.

Humboldt's own early "unfolding" took place in a situation of high privilege. He was born in 1767 into the family that owned Tegel, a sixteenth-century mansion beautifully set near a lake on the edge of Berlin. There, he had his education from private tutors, as did his brother Alexander. Despite being two years behind him in age, and also despite doing very little work at his books, Alexander tended to attract more attention. While Wilhelm was a quieter, "inward" type, as he admitted himself, Alexander was mercurial and outgoing. Alexander went on to become an explorer and scientist, renowned for an intrepid five-year expedition to Central and South America and for his multivolume science book *Cosmos*; he would have literally hundreds of things named after him, from mountains to plants to penguins. Johann Wolfgang von Goethe said of him later, still reeling after one of Alexander's visits, "What a man he is! . . . He is like a fountain with many pipes, under which you need only hold a vessel; refreshing and inexhaustible streams are ever flowing."

Wilhelm had his own charm, but it ran in a smooth stream rather than bubbling like a fountain. Although he also had some interest in the sciences and natural history, what really excited him were the humanities, especially languages, the arts, and politics. In those fields, and in his "inward" way, he became just as adventurous and just as much of a maverick as Alexander, determined to live by his own lights. He was studious but not solemn: his daughter later described him as being habitually "merry and witty," as well as showing "perfect goodness and kindness." Things would be named after him, too. It is just that they were schools and universities rather than penguins.

As the two boys grew older, they went to university together, their tutor rather oddly accompanying them. In 1789, two things happened in Wilhelm's life. While he and another tutor were traveling in France, the French Revolution broke out. They rushed to Paris so Wilhelm could have the educational experience of witnessing it. What he saw did not convert him to revolutionary politics, but he was struck by the general atmosphere of freedom in the air, as well as by the extreme poverty still so evident in the city. This led Wilhelm to write: "How few people study human misery in all its horrible extent, and yet what study is more

necessary?" The feeling that it was essential to study human life and experience remained with him.

The other event of 1789 had its origin in his own reasonings, rather than in outward events. He laid out these thoughts in a tract, "On Religion," written while he was still a student. It discussed the contentious issue of whether the state was entitled to tell people what to believe, an idea once thought obviously true (at least by the authorities), but questioned through the long Enlightenment period by philosophers including John Locke and Voltaire. The young Humboldt was also inclined to question it. Two years after that first tract, he incorporated his conclusions into a longer political work: *Ideas for an Attempt to Define the Legal Limits of Government.* That is a literal translation from the German, but it came out in English in two alternative versions, called *The Sphere and Duties of Government* and *The Limits of State Action*, respectively. It doesn't matter what you do with it; the title remains less than thrilling. The contents, however, were bold.

Humboldt's subject was the state in its self-appointed role as moral and ideological arbiter for people's lives. Government authorities, he writes, seem to feel it their duty to impose some particular religion or dogma on their society, because they think that otherwise everything will turn into immorality and chaos. Humboldt disagreed, and for humanistic reasons. He had a humanist's view of morality: he thought that its seeds lie in our own natural predisposition toward kindness and fellow feeling. Such impulses need guidance and development, but they do not need replacing by state-imposed commandments. For Humboldt, principles such as love or justice harmonize "sweetly and naturally" with our very humanity, but for this harmony to have any effect, there must be a free field of operation. If the state imposes moral principles by diktat, it obstructs their natural development. Thus, in effect, a state that enforces a particular belief is denying people the right to be fully human.

So Humboldt advises the state to *limit* itself, at least where matters of individual humanity and morality are concerned. People should be able to explore these things in their own way—with one proviso, however. If their actions lead them to encroach on the development or well-being of others (say, through violent or destructive behavior), then the state should intervene to stop them. Humboldt thus asserts the key principle of political liberalism. The government is not there to tell people whom to marry, or what to believe or say, or how to worship, but mainly to make sure their choices do not harm others. We do not need a grand moral vision from our state; we need it to provide the underlying conditions for a decent life, and for our freedom.

And similar principles apply for Humboldt in matters of education. Human character develops best when it is "unfolded from the inner life of the soul, rather than imposed on it or importunately suggested by some external influence." For that to happen, we need good humanistic teachers, but we do not need or want intrusive rules by the state.

This is not a philosophy likely to appeal to any traditionalist regime. (It has little to offer revolutionaries, either; they are more likely to want a radical transformation in every aspect of society, which does eventually mean intruding on individuals' quiet lives and private choices.) It may seem strange that the man who wrote this book would one day be entrusted by the authorities with the job of designing a major national educational program. But almost no one knew that he had written it, because the book was unpublishable. He did try to get it into print, with help from his friend the playwright Friedrich Schiller, but Schiller managed to have only a few sections published in periodical form. The work as a whole did what humanistic works frequently do: it went into the author's desk and stayed there for decades. Occasionally Humboldt would look through it again and make amendments, but mostly it just waited.

In the meantime, he became an eminent Establishment figure. He moved around Europe, taking up governmental and diplomatic postings: he lived at various times in Rome, Vienna, Prague, Paris, and London. This solid career was what made him a good choice when the Prussian education project came up in 1809. Humboldt applied himself to it systematically—but he also seems to have seen an opportunity at last to put some of his liberal ideas into practice. His reforms combined his love of *Bildung* with his belief that young people would develop their "humanity" best if they could have as much freedom as seemed feasible.

For the earlier age groups, he believed that everyone should start with the same all-around foundation. (All boys, that is, since like everyone else in his world, he did not think to include girls in the system.) Instead of working-class children being immediately trained for a vocational skill, they would start with a general *Bildung* aimed at forming good character. Education at all levels was not to be primarily about acquiring skill sets, but about creating human beings with moral responsibility, a rich inner life, and intellectual openness to knowledge. Having all this, people would be able to continue in a well-formed way in whatever course of life they adopted.

Those with scholarly aptitudes could advance to higher levels. By the time they reached university, they were expected to be able to manage most of their learning for themselves, seeking knowledge through seminars and independent research more than by passively listening to lectures. University education, Humboldt said, should mean "an emancipation from being actually taught." Even after students graduated, that should not mean the end of education. He believed in lifelong learning, rather than in getting through school and then forgetting the lot.

In some ways, this was a vision very much of its time, not least in its taking no account of girls. But in parts it almost sounds like some of the radical educational experiments of the mid-twentieth century—although they would take the freedom element a good deal further. Humboldt's principle was not "anything goes"; he sought to allow and foster the development of truly harmonious, many-sided humans. His vision of humanity and freedom remained at the heart of the Prussian educational system and went on to influence educational thinking elsewhere. Questions were raised that we are still wrestling with in our own time: What *is* a humanistic education for? If the aim is to create fully rounded, responsible citizens, how do you quantify this target? How do you justify it financially, or politically? What is the right relationship between useful-skill learning and the more nebulous benefits of an all-around *Bildung*? How much freedom should the student have, and what is the role of the teacher as a personal presence in the student's life? And how do you put a value on continuing to learn after the career-training years? These questions go beyond educational theory to touch on deeper questions of what we want in life generally.

Humboldt himself certainly loved pursuing his own lifelong learning. He was never happier than when left quietly to research some intellectual project—and the subject of his researches was often, in one form or another, that elusive thing: the *human*. As he wrote in a letter:

> There is only one summit in life: to have taken the measure in feeling of everything human, to have emptied to the lees what fate offers, and to remain quiet and gentle, allowing new life freely to take shape as it will within the heart.

This pursuit gave him so much pleasure that, perhaps naively, he imagined that it would be fulfilling for many other people, too—but he knew it could only be encouraged, never forced. Life must *freely* take shape in each of us. And, besides applying his belief in freedom to education, government, and religious belief, Humboldt applied it in his personal life.

He was married, to Caroline von Dacheröden (or "Li," as he always called her); they had children and seem to have been happy together. But both his ideas and their practice were unconventional. In the secret tract on the role of the state, Humboldt had already suggested that freedom should also mean trusting people to work out their own choices in marriage and sexuality—again, so long as no harm was done, and so long as the situation was consensual. Otherwise, each marriage should mostly be allowed to follow its own course, just as each human individual should. A marriage has its own character; it comes from the characters of the two people involved. Making it conform to an external rule is unhelpful. The state's task, as always, is to protect people from harm and otherwise to allow them to do as they wish.

Thus, Caroline took other lovers, sometimes spending more time with them than with him. And Wilhelm pursued his fantasy life. I mentioned that his sexuality was unorthodox; we know about this only because he wrote about it—not in published form, of course, but in his journal, where he recorded his daydreams. What fascinated him was the idea of struggling to subdue physically strong working-class women, in various situations. One woman, for example, particularly caught his eye when he saw her working on the ferry that crossed the Rhine. Sometimes he explored such scenarios with prostitutes, but at other times he just fantasized. What makes this so interesting is that, in writing about it, he also reflected on both its origins and its effects in his own psychology. Long before Sigmund Freud made such an idea seem obvious, Humboldt wondered in his journal whether such desires might shed light on other aspects of human nature. He speculated that leading a life of such vivid sexual imagination had also helped to form his whole path in life: it made him more "inward." It also fed his interest in human relationships, and in "the study of all character"—the central pursuit of his intellectual career.

So, does the Prussian educational system owe something to Wilhelm von Humboldt's sex kinks? Yes, in a way! But even more interestingly, both sides of his life show how engrossed he was in the general question of human nature, in all its complexity and changeability.

The unusual aspects of his relationship with Caroline had another fortunate consequence: as they were often apart, we have a voluminous correspondence between them, which we would not have had if one of them had always been in the drawing room and the other in the study. His letters to her are a rich resource, filled with his reflections on humanity, on education, and on his other research interests. He was a good correspondent in general—one of those copious letter writers to set alongside Petrarch, Erasmus, or Voltaire. Having lived in so many parts of Europe, he knew people everywhere, and was always interested in them, despite his inwardness. As he wrote in one of his letters to Caroline:

> The more in life one searches for, and finds, human beings, the richer, more self-sufficient, more independent one becomes oneself. More humanized, more readily touched by all that is human in all the facets of one's nature, and in all aspects of creation. This is the goal, dear Li, to which my nature urges me. This is what I live and breathe. Here for me is the final key to all desire . . . Who, when he dies, can tell himself, "I have comprehended as much world as I am able, and have transformed it into my humanness," has fulfilled his aim.

After all these experiences, however, what he loved most was to go home to the estate of Tegel—which he and Alexander had now inherited from their parents. Wilhelm had the place completely rebuilt in the early 1820s, turning it into a mansion in the neoclassical style. He and Caroline spent time together there; they developed an art collection, which especially featured a form very popular in German lands at that time: copies made in plaster of the great classical sculptures and statues of Rome and Greece. Wilhelm enjoyed the company of their children, and later of his grandchildren. He read and wrote and studied.

Above all, he pursued his greatest intellectual passion: the study of language. He considered this the key to studying humanity itself, since we are cultural creatures who live largely in the world of symbols, ideas, and words. He wrote to Caroline: "It is only through the study of language that there comes into the soul, out of the source of all thoughts and feelings, the entire expanse of ideas, everything that concerns man, above all and beyond everything else, even beauty and art."

One benefit of his jobs in other countries had been the opportunity to immerse himself in their languages. He had learned Basque while spending time in or near the Spanish peninsula, and he worked on Etruscan inscriptions during his period in Rome. He studied farther-flung languages, too: Icelandic, Gaelic, Coptic, Greek, Chinese, Sanskrit. Alexander brought back materials from his travels so that Wilhelm could learn a little about Native American languages.

As time went on, Alexander became a more frequent visitor at Tegel— a place he had mostly avoided earlier in life. He would come and amuse Wilhelm's family by bringing stories and political news from the world outside. Wilhelm, by contrast, liked to claim that he never read a newspaper: "You are sure to hear what is important, and can spare yourself the rest." The contrast between the two brothers was as clear as ever: one looking outward, one inward; one following the fountain flow of current events, the other immersing himself in deep, long studies of culture.

Caroline died in 1829, and Wilhelm's remaining years at Tegel were dedicated to his final project: the study of Kawi, the priestly and poetic classical Indonesian language of Java. He hoped to write an authoritative study, and began by writing an introduction, which became as long as any ordinary book. It discussed his general theory of languages: with his usual holistic approach, he saw them as expressions of each particular culture's entire view of the world.

But time ran out on him, and he never finished the rest of the book. Five years after Caroline's death, his own health went into a decline. His daughter Gabriele von Bülow came over from her home in England to help him, bringing her children; ever the linguist, Humboldt was impressed by the careless way these cosmopolitan youngsters mixed German and English in their speech. In March 1835, he developed a fever and drifted into semiconsciousness, during which he, too, murmured multilingually, in French, English, and Italian. At one point, he said clearly, "There must be something to follow—something to come still—to be disclosed—to be . . ." The family gathered around him in his final days. On April 8, he asked for a portrait of Caroline to be taken off the wall and brought to him. He pressed a kiss to it, with his finger. Then he said, "Good-bye! Now hang her up again!" With these last words, he died.

The Humboldtian model of education would have a widespread influence, and in large parts of German-speaking territory it remained dominant well into the twentieth century—until 1933, that is, when the Nazis came to power and threw out its humanistic ideals entirely. They replaced Humboldt's model with a giant indoctrination machine, designed to turn boys into warriors and girls into mothers for producing more warriors. The forming of well-rounded, fully human, free, cultured individuals had no place in the Fascists' world. They had no wish to "humanize" anyone; quite the opposite.

Along with the afterlife of his educational ideas, Humboldt's youthful political ideas about freedom would have an afterlife, too. When he died, his heirs began going through the papers in his study, and they found—still there after half a century—the tract on the limits of the state. It finally saw publication, thanks to Alexander, who did the formidable labor of preparing a multivolume collected edition of Wilhelm's works. The *Limits* came out as part of that, in 1852.

It was translated into other languages, including English, and promptly caught the imagination of English readers. Among those who read it was one of the most important liberal thinkers of that later generation, John Stuart Mill, along with the collaborator and partner whom he had just married: Harriet, formerly Taylor, now Mill.

We met the Mills in the previous chapter, in the context of their feminism. Harriet's arguments for women's right to aspire to the largest and highest "proper sphere for all human beings" struck a strongly humanist note. John, meanwhile, developed a full-scale theory of political liberalism. His own feminism and his discussions with Harriet were powerful influences on this, and so was his reading of Wilhelm von Humboldt. In 1859, when he published his own very influential short work, *On Liberty*, he prefaced it with a quotation from Humboldt's rediscovered book on the state:

> The grand, leading principle, towards which every argument hitherto unfolded in these pages directly converges, is the absolute and essential importance of human development in its richest diversity.

Mill's subject is liberty, but by quoting this at the outset, he plants that liberty firmly in a broader humanist tradition. The two words featured in those lines, *diversity* and *development*, would always go together with the word *freedom* in Mill's thinking. Each of those three nourished the others. For him, we become fully developed human beings if we have freedom, but also plenty of contact with the diversity of ways in which one can live a human life—including even the most eccentric possibilities. A liberal society lets us develop our own such possibilities through contacts with diversity, all taking place in a culturally rich environment and without state interference. Except, of course, if what we do hurts others. For Mill, as for Humboldt, the state's task is to step in if my own pursuit of freedom and experience is damaging yours. The state has no business telling people what they *should* do: it is no part of its role to define a single perfect form of life or morality. Its role is to enable each of us to have the space we need to stretch ourselves, without robbing others of their space.

For Mill, too, the right approach to education is crucial, and here again, he stressed diversity. We need experiences that make us expand,

and this means making "experiments in living." Humboldt, too, had written of how we learn best through a "variety of situations," rather than through aspiring to a unitary model of life. Moreover, the encounter with variety helps make us more tolerant: as Montaigne had said, speaking of the benefits of travel, "So many humours, sects, judgments, opinions, laws, and customs teach us to judge sanely of our own."

Thus, Mill recommends that a liberal society support "absolute freedom of opinion and sentiment on all subjects, practical or speculative, scientific, moral, or theological." This includes supporting the freedom to express all this openly, since a freedom that must be kept secret is no freedom at all. He does note that such expressions may offend sensibilities; it may mean that people will do things that others consider "foolish, perverse, or wrong." That is not a problem unless it causes real harm to those others. (Of course, defining "harm" is so complicated that we are still arguing about it today.)

On Liberty also hinted at other implications, especially for sexuality and religion. Mill believed, like Humboldt, that individuals should be free to work out their relationships for themselves, with the usual no-harm clause. Like Wilhelm and Caroline, he and Harriet had an unconventional relationship, although this time no ferrywomen were involved (so far as we know). For twenty years after they met and fell in love, the couple were unable to marry, because Harriet was already married to someone else and divorce was almost impossible at the time. Her husband, John Taylor, sounds like a nice chap, but they had married when Harriet was only eighteen, and she realized only later that they were not well matched. When she met Mill, she fell for him mainly because he was someone with whom she could talk philosophy and politics and morality for hours. They developed from being passionate friends to being lovers, and eventually they began (more or less) living together, by discreet agreement with John Taylor. To avoid distress all around, they kept to a quiet life in a suburb well away from fashionable society. This continued for some fifteen years, until John Taylor died, of cancer, in 1849. Once a decent period of mourning had passed, she and Mill married, but with some adjustments added to the standard wedding vows. Marriage, at that time, gave the husband almost total control over his wife's affairs, including over her property. Such control could not legally be renounced, but at the wedding Mill read out a "Statement on Marriage," noting that he disagreed with those rights and promising never to exercise them. Thus, like the Humboldts, they rejected the predefined path laid down by the state, and chose the principles that suited their views.

The other delicate matter was religion, and here Mill's feelings varied through his life. In his late years, he seems to have considered the possibility that there was an abstract, deist-style God out there somewhere, remote from human affairs. But on the whole he showed no sign of even that belief. Very unusually for the time, he had been brought up without religious indoctrination: his father, James Mill, was an agnostic who had rejected his own Presbyterian upbringing in favor of the utilitarian philosophy of his friend Jeremy Bentham. So John was indoctrinated with that instead. Let us wind back to his childhood for a moment.

Immersion in utilitarian theory had been just one part of what was

surely one of the strangest experiments in child-rearing since Montaigne's
father had tried to make his son a native Latin speaker. James did not do
that, but he did homeschool his children and gave John an astonishingly
early start on the classics. The toddler was learning Greek by the age of
three, using Aesop's *Fables*; afterward he moved on to Herodotus, Xeno-
phon, and Plato. Latin was added when he was about seven. He also acquired the job of teaching what he learned to his younger siblings as they
grew up behind him. Each morning, his day began with a pre-breakfast
walk, taken with his father in the pleasant, still-rural area around their
north London home at Newington Green. This should have scored high
on the happiness-o-meter, except that while they walked John had to give
a verbal report on whatever he had read the day before, then listen as
James held forth on "civilization, government, morality, mental cultivation." Finally, John had to repeat the gist of these arguments back in his
own words. It would be nice to know what his mother, Harriet Barrow
Mill, thought of all this, but—oddly for a feminist—John never mentions her in his autobiography.

At first, John absorbed his father's influence, and as a youth he
founded his own little Utilitarian Society with a membership of three.
He continued to develop and use utilitarian ideas later: you can see them
at work in the balance of liberal benefits and harms described in *On Liberty*. At the age of about twenty, however, he went through an experience
that changed his perspective on such balances. He fell into a depression.
It produced the sort of *accidia* that Petrarch had suffered five centuries
earlier: an inability to feel pleasure in anything. This threw doubt on the
felicific calculus. What was the point of counting happiness units if, for
deeper reasons, you could not *feel* that happiness?

Mill's path out of this came partly through an unexpected discovery:
poetry. Neither his father nor Bentham had ever seen the point of it;
Bentham flippantly defined a poem as writing with lines that failed to
reach the margin. Now, rebelliously, John fell in love with the form, and
particularly with the work of William Wordsworth, filled as it was with

gushing emotion and love of nature. Wordsworth also tried, in his *Prelude*, to trace the unfolding and development of an individual's inward experience from childhood on: a very *Bildung*-ish thing to do.

Reading Wordsworth made Mill reflect that humans need such deeper satisfactions, in a way that other animals do not seem to. We long for meaning; we crave beauty and love. We seek the fulfillment to be found in "the objects of nature, the achievements of art, the imaginations of poetry, the incidents of history, the ways of mankind, past and present, and their prospects in the future"—all the aspects of *culture*. (One thinks of Giannozzo Manetti, in his treatise *On Human Worth and Excellence*: "What pleasure comes from our faculties of appraisal, memory and understanding!") Happiness is still the good to be sought, but from now on, Mill knew that some forms of happiness were more meaningful than others. One such form is that feeling of being free, "alive," and "a human being," which he would write about in *The Subjection of Women*. Strict utilitarianism cannot easily accommodate this: instead of countable happiness units, we are taken back to qualities that are incalculable and immeasurable. But what Mill's new approach loses in rigor, it gains in subtlety. His version is more *human* than Bentham's.

As well as improving utilitarianism, Mill's human element improves liberalism. It distinguishes it, for example, from the travesty now described as "neoliberalism," which allows the rich to pursue profit without regulation while the rest of the population is left to deal with the consequences of such ravaging of society. For Mill, as for Humboldt, this is not what freedom means. A truly liberal society both values and enables deeper fulfillments: the pursuit of meaning and beauty, the diversity of cultural and personal experiences, the excitement of intellectual discovery, and the pleasures of love and companionship.

Mill always said that Harriet contributed much of the thinking that went into *On Liberty*, as well as into the much later *Subjection of Women*, although he did not go so far as to put her name on the title page of either work. Had he done so, he would have had to do it posthumously, since she

MILL'S LOGIC; OR, FRANCHISE FOR FEMALES.

"PRAY CLEAR THE WAY, THERE, FOR THESE—A—PERSONS."

did not live to see the publication of either. She died in 1858 of a respiratory disease that was probably tuberculosis, while they were in Avignon on their way farther south in search of sunshine and healthier air. In his grief, having buried her there, Mill even bought a house nearby, so that he and her daughter (by Taylor) could remain in the area. He wrote an inscription for her tomb. Full of praise for her achievements, it includes the line "Were there but a few hearts and intellects like hers, this earth would already become the hoped-for heaven." He does not mention any other kind of heaven: her afterlife, as with that of other humanists, was to exist solely in human memory, through the effects of her deeds and writings.

Mill continued his work in politics and philosophy, and put his feminist ideas into practice in 1865 by running for the British parliament, partly on a platform of extending the vote to women. He won the seat, but when he proposed a women's suffrage amendment to an electoral reform bill of 1867 (he suggested changing the word "man" to "person"), it failed. The parliamentary debate around it was a step forward, however, and he came to look back on this as his most important achievement in this role. Five years later, in 1873, he died, and was laid to rest with Harriet in the Avignon grave.

The ideas of Humboldt and the Mills remain at the foundation of liberal society today, not only for their thoughts about freedom but for their humanism: their vision of a society based on human fulfillment, in which each of us can unfold our lives and realize our humanity to the utmost. No society can claim that it has achieved such a thing to perfection—far from it. But arriving at static, ideal perfection never has been a liberal goal, or a utilitarian one. Or, indeed, a humanistic one. The goal in all three cases is to create just a little more of the good stuff in life, and less of the bad stuff.

Also inspired by Wilhelm von Humboldt was another Englishman, Matthew Arnold. A poet, a critic, and a witty and controversial essayist, he was also a professional educator who spent thirty-five years inspecting schools around the country, as well as writing reports on the systems of other countries—all in the attempt to improve the level of human unfolding.

There was certainly a lot of room for such improvement. Schools for the poor in Britain were of variable quality. Arnold argued for bringing them all to a consistent standard, and raising that standard several notches, mainly by introducing better cultural materials into classrooms. You can tell he has been reading Humboldt when he writes, in his 1869 study *Culture and Anarchy*, that the goal of such reforms is to make it possible for us to develop "all sides of our humanity." Also Humboldtian is that he takes this to mean *all* levels of society developing their humanity together. No one should be left behind: we are "all members of one great whole, and the sympathy which is in human nature will not allow one member to be indifferent to the rest, or to have a perfect welfare independent of the rest." Instead of being content to develop alone, the individual should be "continually doing all he can to enlarge and increase the volume of the human stream sweeping thitherward." Arnold has me at "thitherward." I've long thought the family of terms including *thither* and *thence* ("to there" and "from there") should be brought back into usage, and here he is doing something even better.

Matthew Arnold had grown up in an educational environment, as his father was Dr. Thomas Arnold, the vigorous and very Christian headmaster of Rugby School. Matthew went on to study at Oxford, and may have developed doubts about religion while there; the theme continued to trouble him, and often crops up in his poems. (We will return to that point in the next chapter). He married a devout woman, Frances Lucy Wightman, known as "Flu." Unlike the Humboldts and Mills, the Arnolds' marriage followed a more conventional path—but one marked by much sorrow. At the time Matthew was revising *Culture and Anarchy* from a lecture into a book, they were in mourning for two children lost within a single year, most recently their oldest son, Tommy, who died after a fall from his pony.

Yet somehow, *Culture and Anarchy* came out sparkling with wit and playfulness, as well as advancing serious arguments. Arnold's overall point is that anarchy, which he deplores, can be warded off by means of culture, which he admires. But much happens along the way. He surprises and amuses the reader with his turns of phrase; he knows how to make the humanistic heart swell with enthusiasm at regular intervals. He can charm you into assent even when making somewhat absurd or ill-supported claims. At times, you can only look on perplexed as he rides some idiosyncratic hobbyhorse off into the distance for a page or two; eventually he trots back. Above all, he shows an almost willful tendency to confuse people by using words to mean things they normally don't mean. Thus, he borrows the term "Hebraism" from the German Jewish poet Heinrich Heine, but mostly uses it to denote Christian Puritanism. When he speaks of the "Barbarian" social class, a careless reader may think he is talking dismissively of the lower orders, but no; he uses it for the aristocracy. (The working class is "the Populace," and the middle classes are "Philistines.")

Also misleading are two key phrases that he repeats often in the book. One is the statement that "culture" can be defined as "the best which has been thought and said in the world." The other is also a definition of culture, this time as whatever brings "sweetness and light."

The first of these, "the best," sounds elitist, implying high things accessible only through rarefied tastes and an exclusive education. But Arnold is emphatic in rejecting the tendency of the middle and upper classes to feel that all culture somehow belongs to them by birthright, whether or not they ever touch a book or look at a work of art. For him, real culture is accessible to all, and it comes from an "eagerness about the things of the mind." It means curiosity and the questioning of received ideas; it means "turning a stream of fresh and free thought upon our stock notions and habits, which we now follow staunchly but mechanically." This is the exhilarating sense of *expanding* into the human world that Humboldt described in his letters. It is also the widening of life that Mill believed came from encountering diverse life experiences. You can be cultured even if you only read a newspaper, said Arnold, so long as you read it with a free, fresh, and critical mind.

Developing such a mind is difficult, however, if you have not had sufficient exposure to high-quality material, which is why education is important. And it should be the right kind of education. Even the poorest members of society should have access to good, original works of art and literature, not the dumbed-down pabulum that is often given to them in the belief that pre-chewed and undemanding things are all they can handle. For Arnold, there is a challenge for the educator here: to find ways of presenting the best culture in its original richness, while *also* making it accessible. What must be done with culture is "to humanise it, to make it efficient outside the clique of the cultivated and learned"—and still to keep it "the *best* knowledge and thought of the time."

The other phrase, "sweetness and light," is even worse in its suggestion of fairy-like sugary fluffiness. In fact, it comes from a scene in Jonathan Swift's "Battle of the Books," itself drawn from sources in the Latin poetry of Horace. In Swift's satire, a spider and a bee have an animated

discussion about which of
them is better. I am, says
the spider, because I am
an original creator. I build
from my own silk, need-
ing nothing else. *I* am,
says the bee. You may be
more original, but all you
can create is cobwebs and
venom. Instead, although
I collect my pollen from
flowers, I use it to produce
honey (sweetness) and wax
for candles (light). For Arnold, too, culture feeds on
many secondhand experi-

SWEETNESS AND LIGHT.

ences but turns them into something fresh and illuminating. There is
nothing fey about the "light" he means; it is more like the intellectual
light that the Petrarchan humanists felt they were liberating from the
monastic cells—or perhaps the Enlighteners' light of reason.

Culture and Anarchy is a book from which you can read different
messages, depending on your inclinations. Conservatives often took it to
heart because they shared Arnold's horror of "anarchy," specifically the
public disorder and street demonstrations that were a feature of British
life at the time of publication. Privileged himself, Arnold could see no
call for people to behave in such an uncouth and unharmonious way
when they could be reading Horace instead. Yet some of what he says is
remarkably forward-looking: he is against exclusivity, and open-minded
in his support of critical and curious thinking. He also describes himself
as a liberal. At the heart of *Culture and Anarchy* are humanist ideas of an
enduring vintage: that our shared humanity connects us all, and that no
one has a right to condescend to others or dismiss them as unimportant.

Arnoldian thinking does have a certain air of earnestness, which was carried forth during its long afterlife of influence in Britain and elsewhere. It was a force behind the foundation, in the twentieth century, of the British Broadcasting Corporation, which aimed at enlightening and informing as well as entertaining the masses. It lay at the center of countless institutions of adult education founded earlier in that century, such as the Workers' Educational Association, established in 1903.

It also had an impact on the publishing industry, which had a very Arnoldian phase in America and Britain alike. Sets of "Great Books" could be good earners for publishers, since Shakespeare and Milton required no royalty payments. Even translations could work well, despite the need for translators. One early series, Bohn's Standard Library, published many Greek and Roman classics in English, although it did frustrate readers by leaving any lines referring to sex in their original languages.

Then came such outstanding productions as Dr. Eliot's Five-Foot Shelf of Books, the name bestowed on the fifty-one-volume set of literature edited in 1909 by Charles W. Eliot, the president of Harvard University. In Britain there was the Everyman's Library, founded in 1906 by J. M. Dent, the working-class son of a housepainter. Unfortunately, Dent's own habit of shouting "You donkey!" at members of his staff on a regular basis suggests that he was not a fan of every man or woman himself. Those employees were, in fact, the secret of the publisher's success, especially the series editor Ernest Rhys, a coal-mining engineer who had run reading groups for miners before shifting to the book world. He gave the series its ethos: the books must be cheap yet designed to the highest standards. Each sported an attractive woodcut title page and the dolphin-and-anchor printer's device of Aldus Manutius—a tribute to that pioneer of clear, well-printed, portable books.

To help readers find their way around such abundance, lists of Arnoldian "bests" began to appear, such as the "Best Hundred Books," chosen in 1886 by the director of the Working Men's College, Sir John

Lubbock. Besides the usual Eurocentric choices, he recommended such works as Kongzi's *Analects* and potted versions of the *Mahābhārata* and the *Rāmāyana*. He did admit that he had not personally enjoyed everything on the list: "As regards the Apostolic Fathers, I cannot say that I found their writings either very interesting or instructive, but they are also very short."

The list included other ideas, added by well-known figures whom Lubbock approached for suggestions. John Ruskin said he wanted to see more books on natural history: "I chanced at breakfast the other day, to wish I knew something of the biography of a shrimp." Henry Morton Stanley, the adventurer who had gone to Africa to retrieve David Livingstone, told a swashbuckling story about doing that journey accompanied by Darwin, Herodotus, the Quran, the Talmud, *The Thousand and One Nights*, Homer, and much else. But as his porters left him or fell ill, he had to throw books away, until, he said, "I possessed only the Bible, Shakespeare, Carlyle's 'Sartor Resartus,' Norie's Navigation, and Nautical Almanac for 1877. Poor Shakespeare was afterwards burned by demand of the foolish people of Zinga."

Working-class people themselves reflected on Arnold's belief in fulfillment through reading and culture, and they diverged in their responses. Some feared that—as the radical author and former cotton-mill worker Ethel Carnie put it in a letter to the *Cotton Factory Times* in 1914—too much culture would "chloroform" working people, distracting them from the task of agitating to bring about real changes to their lives. For such readers, working-class people would do better to read Karl Marx, not Kongzi or shrimp biographies, and to turn to revolutionary political action to change their living conditions.

But others did not see any contradiction: they argued that reading and studying were the best way of opening one's eyes to the exploitation going on in society and equipping oneself to fight against it—thus, not being chloroformed into sleep, but emerging into wakefulness. George W.

Norris, a post office worker and union official who spent twenty-two years taking Workers' Educational Association courses, looked back on the effect they had had on him, and wrote: "Training in the art of thinking has equipped me to see through the shams and humbug that lurk behind the sensational headlines of the modern newspapers, the oratorical outpourings of insincere party politicians and dictators, and the doctrinaire ideologies that stalk the world sowing hatred."

And there was another factor involved. Studying, reading, looking at art, exercising one's critical faculties: all these things could generate *pleasure*.

Humanists had always emphasized the hedonistic aspect of cultural life. Manetti had written of the enjoyment that came from thinking and reasoning. Cicero had argued for giving Roman citizenship to the poet Archias because of the pleasure as well as moral improvement he gave Romans. All three of our humanists in this chapter were in agreement that pursuing culture and developing one's humanity to the utmost were deeply satisfying things to do. For Arnold, it brought life a taste of honey. In Mill's case, personal experience of "the imaginations of poetry" and the study of "the ways of mankind" had given him back his ability to feel anything at all. Humboldt was the most blissed-out of the three, writing in a letter: "An important new book, a new theory, a new language appears to me as something that I have torn out of death's darkness, makes me feel inexpressibly joyous."

Inexpressible joy! To appreciate the difference between this sensibility and some of the narrow notions of culture that have held sway among duller pedagogues, it suffices to look at an ideology that briefly flourished in some American universities in the early twentieth century, known as "the New Humanism."

That name for it came later, but the ideology was mostly the invention of Irving Babbitt, another Harvard scholar, though of a very different mentality from that of its president Charles Eliot. Babbitt argued for moral training based entirely on a monocultural canon: mainly the literature of the ancient Greeks, with perhaps a few Romans. Any other cultural sources were of no interest, and there was to be no talk of freedom in education. He began his polemical career with a published attack on Eliot's educational philosophy; it appeared the year before the arrival of the Five-Foot Shelf. Such outreach projects, for Babbitt, were an abomination. In some ways he agreed with Arnold's vision, but emphatically not in others: he had no wish to sweep the whole of humanity thitherward. For him, it did not matter whitherward the general public went. The humanist's job was only to train an elite, who should be encouraged to have a "selective" and disciplined sympathy for others, tempered by judgment—not an empathetic free-for-all. We are *not* all connected by our humanity. Of Terence's line "I consider nothing human alien to me," Babbitt wrote that it was a mistake: it fails to be sufficiently selective. That line, for him, was responsible for the excess of weak-minded, wishy-washy do-goodery he saw everywhere around him in society. For him, and for the New Humanists who followed, the "best" was something to be shored up with ramparts and defended against outsiders.

Such ways of talking lose sight of everything that makes cultural life worthwhile for a genuine humanist: the ability to connect to others' experiences, the free pursuit of curiosity, the deepening of appreciation. In particular, it loses joy, replacing it with compulsion—or a kind of *accidia*, if you will. When the novelist Sinclair Lewis (whose choice of the name *Babbitt* for one of his novels and its protagonist was surely a piece of deliberate mischief) won the Nobel Prize in 1930, he scolded the New Humanists in his acceptance speech. "In the new and vital and experimental land of America," he said, "one would expect the teachers of literature to be less monastic, more human, than in the traditional shadows of old Europe." Instead, what do we find? The old dryness and negativity.

Much later, Edward Said would observe in the context of another culture war that such a "sour pursing of the lips," such a "withdrawal and exclusion," and such disconnection of humanities from any concern with the "humane" produced a joylessness that no humanist such as Erasmus or Montaigne would recognize. Nor would a Humboldt, a Mill, or an Arnold, he might have added. Instead, as Montaigne wrote, speaking of the schools of his time:

> How much more fittingly would their classes be strewn with flow-
> ers and leaves than with bloody stumps of birch rods! I would have
> portraits there of Joy and Gladness, and Flora and the Graces, as
> the philosopher Speusippus had in his school. Where their profit
> is, let their frolic be also.

This may seem a long-ago quarrel, and the New Humanists are mostly forgotten. Yet they have contributed to leaving a bad odor hovering around humanism, in some quarters. For some of those who now seek a diverse and more generous approach to culture, the very word *humanism* suggests a narrow elitism. Thus, if one ever sees humanism in academic life today being dismissed as conservative and opposed to the values of diversity and inclusion, some of the blame, at least, must go to the lack of *humanitas* in the New Humanists.

In fact, even as Irving Babbitt and his supporters were writing their polemics, they had lost their case. An explosion in access to reading, writing, and cultural life was already under way around the world. The cheap and popular books, the new circulating libraries that lent them to all and sundry, the courses accessible to anyone who wished to sign up: these were not going away.

Also, those lending libraries, cheap books, and courses provided a way for a large number of people to encounter some of the most radical of ideas to emerge in that century. For a few shillings, one could read skeptical investigations of God, works of Marxist economics, and scientific reevaluations of the origins of the Earth or of the living species to be found on it. You could read about *human* origins. All these fresh departures proceeded from what Arnold called "turning a stream of fresh and free thought upon our stock notions and habits." And they, in turn, would take humanism itself down a new path.

9.

Some Dream-Country

Mostly 1859–1910

Humanism turns scientific—Charles Darwin and Thomas Henry Huxley—on being an agnostic—Leslie Stephen's five minutes in the Alps—"vicars with problems, vicars with doubts"—Mary Ward's Robert Elsmere—*some strange answers to the problem of humanity—Ernest Renan and Auguste Comte— a transformative period.*

Some of the new discoveries reaching the public in the era of Mill and Arnold carried such major implications for how we think about humanity that religious authorities had a hard time keeping up. First the geologists came for them, brandishing evidence that the Earth was both older than the Bible implied and in a state of constant movement and transition that did not fit with the one-off Creation story. Then the paleontologists came for them, with their fossils of vanished or altered species. Even the speleologists came for them, finding remains of an extinct hominid type in Neander Valley caves in Germany.

Then it was the turn of Charles Darwin, with his 1859 book *On the Origin of Species by Means of Natural Selection*. His theory of the variety of life was elegant: as members of a species reproduce themselves over an immense period of time, random variations occur, generating a bigger beak, a longer toe, or some new, fluffy ear hair. These can be passed on to offspring. If the variation works well in their environment, those individuals thrive and go on to produce more such offspring. If it does not work, they often die without issue. This is how, as he concluded the book, "from so simple a beginning endless forms most beautiful and most wonderful have been, and are being, evolved." It is a vision of majesty, but also of horror, since Darwin admits that it all depends on cycles of failure and suffering. "Thus, from the war of nature, from famine and death, the most exalted object which we are capable of conceiving, namely, the production of the higher animals, directly follows." Not only does this tell us that life comes from death but also that *we* might be those "higher animals," and thus results of such a process, too. At this stage, he says nothing more overt about us than that. He would not do so until 1871, with *The Descent of Man, and Selection in Relation to Sex*, and that was amid much distracting material about the last-named topic. It could have been even more distracting: Darwin wanted to use the more economical "sexual selection" in the title but was stopped by the publisher, who thought "sexual" sounded more shocking than "sex." Still, even at the first appearance of the *Origin*, the implications for humanity were not hard to see.

The *Origin* found a wide readership, in Britain especially because it was made a featured title at Mudie's, one of the most important of the new circulating libraries. John Stuart Mill, whose *On Liberty* appeared in the same year, read it with interest. So did George Eliot: she and her partner, George Henry Lewes, were intrigued by Darwin not least because they were keen natural historians and had recently spent the summer of 1856 exploring seaside areas and writing about rock pools and fossils. A different kind of reader was Karl Marx, who thought he could see connections between Darwin's ideas and his own theory of the struggle between social classes. "Although developed in the crude English fashion," he commented to Friedrich Engels, "this is the book which in the field of natural history, provides the basis for our views." Later, having published *Das Kapital*, he sent Darwin a copy, which then remained with uncut pages on the naturalist's shelf, although he did write Marx a warm thank-you letter.

Another reader saw immediately that the *Origin* was going to originate a fight: Thomas Henry Huxley. As a zoologist, an educator, and an eloquent essayist and polemicist, he would do more than anyone else in that period to promote Darwinism, and, in the process, to bring together two great nineteenth-century currents: the boom in education and free-thinking, and the turn toward science-based ways of thinking about ourselves. He thus inaugurated a new type: the scientific humanist.

In this chapter, we shall see what came out of that merging of humanistic currents and what effects it had on people, especially in Britain. It brought responses from vicars and poets, from novelists and naturalists, from those who wanted to make humanity divine, and from those who, conversely, wanted to make divinity more human. We will meet a few of all these types. But first: Huxley and the fight. Fortunately for the Darwinist theory, fighting was exactly what Huxley was good at—far more so than Darwin himself, who hated such things.

Huxley's friendship with Darwin had started a little earlier, when Darwin invited him to Down House, his home in Kent, to see his collection of sea squirts.

Huxley loved sea squirts. A naturalist who had originally trained as a physician, he had just returned to Britain after a four-year voyage around the Pacific in the official post of ship's doctor. Having devoted his time on the voyage to collecting marine and other species, he had now been taken on to produce the British Museum's catalog of its sea squirt specimens. So he eagerly accepted Darwin's invitation, and enjoyed his tour of the house's grounds, with their plantings and greenhouses, their exotic pigeon breeds, and their many experiments and collections in constant expansion. Darwin seemed to be a harmless, diligent enthusiast. Huxley, like almost everyone else, had no idea that he was using all this as material for a dramatic new theory of life.

When the book was unveiled and Huxley realized what Darwin had been up to all that time, he was keen to help. Unlike the gentlemanly Darwin, Huxley was of more socially modest origins, and *everything* in his career had been a fight for him. First, he reviewed the book, raising the drama level to the maximum with remarks such as: "Extinguished theologians lie about the cradle of every science as the strangled snakes beside that of Hercules." Then he gave lectures, making use of newsworthy props: at the Royal Institution, to show the effects of selection processes in breeding, he released a range of live pigeons from a basket before the audience's eyes, like a magician in a stage show.

Next came the 1860 meeting of the British Association for the Advancement of Science, at the beautiful new Museum of Natural History in Oxford. Darwin did not attend: he made his excuses after an attack of a recurring stomach ailment, thus saving himself from having to confront anyone. Representatives arrived from the worlds of religion, culture, and science, all with their witty sallies at the ready. Robert FitzRoy, former captain on Darwin's *Beagle* voyage, was there; he had written to Darwin saying, "My dear old friend, I, at least, *cannot* find anything 'ennobling' in the thought of being a descendant of even the *most* ancient *Ape*." A similar remark was made at the meeting itself by Samuel Wilberforce, bishop of Oxford, a bluff, beefy man so renowned for his quips that people often started laughing even before he opened his mouth. That, presumably, was what they did when he stood up ready to present his question to Huxley: Is it through your grandfather or your grandmother that you claim simian heritage?

Huxley replied neatly that he would rather have an ape for an ancestor than a person who used his merit and influence only to introduce ridicule into a scientific discussion. At least, that was Huxley's account of it—and he described the room as erupting into laughter. As usual with

HUXLEY ON MOUNTIN' KIDS.

"Having anatomically gauged the capabilities of the knowledge-box (*genus homo*), he believes an infant could learn to spell 'pap' fluently, and at the age of seven embark in surgery, music, and the study of natural phenomena, including, of course, itself." (*See Article.*)

much-told tales, versions differed. The botanist Joseph Dalton Hooker thought *he* was the one who had "smashed" Wilberforce with a smart response, while Wilberforce himself left the meeting elated, apparently feeling he had come out on top. Darwin was grateful to Huxley for all this partisanship, but also nervous. "For heaven's sake don't write an anti-Darwinian article," he said. "You would do it so confoundedly well."

Huxley himself became ever more famous, thanks to such performances. He went on to write successful popularizations of Darwinian theory, notably his *Evidence as to Man's Place in Nature* of 1863, with a frontispiece showing a series of skeletons of apes marching along in formation and culminating in a human figure.

Less well remembered now is his role as an all-round public intellectual and a communicator of humanistic as well as scientific ideas. He took a great interest in education. Like Arnold, he was adamant that all social classes should have access to good-quality material; like Humboldt, he believed that learning should continue throughout life. In accordance with these ideas, he helped found the South London Working Men's College in 1868—and it would be to workers' educational institutions like this, not to elite or professional audiences, that he delivered some of his own most important lectures.

In one talk to the South London Working Men's College that same year, "A Liberal Education and Where to Find It," he presented his views on education itself. First, he criticized the way schools currently seemed to feel they had done their job if they imparted a few simple moral precepts, along with Middle Eastern history and geography, because the latter related to the Bible. (In *Bleak House*, Charles Dickens also wrote ironically of how the education of the poor seemed to consist mainly of a course in the history of the ancient Amorites and Hittites.) For Huxley, this did not even make a good grounding for the humanities, never mind the rest of human knowledge. It was not that he disliked such studies: he said that he loved learning about ancient cultures himself, because it formed part of the whole story of studying the traces of the human past. And elsewhere he cited Terence: nothing human could ever be alien to him—or uninteresting.

It was just that he had a wider perspective on human studies. He agreed with Arnold and Humboldt that the purpose of education was to produce well-rounded human beings with a rich mental life and an insightful understanding of the world. He did not agree with them about the humanities being the only place to start. Instead he suggested that a better foundation might lie in studying the sciences. These taught children the basics of the physical world and *also* gave them humanistic skills, in the form of an inquiring attitude. It taught them to observe phenomena closely and to learn actively through experiments, as opposed to taking everything from the authority of ancient texts—or even of teachers. It would therefore also equip them better for understanding those texts and teachers. John Stuart Mill had once said that studying classical literature and dialectics provided a good training in general critical thinking. Huxley, in another lecture, quoted Mill's remarks—but with a difference: he took every mention of "dialectics" and the like, and changed it to "science." The love of free thought and investigation was the same; the means were different.

After an 1880 talk by Huxley, again giving his arguments for starting education with a scientific foundation, Matthew Arnold came back with the essay "Literature and Science." Science was indeed important, he said, but the humanities were even more so, not least because they held the key to making human *sense* out of science's discoveries. For example, if we hear science telling us that our ancestors resembled monkeys, we will leap (sorry) to conclusions about ourselves and our human nature. If we are not guided in more constructive directions, those conclusions might be dangerous and negative. For example, we might think: Well, we are only animals anyway—we cannot expect high moral standards of ourselves. Instead, wrote Arnold, a good education founded on ethics and the humanities helps us to deal more subtly with the human and ethical world. It also provides us with high standards to live up to.

It is a good argument, in fact. Arnold is not anti-science; he does not say that the scientific way of thinking about ourselves is wrong. He only says that we need a good armory of cultural understanding to respond to it in the best way. Few would disagree with him.

But Huxley's argument is good, too. For him, we will do a better job of coming up with such moral and human responses if we also start with a good grounding in science itself, so that we know what we are talking about. A little scientific training protects us against a tendency to go storming off into foolish interpretations based on misunderstandings of the facts, or of how matters of evidence or experiment work. I find this very convincing, having written a lot of this book during a global pandemic characterized by waves of misinformation and superstition, which had damaging effects on such lifesaving factors as the acceptance of vaccines. Better education in science could have helped flatten those waves. But an Arnoldian could argue that the COVID-19 pandemic has equally shown the importance of such classically humanistic matters as good government and moral engagement with others. In truth, we need both.

The Arnold and Huxley debate, playing out between two cultured and eloquent writers, each imbued (if in slightly different ways) with the spirit of their time, captures a moment when the atmosphere was changing in humanistic thought. From now on, both "humanities-humanism" and the meliorist humanism of the Enlightenment would find themselves in the company of the new arrival, scientific humanism. The principles of the latter—an interest in modern scientific methods and reasoning, along with a naturalistic interpretation of how humans fit into the picture—would remain a part of the larger humanist worldview into our own time.

Humanities-based, ethical forms of humanism remind us that we are spiritual, cultured, and moral beings: we are formed by our human environment as well as by our physical nature. Scientific humanism reminds us that we are animals, too, and that we live in a constant process of transition on a changing Earth, in a very large universe. If everything is in a good balance, these visions of ourselves do not work at cross-purposes; they inform and enhance one another.

In the closing passage of the *Origin*, Darwin had marveled at the way simple natural processes could produce extraordinary and beautiful results. But he also realized that his theory of natural selection and survival did not provide an obvious basis for human morality.

It provided no *direct* basis, that is, but in *The Descent of Man* he did come up with a possible, indirect explanation for how morality entered our human world. His theory owed a lot to humanists of the Enlightenment era, such as David Hume, because he thought—as they did—that morality probably emerged from our tendencies to fellow feeling and "sympathy." These in turn emerged from our nature as group animals. Like all social species, early humans had to negotiate the interpersonal challenges of the group; this has made us sensitive to others' responses. When they treat us positively, we feel good. Other animals share such sensitivity, but in our case, we also have language, so we can go further in expressing feelings in terms of praise or blame. Our moral world deepens, because we can also look back on past situations to make comparisons between the things we have done before and the responses they evoked. Out of this, general ethical opinions begin to form, and these are shared with others. Thus, emerging from a combination of "habit, example, instruction, and reflection," a moral system comes into being.

Darwin's explanation for morality is a thoroughly humanistic one: it emerges from social feelings and behavior, and need not rely on anything coming from God. If anything, he sees the process as operating in the reverse direction; he speculates that, at some later stage of cultural development, the general moral gaze of others becomes identified with an imagined figure: that of "an all-seeing Deity."

Darwin took humanistic morality as a guide in his own life, too. He had lost his Christian belief as a young man, not least because he could not bear the thought of there being a Hell—that most unempathetic of ideas. Writing private notes, he reflected that he had always felt his deepest satisfactions when he had helped others, and then when they had thought well of him because of it—especially if they were people to whom he was close. For him, these feelings amply compensated for the lost idea of God. He did not go so far as to call himself an atheist, even in private notes, but he did call himself an *agnostic*.

The person who did the most to popularize this term was, again, T. H. Huxley. He wrote an essay headed simply "Agnosticism" in 1889, and there explained that he had arrived at this label after going through other possible ways of describing himself. Was he, perhaps, "an atheist, a theist, or a pantheist; a materialist or an idealist; a Christian or a freethinker"? None of these felt right, although the last one was not bad. The rest all seemed to name some definite belief in how the world was, but he had no such belief. He settled on "agnostic," because it was the opposite of a "gnostic"—that is, someone who claims *gnosis*, or knowledge.

Actually, agnosticism is more of a definite and positive position than Huxley makes it sound. His contemporary Richard Bithell stressed in a book titled *The Creed of a Modern Agnostic* that it did not mean floating off into a mystical cloud of unknowing. For him, agnostics do think that humans can have definite moral principles. They also believe that they can learn things about the world, by trusting the scientific method of advancing hypotheses and testing them against evidence. It is just that they retain more modesty than usual about the results. More recently, another agnostic, the philosopher and broadcaster Bryan Magee, wrote in his short final testament, *Ultimate Questions*, that the word meant to him "an openness to the fact that we do not know, followed by intellectually honest enquiry in full receptivity of mind."

Another noted agnostic of the nineteenth century, Sir Leslie Stephen, was more flippant about his reasons for choosing the term: he said he preferred *agnostic* because *atheist* still savored too much of "the stake in this world and hell-fire in the next." But agnostics could carry a whiff of that destination as well: the educational reformer Frederick James Gould recalled once chatting about the afterlife with an amiable Salvation Army officer over tea and sandwiches: "I asked him what became of sincere Agnostics. He pointed dramatically to the floor, and calmly munched bread-and-butter and water-cress."

Sir Leslie Stephen was known as the compiler of the very Victorian *Dictionary of National Biography*; he would also later be remembered as the father of the resolutely non-Victorian experimental novelist Virginia Woolf. He also found time to be a noted mountaineer. One of his Alpine experiences became the basis for an entertaining essay

of 1872, "A Bad Five Minutes in the Alps." It sums up his mental tour of possible beliefs, and the conclusions he reached about them, all while telling a literally cliff-hanging story.

One Sunday, he says, while staying in one of the mountain resorts there, he went out for a bracing pre-lunch walk. It was windy, and then it started to rain. Trying to return, Stephen took what he thought would be a short-cut. At one point on it, the track seemed to disappear on a stretch of rock face above a torrential stream, before resuming visibly on the other side. He decided to risk it and started scrambling across. At first it was easy, but as he took a large step and reached for an outcrop above him to steady himself, he slipped. As he slid down toward the stream far below, he had time for just one thought, and it was, "At last!" He had feared and wondered about death for so long; now it was upon him.

But he flung out a hand just in time and managed to grab the ledge his feet had been on, stopping his fall. Then he managed to get the tip of his right foot onto another jutting rock, for more support, but he could neither pull nor push himself any farther up. He hung there, by a hand and a foot—and they were already beginning to tire. It seemed that he would have about twenty minutes before his strength gave way. There was no point in shouting, as no one would hear, and it would weaken him faster. He imagined his fellow guests entering the dining room, sitting down and joking about his absence. By the time anyone became worried enough to come look for him, he would be rolling down the stream as "a ghastly mass."

Since he appeared to be doomed, Stephen applied himself to seeking a suitable state of mind for dying in. But none of what he had been taught about this solemn process seemed to work. His mind wandered; mainly he just felt annoyed at himself for making such a mistake. He reminded himself that he had about a quarter of an hour to answer the questions of life: What is the universe? What part should we play in it?

All the religions and denominations he had come across—Protestantism, Catholicism, Pantheism—pointed in different directions. He ran through them in his mind, one by one, and had a terrible thought: what if they were *all* true and he was supposed to believe in all of them at once, but had accidentally failed to believe in one single clause in, say, the Athanasian Creed? God would greet him by saying: Sorry, you have been good and kind, but you forgot that clause and must now go to Hell.

Fortunately, Stephen reflected, such uncompromising rules were now out of fashion, like other old ideas, such as the view that human life was vile and despicable. But too much Panglossian positivity seemed wrong, too. Did it even matter? Was Leslie Stephen a mere grain of dust in the universe, about to be thrown aside with indifference? He knew that the atoms of his flesh would be dispersed through the stream and would recombine to form other things: the Epicurean view. But it was hard to feel much personal involvement in this. Nor could he find comfort in the thought that a general shared "humanity," of which he had been a part, would go on without him. Still, he craved "something like a blessing to soothe the parting moment—some sense of sanctification."

Thinking this, he found a memory arising of a time when he was taking part in a boat race on the Thames, and his boat was well behind the others. As they neared the finish line, it was obvious that he could not win. Yet he continued to row as hard as ever, out of an obscure sense that it was his "duty" to try his very best. Now, hanging on the rock, he had the same feeling. The game was up, yet he must cling on until the last moment, resisting. This gave him a moral foundation of sorts: one that required no God, nor even any sense of meaning in the universe. It was his own human need to do his duty.

The Victorians had a great feeling for "duty" as something almost transcendental. George Eliot held it in high regard, too: one day, out strolling with a companion, she remarked that out of the three words "God, Immortality, Duty," she considered the first inconceivable and the second unbelievable, but the third was "peremptory and absolute." Darwin also wrote of the "deep feeling of right or duty" as the "most noble of all the attributes of man" (and, as with moral attributes in general, he speculated about its origins in the social group). Leslie Stephen himself seems to have been thinking of something similar when he noted, some years earlier and à propos his loss of faith: "I now believe in nothing, but I do not the less believe in morality." He added, "I mean to live and die like a gentleman if possible."

Today, many of us feel strongly about duty, but it is more likely to be in the context of a specific situation, perhaps in relation to the needs of family or work. To the Victorians, it was almost an entity in itself. Yet it was essentially humanistic: it needed no God to guarantee it but emerged from our own moral nature. It was a human-centered wish to do the right thing, not just by each other, but by our own lives—our own humanity.

The ending to the Alpine story (as one might guess from the author's being alive to tell it) was a happy one. Having had his epiphany about duty, Stephen noticed that he might just be able to reach for another handhold if he lunged for it. It would mean taking a swing and abandoning his existing handhold. Still, he had nothing to lose. He reached—missed—and began sliding downward. But almost immediately, he came to a halt. It turned out that another ledge had been there all the time, just below him; it supported him more firmly, and he could step back onto the path again from there. Looking at his watch, he saw that the whole drama had taken five minutes—a bad five minutes in the Alps—and that he would be in time for lunch.

At the end of the story, Leslie Stephen hints that it was just that: a story. His account may also have inspired a more overtly fictional scene:

an incident in a novel by Thomas Hardy. In *A Pair of Blue Eyes*, which began to appear in serial form that year, 1872, Hardy has his character Henry Knight go out for a walk on a coastal clifftop with the young woman he fancies, Elfride Swancourt. Henry misses his footing and slips off the edge, but catches himself on an outcrop, where he remains hanging over the beach. Elfride leaves—to get help, it seems, which is likely to mean a long wait as there is no one else anywhere nearby. Dangling there, his grip gradually loosening, Henry notices a fossil of a trilobite, embedded in the rock just before his eyes. Here we both are, he thinks, separated by millions of years, yet brought close in this moment of death.

In fact, Elfride reappears almost immediately. Instead of going for help, she has merely gone behind a bush to remove her long knickers. She knots them into a rope, throws the end down, and rescues him very efficiently, thus proving that underwear is not just for making manuscripts.

Hardy was a poet as well as a novelist, and several of his poems touch on the gradual withdrawal of God from the human mental landscape. He wrote some verses that are filled with yearning for the old certainties—the cozy village church, the hymns—as well as other poems that suggest a great liberation. "God's Funeral" and "A Plaint to Man" show God fading away, like the picture cast by a magic-lantern slide when the light behind it is turned down. Of course, the light was of human origin all along. As he goes, God tells Man to seek strength and consolation in human fellowship instead:

> In brotherhood bonded close and graced
> With loving-kindness fully blown,
> And visioned help unsought, unknown.

Other poets also captured this sense of something fading from view, including Matthew Arnold. In his poem "Dover Beach," started around 1851 and published in 1867, the poet looks out of a window onto a beach at night. He hears the pebbles rolling as the tide goes out, and imagines it as a Sea of Faith, similarly receding and leaving a conflict-ridden world lacking sense or meaning: "And we are here as on a darkling plain / Swept with confused alarms of struggle and flight, / Where ignorant armies clash by night." If there is some faint hope, he concludes, it can be found only in our fidelity to one another. (Apparently, he was inspired by the view from the bedroom window on his seaside honeymoon, which makes you wonder whether that was an entirely heartening experience.) Elsewhere, Arnold took a more pragmatic view: in *Culture and Anarchy* he advised sticking with the Church of England faith because it was nicely bland, and also officially established as the national religion, so it could safely be ignored most of the time, leaving one free to think about other things.

Other writers were more earnest and more violent in their imagination. If God was dead, suggested some, then a murder must have taken place. The English poet Algernon Charles Swinburne wrote a "Hymn of Man" in 1869–1870, depicting humans as first making God, then sitting in judgment against him, and finally killing him. This calls to mind a better-known passage by Friedrich Nietzsche, not published until 1882: A madman runs through a marketplace with a lantern, looking for God, and crying, "We are all his murderers. But how did we do this? How were we able to drink up the sea? Who gave us the sponge to wipe away the entire horizon? . . . Is the magnitude of this deed not too great for us? Do we not ourselves have to become gods merely to appear worthy of it?" This is not the kind of murder for which one is condemned to prison or execution; it is the kind for which one is condemned to take over the task formerly belonging to the murderee.

Other nineteenth-century metaphors for describing loss of faith evoked feelings of vertigo or disorientation. The novelist and biographer J. A. Froude described his generation as finding "the lights all drifting, the compasses all awry, and nothing left to steer by except the stars." He had been through a disorienting experience himself: as a young fellow of

Exeter College, Oxford, he had published a novel about the complexities of religious doubt, *The Nemesis of Faith*. A colleague at the college built a bonfire and staged a public book burning; Froude was forced to resign as fellow. The Oxford and Cambridge colleges were, in general, difficult places to come out as a skeptic about religion. Little changed during the nineteenth century. At the beginning of it, Percy Bysshe Shelley had been sent down from University College, Oxford, for coauthoring a tract called *The Necessity of Atheism*; at the end of it, Bertrand Russell would find himself blocked from becoming a fellow at Trinity College, Cambridge, because his atheism was well known. Since some colleges were designed as training institutions for the Anglican clergy, losing your faith would also mean the abandonment of your career. If you admitted to it *after* becoming a clergyman, you lost your livelihood and could even face prosecution. In 1860, six clergymen contributed to a collection of critical reflections on religious matters, *Essays and Reviews*; at the instigation of Bishop Samuel Wilberforce, two were convicted in ecclesiastical court on charges of heresy (although the verdict was later overturned).

Outside that rarefied world, admitting to doubts was likely to cause a traumatic break with family. When the young Robert Louis Stevenson told his father he had lost his religion, his father responded with the terrible words: "You have rendered my whole life a failure." Another writer, Edmund Gosse, took years to extricate himself from the austerities of the Plymouth Brethren, of which his father, Philip Henry Gosse, was a member. In its most extreme phase, Edmund's childhood had been devoid of visitors, or games, or any books apart from the Bible. As he wrote, alluding both to humanistic culture and to companionship: "I had no humanity; I had been carefully shielded from the chance of 'catching' it, as though it were the most dangerous of microbes." He later looked back in sorrow on the affection he and his father could have had without that belief system, especially since they both enjoyed that great pursuit of the time: exploring seaside rock pools and collecting specimens. Indeed, the elder Gosse was far more than an amateur in these activities: he was a renowned naturalist, but he used his books to put forward bizarre explanations of how the biblical Creation story *and* the discoveries of paleontologists and geologists might both be true. His theory was that God had created the world to look ancient even though it wasn't. He was hurt when even devout clergymen failed to find this convincing, or took umbrage at the idea of God as a deliberate deceiver.

In the Church of England, many of these clergymen in fact showed a more open-minded interest in Darwin and other new ideas than one might expect. They were educated men and thoughtful readers of literature of all kinds. Besides, they often had their own butterfly-collecting or rock-pool-dabbling interests. They may well have been the first in line at the bookshop or lending library for Darwin's books.

Still, those books did not make peaceful reading, and the butterfly nets sometimes became entangled on the horns of a dilemma. As Huxley's biographer Adrian Desmond has put it, "Letter after letter dropped through Huxley's mailbox from vicars with problems, vicars with doubts, vicars who held him responsible." Some of them were swept back and forth by changes of heart, like the clergyman father of the family in Rose Macaulay's novel *Told by an Idiot*. The book opens with the mother announcing to her six children: "Well, my dears, I have to tell you something. Poor papa has lost his faith again."

"Oh, I do think papa is too bad," laments one of the daughters. "Mamma, *must* he lose it just this winter—his faith, I mean? Can't he wait till next?"

The family's problem is, of course, that if he admits to loss of religion, he will become unemployed, and they will all suffer. But another daughter is more hopeful: "By next winter he may have found it again."

The nineteenth century was the great era of the long, in-depth, socially responsible novel, and so many such books included these themes of doubt and Darwin-reading that they amounted to an identifiable literary genre. Let us take one example as representative of them all: the 1888 novel *Robert Elsmere*, by Mary Augusta Ward—a prolific author who demurely chose to write under her full married name of Mrs. Humphry Ward. She was actually an Arnold. Matthew Arnold was her uncle, and she also became linked to the Huxley family when her sister married T. H. Huxley's son.

As for being demure, that would not have been the first word to come to mind when you saw her grand, formidable Victorian figure sailing around a corner. On seeing just that, Virginia Woolf (formidable enough herself), once hid behind a nearby post. Part of the reason for her avoidance was that Mary Ward disagreed with her on the subject of women having the vote. Woolf was very pro, whereas Ward opposed it, and was a force in the Women's National Anti-Suffrage League. Yet she campaigned for women's education, cofounding the Association for the Education of Women and giving support for women studying at Oxford. In the Arnoldian spirit, she also believed in better education for the poor; a Mary Ward Centre for adult education can still be found in London.

Ward was by no means irreligious, but she was fascinated by the developmental stages of doubt and by its consequences in people's lives. *Robert Elsmere*—the most durable of her twenty-six novels—concerns the title character, who is a clergyman, and his wife, Catherine, a fervent believer. Their marriage is a happy one, but Robert undergoes a long slow alteration in his faith. Neglecting his sermons, he instead spends time providing medicines for the sick of his parish and trying to improve unhealthy living conditions. Catherine calls this work his "dirt and drains."

He also entertains his flock with stories, retelling the plots of Shakespeare and Dumas for their enjoyment, introducing them to a new experience of literature and allowing them to "live someone else's life" for half an hour. Without yet having become a doubter, he is becoming a humanist. The process continues. Elsmere reads Darwin. He studies history and is troubled by the way Christianity seems to have caused more violence and suffering than it has prevented. He wonders what a Christ who was only human would be like, and imagines "a purely human, explicable, yet always wonderful Christianity. It broke his heart, but the spell of it was like some dream-country wherein we see all the familiar objects of life in new relations and perspectives."

This "purely human" world was the dream-country, or alternative wonderland, into which, like Alice, many thoughtful people were now venturing. The world looked different after reading Darwin or Huxley. Yet everyone's human needs continued to be the same: people still required medicines and drains; they still longed for reassurance and meaning. For those following Robert's path, it began to seem that humanist values or a "human Christ" could provide those things just as well as traditional theology, and perhaps better.

Thus, performing a "catechism of himself," Robert concludes that he believes in Jesus, but only as a wise man and teacher, not as a miracle worker or direct mediator with the Deity. Even God, he feels, should be thought of as a synonym for "the good": the quality that emerges whenever people help their fellows, or sacrifice themselves for others. These thoughts build in him, until he decides: "Every human soul in which the voice of God makes itself felt, enjoys, equally with Jesus of Nazareth, the divine sonship, and *miracles do not happen!*" There. "It was done."

He has to leave the church, but as a replacement he becomes involved with a non-theological Sunday school for working-class boys. He teaches classes demonstrating the marvels of electricity or chemistry, or introducing the children to natural history collections. He gives talks at workingmen's clubs. In short, he becomes very much like T. H. Huxley, or even

Mary Ward herself—except that he goes further and sets up an alternative churchlike organization, based on meliorism and reform of conditions for the poor. Ward here was inspired by the real-life ideas of a social reformer named Thomas Hill Green, called "Grey" in the novel.

Robert Elsmere's conversion (as it were) gives the book its long but clear narrative line. Along the way, other characters are woven in, each showing a different perspective on the same questions. Catherine's sister Rose is a talented musician who chooses, life-affirmingly, *not* to give up her art for the sake of religious self-denial, as Catherine would have preferred her to do. Robert's old Oxford friend Langham, who falls in love with Rose, is a freethinker, too, but he is more disturbed by his doubt than the more robust Elsmere. At the other end of the spectrum entirely is Mr. Newcome, a clergyman of the "Ritualist" tendency, which was obsessed with strict ceremonial practices. Confronted with Elsmere's idea that different beliefs might all be tolerated together, he fulminates: how can we go around idly choosing what to believe, as if it were a game, when all the time we are in desperate danger, pursued by the two "sleuth-hounds" of Sin and Satan? He says, "I see life always as a threadlike path between abysses along which man *creeps* ... with bleeding hands and feet towards one—narrow—solitary outlet." He illustrates the word *creeps* with clawlike hand gestures as he speaks. "What a maimed life!" thinks Elsmere calmly.

His wife, Catherine, is, I think, the most moving of the characters. She is never fanatical in the ugly way of Newcome. She even tries to tolerate Robert's change of views, but she finds it hard for the most loving of reasons: fear of what will happen to him after death. The same concern was felt by Darwin's wife, Emma: Charles had warned her before the marriage that he was not a believer. She thanked him for his honesty but was afraid because it meant she would never see him in the afterlife. The Christianity of a Tertullian or Bernard of Cluny has come a long way: the prospect of one's nearest and dearest going to hell is not so delightful after all.

Catherine Elsmere grieves for her husband's future, and in more immediate terms she also has to cope with his losing his job. Ward conveys these spiritual and practical perils vividly. How can anyone who loves her husband look at him, across the hearthrug, and know with all one's being that he is going to end up in Hell? Yet this was the drama of many Victorian households.

Robert Elsmere is not short, even by the standards of its time, and it met with exasperated reviews from such highly respected critics as William Gladstone, who found it religiously disturbing as well as overdidactic. Henry James compared it to a slow-moving ship with a close-packed cargo—and he should know!

In fact, having approached it with trepidation, I was surprised by how engrossed I became in it. Perhaps it helps if you have a prior interest in that era's crisis of belief and doubt. But I'm not alone. *Robert Elsmere* became a word-of-mouth success on publication, selling around forty thousand copies in Britain and two hundred thousand in America in its first year alone. Some of these were pirated editions—so many of them that the book became a test case for campaigners trying to introduce international copyright protections for authors and publishers. They succeeded, and the protections were won in 1891: a small humanistic victory in itself.

Most interesting, from a humanist point of view, is that Robert does much more than fall into doubt's sea, or lose himself on the darkling plain. He loses one version of himself, but that is not what the story is finally about. It is about finding a positive, humanistic set of values to take its place. For him, those values are worthy of being called a new religion.

Others were in search of a new, humanized religion as well. Some of the results of that quest were distinctly strange.

One approach, if you wanted to redesign Christianity to fit the new ideas of humanity, was to take the existing Jesus story and strip it of everything supernatural, leaving only an inspiring story about a great moral teacher who lived long ago. There were already precedents for this, the most notable operation having been done by the American founding father Thomas Jefferson. In 1819, he literally cut up copies of the New Testament and reassembled selected passages to form a single account of Jesus's life, relieved of elements such as the Virgin Birth, the miracles, and the Resurrection. The remaining text allowed more emphasis to remain on Jesus's moral teachings, especially the Sermon on the Mount. Jefferson called the new text *The Life and Morals of Jesus Extracted Textually from the Gospels in Greek, Latin, French & English.* Once it was published, it became known more handily as the Jefferson Bible. His intention, as he had said in a letter, was to isolate "the most sublime and benevolent code of morals which has ever been offered to man," by removing what he called "amphibologisms," or ambiguous elements, including stories that he suspected had been added by various hands or were generally bogus. In a way, he was working in the tradition of a Valla or an Erasmus: questioning texts and trying to get back to something purer and more beneficial. He just took the idea a good deal further.

Others did not actually slice up pages, but they did consider ways of retaining the Bible's uplifting ideas and stories while liberating it from its supernatural part. One such person was Matthew Arnold, whose long essay *Literature and Dogma* argued for approaching the sacred texts mainly as literature—thus, as purely human sources of cultural sweetness and light. He hoped that this might be a way to lure back some of the people who had drifted away from religion, and stop even more from leaving. But what would they be lured back *to*, without the supernatural material? Merely to the materials of good literature: a fine moral message and a memorable central character.

For some, Jesus was of such mesmerizing interest as a protagonist that this took over even from the moral purpose. Two influential biographies were written of him in the mid-nineteenth century, placing him in his own historical context as well as examining his life and its meaning as myth. The more heavyweight of the two was German historian David

Friedrich Strauss's *Life of Jesus* of 1835 (translated into English by George Eliot). The more readable was by a Frenchman, Ernest Renan: his *Life of Jesus* appeared in 1863.

It was reading Strauss's book that had set Renan on this path: he came across it when he was a young man studying for the priesthood in his native Brittany. The impact was immediate: he decided to leave the seminary. He did remain a biblical scholar and historian, and more of a deist than an atheist—he believed that God had created the world and filled it with "the divine afflatus" before retiring from the scene. Jesus was merely a human being, but no ordinary one. Renan conjures up an extreme, visionary figure who gradually moves further and further from any attachment to the world and toward the drama of a heaven that only he can see. By the end, Jesus is no longer quite of this planet. Renan makes us *feel* why people were so enthralled by him; he uses the skills of a psychological novelist to show Jesus's character as it develops away from normal humanity without ever fully leaving it. Yet he also uses his formidable erudition (and much traveling around the original sites) to keep

Born Feb. 27, 1827   Died Oct. 2, 1892
THE LATE M. ERNEST RENAN

Jesus rooted in his historical and geographical context. He vividly conveyed what it might have been like to grow up in a world so remote from the cultural worlds of Greece or Rome.

The book caused a furor (as Strauss's had), even though Renan claimed he had toned it down before publication, to cause less offense. He fled Paris for Brittany but found his notoriety had preceded him. "I always thought you were reading too hard," said one of his former teachers. Secretly, Renan seems to have quite enjoyed the fuss: a later witness to his lectures observed how his eyes would twinkle in his round face every time he opened his mouth (revealing a set of "very small teeth") to say something more than usually daring. The American free-thinker Robert G. Ingersoll, who knew him and shared his tendency to twinkle, was amused at the way bigots became incensed by Renan's merry and modest demeanor: "Such cheerfulness, such good philosophy, with cap and bells, such banter and blasphemy, such sound and common sense," wrote Ingersoll. "His mental manners were excellent."

Ingersoll himself was of a different school of thought: he did not find Jesus either exciting or morally wise. For him, it was a personal failing in Jesus to have shown so little interest either in understanding the physical processes of the world or in improving the conditions of life in it. E. M. Forster would feel the same way: he admitted to disliking Jesus's un-worldliness and his rejection of intellectual curiosity, and found in him "such an absence of humour and fun that my blood's chilled." Forster did not think he would have liked Jesus as an individual, and that was a deal-breaker, since personal responses were everything to him. The problem, perhaps, was that something of the divine *did* still cling to Jesus, whether you believed in that divinity or not. One could try to make him "human, all too human," but he remained the sort of human who was entirely dedicated to redemption in the beyond and to submission to and love of God the Father.

Another option, for those who preferred their religion even more hu-manized, was to set up humanity itself in the place of God or Jesus and worship that instead.

There were precedents for this, too. In France, just after the Revolu-tion, a secular "religion" had briefly held sway, designed to replace the Catholic religion, which the revolutionaries hoped to eradicate. They began by ransacking the churches. They even briefly considered demolishing huge cathedrals, such as the one at Chartres, until an architect pointed out that the rubble of such a building would block the whole of the town

LA FÊTE DE LA RAISON, DANS NOTRE-DAME DE PARIS, LE 10 NOVEMBRE 1793
D'après le tableau de M. Ch. L. Muller, dix-neuvième siècle.

center for years. But they were also aware that people might need a substitute, so they set up personifications such as Reason, Liberty, or Humanity as a focus for devotion. The altar at Paris's Notre-Dame was replaced by one dedicated to Liberty, and the building hosted a Festival of Reason on November 10, 1793. This included a parade by the Goddess of Reason, played by Sophie Momoro, wife of the organizer Antoine-François Momoro. The year after that, the religions of humanity and reason fell out of favor with Maximilien Robespierre, who showed his disapproval by having Antoine-François Momoro and others guillotined, and then introducing his own, more deistic Cult of the Supreme Being instead. That continued until 1801, when Napoleon banned that, too, and brought back more conventional religious practices.

The idea of venerating abstractions of this sort lived on. In Germany, the philosopher Ludwig Feuerbach suggested following a human religion in his 1841 book *The Essence of Christianity* (another work that would be translated into English by George Eliot). Feuerbach thought that monotheistic religion had anyway resulted from humans' choosing their own best qualities, naming those qualities "God," and worshipping them. So one might as well cut out the middlegod and worship Humanity directly, or at least our moral side. Feuerbach did not attempt to organize such a religion, but others did, notably the French thinker Auguste Comte.

Comte had some excellent ideas: he founded the discipline of sociology and coined the term *positivism* to describe his belief that our lives could be better governed if they were based on empirical (that is, "positive") science. His scientific worldview led him to reject traditional religion, but his sociology told him that people seemed to need something ritualistic in their lives to replace it. He therefore designed what became known as the Positivist religion, or the Religion of Humanity. It was dedicated to an abstraction, but there was nothing abstract about its practices.

First, being a Catholic by upbringing, Comte was certain that this religion would need an idealized feminine figure to replace the Virgin Mary. He found such a figure in a woman with whom he happened to be personally fascinated: Clotilde de Vaux. After a life unhappily married to a man who abandoned her, she died young, all of which made her the perfect symbol of gentle, anguished female virtue. In the Religion of Humanity, she loomed larger than humanity itself, it sometimes seems. But for living women, Comte's religion had less to offer: they were expected to devote themselves exclusively to bringing up children.

Then there had to be saints, to replace the Catholic ones. Comte chose a range of artists, writers, scientists, and even some religious thinkers who had shown outstanding human qualities, such as Moses. He named the months of the year after them—an idea borrowed from the Revolutionary calendar. And of course, there must be a pope at the head of it all. He seemed prepared to consider himself for this role, but had no time to make it official before he died, in 1857.

After this, the Positivist religion snowballed away and found followers in countries around the world. It had a lasting success in Brazil, because it was adopted by some of the new republic's founders after their coup of 1889. They were attracted by the positivist philosophy of rationalism and its opposition to war and to slavery. A fine Templo da Humanidade was built in Rio de Janeiro, modeled on the Paris Panthéon and featuring a giant painting of Clotilde de Vaux holding a child. Sadly, its roof collapsed in a storm in 2009. Other Positivist churches are still standing in other parts of Brazil.

Another country where Positivists did well was Britain, where so many were already swimming in doubt's boundless sea. In 1859—the year that also saw publication of both the *Origin of Species* and Mill's *On Liberty*—Comte's English translator Richard Congreve opened a London branch of the Religion of Humanity. Meetings were held mostly in his own home at first. A small congregation listened to sermons and recited the Positivist Creed, with lines such as "I believe in the coming of the reign of Humanity." Congreve even spoke, in one sermon, of Humanity as the "Great Power whom we here acknowledge as the Highest." Music was played; poetry was recited. One popular choice was "The Choir Invisible" by George Eliot, expressing her wish to live on in human memory rather than in a heavenly afterlife. The Positivists set it to music, so it could be sung as a hymn:

> O may I join the choir invisible
> Of those immortal dead who live again
> In minds made better by their presence: live
> In pulses stirr'd to generosity,
> In deeds of daring rectitude . . .

George Eliot herself took a deep interest in humanist and secular ideas, as one can tell from her choice of books to translate. But having met some English adherents of the Positivist church, she steered clear of it. Partly this was because of the same difficulty Forster would have with

Jesus Christ: she did not personally like its leader. She and Congreve were neighbors, but she felt that his superficial amiability hid a cold heart.

The other great intellectual figures engaged with themes of religion and science at the time were wary, too. John Stuart Mill wrote an exposé ridiculing the Comtist attachment to ritual. He singled out the way Comte made such a cult of femininity while showing no regard for women's real-life opportunities. T. H. Huxley took one look and summed up the religion as "Catholicism minus Christianity."

In fact, some members of the English church of Humanity also had reservations about the excess of ritual, and the result was that must-have feature of all religions: a schism. The split occurred at a meeting in 1881, with the joke going around that—according to T. R. Wright's entertaining account *The Religion of Humanity*—"they had come to Church in one cab and left in two."

The group that departed from Congreve's was led by Frederic Harrison. He preferred a slightly less elaborate set of imagery and paraphernalia, and thought that "mumbling Catholic rites in a sordid hole" made Positivism look ridiculous. There would still be hymns: his wife, Ethel, edited an anthology of them, including numbers such as "Hail to Thee! Hail to Thee! Child of Humanity!" But they met in a physically brighter location, Newton Hall off Fetter Lane in London, and Harrison's whole approach was warmer. No one called him coldhearted; he was exceptionally hearty and humorous. Having seen him out riding one day, Anthony Trollope described him as looking like "a jolly butcher on a hippopotamus." Harrison's son Austin left a wonderful portrait of him in his memoirs, recalling his father's hilarious and melodramatic home performances of his favorite author, Shakespeare, continuing until the children had collapsed into too many giggles to go on. He also took on a tutor for them: the hard-up novelist George Gissing, who would enthrall them with horror stories from his own very different schooldays, complete with loud "Thwack!" sounds as he recalled the floggings.

Despite such appealing personalities and the pleasures of exuberant hymn-singing, the Religion of Humanity in general left an unfortunate legacy. Even today, a common view of humanists is that they just want to replace one religion with another and to make an idol out of humanity, looking down on all other species as inferior. These things were mostly true of Comte's religious confection. But they do not feature in modern humanism, which rejects dogmatic systems of all kinds, and stresses its respect for non-human as well as human life.

It seems to me a pity that Comte's perfectly good humanist ideas about reason and morality should have gone along with another, rather insulting one: the notion that human beings *must* have saints and virgins, or they will not be able to cope. Mill expressed this objection to Comte's thinking when he asked, "Why this universal systematizing, systematizing, systematizing?" And why this attachment to ideologies, rites, and rules? Everything in Mill's own philosophy of freedom, diversity, and "experiments in living" went against this. It appalled him to see that a philosophy starting out from a desire for human "evolution" had ended, instead, in subjugation to dogma.

The nineteenth century was such a transformative period, in the sciences and humanities alike, that it need not surprise us to see wayward responses emerging. The humanized Jesus and the Religion of Humanity were just two of them; many more possibilities existed. The memoir by Frederic's son Austin Harrison has given us a vivid portrait of this free-roaming intellectual world of Victorian London in which he grew up. It was, he said, so full of radicals and evolutionists and freethinkers and agnostics and Positivists that not to be one of them "was to be just nobody at all." The dramas of the "death of God," the disorientation of losing faith, the wild attempts at substitution, the desire for moral mentors, the scientific excitement—it all went into the mix to form an extraordinary moment in the story of humanism.

Related dramas continue in our own time, too. We still ask similar questions, even if we formulate them in different ways: How *do* humans fit into the rest of the variety of life, or into the physical universe in general? How can we reconcile what emerges from scientific reasoning with what is offered by our heritage of religious thought? Do we need heroes, or saints, or moral leaders? What kind of entity is this humanity, anyway, which so dominates the planet that some have begun to call this the Anthropocene epoch? We certainly do not have answers yet, and perhaps never will. But as any agnostic would say, it is sometimes better not to be too sure about answers.

When the philosopher Bertrand Russell looked back on this period—which was that of his own nineteenth-century childhood, as viewed from the perspective of the very different century that followed—he wrote that it could seem naive and full of "humbug." Yet it had a major advantage: people were driven more by hope than by fear. In his view, if humanity were to flourish, or even continue to survive at all, it would have to deal wisely with the fear and recover some trace of the hope.

10.

~⌒~

Doctor Hopeful

Mostly 1870s onward

*Another trio, this time of humanists with a positive
attitude in an era of hope—Ludwik L. Zamenhof
invents a language—Robert G. Ingersoll believes in
happiness—Bertrand Russell looks around himself
in an energetic way.*

There were many ways to be hopeful in the nineteenth century.
Some people put their trust in political revolution. Some dreamed
of all of humanity ascending on a ladder of progress, led by En-
glishmen. Some believed in nationalist victories or religious transcendence. And some were optimists of a different kind: they hoped to find
rational solutions that would nudge humans into living without bigotry,
without superstition, and without war, for the greater good of all.

This chapter is about three of those heroic hopers. All three were
men of the nineteenth century and carried a lot of that century's spirit,
although two of them lived past its end—a very long way past it, in the
case of one, Bertrand Russell. The third, Robert G. Ingersoll, died in
1899 and did not quite make it.

The other made it just far enough to see his hopes for humanity severely disappointed by the First World War. He is the one we shall meet

first: Ludwik Lejzer Zamenhof, inventor of a language that spoke of
optimism in its very name.

Ludwik Zamenhof was born at
the end of 1859, into a Jewish family in Białystok. This gave
him firsthand experience of what
oppression and national prejudice
did to people's lives. Białystok, currently in Poland, had a long history
of belonging to different nations.
Having started out as part of the then-huge territory of Lithuania, it became Polish for a while, and then turned Prussian. During Zamenhof's
youth, it was under widely resented Russian control. Later, it would twice
be invaded by Germany. Its population was a mixture of Russian, Polish,
German, and Jewish: each group tended to dislike and distrust the others, with the Jews invariably getting the worst of it.

As a boy, Zamenhof noticed that the lack of understanding between
communities in his city seemed exacerbated by the fact that each group
invested an intense emotional sense of identity into its own language,
while seeing the language and identity of others as alien and threatening.
Everywhere he went, he heard people talking about Russians, Poles, Germans, and Jews. He never heard them talk about "people."

The residents of Białystok often did learn a smattering of one another's languages, but this was hard work and meant encroaching on
someone else's territory: no language could be neutral ground. While
still a teenager, Zamenhof wondered if it might help to have a new one
that could be learned without much effort and that was nobody's exclusive property. He did not envisage anyone losing their own primary language or culture; there would simply be an extra bridge-language, giving

everyone a means of communicating and thus helping them to understand others as having human lives similar to their own.

It was a beautiful idea, which also bore the traces of an ancient legend. The Old Testament story of Babel told of how the denizens of that great city, speaking the same language, designed and built a tower that reached almost to heaven itself. God looked down and said, "Behold, the people is one, and they have all one language; and this they begin to do: and now nothing will be restrained from them, which they have imagined to do." Not liking this prospect, he smashed the tower, sent the builders off in all directions, and multiplied their languages so that in future they would always have difficulty working together for the common good. Ever since then, linguistic and cultural incomprehension continued to keep humanity weak, unable to achieve what Forster would call a way to "connect," or what Erasmus called "friendship among many."

For Erasmus, and for others over centuries of European history, Latin had played this role. It played it so well that some medieval linguists, notably Dante, thought that Latin *was* an artificial language, put together by the Romans to get over the scattering of natural vernaculars after Babel. It had the advantage that, having been designed by committee ("formulated with the common consent of many peoples"), it was subject to no individual vagaries and could not change. Lorenzo Valla then rather spoiled this theory by pointing out that Latin had vagarized with vigor.

But Latin was only ever for the educated few and, even among those, it was in decline by the late nineteenth century. It remained common in school education, but the number of people who could use it to communicate properly kept dwindling. Zamenhof did consider Latin or Greek for his purpose, but rejected them, mainly because, like Russian and Polish, they both had complicated verb and noun endings to torment the learner. They also lacked words for modern things—the problem the Ciceronians had faced.

So he assembled notebooks and language guides—he had a good

And they said go to, let us build us a City and a Tower, whose top may reach unto Heaven, and let us make us a name, lest we be scatter'd abroad upon the face of the whole Earth. Gen. 11. v. 4.

grounding in such materials, as his father and grandfather were both language teachers—and began creating his own language, based on ease of learning. He stripped out gender, case endings, and verb conjugations. Instead, he took about nine hundred root words derived from different language families and added a range of consistent prefixes and suffixes to generate more meanings. When he finished this first version of the language, he had a launch party; it was on December 17, 1878, which was just after his nineteenth birthday, so it doubled as a birthday party for himself and for the language. Friends and family assembled around a table artfully arranged with a cake, notebooks, and vocabulary lists, and sang a song:

> *Malamikete de las nacjes,*
> *Kadó, kadó, jam temp' está!*
> *La tot' homoze en familje*
> *Konunigare so debá.*

> Enmity of the nations,
> Fall, fall; it is already time!
> The whole of humanity
> Must be united in one family.

A distressing setback had to be overcome before Zamenhof could unveil the language in a fuller form. After the launch, he went to study medicine in Moscow. (Later, he would specialize in ophthalmology, and continued to run a practice in the Jewish community of Warsaw for the rest of his life.) His father, fearing that language work would distract the young man from his studies, intervened much as Petrarch's father had: he took away his son's notebooks. They were tied in a parcel and locked in a cupboard at home. Ludwik accepted this, but, while home for the holidays a couple of years later, he asked for permission to take the notes out again so he could at least work during the break. It was then revealed that his father had not kept the material in storage, but had removed and burned it. It was indeed the story of Petrarch's father again, but this time nothing at all survived the flames.

Zamenhof had no choice but to re-create the whole language from memory, so that was what he did. In 1887, he produced the first primer. Generally known by the title *Unua Libro*, or *First Book*, it was signed with the pseudonym "Doktoro Esperanto." This means "Doctor Hopeful," and from this the language itself became known as Esperanto—the hopeful language.

To go with it, Zamenhof later tried to create a hopeful religion. Immanuel Kant had observed in 1795 that religion and language were the two main sources of human division, and therefore also of war, because they threw the differences between people into such obvious contrast. Just as with the language problem, Zamenhof hoped that people would find it easier to cross over such differences if there were a shared, secondary religion that they could add to

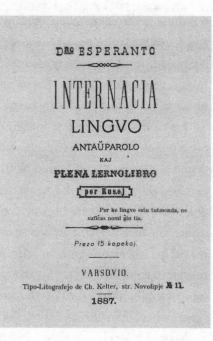

their own cultures and practices. The idea behind it was that everyone shared a basic spiritual humanity, and to some extent also basic values. For example, one could find a key to universal ethics in the Golden Rule espoused by the Jewish theologian Hillel as well as others: "That which is hateful to you, do not do to your fellow." Variations on this rule were found in so many cultures, and it was so simple to remember, that it made a good starting point in creating a sort of Esperanto for the spirit. Zamenhof named the religion after Hillel at first, and published the introductory guide *Hillelism* in 1901. He chose a new pseudonym for himself to go with it: "Homo Sum," from Terence's line. Later, the name of the religion would change, too: it became (in the Esperanto language, of course) *Homaranismo*, which translates as "Humanism."

Not everyone in the Esperantist movement liked the idea of meddling with religion, and Zamenhof heeded advice to downplay this part of his ideal, even when addressing Esperantist gatherings. Yet the thinking was the same: *Homaranismo* should merely add a level of communication and shared humanity, not take anyone's religion away from them. Zamenhof himself had been a Zionist in his youth; he was firmly rooted in the Jewish community where he worked, and had no lack of pride in his Jewish identity. He simply added that extra idea: nothing human is alien.

Esperantists were the first to admit that their projects required a lot of optimism. *First Book* had opened with the admission: "The reader will doubtless take up this little work with an incredulous smile, supposing that he is about to peruse the impracticable schemes of some good citizen of Utopia." (Or, as a charming early translation into English had it: "The reader will doubtless take with mistrust this opuscule in hand, deeming that he has it here to do with some irrealizable utopy.") Many people have continued to smile, viewing Esperanto as a quixotic fantasy predicated on a view of humans as beings who can actually *teach* themselves to embrace each other in universal friendship.

Must that idea be laughable? It depends how you approach it. True: after well over a century of Esperanto's existence, we have still failed to attain world peace or even to head consistently in the right direction. As for *Homaranismo*, few have even heard of it. Fatally, governments never took much notice of Esperanto—at least not in a good way. (More on that later.) It was never adopted by any international organization, apart from that of the Esperantists themselves. In 1908, an Esperantist physician named Wilhelm Molly did try to create an Esperantist microterritory in his hometown of Neutral Moresnet, an area of Belgium frequently contested by Germany (thus in a vulnerable situation, not unlike that of Białystok, albeit on a smaller scale). Dr. Molly planned to rename it Amikejo, or Place of Friendship. But the twentieth century left little room for a micro-land of friendship and peace, and the plan foundered with the beginning of the First World War. Much later, in 1967, Esperanto was chosen as the official language of Rose Island, a nation founded on a sea platform off the coast of Rimini in Italy. But the country's main purpose was the not very idealistic one of evading Italian taxes and laws; it was dynamited by the Italian government.

Yet Zamenhof and the Esperantists always found the ideal of the language, and to some extent the religion, worthwhile, primarily because it *was* a sign of continuing hope. Esperanto and *Homaranismo* may never be projects that large numbers of people are going to adopt, but they do raise the idea of such a possibility. They are *attempts*, like Montaigne's "essays." Even if they don't change the world much, it is cheering that such attempts exist. Esperantism also provides an international network of mutual engagement and connection for those who do get involved.

And sometimes Esperantism crops up where you least expect it. Visiting the site of Petrarch's home at Vaucluse while writing this book, walking on the path along his beloved stream, I was surprised and delighted to see a wall plaque in Esperanto. Translating a nearby plaque in French, and dated 1937, it commemorates Petrarch's poetry and historical researches, and his decision—exactly six hundred years earlier—to build his house in this beautiful spot.

Another, slightly earlier figure who was also driven by hopes and possibilities was outsized in every sense. We have met him before in our story: he was Robert G. Ingersoll, creator of the happiness credo cited in the introduction:

Happiness is the only good.

The time to be happy is now.

The place to be happy is here.

The way to be happy is to make others so.

Thanks to his era's technological innovations, we can hear him saying these words, in a faint and crackly form. He recorded them in 1899, in Thomas Edison's sound studio, and the phonographic cylinder is preserved in the museum at Ingersoll's birthplace in Dresden, New York—along with another recording of him speaking about that great theme: "Hope."

Ingersoll was an agnostic and a rationalist, and typical of his era's charismatic traveling speakers on such subjects. I almost wrote that he was one of its traveling *preachers*, and in his case any resemblance to that breed was no accident. He had grown up on the road with his father, a Congregationalist minister who moved frequently from one location to the next—not least because he kept upsetting people in each place with his outspoken views, especially against slavery. When Robert was born, his birthdate was recorded in a family Bible: August 11, 1833. In another family Bible, the date was given as August 12. "So," he once quipped, "you will see that a contradiction was about the first thing I found in the Bible."

From his upbringing, he had a chance to observe the many ways one could use language and sheer physical presence to amuse, seduce, challenge, and inspire a crowd. As he grew up, he pursued careers that honed these abilities still further. First, he became a schoolteacher, although he was soon drummed out of that line of work because of his tendency to make unsuitable jokes in class—remarking, for example, that baptism was a healthy practice, as long as it was done thoroughly with soap.

Next, he trained as a lawyer, apart from a gap during which he fought and was taken prisoner in the Civil War, an experience that left him with a lifelong hatred of all war. During his legal studies, a friendly judge gave him access to his personal library, consisting of books of Chinese and Indian philosophy, as well as works by Lucretius, Cicero, Voltaire, Paine, Spinoza, Hume, Mill, Gibbon, Darwin, and Huxley—the perfect reading list for a budding "freethinker," to use the term of the time. Ingersoll, who had missed out on earlier opportunities for a general humanistic education, now worked his way through the shelves. It horrified him to learn that people had been accused of blasphemy for expressing such ideas in the past, and then it horrified him even more to realize that similar persecution was still taking place in America. He began taking on such cases at trial. In court, he perfected a rousing, orotund manner that other young lawyers tried to imitate, though with little success. Among those who quickly gave up the attempt was Clarence Darrow, later famous as the defender of the biology teacher John T. Scopes, prosecuted in 1925 for defying a Tennessee law against teaching Darwinism. As Darrow reminisced about Ingersoll: "I have found a few who mastered his form of expression, but they lacked what Ingersoll never lacked and that was something worth saying."

Ingersoll did have plenty to say, and increasingly he said it outside the courtroom as well as inside it. He began writing articles and hitting the road with his lectures, beginning in 1860 with one in Pekin, Illinois, on another great subject of the time: progress. Such speaking and writing became the main activity of his life, and remained so for thirty years. Besides hope, progress, and happiness, his other subjects included the ways in which (he felt) conventional religion blighted and limited the scope of people's lives, and the desirability of freeing ourselves by trying to think more rationally.

To that cause, he brought all the rhetorical skills he had developed in his various careers. Cicero and Quintilian would have been impressed with Ingersoll's range. He used logic, pointing out contradictions in stories of miracles or of answered prayers. He used humor, often sounding like a stand-up comedian. Once, when a woman saw him leaving a saloon bar and said in shocked tones, "Why, Mr. Ingersoll, I am surprised to see

you come out of such a place," he shot back: "Why, my dear madam, you wouldn't want me to stay in there all the time."

At other moments, he could lay on the melodrama, speaking, for example, of the "ghosts" of religion that dominate history: they have "spared no pains to change the eagle of the human intellect into a bat of darkness," he intoned. But lo, let the specters now depart! "Let them cover their eyeless sockets with their fleshless hands and fade forever from the imaginations of men."

All these elements—drama, argument, laughs—were enhanced by his delivery, which was all the richer because it issued from a substantial physical frame. Quintilian himself had recommended cultivating whatever natural advantages one had, "such as voice, lungs and grace of carriage and movement." Ingersoll had all of these, even if his grace was that of a bear. He loved to eat and drink heartily: "Good cooking is the basis of civilization. . . . The inventor of a good soup did more for his race than the maker of any creed. The doctrines of total depravity and endless punishment were born of bad cooking and dyspepsia." So well did he eat that a journalist in the *Oakland Evening Tribune* commented on what a "spectacular auto da fé" his body would have made had he lived in a different era and ended up burned at the stake.

For Ingersoll, there was nothing abstract about humanistic ideas; they affected his entire style of living. Along with good food, he enjoyed good culture. Like Frederic Harrison, he adored Shakespeare. He was with Matthew Arnold in valuing "the best that all the men and women of the world have said, and thought and done." Those best productions were the real "scriptures" of humanity, he said, along with the best mechanical inventions and the best laws, since those two fields of human creation also had such a positive effect on people's lives.

He voiced his exuberance at simply being on this planet:

> Is life worth living? Well, I can only answer for myself. I like to be alive, to breathe the air, to look at the landscape, the clouds, the stars, to repeat old poems, to look at pictures and statues, to hear music, the voices of the ones I love. I enjoy eating and smoking. I like good cold water. I like to talk with my wife, my girls, my grandchildren. I like to sleep and to dream. Yes, you can say that life, to me, is worth living.

Such mentions of his wife, Eva Parker, and their family filled his work. The couple enjoyed thirty-eight years of marriage and had two daughters, of whom the elder, Eva Ingersoll-Brown, went on to be a noted campaigner for feminism as well as a freethinker. Robert himself supported the feminist cause and also defended the rights of children. Parents who beat their offspring, he said, should get someone to take a photograph of their red, angry, ugly faces as they do it, so they can see for themselves what they have become. Instead of finding justifications for violence, he asks, why should we not just treat children "as though they were human beings"?

In another credo, to add to the one about happiness, he said:

> I do believe in the nobility of human nature. I believe in love and home, kindness and humanity. I believe in good fellowship and cheerfulness, in making wife and children happy. I believe in good nature, . . . I believe in free thought, in reason, observation, and experience. I believe in self-reliance and in expressing your honest thought. I have hope for the whole human race.

Naturally such views attracted enmity and suspicion. His opponents called him "Robert Injuresoul," and he was pelted with fruit and vegetables at his lectures. It all bounced off him: the insults, the nicknames, the cabbages, the tomatoes. He even turned fruit to good use in his metaphors. Storing up riches for heaven was a waste of his time on earth, he said. Instead: "I want to suck the orange dry, so that when death comes nothing but the peelings will be left. So, I say: 'Long life!'"

His own life would not be exceptionally long: Ingersoll died of heart failure at sixty-five, in 1899. He left behind admirers, followers, and imitators, as well as many correspondents, in a network rivaling that of a Petrarch, Erasmus, or Humboldt. It grew ever larger, thanks to the newspaper attention his appearances received, which in turn prompted letters from the curious or angry or anguished. Of his responses to these, I find the one that stays in my mind the most was the letter he wrote in 1890 to a man who had approached him saying that he had suicidal feelings. Ingersoll advised him: "No man should kill himself as long as he can be of the least use to anybody, and if you cannot find some person that you are willing to do something for, find a good dog and take care of him. You have no idea how much better you will feel." I hope the man took his advice.

Ingersoll's happiness credo has remained popular with humanist organizations. Although it is expressed as a series of answers, it also prompts us to ask questions of ourselves: Why should we not be happier than we are? Why accept the miseries of religious dread, or patriarchal cruelty, or unreason, rather than just take it on ourselves to find a better way to live? That was Zamenhof's hope in inventing his language. And as Bertrand Russell wrote, "It is not the whole duty of man to slip through the world so as to escape the wrath of God. The world is *our* world, and it rests with us to make a heaven or a hell."

Which brings me to my third hopeful humanist in this chapter. He, too, was formed by the world of the nineteenth century and its experiments, being born firmly Victorian in 1872, but then he lived until 1970, a world of hippies and rock music and computers.

Almost as soon as Bertrand Russell was born, according to his mother, he began to look around himself "in a very energetic way." That was exactly what he continued to do for his ninety-seven (almost ninety-eight) years, as a philosopher, logician, mathematician, polemicist, political activist, sexual liberationist, feminist,

rationalist, atheist, ban-the-bomb campaigner, and much else.

He arrived in the world apparently surrounded by propitious omens, if one believed in such things, which he would never do. His mother, Katharine Russell, Viscountess Amberley, worked to improve women's access to education and had the distinction—after a speech she gave in Stroud in 1870—of being described by Queen Victoria as deserving "a good whipping." Katharine's husband, John Russell, Viscount Amberley, was the son of the former prime minister Lord John Russell, and was himself a Member of Parliament who promoted socially progressive causes. He lost his seat in 1868, in part because of his support for improving access to birth control. This pair of dauntless, aristocratic freethinkers also had an open relationship: the viscountess took a lover, with her husband's knowledge and acceptance.

The birth of "Bertie" was presided over by a pioneering female doctor, Elizabeth Garrett Anderson, who was a family friend. As godfather, another friend was chosen: John Stuart Mill. The choice was a meaningful one. If his task was to guide the boy spiritually, it was unlikely to be into traditional religion.

Unfortunately, Mill died when Russell was less than a year old, so he could not influence him much at all. At least not directly. Through his writings, he had plenty of influence. Russell said that reading Mill's autobiography at age eighteen liberated him from the last remnants of his earlier childhood belief in Christianity.

And Mill's death was not the most significant one in Russell's early life, for his mother died when he was only two, followed by his father, who died a year and a half later. Russell and his older brother were brought up by their paternal grandmother. She was ascetic and traditional: Russell remembered particularly that she would never sit in a comfortable chair until after teatime. That must have been a contemporary obsession; in Anthony Trollope's novel *Can You Forgive Her?*, the character Lady Macleod is described as having been "educated at a time when easy-chairs were considered vicious, and among people who regarded all easy postures as being so; and she could still boast, at seventy-six, that she never leaned back."

Yet Russell also learned something important from his stern grandmother. "She gave me a Bible with her favourite texts written on the fly-leaf. Among these was 'Thou shalt not follow a multitude to do evil.'" That, he said, remained a guiding motto all his life. He certainly lived up to it. If reason told him an argument was right or wrong, he would always say so, even if it might land him in a world of trouble. He aptly called one of his most provocative publications *Unpopular Essays*.

This principle went along with another one: Russell considered it "undesirable to believe a proposition when there is no ground whatever for supposing it true." He supplied a good metaphor for this in 1952, though it was not actually published at the time. In response to a journalistic question, "Is there a God?," he asked the reader to consider an orbiting teapot:

> If I were to suggest that between the Earth and Mars there is a china teapot revolving about the sun in an elliptical orbit, nobody would be able to disprove my assertion provided I were careful to add that the teapot is too small to be revealed even by our most

powerful telescopes. But if I were to go on to say that, since my assertion cannot be disproved, it is intolerable presumption on the part of human reason to doubt it, I should rightly be thought to be talking nonsense. If, however, the existence of such a teapot were affirmed in ancient books, taught as the sacred truth every Sunday, and instilled into the minds of children at school, hesitation to believe in its existence would become a mark of eccentricity and entitle the doubter to the attentions of the psychiatrist in an enlightened age or of the Inquisitor in an earlier time.

Here we have one of Russell's strongest convictions: that accepting assertions on the basis of authority alone is never good enough. We also get a wonderful example of Russell's tone. He had, as Thomas Paine once wrote of Voltaire, a high capacity for spotting folly, combined with an "irresistible propensity to expose it." Just as with Voltaire, and Ingersoll as well, this could be entertaining or irritating, depending on your mood and also on whether you were the one whose folly he was exposing.

Behind the puckish exterior, Russell's thinking was based on a deep understanding of formal logical reasoning—logic and mathematics being his great (and interconnected) loves. Mathematics came into his life when he was eleven and his brother gave him a copy of Euclid's geometry. Russell was in ecstasy: "I had not imagined that there was anything so delicious in the world." He went on to teach both subjects and to cowrite, with Alfred North Whitehead, the magisterial *Principia Mathematica*, which investigated the logical foundations of mathematics. He investigated the logical foundations of many other things, too—nationalism, jus-

tifications for war, opposition to birth control, the denial of women's rights, the justifications for church power—and found them all wanting.

It was logic, as well as family tradition, that led him to an early involvement in the women's suffrage fight. He stood for election as MP for Wimbledon in 1907 on this single issue, knowing he would lose but wanting to publicize the cause, just as Mill had done with his parliamentary arguments in 1867. What shocked Russell was not the loss itself but the ugly behavior of the opposing forces. Organized mobs turned up to his speeches to throw rotten eggs or, in one incident, to release live rats among the audience, plus a dead one thrown into the campaigners' meeting room afterward. Like Zamenhof and Ingersoll, Russell was perplexed as to why things could not be managed more rationally; *why* could people not see the path to well-being and happiness, when it was all so *logical*?

Yet Russell's own life was not guided exclusively by reason or logic, either. He suffered from depression at times. During one episode when he was young, he stood watching the sunset and thought about suicide— but he was saved, he said, by the fact that he still wanted to learn more mathematics. Intense emotions swept through him; he was once described as being "a good hater," and he was equally prone to sudden loves or infatuations. In one strange moment, seeing the wife of his colleague Whitehead visibly ill and in pain, he understood all at once that

> the loneliness of the human soul is unendurable; nothing can penetrate it except the highest intensity of the sort of love that religious teachers have preached; whatever does not spring from this motive is harmful, or at best useless; it follows that war is wrong, that a public school education is abominable, that the use of force is to be deprecated, and that in human relations one should penetrate to the core of loneliness in each person and speak to that. . . . Having for years cared only for exactness and analysis, I found myself filled with semi-mystical feelings about beauty, with an intense interest in children, and with a desire almost as profound as that of the Buddha to find some philosophy which should make human life endurable.

This was not logic; it was an epiphany. The experience also made him realize that he had fallen out of love with his own wife, Alys, and they divorced a while later; he would go on to three more marriages, as well as many affairs. Through most of his life he was exceptionally lustful, and perhaps a sex addict. He had a tendency to try his luck with almost any woman he met; so far as we know, he never crossed the line into being coercive, but his behavior could be tiresome for women around him, as well as somewhat wearying for himself. The fact that Russell was all too human is also evident from the very personal emotional intensity that he put into his quest for the truths of logic and mathematics. He loved both subjects because they had a transcendental validity that went beyond human lives, yet they also provided a source of emotional meaning for him, as poetry had done for the young Mill. Russell made a joke of it: when asked by Chicago's *Little Review* in 1929 which things he loved most, he answered: the sea, logic, theology, and heraldry. "The first two because they are inhuman, the last two because they are ridiculous."

He could never resist such neat turns of phrase, but his dislike of theological tradition ran deeper than this affectionate ridicule suggests. Like the long-ago Epicureans, or the Baron d'Holbach in the Enlightenment era, or Ingersoll in more recent times, Russell thought escaping from religious anxieties, especially about the afterlife, was necessary if human beings were to be happy. Fear was the greatest enemy of happiness, and religion in turn was one of the biggest sources of fear. The idea of using such phrases as "God-fearing" in a positive sense repelled him. Sometimes, of course, a state of alarm is useful, as when confronted by a physical threat from which we must escape, but in most situations in modern life, he thought, we need it less than we need courage. "We ought to stand up and look the world frankly in the face." In general, like Ingersoll, he wanted human life to be bolder, freer, more constructive, more joyful—and felt that it was largely up to us to make it so.

Another fear that ruined many lives was the fear of the stranger, or of anyone different from oneself: feelings that were stoked by nationalists as well as racists. In 1914, the year after the last volume of the *Principia Mathematica* came out, the world fulfilled Russell's own worst fears in this respect with the start of the First World War. Writing to his lover Ottoline Morrell in the initial few days, Russell voiced his horror. "I seem to feel all the weight of Europe's passion, as if I were the focus of a burning glass—all the shouting, angry crowds, Emperors at balconies appealing to God, solemn words of duty & sacrifice to cover red murder & rage." Even some of his own liberal-minded friends seemed to be throwing themselves into this frenzy, changing overnight into German-haters.

All over Europe, peaceable and rationalist types were suffering a similar shock. The Austrian writer Stefan Zweig recalled how he and his friends, who had always enjoyed a world of reason and technology, of electric lights and horseless carriages, of good health and social welfare, were stunned by the sudden relapse into the "barbaric." In Hungary, when the young artist Béla Zombory-Moldován saw a poster announcing war—which meant he would have to present himself for military service within days—he could not believe it. "This was the twentieth century!" It was the time of "enlightenment and democratic humanism." How could it be true? "They were going to shoot at me, or stab me, or I was going to shoot at a complete stranger with whom I had no quarrel, whom I didn't even know." It made no sense. The shock to Europe was like that of the Lisbon earthquake to the "optimistic" philosophers of the eighteenth century, but this time the cause was human rather than geological instability. It was the sort of stupid, accidental slide into war that Erasmus had warned about.

Russell thought that Britain, at least, should stay out of it. He was in no danger of having to fight in the trenches himself: when conscription was introduced at the beginning of 1916, he was forty-three, thus over the age limit of forty. I have to take a moment to boggle at this. Russell still had so many decades of high-profile public life and protest to come, and he saw so many social changes (many of them helped along by his own activism) that it is impressive to realize that he was already at a mature stage of life so early in the century. Having opposed the First World War in his forties, he would then live long enough to also oppose the Vietnam War in his nineties.

Although Russell did not need to define himself as a conscientious objector to avoid the front, he worked to defend those who did. In 1916, he was fined £100 after admitting authorship of a pamphlet supporting an objector's case. As a result of the conviction, he lost his teaching post at Trinity College, Cambridge. (He would be reinstated after the war, thanks to colleagues' support.) That was not the end of his civil disobedience. In 1918, police came to arrest him while he was in his bath, because of an article he had written arguing for a quick peace deal. The specific offense was an aside in the article wondering whether the U.S. troops currently in Britain and France would end up being deployed to intimidate workers on strike, as they had been at home. Russell was charged with publishing "statements likely to prejudice His Majesty's relations with the United States of America." He was found guilty and sentenced to six months, of which he would serve five.

Recalling his prison experience later, he showed his usual levity. On arrival at the prison gate, he had to give his details to the warder. "He asked my religion, and I replied 'agnostic.' He asked how to spell it, and remarked with a sigh: 'Well, there are many religions, but I suppose they all worship the same God.'"

Once inside, Russell took an interest in his fellow prisoners—"though they were on the whole slightly below the usual level of intelligence, as was shown by their having been caught." He was allowed to continue with his reading and writing, on condition that he write nothing subversive. Reading Lytton Strachey's *Eminent Victorians*, a work savagely debunking the staid virtues of the high Victorian era, he laughed so loudly that the warder came to remind him that prison was supposed to be a place of punishment. One wonders how prisoners and guards alike put up with him.

While he was still incarcerated, the conscription age threshold was raised to include over-forties, so the order went out for him to report for his medical examination. But, he wrote, "the Government with its utmost efforts was unable to find out where I was, having forgotten that it had put me in prison." By the time he was released in September, the war was nearly over.

For all his jests, Russell was shaken by every aspect of his experience during this time; he said later the war changed everything for him. From then on, he chose to write a different sort of book. He did not abandon formal philosophy or logic, but as he noted in an essay called "From Logic to Politics," he found a new desire to write about peace and society, and the psychological question about why people felt such attraction to violence and cruelty. This did not mean that he despaired of humanity. On the contrary, he felt "a new love for what is living" and a greater awareness than ever of the ubiquity of suffering. He recognized that human destructiveness must always be part of the picture, but he hoped to find an equivalent urge toward "joy."

Even before the war ended, the most urgent question for him was how to *redirect* the forces that had driven humans into fear and bellicosity. He did not quite share Zamenhof's hope that people could be brought together by something as simple as a shared language or belief system—or even by a spirit of friendship, as Erasmus had thought. Nor would reason be enough, at least not on its own. In a series of wartime lectures delivered in early 1916, *Principles of Social Reconstruction*, Russell wrote that we cannot simply *will* war to be gone from our lives. War comes from human emotional drives, but so do science, art, love, and the spirit of cooperation. These are all forms taken by human creative energies. We need to learn not how to remove our passions but how to direct them to ends more constructive than war or fanaticism. "It is not the weakening of impulse that is to be desired, but the direction of impulse towards life and growth rather than towards death and decay." Or, as one might say, toward hope rather than despair.

But how? In Russell's view, as for so many humanists before and after him, an essential move was to change the way we bring up children, and generally how we sustain people throughout life. *Education* must change.

In his ensuing writings on this subject, Russell sometimes channeled Wilhelm von Humboldt: education should encourage the young to unfold their humanity freely and to pursue curiosity instead of sitting passively, being crammed full of facts. Other educationalists had worked out radical approaches since Humboldt, too—such as the poet Rabindranath Tagore, who had founded a school at Santiniketan in India where classes were held under trees in the open air and artists and scholars were brought in to share their work with the children. Tagore believed in giving Indian children an education based on freedom and on their own recognizable world, rather than on an imported British model. In general, he wrote, education should encourage "mental nourishment, expansion of conscience and strength of character."

Russell shared this vision of education as free development. He also shared with T. H. Huxley the view that science study was crucial for developing a spirit of inquiry about the world. Scientific literacy helped protect against irrational beliefs, and it stimulated the imagination, encouraging people to think about "what the world might be" rather than focusing on the one already existing. Classics-based study treated the ancient authors as fixed in eternal perfection, impossible to improve upon, but for scientists any idea can be developed and changed.

Where Russell departed from Humboldt was in having a much more radical vision of the learner's freedom. He and his second wife, Dora Russell, put this vision into practice in 1927 by founding an experimental school at Beacon Hill in Hampshire, to be based on giving children all the freedom they could handle—and more. Starting with some twenty pupils as well as their own two children, they allowed them to learn about what appealed to them in their "free mental life," and to pursue their own questions and curiosity. For Russell, children who were taught to inquire into what was new, not to obey rules and cling to apparent certainties, would be less likely as adults to be drawn into ideologies offering "safety in return for servitude."

It was a risky experiment, and Beacon Hill had problems. The lack of discipline allowed bullying behavior to go unchecked; in the worst incident, some children tried to burn to death a pair of rabbits given to another child, and in the process started a fire that almost destroyed the house. The Russells hastily tightened up the management.

Such events caused scandal, but even more was generated by the Russells' overall ethos. They did not teach religion; perhaps even worse, they refused to impart the cant about nation and empire that still filled the classrooms of more conventional schools. Russell also believed that, when children asked questions about sex, they should be told the truth—a controversial view. He did point out that, when talking to children about sexuality, it was important to stress the need to respect the freedom and consent of others at all times; this was contrary to the teaching of the church, he remarked, since at the time it held that "provided the parties are married and the man desires another child, sexual intercourse is justified however great may be the reluctance of the wife."

There was more. In hot weather, the children were allowed to go unclothed. One story had it that a journalist rang the doorbell and saw the door opened by a naked child. "Oh, my God!" exclaimed the journalist, to which the child replied, "He doesn't exist," and closed the door. Russell's daughter Katharine Tait commented in her later memoir, "We treated this story with the contempt it deserved because we knew we didn't have a front doorbell."

Juicy tales of this kind would come back to haunt Russell. In 1940, when he was separated from Dora (who continued running the school for a while) and teaching in California, he was given the impression that a new post at the City College of New York was his for the asking. He resigned in California and went to New York, almost with his last cent, only to find that the job was not his, after all: his reputation had scuppered it. The college withdrew the offer on the pretext that he was not a

U.S. citizen. The matter came to court, where the lawyer Joseph Gold-
stein described Russell's works as "lecherous, libidinous, lustful, vener-
ous, erotomaniac, aphrodisiac, irreverent, narrow-minded, untruthful,
and bereft of moral fiber." Russell's family ran around naked in England,
he said. Moreover, "Russell winks at homosexuality. I'd go further and
say he approves of it."

Russell lost, because technically it was true that he was not a U.S. citizen, which invalidated any claim to the job. He was left stranded, aged
sixty-seven, penniless and with considerable family commitments, and
with the Second World War under way on the other side of the Atlantic.

But Russell's lucky stars worked for him again, producing salvation in
the form of a wealthy chemist: Albert C. Barnes. Using a fortune earned
from coinventing the antiseptic later marketed as Argyrol, used for eye
diseases, Barnes had set up a foundation to advance education, art, and
the study of botany. (The Barnes Foundation still exists today, as a gallery in Philadelphia.) He hired Russell, for a generous fee, to deliver a series of lectures on philosophy through the ages. These eventually turned
into a book, *The History of Western Philosophy*, which became an enduring bestseller. The money it brought in helped to keep Russell solvent
and independent for the rest of his life—thus funding much of his future
activism.

Russell was of course too old to fight in the Second World War, just
as he was in the First, but this time he was not a pacifist. Whereas
the First World War had seemed to him avoidable, he considered the dangers of Nazism far worse than those of fighting to stop it. Hitler's ideology
represented everything Russell hated—racism, militarism, nationalism,
thuggery, stupidity—all taken to the most extreme level. It was what
Milton had called (in a rather different context!) "Chaos and Old Night."
Battling against those two things, said Russell, is "our one truly human
activity."

Zamenhof, who had also dedicated his life and powers to that human fight, did not live to see the Second World War, or even the end of the First. Having served his community in Warsaw in his ophthalmological profession to the end, he died in 1917. The Esperanto language would survive, but only just, and so did some of his family, after terrible losses.

First, the language. After the Nazi regime established itself in Germany in 1933, Esperanto organizations in the country went two different ways. The German Workers' Esperanto Association was anti-Nazi from the start, and was in any case instantly outlawed for being a socialistic movement. The main German Esperanto Association continued to operate for a couple of years, adjusting to the Nazi element. It obeyed new laws by expelling all members identified as Jews, an extraordinary act for an organization whose Jewish founder had been driven entirely by the desire to counter prejudice and racism.

If it hoped to placate the regime by these means, it did not work: the Nazis were never going to tolerate a movement created in order to seek global peace by means of a cosmopolitan language. To Hitler and his followers, Esperanto was a Jewish trick aimed at world domination. In 1935 all teaching of Esperanto was stopped in schools, and in 1936 Esperanto organizations were banned entirely. Somehow, a few teachers of the language managed to keep it going even in the worst situations through the coming years: one gave Esperanto classes in the concentration camp of Dachau, and another did so in the Dutch concentration camp at Amersfoort, on the pretense that it was Italian—a language considered acceptable since Italy was then a German ally.

Ludwik Zamenhof's youngest daughter, Lidia, spent much of the 1930s in France, writing articles warning about the dangers she saw coming. She tried to get a visa to stay in the United States, where she had taught briefly, but this was denied, and in November 1938 she returned to Poland. After the Germans invaded in 1939, Lidia Zamenhof was arrested and imprisoned; so were her brother, Adam, and sister, Zofia. Adam was shot the following year, as part of reprisals for others' resistance activity. Both sisters were released and lived in Warsaw's ghetto, until in 1942 they were separately sent to Treblinka and murdered.

Adam's widow and son, however, made an extraordinary escape. They were to be sent to Treblinka at around the same time, but somehow managed to flee just before boarding the train, and then survived the rest of the war in hiding. The son, Louis-Christophe Zaleski-Zamenhof, lived until 2019, dying in France. His two daughters, Hanna Zaruski-Zamenhof and Margaret Zaleski-Zamenhof, now live in the United States and France, respectively—and are both Esperantists.

Esperanto did not fulfill its greatest hopes. Although designed to be easy, it still takes some effort to learn (what language doesn't?), and those who are most inclined to exclude or massacre others on the basis of race, language, or other grouping are probably not those most likely to bother to take classes for the sake of peace and enlightenment.

Yet the language *is* still alive, and still hopeful. And as Robert Ingersoll said in his phonograph recording on that theme in 1895: "Hope builds the house and plants the flowers and fills the air with song."

11.

~~~~~~~~~

The Human Face

Mostly 1919–1979

*Anti-humanism in the ascendant—engineers of human
souls—Giovanni Gentile and Benedetto Croce—but
what can a humanist do?—the Manns—exiles—Aby
Warburg's library and other rescues—more horrors, and
much despair—international organizations and
pragmatic recoveries—Russell is hopeful again.*

If you wanted a manifesto for Chaos and Old Night, you could start
with the two-part summary of Italian Fascist ideology published in
1932, cowritten by Benito Mussolini and his philosophical sidekick,
Giovanni Gentile.

Gentile, who was the author of the main theoretical parts, explained
that a Fascist state does not aim at increasing human happiness or well-
being, and it is not interested in the idea of progress. If life were always
gradually improving, why would anyone be motivated to fight or die for
a transcendent, glorious purpose? Peace is not desirable, either: there is
nothing good about making compromises and seeking equilibrium with
other nations, as Erasmus, Kant, or Russell would have wished. The same
goes for individual development or freedom, the goals sought by a Mill or
a Humboldt. Far from the liberal vision of the state as intervening mainly

to stop individuals from hurting one another, the Fascist state *does* sometimes want to hurt people, to advance national interests. Instead, it offers something bigger than happiness or well-being: it offers self-sacrifice. The state, becoming the ultimate source of value for each person, plays a role similar to that of God: Fascism is avowedly "a religious conception." As with most monotheistic gods, the state demands a "discipline and an authority which descend into and dominate the interior of the spirit without opposition." Through submission, individuals gain true freedom, "the only kind of liberty that is serious."

You can generally be sure, whenever ideologues speak of true or serious freedom, that it will be at the expense of actual, ordinary freedom. And when the rhetoric is transcendental, the reality will probably be miserable.

Indeed, Italian Fascism had itself grown from misery. Originating in 1919, the National Fascist Party appealed initially to a cohort of disoriented young men who had fought in the First World War and then returned to find themselves ignored again and abandoned to their poverty. The party restored their sense of belonging and meaning. The very name of Fascism evoked belonging: it came from the Roman symbol of the *fasces*, or bundle of sticks, which represented the tying together of individuals to create a powerful unity.

At first, there was little philosophy or classical imagery to be found among the Fascists: their main occupation was violent street fighting against rival groups of socialists and communists, who were similarly radicalized by their war experiences. Yet the party would take control of Italy in 1922, with Mussolini becoming prime minister—at least partially thanks to naive liberal politicians who thought they could tame and neutralize him by allowing him a taste of coalition government the previous year. (German politicians would soon make a similar mistake.) Mussolini hoped to acquire a better intellectual gloss by appointing the philosophy professor Gentile his minister of education as well as unofficial theorist.

Education was important because, in the Fascist vision, ordinary human beings as we know them need to be *transformed* to fit the state's needs. As Gentile wrote, Fascism offered a complete transfiguration of the human: it sought to rebuild "the man, the character, the faith." This goal of altering humanity recurs frequently in anti-humanistic regimes. Leon Trotsky, the Russian revolutionary, wrote in 1924 of raising humans into a greater type, transforming them socially and perhaps even biologically. In the coming era, he predicted, the human species "will once more enter into a state of radical transformation, and . . . will become an object of the most complicated methods of artificial selection and psycho-physical training. . . . Man will make it his purpose to master his own feelings, to raise his instincts to the heights of consciousness, to make them transparent, to extend the wires of his will into hidden recesses, and thereby to raise himself to a new plane, to create a higher social biologic type, or, if you please, a superman." Joseph Stalin later also called writers "engineers of the human soul," because of the work they were called to do in mentally remodeling people to fit the "New Soviet" type. Such types were physically depicted in sculpture and photography as pumped-up Vitruvians, with masculine chins held high and shoulder muscles bulging. (And those were just the women.)

As Erasmus and others had observed long before, if you want to mold humans into particular shapes as a mother bear does with her cubs, you must begin with early education, at home and at school. In Italy, Gentile therefore organized the opening of new elementary schools all over the country—in some ways a good thing, as it raised basic education levels. But the syllabus was highly ideological, impressing on young minds the grandeur of imperial Rome and a general sense of Italy's unique destiny. A similar educational program was launched in Germany after Adolf Hitler came to power in 1933. As described by Erika Mann in her study of Nazi education, *School for Barbarians: Education under the Nazis*, this abandoned the idea even of imparting knowledge, let alone encouraging inquiry. Its main purpose was to produce children incapable of imagining anything much beyond nation and race. It also habituated them to images of war, long before the actual war began: in art classes, she wrote, they drew pictures of gas masks and bomb explosions, and there was constant marching in soldierlike formations. The philosopher Hannah Arendt put it neatly in her postwar study of totalitarian life: "The aim of totalitarian education has never been to instill convictions but to destroy the capacity to form any."

The Humboldtian model that had previously been so important in Germany, with its talk of free *Bildung*, was abandoned. If a Humboldtian education aims at creating a person who is humanized, "touched by all that is human in all the facets of one's nature" as its creator had said, a fascistic education instead aims at creating a *de*humanized one. It was education as transformed by what the German art historian Erwin Panofsky called "insectolatrists": those who thought an antlike hive-mind, centered on race, class, or nation, was better than a messy plurality of independently thinking beings.

Some educationalists dared to speak up against such plans. In Italy, when Gentile became the minister of education, he was taking on a role that had recently also been held by a colleague and friend of his, Benedetto Croce. He and Gentile shared many philosophical interests and had long worked together on the cultural periodical *La critica*. In the Fascist era, however, they became light-and-dark reversals of each other: case studies in how two broadly humanistic intellectuals could respond differently to the rise of an anti-humanist political movement.

Croce was a humanist in several senses: besides being a scholar of the humanities (as was Gentile), he was a liberal thinker in the tradition of Humboldt and Mill. He was also a person who lived without religious belief.

His move away from traditional ideas of God may have had something to do with a personal catastrophe he survived at the age of seventeen. While his family was on holiday on the island of Ischia in July 1883, an earthquake struck, and their hotel collapsed, burying them all under

the rubble. Trapped, and with broken bones, Croce listened all night to the sound of his father's distant cries for help—until they faded. His mother and sister also died. The disaster left Croce as the sole representative of the family: mentally traumatized but suddenly wealthy. Because of this, when he realized a year or two later that he could not cope emotionally with university, he was able to support himself through years of private study instead. The nonstandard education did not hold him back. He went on to an eminent career as a historian and philosopher and also entered politics.

Croce served his stint as education minister under the liberal government that preceded the Fascist one. Like others in the former party, he was initially fooled into thinking that Mussolini could somehow be made genteel if brought into the inner circle of power. The real nature of the threat became more apparent in June 1924, when Fascists murdered the courageously outspoken socialist Giacomo Matteotti. Croce continued to be cautious for a while—the dangers of opposition were now undeniable—but he eventually took a stand. His friendship with Gentile was over, he announced. As he put it in a letter written later that year, he had no intention of watching passively while the "white robe" of philosophy was reduced to "a mop for the kitchen of fascism."

The following April, Gentile issued a "Manifesto of Fascist Intellectuals," a pseudo-religious exaltation of Fascism and the state. Croce responded with what became known as his "Manifesto of Anti-Fascist Intellectuals." He attacked Gentile's text as "a piece of half-baked schoolwork," filled with bad arguments and intellectual confusion. Gentile talked about "religion," wrote Croce, but this really meant a low mixture of aggression and superstition. Was Italy supposed to give up its *real* religion? By this Croce meant not Catholicism but the ideals accompanying Italy's unification in the previous century: to wit, "love of truth; hope for justice; a generous human and civic sense; zeal for intellectual and moral education; and eagerness for liberty."

After his protest, Croce retired to his home in Naples, but he continued to study, write, and even to host fairly open anti-fascist meetings there. The regime mostly did not interfere, except when a gang broke in late one night in 1926, damaged works of art on the walls, and shouted at Croce and his wife as they came out of their bedroom. Subsequently, with the excuse that Croce would need protection against such random attacks, two policemen were permanently posted outside the house, watching comings and goings. But Croce continued his work, and he survived the entire Fascist period without coming to harm.

Throughout those years, Croce urged his readers to maintain their sense of humanity and of hope in the future. He believed that the long sweep of history was still leading toward ever greater freedom and progress, even if major detours occurred at times. The important thing, he wrote in an essay of 1937, is to understand that these detours are bound to occur, and therefore not to fall into despair when they do. At the same time, one cannot take this as a reason to sit back and just wait for the good years to return of their own accord. Freedom is identical to life itself; it must always be fought for, even if the fight never ends, and even if at times it is tempting to give up hope.

By the mid-1930s, many humanists around Europe were finding it hard to maintain that level of optimism. Their initial response, especially when Hitler came to power more than ten years after Mussolini, was to feel stunned and unsure where to turn. As Stefan Zweig wrote in his autobiography, *The World of Yesterday*, he and his civilized friends in

Vienna could not at first believe that the danger was real. "It is difficult to rid yourself, in only a few weeks, of thirty or forty years of private belief that the world is a good place," he wrote. It seemed that such "inhumanity" must quickly self-destruct "in the face of humane standards." This, however, did not happen. Austria already had many Nazi sympathizers; Zweig was both Jewish and known for his humanistic and pacifist views, so it was clear that he might be an early target. When his books were burned in public and the police raided his house, it was his signal to leave the country.

In that same year, 1934, Zweig published a short biography of Erasmus, filled with his admiration for the great humanist, but also ending by asking the question of why the Erasmian values of peace and reason were so hard to maintain. They had fallen apart in Erasmus's time; they were falling apart now. Why did humanism have this fatal "weakness"? Humanists seemed to suffer from a "beautiful error": they allowed themselves to believe that better learning, better reading, and better reasoning would be enough to bring about a better world. The world kept proving them wrong.

But what *does* a humanist do? This was the question over which so many were now puzzling. Do you involve yourself in government and hope to minimize the damage from within? Italians had learned the dangers of that: trying to tone down fascists can merely make you complicit with them. Do you go out on the streets, ready for physical battle? That was not the humanistic way. Do you, then, deplore the rise of barbarism in elegant prose, reminding readers of their humanity in speeches and articles? But most of those who hear the speeches and read the articles probably already agree with you.

Perhaps, if you want to live and you are in danger, you start by emigrating, as Zweig did. The emotional cost of this was so high, however, that by the time he and his wife, Lotte Altmann, reached their third country of refuge, Brazil, they were mentally as well as physically exhausted. Zweig had lost his library and his notes. He continued writing in Brazil without them; among his last works was a biographical essay on Montaigne, presenting him very much as he had Erasmus: as an anti-heroic hero in terrible times, who somehow keeps the humanistic spirit going without despair. But Zweig did despair. He and Lotte took their own lives together in Brazil in 1942. In a radio tribute, E. M. Forster said that Zweig, too, was one of the non-heroic heroes he had so often written about. "He is the humanist who hopes for the continuance of civilisation, and civilisation to-day is a far from encouraging spectacle." As it happens, Forster himself had been described in almost identical terms earlier in the 1930s by his friend Christopher Isherwood: "The antiheroic hero, with his straggly straw moustache, his light, gay, blue baby eyes and his elderly stoop."

Roger-Pol Droit, in his history of the postwar organization UNESCO, has written:

> There is something truly poignant in some of the debates and testimonies of the 1930s. The intellectuals concerned have diagnosed the essential elements in the crisis of humanism and modern society and have started to propose remedies. Yet they find themselves the helpless spectators of an inexorable chain of events. . . . The tragedy arises here, as in Antiquity and in the classical theatre, from the combination of lucidity and powerlessness.

One of these spectators, and a reader of Zweig's Erasmus book when it came out, was the grandly successful German novelist Thomas Mann (father of, among others, the Erika Mann mentioned a few pages ago on the subject of Nazi education). Making notes on Zweig's book in his diary, Thomas reflected that what Erasmus apparently had not understood was a strange fact. It was not just that humanism could not assert itself; it was that so many people actually seemed to *long* for a world of violence and unreason. But humanists' failure to be bold came into it, too: in a lecture of April 1935, Mann said, "In all humanism there is an element of weakness, which . . . may be its ruin." He blamed its tendency to be too flexible. Humanists give in too easily. "Intimidated, stunned, ignorant of what is happening, with disconcerted smiles they abandon position after position and seem to want to agree that they 'no longer understand the world.'" They even adjust themselves to the style of their enemy—"to the malignant stupidity of his whims and propagandist formulas." Worst of all, they always try to see the other side of any question. When dealing with murderous fanaticism, that is not necessarily helpful.

Mann himself had been aware of the magnetism of extreme ideas for some time and had explored it in his fiction. His most direct treatment was in the 1929 short story "Mario and the Magician," in which a sinister stage conjurer, Cipolla, exerts an uncanny power over the crowds who come to see him, just as Mussolini and Hitler did. Before this, Mann had also written about twentieth-century irrationalism and anti-humanism in his masterpiece, *The Magic Mountain*. This had started life as a novella in 1912, but then he paused it for about five years. He resumed work on it in a changing world: the First World War came and went, and Fascism began to grow. These changes informed the book, which grew to a huge size and appeared in 1924, the year after Hitler tried and failed to launch a coup in Munich—home to the Mann family at the time.

The Magic Mountain's young hero, Hans Castorp, travels to a tuberculosis sanatorium in the Swiss Alpine resort of Davos to visit his ailing cousin Joachim. He means to stay for three weeks, but almost before he has noticed, those three weeks have become seven years. His own mild (perhaps imaginary) case of the disease is diagnosed. Meanwhile he falls in love with a charismatic Russian, Clavdia Chauchat, and engages in philosophical conversations with two opposed and talkative men who represent two tendencies in European culture. One is Ludovico Settembrini, an arch, exuberant, pedagogically minded humanist from Padua—something like a Paduan version of Bertrand Russell, minus the mathematics. The other is the menacing proto-totalitarian Leo Naphta, a Jesuit of Jewish origin who represents both a lingering medieval darkness and the coming wave of anti-humanist irrationalism in Europe.

The two men compete to gain influence over the naive Castorp, who absorbs everything they say. Settembrini is highly civilized, but his belief in reason and in the essential goodness of humanity seems doomed to obsolescence. Naphta, on the other hand, has no faith in humanity and even keeps a handy copy of Innocent III's *On the Misery of Man* in his apartment; he lends it to Castorp. Naphta shows as much concern with the young man's education as Settembrini does, yet he also rejects the whole concept of education, at least in the Humboldtian sense. The young, Naphta says, have no interest in learning to be free; they want only to obey. Besides, the humanistic structure of schooling will soon be replaced by public learning through lectures, exhibitions, and cinema. Settembrini is horrified: won't that result in mass illiteracy? No doubt, says Naphta, but what's wrong with that?

There is no future for *Bildung* in Naphta's dreaming, yet the novel itself is a *Bildungsroman*: an example of the literary genre in which a young hero goes through a series of life experiences, learning something from each of them, until he is ready to take up his mature role in the world. Castorp advances through these stages with his mentors, and he does reach a climactic insight. One day, lost in a mountain blizzard and convinced he is about to die—like Leslie Stephen on his precipice—he decides to choose "life," a third option belonging neither to Settembrini nor to Naphta. Again, like Stephen, he discovers that he has only dozed off in the snow for ten minutes and is not dying at all. He finds his way back to the safety of the hotel with its enormous lunches. Eventually he completes his seven years and leaves Davos entirely, no longer ill. He seems destined to become a good bourgeois like the rest of his family in the "lowland"—but what he actually does is go off to fight in the First World War. We see him from afar, at the front, his future uncertain. There is a chance that he will not survive: an undoing of the very idea of a *Bildungsroman*.

Mann himself had come out of the First World War with fairly right-wing views and a belief that writers should be "apolitical." That put him at odds with his older brother, the novelist Heinrich Mann, a dedicated socialist who believed that writers had a moral duty to speak out for a better world. Heinrich and Thomas were like Naphta and Settembrini in that they never stopped arguing. Heinrich did not convert his brother to radical socialism, but in the 1930s Thomas did repent of his former view that a writer need not engage in politics. Seeing the disaster unfolding in Germany, he began giving anti-Nazi talks. He was more cautious than Heinrich, but still attracted the Nazis' attention. At one speech in 1930, titled "An Appeal to Reason," he was heckled by SA men disguised in civilian suits. In 1932, he opened a parcel to find a half-burned copy of his own first novel, *Buddenbrooks*, sent by a young Hitler supporter with a note suggesting that he finish the burning job himself. Mann saved the blackened leaves and told his friend Hermann Hesse that one day these would testify to the state of mind of the German people in the year 1932. These words imply that he thought the madness might pass soon rather than get worse. Instead, the Nazi takeover was accomplished in full the following year. Heinrich, seeing the scale of the danger immediately, fled Germany. Thomas was less sure how to respond.

The problem was resolved for him partly by the fact that he happened to be in Switzerland when the takeover happened, enjoying a break there with some of his family. After much urging by his daughter Erika, he decided not to return. She was in danger, too, being a theatrical performer and a flamboyantly cross-dressing lesbian, renowned among other things as a champion racing driver. Her brother Klaus was also gay and involved in the theatrical demimonde. Thomas himself was not as heterosexual as he pretended to be. It was clear that the whole family would be better off having nothing to do with Nazi Germany—although Thomas did choose to continue publishing his works there for some time. On the other hand, he was persuaded that it was better to stay out of the country himself and work against the regime with his writings and lectures.

One thing bothered him: he had left half-finished manuscripts at their home in Munich, including the latest volume of his multipart Old

Testament epic, *Joseph and His Brothers*. Erika got into her car and ran a swashbuckling nighttime mission, alone, back across the border to get her father's work. Since the car was well known in town, she parked it on the outskirts and went the rest of the way by foot, donning a pair of dark glasses that she thought would prevent her being recognized, although if anything they probably made her even more conspicuous. She made it to the house, which appeared to be under surveillance, so she waited until sundown. Then she sneaked inside, packed the manuscripts in her bag, and sat in the darkness of her own former bedroom until one o'clock, the dead of night. She crept out and ran through the streets, passing groups of drunken Nazis in celebration. Instead of the sunglasses, she pulled her hat down over her eyes. Once safely back at the car, she wrapped up the papers and stuffed them under the seat with some oily tools, then drove for the Swiss border. It was not, at this stage, too difficult to cross there: the guards even said to her that "they could quite understand anyone's wanting to get away for a trip to the mountains."

Another of Thomas's children, Golo, managed to bring some more material a month or so later. Thus reunited with at least some of his papers, Thomas stayed in Switzerland for several years, writing pieces with

such titles as "Achtung, Europa!" (Europe, Beware!). In 1938, he did a tour of America, delivering one of his most eloquent lectures, "The Coming Victory of Democracy," and decided to move there permanently. Klaus and Erika went, too. Thomas initially found work teaching at Princeton; then the family moved to Los Angeles. Along with Golo, Thomas's brother Heinrich also managed to join them, after a grueling journey across the Pyrenees and through Spain. Heinrich would always find life in America challenging. He got by, with help from Thomas and from a contract to write Hollywood film scripts—a common financial lifeline for artistic émigrés. But it was difficult work for a committed socialist with limited command of English. Thomas, instead, had a good exile. He continued writing novels and was taken on as a consultant in German literature at the Library of Congress, with help from the Librarian, Archibald MacLeish—himself a poet and a strong believer in the duty of libraries to support writers in such times.

Erika and Klaus jointly wrote *Escape to Life*, which told their own stories and those of many other exiled artistic and theatrical friends. As well as her study of Nazi education, Erika published *The Lights Go Down*, a collection of gripping semifictionalized accounts of ten real-life individuals whom she knew, showing how each reacted differently to the coming of the Nazis. Some of her characters fall victim to the regime; some try to adjust and thus become drawn into moral compromise. A manufacturer, meaning no harm by it, ends up dismissing his half-Jewish assistant to protect himself; he never quite understands what he has done. Others escape entirely, including the journalist of the title story, who begins as a Nazi sympathizer but realizes he is also in danger after his editor catches him with a red pencil, idly correcting thirty-three grammatical errors in one of Hitler's transcribed speeches. He plans his strategy for years, and eventually manages to get away to America with his family—but only after losing the valuable art collection he hoped would finance their new life and almost drowning in a torpedoed ship. The family will have to start again with nothing, but they are alive.

The community of such escapees in America now included many notable European humanist scholars, as well as writers and artists. One of the greatest experts in Renaissance humanism, Paul Oskar Kristeller, was helped on his journey by—of all people—Giovanni Gentile. Kristeller had been doing research in Italy when the German racial laws of 1933 came in, thus depriving him of his university position in Germany. Gentile helped arrange for him to stay and teach in Florence, and then at the Scuola Normale Superiore in Pisa—Italy not yet having such extreme discriminatory laws. Kristeller's teaching also brought him the perk of free Italian rail tickets: during breaks he could visit libraries all over the country to dig out neglected manuscripts by the old literary humanists. He became a sort of modern-day Petrarch or Poggio with a rail pass. The notes he made would generate his most monumental work, *Iter Italicum: A Finding List of Uncatalogued or Incompletely Catalogued Humanistic Manuscripts of the Renaissance in Italian and Other Libraries.*

But Mussolini brought in his own anti-Jewish laws in 1938, and Kristeller lost his job in Italy too. Gentile liaised with Mussolini himself to procure some financial compensation for him, although he neglected to tell Kristeller what he was doing. Thus, when Kristeller received a summons to report to police headquarters in Rome, he was sure that it meant he would be arrested. Failing to show up could be even riskier, however, so he went—and, to his amazement, was handed an envelope full of cash. By now he felt that he had had enough of life under Fascism. He asked Gentile to give the money to the Scuola Normale, except for an amount sufficient to pay for his passage to America. He sailed for New York in February 1939 and became established at the universities of Yale and Columbia as the doyen of Renaissance humanist history.

Others who went to America included the philosopher Ernst Cassirer, who later collaborated with Kristeller and with John Herman Randall Jr. on *The Renaissance Philosophy of Man*, a 1956 compilation of humanist texts that remained a staple of undergraduate courses for decades. Another philosophical exile, Hannah Arendt, went on to write studies of totalitarian politics and of the question of political commitment. Hans Baron, a historian from Berlin, wrote about political commitment, too, defining it as crucial to the fifteenth-century humanist vision of life. He settled in Chicago and became a bibliographer and librarian at the city's independent library of the humanities, the Newberry Library. Then there was the art historian who spoke of "insectolatrists": Erwin Panofsky. He had been at the University of Hamburg but happened to be teaching a course on Albrecht Dürer in New York when the 1933 Nazi laws led to Hamburg firing him by telegram. He stayed where he was and went on to a long career at Princeton.

During his Hamburg years, Panofsky had been part of a network of scholars who saw art history as part of a wider cultural field of study centered on the "symbolic"—that is, the whole realm of language, visual images, literature, and beliefs, as preserved and transmitted through the generations. (Ernst Cassirer also wrote of humans as the distinctively "symbolic" animal.) Before the Nazis, this art historical community had found a congenial home at an extraordinary Hamburg library and institute, named for its creator: Aby Warburg.

Warburg came from a renowned banking family in the city; as the eldest son, he should have been the sole heir to their operations. But from childhood he hated everything to do with banking; what he loved was looking at pictures and reading. Therefore, at the age of thirteen, he came to an agreement with Max, his younger brother. Max could have Aby's whole inheritance. In return, he only had to promise to buy Aby any book he wanted, for the rest of their lives.

Max had no idea what he was letting himself in for. By the time of the First World War, Aby's collection had grown to over fifteen thousand books, as well as a wealth of images in original, engraved, and photographic forms. Art history was his first and greatest love, but he was interested in mythology, philosophy, religion, ancient languages, literature—anything connected to human symbolic activity. He collected from cultures other than European ones, and was especially intrigued by Hopi and Zuni art

from North America. Toward the end of his life, he created large mounted displays of images from his collection, arranged by theme and incorporating everything from reproductions of great art to modern advertisements. The idea was to use them as visual aids for lectures. He called them his *Mnemosyne Atlas*, after the Greek goddess of memory. Before he could finish the project, however, he died, in 1929. The sixty-five panels that he did complete have survived—an artwork in themselves. The library, too, almost amounts to a work of art, being a personal expression of one man's vision, although it did also acquire a knowledgeable, professional staff, and it continued to grow considerably after Warburg's death. In 1920, after a tour given by its librarian Fritz Saxl, Ernst Cassirer concluded: "This library is dangerous. I shall either have to avoid it altogether or imprison myself here for years."

The library continued to flourish, maintained by its staff and the many scholars who roosted in it—but then came the Nazis. The threat they posed to the library and its personnel alike was obvious, especially as many of the latter were Jewish. An astonishing, ambitious plan was formulated: the library in its human and archival entirety would become—like so many individuals—an émigré.

In a feat of organization, the library team, headed by chief curators Fritz Saxl and Gertrud Bing, packed up the books, the images, the Mnemosyne panels; they even packed the iron shelving, the desks, and the photographic and bookbinding equipment. It was all shipped to London, and many of the people involved went, too. Even now, the challenge was only beginning. As Saxl recalled later, "It was a strange adventure to be landed with some 60,000 books in the heart of London and to be told: 'Find friends and introduce them to your problems.'"

That was an adventure, all right, but they were aided by some friends they already had in the city, such as Samuel Courtauld of the Courtauld Institute. He helped them find accommodation at Thames House on Millbank, and then a more permanent home in University of London buildings in Bloomsbury. The two institutes jointly launched a journal in 1937, with the aims of bringing together all "symbolic" studies in an interdisciplinary, holistic vision and taking "the study of Humanism, in the broadest possible sense, for its province." The staff also looked for ways of getting Londoners interested; a memo of 1934, probably written by Saxl, observed that this might require a change of style, since the English seemed averse to anything too abstract or theoretical. In fact, many of those who found an intellectual home in the Warburg Institute had themselves come from other countries. It became an international, humanistic home for all.

And it remains so today. While Warburg's original Hamburg house has once again become an institute and center of archives, offering events and courses, the transplanted Warburg Institute in London is still a great humanistic home. As I write, the building is being modernized, in an attempt to make it more public-friendly—still trying to lure those Londoners in. It is still driven by a spirit of connection, making links between scholars, ideas, histories, and images. Many of the studies of humanistic history I've used in writing this book were written by people who have studied and worked there. I've written much of it there myself.

Its identity as an exile library has also continued to be honored. In

2020, the ceramicist and sculptor Edmund de Waal presented it with his artwork *Library of Exile*, a room that records the names of the world's lost and scattered libraries on its walls. It originally also housed some two thousand books by exiled authors, but the books have now gone to Iraq to help rebuild the University of Mosul Central Library, which was severely damaged in 2015.

The whole of the Warburg collection is, of course, also filled with works by and about exiled authors: from Petrarch (born already in family exile from his ancestral home) to the many fifteenth-century humanists who fled from city to city in Italy, and on to the French *lumières* who sought refuge in Holland or England, and to the works of the twentieth-century scholars who fled Fascism and other oppressive regimes. One may see the Warburg Institute as standing against the whole principle of loss, forgetfulness, and the falling-apart of things—those losses that Petrarch and Boccaccio lamented so eloquently.

Other libraries and cultural heritage sites around Europe also worked hard through the 1930s to shore up their collections against the coming destruction. When the Nazis started burning books, German exiles in Paris (notably the writer Alfred Kantorowicz) set up a German Freedom Library—the Deutsche Freiheitsbibliothek—to collect the very works the Nazis were trying to destroy, and also to preserve the regime's own posters, pamphlets, and other outpourings for future historical study. Its supporters included Bertrand Russell, and its president was Heinrich Mann. After the war ended, it was long thought that the library's contents had been entirely destroyed during the Nazi occupation, but in 1990 it emerged that some titles had been saved, after all; they are now in the Bibliothèque Nationale.

Elsewhere, microfilm photographers and archivists traveled around hastily filming as many irreplaceable documents and manuscripts as they could—a story recently told by Kathy Peiss in her 2020 book *Information Hunters*. Some brave souls even continued after the war had begun: the American scholar of medieval philology Adele Kibre stayed on in

Rome photographing works from the Vatican Library and elsewhere as long as she could. She returned to the United States in 1941 with her films in seventeen suitcases, abandoning her other possessions in order to fit in as much as possible. Then she went to Sweden and directed a microfilm unit there for the rest of the war.

Meanwhile, buildings were protected with sandbags; art was stored in hideaways away from main population centers. In Florence, masterpieces from the Uffizi Galleries were moved to country locations. In Chartres, the cathedral's exquisite twelfth- and thirteenth-century stained-glass windows were taken apart piece by piece and buried in the crypt.

Then the war did come, and with it the chaos, death, and loss. The secret stashes of human culture and beauty waited, in their havens, for it to end.

The few people lucky enough to have found havens also waited—and worked. From his California home, Thomas Mann continued to write fiction, notably another drama about the weakening of humanism, *Doctor Faustus*, published in 1947. He also wrote nonfiction. Among his polemical works of the war years were some short pieces aimed at reaching fellow Germans on the other side of the Nazi propaganda wall. Eminent as he was, many in Germany had been unsure at first what his views were on the regime, so it was significant when some of his anti-Nazi writings found their way in. The first was an open letter, written to the University of Bonn after it stripped him of his honorary doctoral degree in 1937; as happened with so many other works over the centuries, manuscript copies of this short text were circulated by hand. The literary critic Marcel Reich-Ranicki recalled attending a hush-hush meeting with trusted friends at which the text was produced and read out loud: "a small package of paper, very thin and written on both sides." Having listened to it, Reich-Ranicki made his excuses and went home early so he could be alone with his happiness; this great figure in German literature was on their side, after all.

More was to come, starting in October 1940, when Mann began to broadcast monthly messages in German via the BBC. Trying to beam his voice into Germany directly from America would not work, because the transmission could be picked up only on shortwave and radios capable of receiving that were banned in Germany and occupied territories. The first few installments were therefore read out by someone else in London, until an elaborate method was found that enabled Mann's real voice to be heard in Germany. First, he recorded each episode onto a gramophone disc at the NBC studios in Hollywood. The disc was flown to New York, and from there it was played over a telephone line to London, where it was recorded onto a second disc. That could then be played and transmitted to the Continent, as other BBC broadcasts were.

Sometimes, in these recordings, he spoke of specific news, reporting on atrocities that German listeners were presumed not to know about—as when, early in 1942, news came through of a number of Jewish people in Holland being rounded up and gassed to death, by way of "experimentation." More often, he concentrated on reminding his listeners over and over that the Reich did not represent Germany, still less humanity in general, and therefore that it could not last. In the April 1941 broadcast, he said:

> Mankind cannot accept the ultimate triumph of evil, untruth, and violence—it simply cannot live with them. The world resulting from a Hitler victory would be not only a world of universal slavery, but also a world of absolute cynicism, a world which would find it totally impossible to believe in the higher and better in man any longer, a world which would belong completely to evil and be subject to evil. There is no such thing; it will not be tolerated. The revolt of humanity against a Hitler world filled with the utmost despair of spirit and good—this revolt is the most certain of all certainties.

There must, at all costs, be hope.

The war did end at last, and the Nazi killing machine ended with it. What was left was the counting of losses, human and cultural. As the American art historian Frederick Hartt put it, looking around at ruined streets in Florence: "Form to formlessness, beauty to horror, history to mindlessness, all in one blinding crash." So much was gone. Much of it would never come back. The end of the war did not bring any smooth return to the humanists' longed-for world of civility and "friendship among many"—although some made heroic efforts to make it happen, as we will see a little farther on in this chapter.

The end of this war also failed to stop the general human habit of behaving inhumanly. New threats had to be reckoned with: the atom bomb, dropped on Hiroshima and Nagasaki, was clearly going to be impossible to uninvent. The hostility between the two great powers of the United States and the USSR turned cold and lasting, and the cultural atmosphere in America suffered accordingly. At the height of the Cold War's McCarthyism, Thomas Mann—seeing signs that he might become a target himself and feeling disgusted by the whole phenomenon—decided to leave the adopted New World home that had once given him refuge and go back to Switzerland.

As for the Soviet Union and its satellites, the degradation of human dignity and freedom continued unabated. Karl Marx had begun his intellectual investigations by imagining that revolution would restore people to their whole, unalienated humanity, but instead the states founded upon his name became vast alienation machines, with people often forced into a life of evasion and doublethink in order to get by.

In China, home of *ren*, Mao's regime did its best to obliterate every sign of that philosophy of "doing one's best to fulfil one's humanity and treating others with an awareness that they, too, are alive with humanity." During the Cultural Revolution of the 1960s, schoolchildren were encouraged first to ignore their teachers, then to report their ideological failings. Anyone who seemed remotely intellectual or cultured was persecuted and banished to the remote countryside. Beautiful and valuable objects—artworks, books, antiques, precious porcelain—were collected and burned, as in Savonarola's bonfires of the vanities, or else packed away in giant warehouses, where pests and water slowly turned paper into mulch. Confucianism itself was suppressed: in Kongzi's hometown of Qufu in Shandong Province, his tomb was desecrated. Around a hundred thousand books were taken from the town's library and burned. (This seems all the more shocking, somehow, when one remembers that Mao himself had once worked as an assistant librarian at the University of Beijing.) Almost every element of life that might bring pleasure fell under suspicion, the kinds of things that had made someone like Robert Ingersoll feel such a love for life: good food, family bonds, social pleasures, and good humor. Instead, a terrible puritanism held sway. "Barbers still opened, but offered nothing but proletarian haircuts (short back and sides)," writes the historian Frank Dikötter. "Restaurants served only cheap, plain meals." And there were deaths: around a million and a half resulted from the Cultural Revolution, even if that figure is put in the shade by the estimated thirty-six million thought to have been killed by the Great Famine shortly before it. Many more lives were ruined in subtler ways. The popular, mostly humorous novelist Lao She was rash enough to say, in an interview with foreign visitors in 1966, that he was not a Marxist. "We old ones can't apologize for what we are," he said. For this, he was assaulted by a mob of Red Guards. They raided his house; when he returned to it, he saw his manuscripts torn up and his collection of paintings and sculptures damaged and scattered around the courtyard. Soon afterward he was found drowned in a canal, apparently by suicide.

Another regime of extreme nihilism was that of Pol Pot's Khmer Rouge, in power from 1975 to 1979 in Cambodia. It caused up to two million deaths (estimates vary), from a total population of just seven million. Some people were executed, but many more were worked to death. The dehumanization was systematic and total. The year of the revolution was designated Year Zero: there must be no other history. One of the first acts of the new government was to clear the capital, Phnom Penh, of all its citizens, sending them out to join work gangs in the countryside. From then on, there were no newspapers, no mail, no traditional music or instruments, no books, no law courts, no money, no private property, no religious ceremonies or rites of passage, no privately chosen marriages, no ordinary human relationships. No medicines or treatments were available, with terrible consequences in human suffering. Food was minimal. As the writer and filmmaker Rithy Panh recalled, "The varieties of rice available in my childhood—'jasmine flower,' 'ginger blossom,' 'pale young girls'—disappeared within a few months. There remained to us only one kind of rice, white and nameless. Later what remained to us was hunger."

Rithy Panh's 2013 film *The Missing Picture* beautifully conveys the Khmer Rouge's annihilation of every aspect of a truly human existence, through memories of his own childhood and family. Before the revolution, they had led culturally rich lives in Phnom Penh: his father was a teacher, his brother played in a rock band, his sister was the deputy director of the national museum. Then, with everyone else, they were exiled and set to work in the fields. Life had been full; now there was only "conquest through emptiness." One by one, they died: his father, then his younger siblings, then his mother. A filmmaker needs images— but there were no images with which to tell the story, since no cameras existed, and only a few official propaganda movies were made. For *The Missing Picture*, Rithy Panh made small clay figures of each member of the family and photographed them in still tableaux, using his voice to narrate the story. "The revolution is pure," he says at one point. "No room for humans."

Given such events, as well as the two world wars and the Holocaust, it is not surprising that some writers looked back on the mid-twentieth century and saw in it an unanswerable refutation of the entire humanist worldview. The novelist William Golding said of the Second World War that "anyone who moved through those years without understanding that man produces evil as a bee produces honey, must have been blind or wrong in the head." His nihilistic and grotesque fable *Lord of the Flies*, depicting the moral degeneration of a group of boys stranded on a remote island, was an expression of that thought. He explained that he had not previously had such negative views, but such was the spirit of those times.

The idea that humans somehow oozed evil took up residence in the cultural atmosphere. Any seemingly civilized or cultured behavior—all the things in which humanists have taken pleasure or pride over the centuries—now looked like a mendacious veneer. Occasionally, humanists could still be given the role Stefan Zweig created for them in his books on Erasmus and Montaigne: fragile resistance heroes who kept a human light burning in dark times. But they could also be seen as either fools or hypocrites, their fine ideals a cover-up for brutal realities.

The humane surface does indeed seem thin when one considers, say, the many officers of the SS and other Nazi organizations who were highly refined products of the Humboldtian educational system—a system intended to form moral, well-rounded human beings. It is shocking to read, for example, of one young soldier who wrote in 1941 from the murderous eastern front that he felt himself driven to the need for such violence by "the struggle for the truly human, personal values." An appetite for looted artworks among some of the top Nazis suggests a superficially humanistic taste, yet with nothing human in it. And, as Thomas Mann asked in September 1945, what utter failure of feeling did it take for people in Nazi Germany to listen to *Fidelio*—Beethoven's opera about prisoners unjustly confined and abused in a dungeon—"without covering their faces and rushing out of the hall?"

This was why the philosopher Theodor Adorno could say, in an essay of 1951, "To write poetry after Auschwitz is barbaric." The idea behind this oft-quoted remark, as well as the longer arguments of *Dialectic of Enlightenment*, the book he wrote with Max Horkheimer at the end of the war, was not to devalue culture itself but to urge a radical critical evaluation of self-satisfied Western thinking: a "redigging" of Enlightenment thought, as Valla might have said.

But these useful tasks could flip over into something more like a total rejection of liberal, humanistic, and Enlightenment values, as if those values were to blame for their own negation. It was a bizarre twist, considering that both German and Italian Fascists defined themselves explicitly by rejecting the principles of reason, internationalism, individualism, humanitarianism, and meliorism, in order to embrace instinct, violence, nationalism, and war. Anti-humanist though those ideologies were, somehow they were supposed to be humanism's fault—which to humanist ears sounds like saying that car crashes still occur despite traffic lights, therefore the traffic lights are to blame.

Such distortions, however, reflect the difficulty intellectuals were having in finding an adequate response to extreme events. Seeing civilized values dismantled and having nowhere else to turn, they seemed to consider nothing adequate as an answer but some kind of even more extreme dismantling of values.

Thus, some writers thought the situation called for a return to religion or to a vague irrationalist spirituality. It is true that the major totalitarian states of the twentieth century tended to be atheistic, thus proving again that there is no automatic connection between questioning religion and being open-minded or humanist. (Their main problem with religion was that they could not stand there being a bigger God out there than themselves and their ideologies.) Now, in the wake of the horrors, some argued that humans should no longer trust themselves to work toward a better world on their own, and instead should return humbly to the old theologies. (In fact, some religious humanists, such as Jacques Maritain and Gabriel Marcel, had been saying this since the 1930s: nothing would go right for humanity, said Maritain, until they accepted that "the center for man is God.") In 1950, *Partisan Review* ran a series called "Religion and the Intellectuals," because, as the introduction announced, there were signs of a new "turn toward religion" everywhere. And when non-religious activists arranged a meeting in Amsterdam in 1952 to found the organization that eventually became today's Humanists International, the newspaper *Elseviers Weekblad* warned them: no one should try to undermine belief at a moment when society was so clearly "craving for character, for roots, for trust in God."

Others turned toward a general obscurantist mysticism, not traditionally religious yet still taking a position in opposition to Enlightenment reason and meliorism. One influential figure behind this was, ironically, a German philosopher tainted by having supported Nazism in the 1930s: Martin Heidegger. He set out his postwar anti-humanist position in his *Letter on Humanism*, written in late 1946 and published in 1947. Like Maritain, but for different reasons, Heidegger wanted to move the human individual out of the center. What he put in its place was not God, but "Being," which he distinguished from all particular, individual beings. The human role is to listen for Being and respond to its "call." Heidegger said that he did not intend Being to be a substitute for God, but it is hard not to see a certain similarity. In any case, the human role in relation to this giant ineffable Whatsit is strictly handmaidenly. Our task is not to manage our own affairs better, or to improve our moral lives, but only to serve something that can barely even be named.

Heidegger's *Letter* was intended as a response to the French philosopher Jean-Paul Sartre, who had delivered a lecture on humanism to a packed hall in Paris in 1945. Sartre's own position on this subject varied over time. Before the war he had mocked old-style humanists as sentimental hypocrites besotted with an abstract "humanity"; this accusation would come and go through his later work, too (under the influence of Marxism). For now, in the immediate wake of the war, he promoted an "existentialist" humanism based on the idea that each of us is radically free and responsible for our actions. Sartre's humanism was a tough-guy version made for the 1940s; it was also genuinely non-religious. It rested on the idea that humans have no preexisting blueprint for our nature, divine or otherwise. It is up to us what we make of ourselves; we must, individually and at every moment of choice, "invent man."

Partly because of Heidegger's influence, and partly because of an even greater fascination with Marxist theory, the next generation of French thinkers would laugh existentialist humanism out of the intellectual fashion pages and speak not of inventing the human but of dissolving it. In 1966, Michel Foucault ended his study *The Order of Things* by showing the figure of "man" about to be "erased, like a face drawn in sand at the edge of the sea." Just as Nietzsche (and Swinburne) thought humans had created God and then killed him, so Foucault thought the Enlightenment had created a Man that was now ready for obliteration. It would be replaced by a more critical understanding of ourselves as constructed by social and historical influences. Religious thinkers had centered humanity on God; Heideggerians had centered it on Being; now the hub was to be structures and processes—still human, in a sense, but treated as if they were more important than the actual humans who lived with them.

These new critical writers knocked humanist thought out of the center but also offered it a valuable overhaul service. They highlighted questions that European humanists had been inclined to think too little about, especially regarding racism, social exclusion, colonialism, and cultural difference. The postcolonial thinker Frantz Fanon wrote in his 1961 work *The Wretched of the Earth*, "That same Europe where they were never done talking of Man, and where they never stopped proclaiming that they were only anxious for the welfare of Man: today we know with what sufferings humanity has paid for every one of their triumphs of the mind."

Yet Fanon, too, approached the tradition of humanism in philosophy and life as being in need of a drastic rehoeing, rather than meriting wholesale rejection. He called for a new, *fuller* humanist philosophy: "Let us try to create the whole man, whom Europe has been incapable of bringing to triumphant birth," he wrote. "Let us reconsider the question of . . . the cerebral mass of all humanity, whose connexions must be increased, whose channels must be diversified and whose messages must be re-humanized." What could be more humanist than that? He also wrote, "No, we do not want to catch up with anyone. What we want to do is to go forward all the time, night and day, in the company of Man, in the company of all men."

Assessing these currents of thought, the Chinese literary scholar Zhang Longxi has written that to go "from one extreme of the concept of man as almost angelic and divine to the other extreme of man as disappearing like a face drawn in sand" is a strangely "absolutist" response to the crisis, especially coming from the sort of thinkers who normally try to avoid such black-and-white oppositions. (It is more like Innocent III versus Giannozzo Manetti all over again.) Instead, Professor Zhang suggests a humanist approach that draws on subtler traditions: "Temperance and moderation are true human virtues as we learn from philosophical wisdom in both East and West."

Rithy Panh also concluded his book about his experience in Cambodia, *The Elimination*, by writing:

> I undertook this project with the idea that man is not fundamentally wicked. Evil's nothing new; nor is good, but as I've written, there's also a banality of good; and an everydayness of good.
>
> As for the good part of that former world—my childhood, my sisters' laughter, my father's silences, the tireless play of my little nephew and niece, my mother's courage and kindness, this country of stone faces, the ideas of justice, of liberty, of equality, the taste for knowledge, education—that part can't be erased. It's not a bygone day, it's an effort and a work in progress; it's the human world.

Benedetto Croce had also stressed the "work in progress" principle. It is a mistake to despair over ourselves, he wrote in 1947; we make that mistake because we have come to expect the world to be reliably benign, with everyone living a civilized and enjoyable life. When that fantasy is shattered, we feel like giving up. The reality, however, is that history and the human world are neither stable and good on the one hand, nor hopelessly tragic on the other. They are *our own work*, so if we want it to proceed well, we have to exert ourselves to make it happen.

While philosophers tried to adjust their ideas of humanity after the Second World War, more pragmatic types worked for the physical reconstruction of cities, or for cultural and political recovery, and everywhere simply for the restoration of human flourishing, so far as was achievable. Among the most immediate challenges was managing some forty million displaced persons in Europe alone. There was also the project of "denazifying" Germany. Along with this came educational programs elsewhere, which were supposed to provide a basis for general moral revival—making that old humanist connection between education and ethical integrity.

In pursuit of this goal, a British government–backed report of 1943 had already prescribed character-building, plenty of exercise, and the study of the humanities, all designed "to bring to full flowering the varying potentialities, physical, spiritual and intellectual, of which [the child] is capable as an individual and as a member of society." In the United States, a 1945 Harvard committee report, *General Education in a Free Society*, likewise followed every humanistic educator in history by saying, "The complete man must be a good man."

Then there were plans for new international structures and institutions. The largest of all was the United Nations, founded in 1945: it was described by the British humanist Harold J. Blackham as "the beginning of genuine common interest, the human interest as such."

Among its offshoots, later the same year, was UNESCO, the United Nations Educational, Scientific and Cultural Organization. Its Erasmian founding text stated that, as wars begin in human minds, peace must start there, too. It set about enabling the latter goal with an ambitious policy of funding and encouraging libraries, museums, zoos, botanical gardens, scientific research institutes, universities, and the like. Its conception was strongly humanistic, not least because its first director-general was the zoologist Julian Huxley, grandson of T. H. Huxley and himself a proponent of "scientific humanism." In fact, the introductory booklet he wrote before taking up office—*UNESCO: Its Purpose and Its Philosophy*—was so (non-religiously) humanist in tone that some other members objected. He had to insert a last-minute statement in each copy, clarifying that the opinions expressed were his own. But his vision for UNESCO remained humanistic in a broader sense. As he wrote in his memoirs, "The key concept behind all our activities, I felt sure, should be *fulfilment*—fuller realization of capacities by individuals, cities, nations, and humanity as a whole." This remained at the heart of everything UNESCO did.

Unfortunately, the effect could not be as "whole" as hoped, because the Soviet Union and its satellites stayed aloof, rightly suspecting that organizations of this type also advanced another purpose: undermining their influence and ideology in the world. The Soviet bloc also proved awkward collaborators when another UN project was launched a couple of years later: the writing of a Universal Declaration of Human Rights, discussed throughout 1947 and completed the following year.

The drafting committee, headed by Eleanor Roosevelt, took its discussion process seriously, consulting world philosophers as well as representatives of different political views. Principles had to be found that would satisfy everyone, and this meant settling a position on major philosophical questions: whether rights or duties were more important, how individualism could be balanced with community identity, how to be inclusive, and whether one could speak of anything "universal" in humanity at all. These questions are still topics of general cultural debate today.

Then there was the matter of wording. The discussions began with article 1: the Soviet delegate Vladimir Koretsky pointed out (in accordance with official Communist policy on gender equality) that it used the phrase "All men are brothers," which excluded women. Eleanor Roosevelt explained, rather bizarrely, that the phrase was fine because it could be read as "All human beings are brothers"! It remained as it was for the moment, but at a later drafting stage "men" did turn into "human beings," because the Indian representative Hansa Mehta warned that, in some places, it really might be read as meaning only males. But the "brotherhood" stayed. Thus the opening statement became: "All human beings are born free and equal in dignity and rights. They are endowed with reason and conscience and should act towards one another in a spirit of brotherhood."

The term "conscience" in this statement was also considered. The first draft originally spoke only of "reason," but the commission's vice chair, P. C. Chang, a Chinese diplomat and philosopher with a particular admiration for the Confucian thought of Mengzi, suggested adding the term *ren*. Thus, the statement would take in wider implications of empathy and human reciprocity, instead of focusing on reason alone. His idea was taken up, and so the spirit of *ren* is strongly present in the document, even if the English translation "conscience" fails to convey that term's full range of meaning.

The result of all these negotiations was a declaration that is more inclusive and culturally sensitive than most documents of its time. It is not irreligiously humanist in a Huxleyish way, but it is a humanistic text in every other sense. It is also a practical one, designed to be used as a legal support in case of human rights abuses. Almost every nation approved it, but the list of abstentions speaks volumes. They came from six Communist countries, plus South Africa, because the Declaration could not be reconciled with apartheid, and Saudi Arabia, because of a clause providing for equal rights for men and women in marriage.

It may seem easy to take the principles expressed in the Declaration for granted—until they are trampled upon. Then, like humanistic values in general, they suddenly look more worth the effort of protecting. As Thomas Mann had observed in one of his BBC broadcasts to Germany, the real beginning of the Nazi catastrophe could be traced to the moment when,

during the party's victory rally in Berlin in February 1933, Joseph Goebbels announced: "The rights of man are abolished." Those words, said Mann, showed the Nazis' intention of wiping out "all moral attainments of humanity for thousands of years." The purpose of the Universal Declaration of Human Rights was to show the opposite intention: such an annihilation of attainments should not be allowed to happen again.

While these discussions were going on in global meeting rooms, art historians, "Monuments Men," and other volunteers and experts were tackling the task of cultural revival in a more field-based way. They toured the roads of Europe, finding, securing, and protecting the buildings and artworks that had made it through the war reasonably intact. Among them was Frederick Hartt, who described the change from "form to formlessness" and "history to mindlessness" in Florence so vividly. He wrote a very readable account of his adventures touring Tuscany and elsewhere, beginning with the last stages of the German retreat. Often, he followed in the steps of the fearless and energetic Cesare Fasola, a member of the Uffizi staff and himself a partisan of the resistance, referred to by villagers in the area as *il professore*. He thought nothing of cycling alone around the countryside in search of art, even while the Germans were still there; they gave him a special pass. He and Hartt were among the first to arrive at the Castle of Montegufoni (owned by an English literary family, the Sitwells), a storage site for many items from the Uffizi. They found an unnerving scene: the German troops billeted there had now gone, but they had left Botticelli's *Primavera* casually leaning against a wall and turned Domenico Ghirlandaio's circular *Adoration of the Magi* into a drinks table—the same indignity later inflicted on the mosaic from Caligula's ship. One of the Allied visitors, the novelist Eric Linklater, added to the hazards by lovingly pressing kisses to the lips of all the female figures in *Primavera*. He did it when no one was looking—but wrote about it openly in his memoir.

Some heroic German individuals had saved treasures, too. A lot of looting had gone on, but a few officers merely tucked vulnerable artworks away to protect them from damage. This at least was the case at the Benedictine monastery of Montecassino—that great monastic fortress, the library of which Boccaccio had been so delighted to explore some six hundred years previously. With its location high above the route from Naples to Rome, it was clearly of strategic importance to both sides. Two German officers, Maximilian Becker and Julius Schlegel, realized (separately) that this made it a likely bombing target for Allied forces. Therefore, late in 1943, they packed its most precious collection items into some hundred truckloads, to be sent north to the safer stronghold of the Castel Sant'Angelo in Rome. They were right to do it: the Americans did bomb the monastery the following February, with an even more massive bombardment six weeks later. A member of the crew for this second bombing, Walter M. Miller Jr., was so shocked by what he saw that he went on to convert to Catholicism, and also to write a novel, *A Canticle for Leibowitz*. Set in a future world in which most cultural knowledge has been lost, it tells of people finding and investigating a few stray relics of twentieth-century civilization and hoping to use them for a rebirth— very much the project of the fourteenth- and fifteenth-century humanists in Italy. In this case, however, the first relic they find is a note: "Pound pastrami, can kraut, six bagels—bring home for Emma."

Similar destruction almost happened to Chartres, but this time it was an American who saved it. On August 16, 1944, the Germans were still in the town. The Americans were about to enter and were ordered to shell the cathedral heavily as a precaution, in case German forces were using it as a lookout tower. This was plausible: like the Montecassino monastery, Chartres Cathedral has a commanding view over the landscape around it. But an officer, Colonel Welborn Barton Griffith Jr., recoiled at the idea of such destruction being visited upon a 750-year-old building without confirmed evidence. Courageously, he and his driver (whose name I am sorry not to know) sneaked into the town, entered the cathedral alone, and climbed up to the top of the bell tower: no Germans were inside. Griffith gave the all-clear, and the order to shell the building was withdrawn. That was almost his last act in life; later the same day he was killed by enemy fire in the nearby town of Lèves. Through all of this drama, the Chartres window glass remained safely sheltered in its crypt below; when peace came, workers and volunteers retrieved it and reinstalled it in its setting, as carefully as it had been taken out.

A few years ago, I spent two days in and around Chartres, exploring the cathedral and learning some of the stories from its long life, including the story of the brave colonel and driver—and also of that earlier intervention, when an architect dissuaded the French Revolutionary vandals from ordering its demolition.

As well as admiring the beauty of the building itself, I found myself deeply moved by the way it embodies human time. All buildings do this, but Chartres makes its temporal process more visible than most. It rises from the ancient crypt and foundations. Then it reaches its main twelfth- and thirteenth-century space of carvings, buttresses, and windows—all made using the most up-to-date technologies of their time, from the structural engineering of the buttresses to the stained-glass work, much of it featuring a distinctive "Chartres blue." Moving up higher and climbing into the roof, one finds—unexpectedly—a nineteenth-century cast-iron roof support, well hidden from outside view. It was built in 1836 and modeled on the beautiful ironwork of that era's railway stations. Again, the best of modernity has been allied to the greatest possible respect for history. One thinks of the workers who cast it and of the original medieval craftspeople. One thinks, too, of the people from more recent times who patiently numbered and packed away the glass in the 1930s, and those who unpacked and reinstalled it after the war—and those who are still dedicated to working on it and protecting it today. The building holds it all: the human skill and dedication, the political environment of each epoch, the original conception, the centuries of maintenance. It reminds us of the scholarship the cathedral hosted in the "twelfth-century Renaissance," and—yes—of the Christian faith that made it seem worth going to so much trouble to create such beauty in the first place.

I do not share that faith myself, yet I found it impossible to walk around Chartres without feeling a (slightly nervous) faith in humanity. It is true that human beings have several times come close to knocking it down. But other human beings keep trying, even harder, to make it stay up.

The most obvious aspect in which humans needed to pull themselves together, in the aftermath of the Second World War, concerned nuclear weapons. As Jean-Paul Sartre put it in October 1945, the lesson of Hiroshima and Nagasaki was that, from now on, it would always be up to human beings to *decide* whether they wanted to survive or not—the ultimate existentialist decision.

Another public humanist who phrased the problem in a memorable way was Bertrand Russell. He concluded a 1954 radio broadcast, "Man's Peril," with a call to make a choice:

> There lies before us, if we choose, continual progress in happiness, knowledge, and wisdom. Shall we, instead, choose death, because we cannot forget our quarrels? I appeal, as a human being to

human beings: remember your humanity, and forget the rest. If
you can do so, the way lies open to a new Paradise; if you cannot,
nothing lies before you but universal death.

"Remember your humanity, and forget the rest"—the "rest" being national interests, vanity, pride, prejudice, despair, and anything else that
gets in the way of choosing to live—became a much-quoted line, not least
by Russell himself. He repeated it in another of those international conferences, this one taking place in 1955 and hammering out a manifesto to
be signed by concerned scientists, among them Albert Einstein just a few
days before his death. The group went on to hold meetings annually,
starting in July 1957 in Pugwash, Nova Scotia; thus "Pugwash" remained
the name attached to the original manifesto as well as the conferences.
They still meet today, and have the same aims: minimizing proliferation
of weapons and promoting political mechanisms to try to make a catastrophic war less likely.

Bertrand Russell continued to be a stalwart of the anti-nuclear campaign, writing about it and taking part in demonstrations for the rest of
his life. After one such occasion in 1961, when he spoke to a crowd in
London's Hyde Park, he was convicted of "inciting the public to civil disobedience" and sentenced to a week in Brixton Prison. He was now
eighty-nine years old. The magistrate did try to let him off in exchange
for a promise of "good behavior," but Russell would promise no such
thing. Like Voltaire, he became only *more* fearless and provocative as he
went on in life.

Russell worked for many other causes, including environmental ones:
he had a prescient sense of the importance of saving the planet's natural
resources and emphasized the urgency of this as early as 1948–1949 in
his BBC Reith Lectures. (Around the same time, Julian Huxley organized
a UNESCO initiative to create the International Union for the Conser-
vation of Nature, which still works with governments and businesses.)

One part of nature almost swallowed Russell up in 1948, before he had a chance to give the Reith Lectures. During a trip that autumn to Trondheim, Norway, he took a flight in the *Bukken Bruse*, a "flying boat"— a kind of seaplane that touches down in water directly with its hull, instead of having footlike floats. The weather was bad. Just as the flying boat was about to settle in the water, it was hit by a gust of wind and tipped over sideways. A wing came off, and water flooded into the cabin. Nineteen of the forty-five people on board were killed, including everyone in the non-smoking section toward the front. Most of the smokers, being farther back, managed to swim out and were rescued—including Russell, eternal pipe-puffer that he was. He was drenched and had nothing to change into until a kind clergyman lent him a clerical outfit to wear— an amusing sight to those who knew Russell's views on religion. One journalist called from Copenhagen and asked him what he had thought about while in the water. Did he think about mysticism and logic? No, he said. "I thought the water was cold."

Russell's campaigns, by their nature, were often *against* things: nuclear weapons, the depredation of nature, and wars—notably in his opposition to U.S. involvement in Vietnam in the late 1960s, by which time he was well into his nineties. His general attitude toward the world, however, was anything but negative. In an autobiographical talk of 1955, "Hopes: Realized and Disappointed," he looked back on his prewar optimistic liberalism, which he admitted had become harder to maintain. Yet he would not give it up: "I will not submit my judgments as to what is good and what is bad to the chance arbitrament of the momentary course of events." One must adapt to changes in the world, of course, but "it is also a bad thing to assume that whatever is in the ascendant must be right." In any case, as he always emphasized, it is for *us* to decide whether our world becomes more happy than otherwise.

He returned to such thoughts in his autobiography, the final volume of which was one of the last things he published, a few months before his death in February 1970. He closed the volume with a summation of his experience of almost a century of life:

I may have thought the road to a world of free and happy human beings shorter than it is proving to be, but I was not wrong in thinking that such a world is possible, and that it is worth while to live with a view to bringing it nearer. I have lived in the pursuit of a vision, both personal and social. Personal: to care for what is noble, for what is beautiful, for what is gentle; to allow moments of insight to give wisdom at more mundane times. Social: to see in imagination the society that is to be created, where individuals grow freely, and where hate and greed and envy die because there is nothing to nourish them. These things I believe, and the world, for all its horrors, has left me unshaken.

12.

❧ ------------ ❧

The Place to Be Happy

1933–now

*Humanist organizations, manifestos, and campaigns—
Born of Mary—courts, parliaments, and schools—
Relax!—"glory enough"—enemies—architecture and
city planning—Vasily Grossman—machines and
consciousness—the posthuman and the transhuman—
Arthur C. Clarke and the Overmind—the humanist
bark—when, where, and how to be happy.*

Also looking for Russell's "world of free and happy human beings" throughout the twentieth century, and into the twenty-
first, have been people who gather into groups under the name
of Humanists. Some of these groups first developed out of Secular, or
Rational, or Ethical Societies of the previous century. Some were strongly
atheistic; others had links to quasi-religious organizations such as the Unitarians. Some mainly sought to promote scientific and rationalist ideas;
others put more emphasis on moral living. Some were allied with radical
socialism; others avoided political affiliation.

During the crisis of the 1930s it had occurred to a few people in
America, mainly Unitarians, that it would be useful to make connections between groups by writing "some kind of humanist blast." That

blast became the world's first Humanist Manifesto, issued in 1933. It presented humanism as a "religion," partly because that was the Unitarian approach, and partly because it made a handy way to talk about a movement that otherwise fit no obvious category. Not all humanists wanted to be involved, in some cases because they disliked the idea of agreeing to any dogma at all. One of those invited to sign, Harold Buschman, wrote back warning, "There will be 'heresies' and misunderstandings instead of a free checking of experiences, one with another." Another, F. C. S. Schiller, observed ironically, "I note that your manifesto has 15 articles, 50% more than the Ten Commandments."

Thirty-four signatories did put their names to the manifesto. They thus endorsed a statement that showed concern with civil liberties and social justice, and a preference for reason as the best means of governing public affairs. Although the manifesto called humanism a religion, it also said that humanists see the universe as "self-existing and not created," and that they expect no "supernatural or cosmic guarantees of human values." A humanist may have "religious emotions," but these mainly take the form of "a heightened sense of personal life and [a belief] in a cooperative effort to promote social well-being." A humanist, they agreed, is a person whose field of concern "includes labor, art, science, philosophy, love, friendship, recreation—all that is in its degree expressive of intelligently satisfying human living." In short, a humanist values "joy in living" and is someone to whom (to quote Terence) "nothing human is alien."

This statement attracted strong responses from those whose idea of religion was quite different. *The Bristol Press* in Connecticut approvingly cited an anecdote of one student telling another, "Thomas, you say just once more that there is no God, and I will knock hell out of you." The paper added, "Such a dose of medicine is the only argument which these professors are capable of understanding and in our humble opinion they would be cured." In that fateful year of 1933, that was the least of the threats that would face humanists, "professors," and everyone else besides.

In the postwar years, humanist organizations emerged, or old ones were revived, in many parts of the world. They included several notable groups in India—with its ancient freethought tradition going back to the Cārvāka school. The most flamboyant of the Indian activists was Manabendra Nath Roy, the founder of the Indian Radical Humanist Movement. In the earlier years of the century he had been a Marxist and spent time in Mexico helping with the foundation of the Communist Party there. He then spent eight years in the Soviet Union, once (as he recalled in his memoirs) cooking an excellent soup for Stalin. But he became disillusioned with Communism, especially in its Stalinist form, because of its lack of respect for individual lives or for personal freedom. Roy returned to India and became involved in the independence movement, spending six years in prison for his activities. (As Bertrand Russell remarked of the British at this time, they shared with Fascists the belief that one could "only govern by putting the best people in prison.") He knew Mohandas K. Gandhi, but had some disagreements with his approach and formed a breakaway Radical Democratic Party. They differed as much in temperament as in political principle: Gandhi was known for his austere living, but Roy preferred the ebullient Robert Ingersoll tradition. For him, the humanist way of life meant appreciating the pleasures of this planet to the maximum: besides soup, he loved good food in general, as well as good wine, traveling, socializing, freedom, friendship, and "joy in living." To promote these excellent things and his political commitment to internationalism and ethical living, he launched a "New Humanism"—definitely not to be confused with the elitist New Humanism of Irving Babbitt and his associates. Roy's manifesto prominently featured Protagoras's line: "Man must again be the measure of all things."

Other Indian humanists were in the forefront of a new project after the war: the attempt to establish a unified body to support and coordinate the many groups around the world. A key mover came from the Netherlands: Jaap van Praag, cofounder in 1946 of the Dutch Humanist

League. He was Jewish and had survived the war in hiding throughout the Nazi occupation. For him, promoting humanist values was one way of warding off the possibility of such things happening again. He and others organized a congress in Amsterdam in 1952 that convened more than two hundred delegates from all directions, brought together with the aim of founding a lasting institution and, naturally, writing a new manifesto to go with it.

As usual when humans get together with an important purpose in mind, the congress immediately fell to arguing strenuously over ideology and the choice of terms. According to an entertaining account by Hans van Deukeren, the disputes began with the question of what to call themselves. Some delegates wanted to make it an International Ethical Society; for them, "ethical" was a well-established general term for such groups, whereas "humanist" brought to mind Auguste Comte's Religion of Humanity. Others were in favor of "humanist" and thought "ethical" was too bland. Only after fourteen hours of discussion did someone suggest calling it the International Humanist *and* Ethical Union. And so it became—IHEU for short—although it has now changed, to become Humanists International. It has continued to flourish, weathering further ideological disputes, and it remains the hub for the world's humanists with their varied national challenges and battles.

As for the 1952 manifesto, known as the Amsterdam Declaration, this had an enduring success, but in evolving forms; it has been through several updates to add new ideas or adjust the emphasis of older ones. The latest version, issued by Humanists International in 2022, follows the 1952 original in many ways, above all by emphasizing the ethical focus of humanism. Both versions speak of the importance of personal fulfillment and development, as well as of social responsibilities and connections. Both support free scientific inquiry, informed by human values, as our best hope for finding solutions to our problems. Humanists, says the new version, in line with the original, "strive to be rational," but artistic activity and "creative and ethical living" are also important. Both documents remind us of the long, inspiring traditions that lie behind modern humanism. Both also express a guarded optimism for the future. In the 2022 Declaration, this is summed up with the words: "We are confident that humanity has the potential to solve the problems that confront us, through free inquiry, science, sympathy, and imagination in the furtherance of peace and human flourishing."

The 2022 version expands on all this, however, by including new elements that were missing in 1952. It puts more stress on the wide *range* of those humanistic traditions that nourish modern humanism: "Humanist beliefs and values are as old as civilization and have a history in most societies around the world." Humanists, it says, hope for "the flourishing and fellowship of humanity in all its diversity and individuality." Thus: "We reject all forms of racism and prejudice and the injustices that arise from them." The 2022 Declaration follows the original in promoting the life-enhancing effects of arts, literature, and music, but also adds a mention of the "comradeship and achievement" to be found in physical activities. It shows a greater recognition of humanity's connection and duties to the rest of life on Earth—"to all sentient beings," as well as to future generations of humans. Finally, it sounds a new note of modesty in the closing section: "Humanists recognise that no one is infallible or omniscient, and that knowledge of the world and of humankind can be won only through a continuing process of observation, learning, and rethinking. For these reasons, we seek neither to avoid scrutiny nor to impose our view on all humanity. On the contrary, we are committed to the unfettered expression and exchange of ideas, and seek to cooperate with people of different beliefs who share our values, all in the cause of building a better world." (To read the 2022 manifesto in its entirety, see the Appendix at page 371.)

The evolving manifesto reflects changes in how humanists see themselves, as well as broader changes in the world: it provides more subtlety and respect for difference; there is no triumphalism when it talks of humanity. Adding these new levels of complexity has made for a longer text.

But I like the new tone; I like the modesty and inclusiveness, alongside the older elements. Like earlier versions, the 2022 manifesto continues to ground humanism firmly in the realm of ethics and values, and the duty of care we all owe to one another and to our fellow living beings. All versions emphasize this more than matters of belief, irreligion, or even reason—important though those matters are. They focus less on religious doubt than on wider human questions of fulfillment, freedom, creativity, and responsibility. They make it clear that humanism is not primarily about carping at the faithful—an activity that can be alienating for many, and that is anyway not the most cheerful way of spending one's time on Earth. (Carping at those in authority who insist on imposing their faith on others, on the other hand, seems to me an excellent way of spending one's time.) Instead, this is a manifesto for something deeper: a joyful and positive set of human values.

This is also true of a 2003 manifesto issued by the American Humanist Association (founded in 1941, and glorying in the acronym AHA). It speaks of living life "well and fully," guided by compassion as well as reason:

> We aim for our fullest possible development and animate our lives with a deep sense of purpose, finding wonder and awe in the joys and beauties of human existence, its challenges and tragedies, and even in the inevitability and finality of death.

As humanist organizations work to become more positive and more approachable, they have also sought to build better connections with wider communities—including some that may have a high level of distrust or dislike of humanism. Religious institutions and beliefs can be central features of life in these communities, and often bring people a sense of social identity and shared meaning. If humanists are perceived mainly as antireligious, they may be thought of as opposing the validity not just of specific beliefs but of the whole principle of meaning and identity. The Black American humanist Debbie Goddard has described running up against this perception when, as a college student, she openly declared herself an atheist. As she has said: "My closest black friends told me that humanism and atheism are harmful Eurocentric ideologies and implied that if I'm an atheist, I'm turning my back on my race." Atheism was as seen as threatening "black identity and black history." Goddard decided to work toward two goals: "getting more humanism in to the black community and more people of color into the humanist community."

One of the things that modern humanist organizations—such as African Americans for Humanism, of which Goddard is now director—have tried to do is to emphasize how deeply Black and other perspectives enhance, inform, and enrich the humanist world, rather than being treated as something separate, supplementary, or distracting. In return, as a 2001 declaration by AAH stated, humanists can work more specifically to promote "eupraxophy"—"wisdom and good conduct through living"—in the Black American community. AAH is not the only U.S.-based organization for humanists of color; others include the Black Humanist Alliance and the Latinx Humanist Alliance, both affiliated with the American Humanist Association. In the UK, the Association of Black Humanists is similarly affiliated with Humanists UK.

Organizations for LGBTQ+ humanists also form part of larger humanist groups. The British version, LGBT Humanists, owes its foundation to an extraordinary case in 1977, when Christian fundamentalists resuscitated old blasphemy laws in order to prosecute the journal *Gay News* after it published a poem by James Kirkup, "The Love That Dares to Speak Its Name."

The poem was certainly shocking to some Christians. It portrayed a Roman centurion kissing and caressing the crucified body of Jesus in a way that is at once sexual and tender. It caught the velociraptor eye of Mary Whitehouse, a conservative campaigner always on the lookout for more battles to fight—her previous ones had included trying, unsuccessfully, to get the BBC to ban the Chuck Berry song "My Ding-a-Ling." Encountering Kirkup's poem (presumably as she browsed innocently through her copy of *Gay News*), Whitehouse got to work organizing a criminal prosecution for blasphemous libel, not against the poet but against the journal and its editor, Denis Lemon.

The case, opening at the Old Bailey on July 4, attracted much interest; perhaps not as much as the *Lady Chatterley's Lover* trial of 1960, but close. It was the first UK trial on a blasphemy charge in fifty-six years. The previous one had been brought in 1921 against the Bradford trouser sales-man and freethinker John W. Gott, after he published a book called *God and Gott*; despite his fragile health, he was given nine months' hard labor. Since then the law had not been used, but it was still officially in force.

Lemon and *Gay News* were defended, respectively, by two high-profile liberal barristers, John Mortimer and Geoffrey Robertson. Leading the prosecution case was John Smyth, who delivered a dramatic opening ac-count of the offense the poem caused to those with Christian belief. After the case, he would rarely appear in the media again until, in 2017, he was obliged to leave the country after accusations of violent abuse of boys attending a Christian summer camp.

An obvious factor to consider in the trial would seem to be that of literary worth. Kirkup was a fellow of the Royal Society of Literature and a university tutor, so his credentials seemed good, and several noted writ-ers offered to testify as to the poem's quality. (The poet himself avoided getting involved in the case, later saying that he disapproved of any po-liticization of art.) But no literary testimony was heard, because the judge, Alan King-Hamilton, ruled it irrelevant. His summing-up to the jury at the end included remarks such as: "There are some who think permissiveness has gone far enough. There are others who may think that there should be no limit whatever to what may be published. If they are right, one may wonder what scurrilous profanity may next appear." He would later recall that he felt "half conscious of being guided by some superhuman inspiration" while delivering this summation. On July 11, the jury duly brought in a ten-to-two guilty verdict. Both defendants were fined, and Lemon was also given a nine-month suspended sentence.

The implication, as John Mortimer wrote afterward, was that making Anglicans blush was a criminal offense. And it *was* only Anglicans: other religions remained unprotected by the British blasphemy laws, as the British Muslim Action Front discovered in 1988, when it tried to use them against the publisher of Salman Rushdie's *The Satanic Verses*.

Meanwhile, with all the publicity, and an excellent BBC docudrama based on the transcript, the main effect of the *Gay News* case was greatly to raise the profile both of LGBTQ+ rights and of the humanist cause. Mary Whitehouse had ranted about a "humanist gay lobby," yet no such thing formally existed. Therefore, gay humanists decided to create one. In 1979 the Gay Humanist Group was born—later LGBT Humanists. In honor of its origin, they took the motto "Born of Mary."

Fighting against blasphemy laws has continued to be a crucial part of what humanist organizations do. In some places the fight seems to be won, or nearly so: in the UK, blasphemy ceased to be a crime in England and Wales in 2008 and in Scotland in 2021, although at the time of this writing it remains illegal in Northern Ireland. In the United States, thanks to the First Amendment's protection of freedoms of speech and belief, no such law ever existed on a national level, but a few do in individual states. The last conviction was almost a century ago: in Little Rock, Arkansas, in 1928, Charles Lee Smith received a prison sentence for displaying a sign reading "Evolution Is True. The Bible's a Lie. God's a Ghost." At the first of his two trials, he could not even testify in his own defense, because, as a known atheist, he was not allowed to swear the necessary oath on the Bible to tell the truth.

A range of other countries have blasphemy laws on the books (in some cases inherited from British colonial laws), and seven currently go further by allowing for death sentences. An international "End Blasphemy Laws Now" campaign was founded in 2015, and the Center for Inquiry in the United States also created a "Secular Rescue" program.

For those emerging from high-control religions and regimes, it offers help, including with asylum claims, immigration, legal needs, and scholarships. It has been described as an "Underground Railroad to save atheists." During the period I have been writing this book, American humanists have also acquired new challenges to deal with in the United States itself, especially from the undoing—largely rooted in conservative religious views—of abortion rights that had once seemed firmly established.

All this lies at the most dramatic end of the activist spectrum, but organized humanists also keep busy working toward more modest achievements in their various countries: more inclusive and humanist-friendly treatment of religious subjects in schools, equal recognition of humanist wedding and funeral ceremonies, access to dignified assisted dying for terminally ill people, and so on.

In Britain, Humanists UK has some particular battles to fight, notably against the bizarre privileges still given to Anglicans in the political system—perhaps not surprising in a country with a long tradition of designating the monarch as "Defender of the Faith." The House of Lords includes seats for twenty-six Church of England bishops, meaning that, in company with a handful of other theocracies, the UK automatically reserves a say in government for clerics. Both there and in the House of Commons, each day starts with prayers, usually led by a senior bishop (in the Lords) and a specially appointed Speaker's Chaplain (in the Commons). Attendance is voluntary, but members who want to be sure of a place to sit on busy days find it advisable to reserve one for the prayer session; otherwise, they risk turning up later to find standing room only.

At least MPs no longer have to swear a specifically religious oath when they take office. The option to choose a secular affirmation was secured for them in 1888 by Charles Bradlaugh, MP and founder of the National Secular Society. Elected in 1880, he refused at first to swear the usual oath, and was not allowed to take up his seat. The theory, as always, was that non-believers could not be trusted to speak honestly in politics or do the right thing for the country, just as they could not be trusted to

AUGUST 3RD 1881.   MARCH 14TH 1888.

speak truly in court. As a paradoxical result, those without acceptable beliefs could prove their reliability only by lying. Bradlaugh offered to do that, giving the religious oath anyway. But now he was told he could not, since he had admitted to not believing in it. Each time he tried to enter Parliament he was ejected. Once he was held overnight in a cell underneath Big Ben, and another time he was forcibly bundled out of the building by security—not easy, as Bradlaugh was (like Robert Ingersoll) built on formidable dimensions. His friend George William Foote described his appearance on the street after his expulsion: there "he stood, a great mass of panting, valiant manhood, his features set like granite, and his eyes fixed upon the doorway before him. I never admired him more than at that moment. He was superb, sublime." With Bradlaugh's seat officially considered vacant, it kept going to by-elections, but he kept standing for it and winning again. At last, in 1886, he was allowed to take it up, making the standard religious oath—but soon after entering Parliament he proposed a bill to have the non-religious affirmation recognized instead. The bill passed and became law.

The United States also has religiosity woven into its political life, but in a different way. In contrast to the UK, it is officially secular, yet a strong assumption reigns that no (openly) irreligious candidate could ever attain high office. The older political foundations of the country were quite different: they were based on the principle of separation of church and state, and were in any case created by people who often had skeptical, deist, or pluralist beliefs themselves. Thomas Jefferson, for example, before creating his de-amphibologized Bible, wrote in his *Notes on the State of Virginia* that "it does me no injury for my neighbour to say there are twenty gods, or no god. It neither picks my pocket nor breaks my leg." Some of the most conspicuous religious elements in the American public realm became established only in the 1950s. The phrase "under God" was added to the Pledge of Allegiance in 1954. "In God We Trust," although used on coinage and elsewhere before that, began appearing on paper currency in 1957, following a law approved in 1956. Also in 1956, it replaced *E pluribus unum* as the motto of Congress.

Even during those pious postwar years, the United States' secular principles meant that, in theory, children should never be obliged to attend religious lessons. In practice, this was often ignored. A quietly determined activist, Vashti McCollum, brought a case in 1948 against her son's school for effectively making it impossible for him to avoid such classes. After repeated losses, she won at last at the Supreme Court. Along the path to that victory, she and her family endured much abuse. People threw rubbish at their door, including entire cabbage plants with roots and mud. Scrawled over both house and car windows was "ATHIST." Letters arrived saying things like "May

your rotten soul roast into hell." When McCollum showed these letters to a woman who knocked at the door, hoping to persuade her to repent, the woman claimed that no Christian could have written such things. McCollum replied, "Well, it's a cinch no atheist wrote them."

In the UK, a similar outcry came in 1955 when the educational psychologist Margaret Knight delivered two BBC radio programs aimed at parents who wanted to teach their children moral principles without a Christian slant. She had to fight internal opposition within the BBC, and afterward the media rushed to deplore her. The *Sunday Graphic* printed her picture with the words, "She looks—doesn't she—just like the typical housewife: cool, comfortable, harmless. But Mrs. Margaret Knight is a menace." In a memoir, she recalled how, in her own youth, she had tried to suppress her religious doubts, until she read Bertrand Russell and realized that it *was* possible to say and feel such things. All she wanted to do with the radio series, she said, was to give parents and children a similar awareness that one could speak openly about matters of belief and doubt.

Raising such awareness still forms part of what humanist groups do today. Even if one lives in a society where non-religious views are widespread, generally, it can be hard to admit to doubts about a religion one has grown up personally embedded in. Humanist organizations hope to promote a general spirit of acceptance and even comfort, reminding people that if they do question their religion, they have company, and that living with a purely humanistic morality is a valid choice.

This was why both British and American organizations ran advertising campaigns in 2008 and 2009, putting posters on billboards and the sides of buses. The American Humanist Association's messages read: "Don't believe in God? You're not alone." And: "Why believe in a God? Just be good for goodness' sake." The British message, instigated by Ariane Sherine, was the one we met in our introductory chapter: "There's probably no God. Now stop worrying and enjoy your life." Not everyone liked that thought. Along with the more predictable letters of complaint re-

ceived by the BHA from the religious were also some from hard-core atheists who thought the word *probably* was a cop-out, and from radical
agnostics who felt that announcing even the *probable* nonexistence of God
was too definite a statement to make. It goes to show that you can't please
all of the people all of the time—a good humanistic principle in itself.

The priority in these campaigns was, as always, to strike a positive
note. Relax! Just be good—you have plenty of company—enjoy your life.
The advertisements were meant not as attacks but as attempts to connect
with people who might already be, to some extent, humanists without
knowing it.

Meanwhile, religious practices and communities still offer many people joy, fellowship, and fulfillment. Why would humanists wish people
not to have such (highly humanistic) forms of satisfaction in their lives?
Indeed, most humanists do not wish this. They concentrate on helping
those to whom religion has brought trouble or fear; they promote awareness of humanistic possibilities, and work for better laws and political
structures to serve the needs of the non-religious.

Humanism should never mean taking anything away from the
riches of human life; it should open up *more* riches. I am with Zora Neale
Hurston, whose Democritan vision of material existence we met in the
opening chapter. In the same passage, she also said:

I would not, by word or deed, attempt to deprive another of the consolation it affords. It is simply not for me. Somebody else may have my rapturous glance at the archangels. The springing of the yellow line of morning out of the misty deep of dawn, is glory enough for me.

My own sense of rapture and glory comes mostly from trying to imagine the grandeur and complexity of the universe, about which we are learning more all the time. Science tells us things that I can only describe as sublime: that we live in a universe estimated to contain some 125 billion galaxies, of which our galaxy alone contains some 100 billion stars, of which our particular star shines upon our planet and fills it with some 8.7 million diverse species of life, of which 1 species is able to study and marvel at such observations. That makes *us* a marvel, too: somehow, our three pounds or so of fleshy brain-substance are able to encompass and develop such knowledge, and to generate a whole mini-universe of consciousness, emotion, and self-reflection.

Atheists may find it simply perplexing that, given all this, so many people instead remain wedded to the idea of merely local gods who seem concerned mainly with collecting tributes and watching to see if we are having sex correctly. The question such atheists ask is: Why should not the human mental landscape reflect what we have managed to learn, so far, about the universe and its life and beauty—as if in a clear, undistorting mirror?

But very little of the human mental landscape is ever remotely like a reflection in a clear, undistorting mirror. Julian Huxley wrote of a human being as a transforming mill, "into which the world of brute reality is poured in all its rawness, to emerge . . . as a world of values." We can try to make ourselves think as rationally and with as broad a scientific reach as possible; it is a good thing if we do. But we will *also* always live in a world of symbols, emotions, morals, words, and relationships. And that will often mean a porous border between non-religious and religious ways of relating to that world.

As the nineteenth-century Russian short-story writer, playwright, and physician Anton Chekhov wrote in 1889, in a letter to a friend—alluding to a song by Mikhail Glinka, with words by Alexander Pushkin:

> If a man knows the theory of the circulatory system, he is rich. If he learns the history of religion and the song "I remember a Marvelous Moment" in addition, he is the richer, not the poorer, for it. We are consequently dealing entirely in pluses.

> Dealing in pluses: that is glory enough for me.

But this does not mean that all is well. A more serious problem occurs not when supernatural beliefs are asserted but when deeper humanistic values come under threat, including in ways touched on throughout this book: cruelties to humans and other living things, the denial of respect to certain kinds of people, the preaching of intolerance, the burning or other destruction of "vanities," and the suppression of freedom in thinking, writing, and publishing. In 1968, the doyen of British humanists, Harold J. Blackham, helpfully supplied a list of what he considered the "enemies" at that time—enemies being a word peaceable types are often reluctant to use, as he acknowledged. Nevertheless, he argued, it *is* necessary to recognize enemies. They are:

> bigots, sectarians, dogmatists, fanatics, hypocrites, whether Christians or humanists, and all those, however labelled, who seek for any purpose whatever to dupe, enslave, manipulate, brain-wash, or otherwise deprive human beings of their self-dependence and responsibility, all those particularly who victimize thus the young and inexperienced. The humanist cause, in the vastest and vaguest of phrases, is "life and freedom," and on the enemy front are all those doctrines, institutions, practices and people hostile to life or freedom.

We could add more for our own time: a whole breed of authoritarian, fundamentalist, illiberal, repressive, war-mongering, misogynistic, racist, homophobic, nationalist, and populist manipulators, some of whom claim devotion to traditional religious pieties, whether or not this is sincere. They show contempt for actual human lives yet promise—always!—something higher and better. As enemies of humanism, and of human well-being, they must be taken seriously.

On the other hand, they may also help us to answer the question "What is humanism?" We can find an answer by looking at the gaps left behind whenever a casual disregard of individuals is in the ascendant. Humanism is whatever should be there instead.

One can see this in specific areas of life, not just on a wide political canvas. For example: What is humanist architecture, or humanist city planning? It is the sort that does not constantly crush the ability to live a decent, satisfying human life. A humanistic civic designer pays attention to how people use a space and to what makes them comfortable, rather than trying to make a big impression with buildings of gasp-inducing size or a field of stylish obstacles that is frustrating to walk around. For humanistic architects, it is better to start with "the human measure." Geoffrey Scott, author of the influential 1914 study *The Architecture of Humanism*, explained this by reminding us of our tendency to talk about buildings in terms of our own bodily experience, saying that they feel top-heavy, or soaring, or well balanced—descriptions derived from our own physical sense of existing in the world. A humanist architect will look for "physical conditions that are related to our own, for movements which are like those we enjoy, for resistances that resemble those that can support us, for a setting where we should be neither lost nor thwarted."

These goals drove the great American advocate of humanistic city design, Jane Jacobs. She began by campaigning successfully in 1958 against a plan by Robert Moses to run an expressway right through the center of Lower Manhattan, demolishing Washington Square Park. She went on to write studies of how people actually live and work in cities— observing, for example, that it may seem a good idea to put large parks on the edge of town, but that people are more interested in walking *through* somewhere nice on their regular routes to work or the shops, rather than making special trips. She also noted that a bustling neighborhood street, filled with bars and frequented by unruly teenagers, may feel chaotic and noisy but is likely to be a safer environment than a clear open space—and certainly one more conducive to human relationships. The work of Jacobs influenced others, such as the Danish city planner Jan Gehl, who spent hours dawdling on Italian streets, taking notes about how the residents walked across a piazza or how they paused to chat while leaning on a bollard. A local paper printed a picture of him at lurk, with the caption "He looks like a 'beatnik,' but he isn't." Then he applied his discoveries to projects around the world, working with local citizens. In one case, after he and residents of the Danish housing project of Høje Gladsaxe had jointly designed a children's play area, the original architects called the results "an act of vandalism against the architecture." For Gehl, that always made more sense than architecture vandalizing people's lives.

What applies in urban design applies in many other fields as well—politics, certainly, but also aspects of medical practice and the arts. Anton Chekhov, whose thoughts on "pluses" we met a few pages ago, took this human-first approach in his work both as a physician and as a writer. His short stories, especially, are humanistic in the close attention they pay to the events (or quiet non-events) from people's everyday lives: moments of love or heartbreak, journeys, deaths, boring days. His views on religion and morality were also those of a humanist: he disliked dogma and was skeptical about supernatural beliefs. As one twentieth-century admirer of Chekhov wrote:

> He said—and no one had said this before, not even Tolstoy—that first and foremost we are all of us human beings. Do you understand? Human beings! He said something no one in Russia had ever said. He said that first of all we are human beings—and only secondly are we bishops, Russians, shopkeepers, Tartars,

workers. . . . Chekhov said: let's put God—and all these grand progressive ideas—to one side. Let's begin with man; let's be kind and
attentive to the individual man.

These words are actually spoken by a fictional character, in a scene
from the novel *Life and Fate* by the Jewish Ukrainian writer Vasily Grossman, another of the great humanist authors. Like Chekhov, Grossman
was a scientist as well as a creative writer: he began in a career as a chemi-
cal engineer. Then he took up writing fiction, much of it light and comic
at first, and journalism during the Second World War, especially by fil-
ing reports from the battle front at Stalingrad. In the 1950s, he worked
on *Life and Fate*, which was much influenced by his war experience and
especially by the loss of his mother, Yekaterina Savelievna, who was murdered by the Nazis. *Life and Fate* plunges us into the very worst that
the twentieth century had to offer: war, mass murder, cold, hunger, be-
trayal, racist persecution in both Nazi-occupied territory and the Soviet
Union—in short, human grief and suffering on a staggering scale. It
takes us to places we can hardly bear to go, including into a Nazi gas
chamber and right into the moment of death. But through all of this,
Grossman imbues the narrative with his humanist sensibility, putting
individuals at the center, never ideas or ideals.

He was a humanist in other ways, too. He did not like religious institutions, which he saw as tending to obstruct rather than encourage people's natural tendency toward kindness and fellow feeling. For Grossman,
those two qualities were all that really mattered. As another character in
Life and Fate says, "This kindness, this stupid kindness, is what is most
truly human in a human being. It is what sets man apart, the highest
achievement of his soul. No, it says, life is not evil!"

In a Communist regime, it was fine to criticize the ideologies of traditional religion, but not those of the state. Grossman particularly courted
disfavor by exposing the Soviet Union's own anti-Semitic tendencies,

which were not acknowledged to exist. When he began *Life and Fate*, Stalin was still alive and there seemed little likelihood that such a book could be pub-  lished. But in 1953, Stalin died and was succeeded by Nikita Khrushchev, who promised a cultural "thaw." So by the time Grossman finished the novel in 1960, it seemed to him that it was worth sending it to a publisher, after all. Friends warned him that he was being too optimistic; they were right. Soon after he dispatched it, he received a visit from the KGB. They searched his house and removed other copies of the typescript, along with all his drafts and notebooks. They also took carbon paper and typewriter ribbons, wanting to obliterate even those faint imprinted ghosts of the words. The book seemed to have been wiped from the Earth.

What they did not know was that Grossman had taken the precaution of giving two other versions to two different friends, who hid them and waited. Grossman wrote other books, including an unfinished novel about the confused emotions of a man emerging from a thirty-year imprisonment in the Gulag, and a beautiful account of his own travels and encounters in Armenia. By that time, he was ill with stomach cancer. He died in 1964, still seeing no prospect of getting *Life and Fate* published.

More than a decade went by. Then, in 1975, one of the friends managed, with help from others, to smuggle a microfilm of the manuscript out of the country. The film was hard to read, but further copies were made, and a partial version of the text appeared from a publisher in Switzerland in 1980. Five years later, a more complete version came out in English translation. It was immediately hailed as a twentieth-century masterwork, comparable to Tolstoy's *War and Peace*—or to an interlinked series of Chekhov stories. Part of its fascination was its own story; one of survival against the odds. Like so many works by our humanists in earlier times, it had been saved by ingenuity, concealment, rescue, and reduplication. And, as Petrarch and Boccaccio and the early humanist printers knew, nothing is so good for rescuing a book as making lots of copies of it.

There are certainly lots of copies of *Life and Fate* around today. If someone asks you "What is humanism?" and a more direct answer does not come to mind, you could do worse than taking that person to a bookshop and buying them one.

Every time a person dies, writes Grossman in *Life and Fate*, the entire world that has been built in that individual's consciousness dies as well: "The stars have disappeared from the night sky; the Milky Way has vanished; the sun has gone out . . . flowers have lost their colour and fragrance; bread has vanished; water has vanished." Elsewhere in the book, he writes that one day we may engineer a machine that can have humanlike experiences; but if we do, it will have to be enormous—so vast is this space of consciousness, even within the most "average, inconspicuous human being."

And, he adds, "Fascism annihilated tens of millions of people."

Trying to think those two thoughts together is a near-impossible feat, even for the immense capacities of our consciousness. But will machine minds ever acquire anything like our ability to have such thoughts, in all their seriousness and depth? Or to reflect morally on events, or to equal our artistic and imaginative reach? Some think that this question distracts us from a more urgent one: we should be asking what our close relationship with our machines is doing to *us*. Jaron Lanier, himself a pioneer of computer technology, warns in *You Are Not a Gadget* that we are allowing ourselves to become ever more algorithmic and quantifiable, because this makes us easier for computers to deal with. Education, for example, becomes less about the unfolding of humanity, which cannot be measured in units, and more about tick boxes. John Stuart Mill's feeling of being fully "alive" and "human" as one comes of age; Arnold's sweetness and light; Humboldt's "inexpressibly joyous" experience of intellectual discovery—these turn into a five-star system for recording consumer satisfaction. Says Lanier: "We have repeatedly demonstrated our species' bottomless ability to lower our standards to make information technology look good."

To see this demeaning thought taken to its logical conclusion, we can turn back by more than a century to—surprisingly—George Eliot. Not normally known as a science fiction writer (or, indeed, as a pessimist), she came up with a terrifyingly pessimistic sci-fi image in her final book, *Impressions of Theophrastus Such*, published in 1879. A character in the chapter "Shadows of the Coming Race" speculates that machines of the future might learn to reproduce themselves. Having done so, they might also then realize that they do not need human minds around them at all. They are able to become all the more powerful "for not carrying the futile cargo of a consciousness screeching irrelevantly, like a fowl tied head downmost to the saddle of a swift horseman." And that is the end of us.

Oh well. These days some think that, if humanity ends in disaster, caused by rogue artificial intelligence or environmental collapse or some other blunder, the world would be better off without us anyway. We are hardly a good influence: we are wrecking the planet's climate and ecosystems, obliterating species with our crops and livestock, and redirecting every resource to the production of more and more humanity. Even our satellites proliferate like a rash over the night sky. Our impact is so great that geologists are debating the possibility of officially designating our epoch the Anthropocene, a period that may be identifiable in the sediment, in part, by a layer of our domesticated chicken bones. That puts the screeching fowl of consciousness in a new light. But if we do humanize everything, in the end we will consume the basis for our own lives, too, and thus dehumanize everything again.

Contemplating this, some human beings seek paradoxical consolation by embracing the prospect. "Posthumanists," as they are sometimes known, look forward to a time when human life is either drastically reduced in scope or no longer around at all. Some propose deliberately bringing about this self-destruction ourselves. That is the message of the Voluntary Human Extinction Movement (VHEMT), founded in 1991 by environmentalist and teacher Les U. Knight. Half serious and half a surreal work of art, the movement advocates doing the Earth a favor by giving up breeding and waiting for ourselves to gently fade away.

Posthumanism has a benign air of modesty about it, yet it is also a form of anti-humanism. Somewhere at the heart of it, I think, is an old-fashioned sense of sin. The desire is to imagine the Earth returned to an Edenic state, with humanity not just expelled from the garden but actually uncreated. It is not all that remote from the idea of a few extreme Christians that we should accept (or even accelerate) the environmental crisis on Earth, because it will bring Judgment Day all the sooner. In a 2016 survey, 11 percent of Americans endorsed the statement that, with the end times coming anyway, we need not worry about tackling the climate challenge. More puzzlingly, 2 percent of those identifying as "agnostics or atheists" agreed with it, too.

Others devoutly wish for a different consummation. "Transhumanists," unlike posthumanists, look forward eagerly to technologies that will, first, extend the human lifespan considerably, and, later, allow our minds to be uploaded into other data-based forms, so that we can ditch the need for human embodiment. Some talk of a moment of "singularity," when the rate of development has accelerated to the point that our machines and ourselves may fuse into one. In the stage after that, as Ray Kurzweil writes in *The Singularity Is Near*, "vastly expanded human intelligence (predominantly nonbiological) spreads through the universe."

Posthumanism and transhumanism are opposites: one eliminates human consciousness, while the other suffuses it into everything. But they are the sort of opposites that meet at the extremes. Both agree that our current humanity is something transitional or wrong—something to be left behind. Instead of dealing with ourselves as we are, both imagine us altered in some dramatic way: either made more humble and virtuous in a new Eden, or retired from existence, or inflated to a level that sounds like that of gods.

I am a humanist; I cannot happily contemplate any of these alternatives. As a science fiction enthusiast, I used to have a weakness for transhumanism, however. Years ago, my mind was blown by a classic science fiction novel: Arthur C. Clarke's *Childhood's End*, published in 1953.

The story begins, as many in the genre do, with aliens arriving on Earth. They promptly shower us with gifts, which include hours of entertainment. "Do you realize that *every day* something like five hundred hours of radio and TV pour out over the various channels?" asks one character in the book, conveying 1953's idea of a cornucopian abundance. But the bounty of the aliens comes with conditions: humans must stay on Earth and give up exploring space.

A few people resist the gilded cage, declining to watch the entertainment and proclaiming defiant pride in human achievements. But as time goes on, this aging minority is forgotten and a new generation emerges. They have new mental gifts, including the first stirrings of an ability to access the "Overmind," a mysterious shared consciousness in the universe, which has outgrown "the tyranny of matter."

That generation in turn gives way to the next, and these beings are hardly human at all. Needing no food, having no language, they simply dance for years, in forests and meadows. Finally they stop and stand motionless for a long time. Then they slowly dissolve upward, into the Overmind. The planet itself becomes translucent like glass and shimmers out of existence. Humanity and the Earth have gone, or rather, they have been transfigured and merged into a higher realm.

Such an ending for humanity is neither optimistic nor pessimistic, writes Clarke; it is just final. So is his novel, in a way. It pushes fiction to its limits. Earlier science fiction writers had also imagined a future in which humanity dies, notably Olaf Stapledon in his 1930 work, *Last and First Men*. But Clarke goes further, into a realm where there can be no more stories at all. Species have vanished; even matter has vanished, at least from Earth. He goes where Dante went in his *Paradiso*—and Dante complained in that work's first canto that this necessarily defeats the powers of any writer. To write about Heaven is "to go beyond the human"—*trasumanar*—and, says Dante, this also means going beyond what language itself can accomplish.

When I first read *Childhood's End*, I loved its finale. Now I feel the melancholy of such a vision far more. It leaves me in mourning for those flawed, recognizable individuals that we are and for the details of our planet and our many cultures, all lost to a universal blandness. Every particularity has gone: the atoms of Democritus, Terence's nosy neighbor, Petrarch's lack of patience and Boccaccio's bawdy stories, the Lake Nemi ships and the fishlike Genoese divers, Aldus Manutius and his exuberance ("Aldus is here!"), students floating down rivers, Platina's recipe for grilled eel *à l'orange*, Erasmus's polite farts, the *Encyclopédie* (all 71,818 articles of it), Hume's games of backgammon and whist, Dorothy L. Sayers's comfortable trousers, Frederick Douglass's magnificently photographed face and his eloquent words, the priestly and poetic Kawi language, sea squirts, bloomers, the Esperanto plaque by Petrarch's beloved stream, M. N. Roy's good soups, ridiculous heraldry, Rabindranath Tagore's classes under the trees, the windows of Chartres, microfilms, manifestos, meetings, Pugwash, busy New York streets, the yellow line of morning. They have all gone up in the ultimate bonfire of the vanities. To me, this no longer says sublimity; it says, "How disappointing."

Where, in all this pure divinity and mysticism, is the richness of actual life? Also, where is our sense of responsibility for managing our occupancy of Earth? (Not that Clarke himself supported abdicating such responsibilities—quite the contrary.) And what about our relationships with fellow humans and other creatures—that great foundation for humanist ethics, identity, and meaning?

These dreams of elevation perhaps emerge from memories of being a small child, lifted out of a cradle by big arms. But the Earth is not a cradle; we are not alone here, since we share it with so many other living beings; and we need not wait to be spirited away. Give me, instead of the Overmind, or the sublime visions of any religion, these words of a more human wisdom by James Baldwin:

> One is responsible to life. It is the small beacon in that terrifying darkness from which we come and to which we shall return. One must negotiate this passage as nobly as possible, for the sake of those who are coming after us.

A sense of sin is of no help on that journey; neither is a dream of transcendence. Dante was right: we really cannot *trasumanar*, and if we have fun trying—well, that can produce beautiful literature. But it is still human literature.

I prefer the humanist combination of freethinking, inquiry, and hope. And, as the late scholar of humanism and ethics Tzvetan Todorov once remarked in an interview:

> Humanism is a frail craft indeed to choose for setting sail around the world! A frail craft that can do no more than transport us to frail happiness. But, to me, the other solutions seem either conceived for a race of superheroes, which we are not . . . or heavily laden with illusions, with promises that will never be kept. I trust the humanist bark more.

Finally, as always, I am brought back to the creed of Robert G. Ingersoll:

> Happiness is the only good.
>
> The time to be happy is now.
>
> The place to be happy is here.
>
> The way to be happy is to make others so.

It sounds simple; it sounds easy. But it will take all the ingenuity we can muster.

Acknowledgments

For conversations, advice, readings, and intellectual generosity of all kinds, I would like to thank the wise and resourceful people who have helped me, particularly Hamza bin Walayat, Andrew Copson, Peter Mack, Scott Newstok, Jim Walsh, and Nigel Warburton. In Florence, I would like to thank Enrica Ficai-Veltroni, Giovanna Giusti, and Mara Miniati for their generosity with their time and expertise. Thank you also to Stefano Guidarini for our conversation about Leon Battista Alberti, and to Peter Moore for much sharing of ideas and inspiration and for passing so many discoveries my way.

Much of this book was written in the realm of marvels that is London's Warburg Institute Library, and in the British Library. Thank you very much to the staff of both, especially Richard Gartner of the Warburg, and to those of the other excellent libraries and archives I used, notably the Bishopsgate Institute Library, the Conway Hall Library, the Wiener Holocaust Library, and, as ever, the London Library.

My thanks to Humanists International and Humanists UK for all their help, including in making the 2022 Declaration of Modern Humanism available to be quoted in full. Thank you especially to Catriona McLellan for her help with the Humanists UK logo.

Many thanks to Becky Hardie, Clara Farmer, and the rest of the team at Chatto & Windus, and to Ann Godoff and the team at Penguin U.S., especially Casey Denis, Victoria Lopez, and my erudite and judicious copy editor, David Koral. I feel very lucky to have had so much expert and warmhearted support from my beloved agents: Zoë Waldie and everyone else at Rogers, Coleridge & White, and Melanie Jackson in the United States.

A special thank-you to Judith Gurewich, especially for our conversations about Petrarch and our shared hero, Lorenzo Valla.

Thank you to all involved with the Windham-Campbell Prizes; receiving such an unexpected honor in the early stages of writing this book made all the difference.

Above all, thank you to my wife, Simonetta Ficai-Veltroni, for the many years of love and encouragement, for her excellent insights and instincts, for reading innumerable versions of the work in progress, and for much, much more.

This book is dedicated to all the people who have quietly (or loudly) stood up for their humanistic beliefs over the centuries, often in situations where doing so has required exceptional courage. There are many such people still doing exactly that today.

Appendix

HUMANISTS INTERNATIONAL
DECLARATION OF MODERN HUMANISM

Agreed at the General Assembly, Glasgow, United Kingdom, 2022

Humanist beliefs and values are as old as civilization and have a history in most societies around the world. Modern humanism is the culmination of these long traditions of reasoning about meaning and ethics, the source of inspiration for many of the world's great thinkers, artists, and humanitarians, and is interwoven with the rise of modern science.

As a global humanist movement, we seek to make all people aware of these essentials of the humanist worldview:

1. Humanists strive to be ethical

We accept that morality is inherent to the human condition, grounded in the ability of living things to suffer and flourish, motivated by the benefits of helping and not harming, enabled by reason and compassion, and needing no source outside of humanity.

We affirm the worth and dignity of the individual and the right of every human to the greatest possible freedom and fullest possible development compatible with the rights of others. To these ends we support peace, democracy, the rule of law, and universal legal human rights.

We reject all forms of racism and prejudice and the injustices that arise from them. We seek instead to promote the flourishing and fellowship of humanity in all its diversity and individuality.

We hold that personal liberty must be combined with a responsibility to society. A free person has duties to others, and we feel a duty of care to all of humanity, including future generations, and beyond this to all sentient beings.

We recognise that we are part of nature and accept our responsibility for the impact we have on the rest of the natural world.

2. Humanists strive to be rational

We are convinced that the solutions to the world's problems lie in human reason, and action. We advocate the application of science and free inquiry to these problems, remembering that while science provides the means, human values must define the ends. We seek to use science and technology to enhance human well-being, and never callously or destructively.

3. Humanists strive for fulfillment in their lives

We value all sources of individual joy and fulfillment that harm no other, and we believe that personal development through the cultivation of creative and ethical living is a lifelong undertaking.

We therefore treasure artistic creativity and imagination and recognise the transforming power of literature, music, and the visual and performing arts. We cherish the beauty of the natural world and its potential to bring wonder, awe, and tranquility. We appreciate individual and communal exertion in physical activity, and the scope it offers for comradeship and achievement. We esteem the quest for knowledge, and the humility, wisdom, and insight it bestows.

4. Humanism meets the widespread demand for a source of meaning and purpose to stand as an alternative to dogmatic religion, authoritarian nationalism, tribal sectarianism, and selfish nihilism

Though we believe that a commitment to human well-being is ageless, our particular opinions are not based on revelations fixed for all time. Humanists recognise that no one is infallible or omniscient, and that knowledge of the world and of humankind can be won only through a continuing process of observation, learning, and rethinking.

For these reasons, we seek neither to avoid scrutiny nor to impose our view on all humanity. On the contrary, we are committed to the unfettered expression and exchange of ideas, and seek to cooperate with people of different beliefs who share our values, all in the cause of building a better world.

We are confident that humanity has the potential to solve the problems that confront us, through free inquiry, science, sympathy, and imagination in the furtherance of peace and human flourishing.

We call upon all who share these convictions to join us in this inspiring endeavor.

Notes

ONLY CONNECT! AN INTRODUCTION

1   **"What is humanism?":** David Nobbs, *Second from Last in the Sack Race* (1983), in *The Complete Pratt* (London: Arrow, 2007), 289–91.

2   **Their worldview has been summed up:** Kurt Vonnegut, *God Bless You, Dr. Kevorkian* (New York: Washington Square Press/Pocket Books, 1999), 9.

3   **They hope to cultivate *humanitas*:** For a definition encompassing such meanings: https://en.wiktionary.org/wiki/humanitas.

4   **The human-centered approach:** Quoted in Diogenes Laertius, *Lives of Eminent Philosophers*, trans. R. D. Hicks (London: W. Heinemann; New York: G. P. Putnam's Sons, 1925), vol. 2, 463–65. A similar line is reported by Socrates in Plato, *Theaetetus*, 160c–d.

4   **Here is the novelist:** E. M. Forster, from a letter to *The Twentieth Century* (1955), quoted in *Humanist Anthology*, ed. M. Knight (London: Rationalist Press Association/Barrie & Rockliff, 1961), 155–56. Forster served as vice president of the Ethical Union in the 1950s, and president of the Cambridge Humanists Society from 1959 until his death; he was also a member of the Advisory Council of the British Humanist Association (now Humanists UK) from 1963.

6   **A notorious case:** Mashal Khan: https://humanists.international/2017/04/humanist -murdered-fellow-university-students-alleged-blasphemy/. As of 2021, thirteen countries in the world still had the death penalty for blasphemy or apostasy.

6   **The organization Humanists UK:** See a letter from Bob Churchill of IHEU (now Humanists International) pointing out the inappropriateness of Plato and Aristotle: http://iheu.org/uk-rejects-asylum-application-humanist-fails-name-ancient-greek -philosophers/ Also: https://www.theguardian.com/world/2018/jan/26/you-dont-need -to-know-plato-and-aristotle-to-be-a-humanist and https://www.theguardian.com /uk-news/2018/jan/26/philosophers-urge-rethink-of-pakistani-humanist-hamza-bin -walayat-asylum.

6   **More generally, they argued:** On the case overall, personal communication with Hamza bin Walayat. Also: https://humanists.international/2018/01/uk-rejects-asylum -application-humanist-fails-name-ancient-greek-philosophers/. And: https://www .theguardian.com/uk-news/2018/jan/17/pakistani-humanist-denied-uk-asylum -after-failing-to-identify-plato.

6   **And, in the wake:** The new Home Office training procedures: https://humanists .uk/2019/05/17/success-humanists-uk-begins-delivering-training-to-home-office-staff -on-asylum-claims/.

9   **The first discussion:** Jeaneane Fowler, "The Materialists of Classical India," in *The Wiley Blackwell Handbook of Humanism*, ed. A. Copson and A. C. Grayling (Chichester, UK: John Wiley, 2015), 98–101, https://en.wikipedia.org/wiki/Charvaka.

9   **The philosopher Ajita Kesakambalī:** *The Long Discourses of the Buddha*, a translation of the *Dīgha Nikāya* by Maurice Walsh (Boston: Wisdom, 1995), 96 (division I, chap. 2). See Peter Adamson and Jonardon Ganeri, *Classical Indian Philosophy* (Oxford, UK: Oxford University Press, 2020), 39.

10   **A key component:** Epicurus, "Letter to Menoeceus," in *The Art of Happiness*, trans. George K. Strodach (London: Penguin, 2012), 159–60.

10   **Then there was Protagoras:** From Protagoras's lost work *On the Gods*, quoted in Diogenes Laertius, *Lives of Eminent Philosophers*, vol. 2, 465.

11   **The biographer Diogenes Laertius:** "Protagoras," in Diogenes Laertius, *Lives of Eminent Philosophers*, vol. 2, 465. Plutarch also mentioned Protagoras's being banished, and explained that it was because of the era's intolerance toward anyone who attributed events to natural causes rather than divine powers: Plutarch, "Life of Nicias," in *Lives*, trans. John Dryden, rev. A. H. Clough (London: J. M. Dent; New York: E. P. Dutton, 1910), vol. 2, 266.

11   **the American author Zora Neale Hurston:** Zora Neale Hurston, *Dust Tracks on a Road*, reprinted in *Folklore, Memoirs, and Other Writings* (New York: Library of America, 1995), 764.

12   **The tradition lives on:** https://en.wikipedia.org/wiki/Ariane_Sherine. Bishopsgate Institute Library, London, BHA papers. BHA 1/17/148, on the atheist bus campaign, including a BHA report, "Atheist Bus Campaign: Why Did It Work?" See https://humanism.org.uk/campaigns/successful-campaigns/atheist-bus-campaign/.

12   **It was even formulated:** Ingersoll's happiness credo appears in various formats, including in *An Oration on the Gods* (January 29, 1872) (Cairo, IL: Daily Bulletin Steam Book & Job Print, 1873), 48. He also recited it on a phonograph record, on January 22, 1899. The cylinder is on display at the Robert Green Ingersoll Birthplace Museum, Dresden, New York, and can be heard online at https://youtu.be/rLLapwIoEVI.

12   **This principle of human interconnectivity:** Terence, *Heauton tomorumenos* (*The Self-Tormenter*), act 1, scene 1, line 77. Betty Radice's translation in Terence, *Phormio and Other Plays* (Harmondsworth, UK: Penguin, 1967), 86, reads: "I'm human, so any human interest *is* my concern."

13   **A similar thought:** "Ubuntu (philosophy)," *New World Encyclopedia*, http://www.newworldencyclopedia.org/entry/Ubuntu_(philosophy). For a modern examination of it as a humanist philosophy, see Stanlake J. W. T. Samkange, *Hunhuism or Ubuntuism: A Zimbabwe Indigenous Political Philosophy* (Salisbury, UK: Graham, 1990).

13   **The late Archbishop Desmond Tutu:** Desmond Tutu, *No Future without Forgiveness* (London: Rider, 1999), 35.

14   **Over the years after his death:** "Ethical wisdom" is Karyn L. Lai's translation in *An Introduction to Chinese Philosophy* (Cambridge, UK: Cambridge University Press, 2008), 24. See Jiyuan Yu, "Humanism: Chinese Conception of," from the *New Dictionary of the History of Ideas* (2005), available at http://www.encyclopedia.com/history/dictionaries-thesauruses-pictures-and-press-releases/humanism-chinese-conception.

14   **When disciples asked Kongzi:** Confucius, *The Analects*, 12:2 (*shu* in relation to *ren*) and 15:24 (as guide to life). See the commentary on the latter by Annping Chin in her translation, *The Analects* (New York: Penguin, 2014), 259.

14   **The Jewish theologian:** Babylonian Talmud, Shabbat 31a, https://en.wikipedia.org
      /wiki/Hillel_the_Elder.

14   **The Hindu *Mahābhārata* and Christian scriptures:** "Men endued with intelligence
      and cleansed souls should always behave towards other creatures after the manner of
      that behaviour which they like others to observe towards themselves." *Mahābhārata*
      XIII: 5571, ed. Pratāpa Chandra Rāy (Calcutta: Bhārata Press, 1893), vol. 9, 562. Book
      XIII is the Book of Instruction; the context concerns vegetarianism. "Therefore all
      things whatsoever ye would that men should do to you, do ye even so to them: for this
      is the law and the prophets." Matthew 7:12. Bernard Shaw, *Maxims for Revolutionists*,
      in *Man and Superman* (Westminster, UK: Constable, 1903), 227.

15   **One of Kongzi's later followers:** *Mengzi: With Selections from Traditional Commen-
      taries*, trans. Bryan W. Van Norden (Indianapolis and Cambridge, MA: Hackett,
      2008), 46–47 (2A6: child), 149–50 (6A6: seed). Van Norden remarks that Mengzi
      does allow for rare cases of damage in childhood, such that the seeds are destroyed so
      early that they are not viable; see 150–52 (6A7–8).

15   **Being well educated:** Confucius, *The Analects*, 2:20.

15   **In Greece, Protagoras was a believer:** Plato, *Protagoras*, 328b. In *Protagoras and
      Meno*, trans. W. K. C. Guthrie (Harmondsworth, UK: Penguin, 1956), 60.

16   **The myth of Prometheus's theft:** The myth is related by Plato in *Protagoras*,
      320d–325d.

16   **The Roman statesman Cicero:** Cicero, *On the Nature of the Gods* (*De natura deorum*),
      with the argument for human excellence in book II.

16   **The genre reached its height:** Giannozzo Manetti, *On Human Worth and Excellence*
      (*De dignitate et excellentia hominis*), ed. and trans. Brian Copenhaver (Cambridge,
      MA, and London: I Tatti/Harvard University Press, 2018), 105–11 (book II).

17   **"Ours indeed are those inventions":** Manetti, *On Human Worth and Excellence*,
      139–41 (book III).

17   **Manetti celebrates the physical pleasures:** Manetti, *On Human Worth and Excel-
      lence*, 205 (book IV). Manetti's work was an expansion of earlier, briefer works by An-
      tonio da Barga and Bartolomeo Facio; see Brian Copenhaver's introduction to this
      translation, vii–xvii. Also see Manetti's book IV, translated by Bernard Murchland in
      *Two Views of Man: Pope Innocent III, On the Misery of Man; Giannozzo Manetti, On
      the Dignity of Man* (New York: Ungar, [1966]), 61–103.

18   **In Confucian thought:** On Xunzi, see Bryan W. Van Norden, *Introduction to Classical
      Chinese Philosophy* (Indianapolis: Hackett, 2011), 163–84. On translating the word *e*
      as "detestable," see https://plato.stanford.edu/entries/xunzi/.

18   **The fourth-century theologian Nemesius of Emesa:** Nemesius, *On the Nature of
      Man*, trans. R. W. Sharples and P. J. Van der Eijk (Liverpool: Liverpool University
      Press, 2008), 50.

19   **But a few years later:** Saint Augustine, *Concerning the City of God against the Pagans*,
      book XIV, chap. 11.

19   **The most devastating attack:** Innocent III, *De miseria humanae conditionis*, trans. Ber-
      nard Murchland in *Two Views of Man: Pope Innocent III, On the Misery of Man; Gian-
      nozzo Manetti, On the Dignity of Man* (New York: Ungar, [1966]), 4–10 (stages of life's
      misery), 13 (book I, §13: vanity), 4 (book I, §1: worms), 9 (book I, §8: "vile ignobility").

19   **"Do not look for satisfaction":** Blaise Pascal, *Pensées*, 182, in *Pensées, and Other Writ-
      ings*, trans. Honor Levi, ed. Anthony Levi (Oxford, UK: Oxford University Press,
      1995), 54.

20   **In lectures of 1901–1902:** William James, *The Varieties of Religious Experience*, in *Writings 1902–1910* (New York: Library of America, 1988), 454.

20   **They took away ordinary human freedoms:** This is one reason Plato is an inappropriate choice as an example of a humanist philosopher, by the way. His *Republic* advocates a society in which all citizens must follow the role allotted to their caste. For some castes, all arts and literature are censored, so that they will not be exposed to ideas inconsistent with the larger state goals. In *The Laws*, he goes still further in his call for censorship and rigid social structures—and people are expected to subordinate themselves not only to the state but also to the principle of the divine. The philosopher Karl Popper, himself a committed humanist, argued in *The Open Society and Its Enemies* (1945) that these two works prefigured his own century's totalitarianism.

CHAPTER 1. THE LAND OF THE LIVING

26   **The older of the two:** The stories from Petrarch's early life come from his letters: Petrarch, *Letters on Familiar Matters / Rerum familiarum, libri I–XXIV*, trans. Aldo S. Bernardo (Albany: SUNY Press, 1975; Baltimore and London: Johns Hopkins University Press, 1982–85), vol. 3, 203 (*Fam.* XXI, 15: exile); vol. 1, 8 (*Fam.* I, 1: near drowning); vol. 2, 59 (*Fam.* X, 3: hairstyles). All subsequent references to Petrarch's *Letters on Familiar Matters* in this chapter are to this edition.

27   **A setback occurred:** This story is told in Petrarch, *Letters of Old Age* [*Rerum senilium*, books I–XVIII], trans. Aldo S. Bernardo, Saul Levin, and Reta A. Bernardo (Baltimore and London: Johns Hopkins University Press, 1992), vol. 2, 601 (*Sen.* XVI, 1). All subsequent references to Petrarch's *Letters of Old Age* in this chapter are to this edition.

28   **Many of these verses:** Petrarch's Virgil manuscript, augmented with his notes and a miniature painted by his friend Simone Martini, is now in Milan's Ambrosian Library: S.P. 10/27 *olim*. Images may be found online at https://www.ambrosiana.it/en/opere/the-ambrosian-virgil-of-francesco-petrarca/. The notes are translated in Ernest Hatch Wilkins, *Life of Petrarch* (Chicago: Phoenix/University of Chicago Press, 1961), 77.

29   **Later retreats included:** Petrarch, *Letters on Familiar Matters*, vol. 3, 22–23 (*Fam.* XVII, 5).

29   **The custom had recently been revived:** Ronald G. Witt, *"In the Footsteps of the Ancients": The Origins of Humanism from Lovato to Bruni* (Leiden, Netherlands: Brill, 2000), 118–20.

29   **A later description by:** Giannozzo Manetti, *Biographical Writings*, ed. and trans. Stefano U. Baldassari and Rolf Bagemihl (Cambridge, MA, and London: I Tatti/Harvard University Press, 2003), 75.

29   **At times, everything seemed:** Petrarch, *Letters of Old Age*, vol. 2, 28 (*Sen.* I, 6).

30   **Sending one such list:** Petrarch, *Letters on Familiar Matters*, vol. 1, 160 (*Fam.* III, 18).

30   **"Who knows if":** Petrarch, *Letters of Old Age*, vol. 2, 603 (*Sen.* XVI, 1).

31   **In a letter, he describes:** Petrarch, *Letters on Familiar Matters*, vol. 3, 64 (*Fam.* XVIII, 12).

31   **At other times, Petrarch found comfort:** "Tormented and sluggish" and the intervention story: Petrarch, *Letters on Familiar Matters*, vol. 2, 199–200 (*Fam.* XIII, 7).

31   **His most important production:** The Livy manuscript is in the British Library, Harley 2493. Facsimile edition: G. Billanovich, *La tradizione del testo di Livio e le origini dell'umanesimo*, vol. 2: *Il Livio del Petrarca e del Valla: British Library, Harleian 2493* (Padua: Antenore, 1981).

32 **A particularly energizing discovery:** Cicero, *Pro Archia* (62 CE), para. 16, in Cicero, *The Speeches*, trans. N. H. Watts (London: W. Heinemann; Cambridge, MA: Harvard University Press, 1965), 25.

32 **Petrarch found the full text:** Petrarch, *Letters of Old Age*, vol. 2, 603–4 (*Sen.* XVI, 1). On this and other such stories, see also L. D. Reynolds and N. G. Wilson, *Scribes and Scholars*, 3rd ed. (Oxford, UK: Clarendon Press, 1991), 131–32.

32 **Another work by Cicero:** He found Cicero's letters to Atticus, Quintus, and Brutus. Giuseppe F. Mazzotta, "Petrarch's Epistolary Epic: *Letters on Familiar Matters* (*Rerum familiarum libri*)," in *Petrarch: A Critical Guide to the Complete Works*, ed. Victoria Kirkham and Armando Maggi (Chicago and London: University of Chicago Press, 2009), 309–20, this on 309.

33 **Some of the letters tell long stories:** Petrarch, *Letters on Familiar Matters*, vol. 1, 172–80 (*Fam.* IV, 1, to Dionigi da Borgo, April 26 [1336]).

33 **The letters are literary constructions:** Petrarch, *Letters on Familiar Matters*, vol. 3, 207 (*Fam.* XXI, 15: hospitality); vol. 1, 8 (*Fam.* I, 1: Metabus and Camilla. The story is from Virgil, *Aeneid*, book XI, lines 532–56).

34 **He actually does direct one:** Petrarch, *Letters of Old Age*, vol. 2, 672–79 (*Sen.* XVIII, 1, "To Posterity").

34 **For Petrarch, books are sociable:** Petrarch, *Letters on Familiar Matters*, vol. 1, 158 (*Fam.* III, 18: "They speak"); vol. 2, 256–57 (*Fam.* XV, 3: frosty air); vol. 3, 187 (*Fam.* XXI, 10: tripping and Cicero); vol. 3, 317 (*Fam.* XXIV, 3: "Why did you choose").

34 **Born in 1313:** Marco Santagata, *Boccaccio: Fragilità di un genio* (Milan: Mondadori, 2019), 13.

35 **When his father contemplated:** Giovanni Boccaccio, *Boccaccio on Poetry* (preface and books XIV and XV of *Genealogia deorum gentilium*), trans. Charles G. Osgood (Princeton, NJ: Princeton University Press, 1930), 131–32 (XV, 10).

35 **What he did excel at:** Boccaccio, *Boccaccio on Poetry*, 131 (XV, 10).

36 **the first serious Dante scholar:** The lecture series was begun late in Boccaccio's life. He had earlier discussed Dante's life and work in *Trattatello in laude di Dante*, and wrote short introductions to each canto of the *Commedia* in his own manuscript copies. Sandro Bertelli, introduction to *Dantesque Images in the Laurentian Manuscripts of the* Commedia *(14th–16th Centuries)*, ed. Ida G. Rao (Florence: Mandragora, 2015), 15.

36 **He called Petrarch:** Boccaccio, *Boccaccio on Poetry*, 115–16 (XV, 6).

36 **Yet when it came to assessing:** Boccaccio, *Boccaccio on Poetry*, 132 (XV, 10).

36 **In one, an abbess is informed:** Giovanni Boccaccio, *The Decameron*, day 9, story 2.

37 **in one, a great lord summons:** Boccaccio, *The Decameron*, day 1, story 3.

37 **While writing this:** James Hankins, *Virtue Politics: Soulcraft and Statecraft in Renaissance Italy* (Cambridge, MA, and London: Belknap Press of Harvard University Press, 2019), 193–94, referring to Laura Regnicoli's research for the exhibition *Boccaccio autore e copista*, at the Biblioteca Medicea Laurenziana, Florence, 2013.

37 **Boccaccio was active:** Mazzotta, "Petrarch's Epistolary Epic: *Letters on Familiar Matters* (*Rerum familiarum libri*)," 309–20.

38 **Boccaccio looked up to Petrarch:** Petrarch, *Letters on Familiar Matters*, vol. 3, 224–25 (*Fam.* XXII, 7).

38 **had made good discoveries:** The works he found were Varro's *De lingua latina* and Cicero's *Pro Cluentio*: see Santagata, *Boccaccio: Fragilità di un genio*, 159.

38   **In one strange episode:** Petrarch, *Letters of Old Age*, vol. 1, 22–25 (*Sen.* I, 5, to Boccaccio, May 28 [1362]). On this difficult period for Boccaccio, see Santagata, *Boccaccio: Fragilità di un genio*, 221–33. For Petrarch on the benefits of (cautiously) reading non-Christian classical literature, see "On His Own Ignorance and That of Others," in *Invectives*, ed. and trans. David Marsh (Cambridge, MA, and London: I Tatti/Harvard University Press, 2003), 333–35.

39   **Less selfishly, he gave Boccaccio:** Boccaccio, *Boccaccio on Poetry*, 123 (XV, 9).

39   **In his *Genealogy*:** Boccaccio, *Boccaccio on Poetry*, 135 (XV, 12).

39   **"a considerable measure to the enjoyment":** Petrarch, *Letters on Familiar Matters*, vol. 1, 291 (*Fam.* VI, 2).

39   **The passion for literature:** Petrarch may have had some beginner's lessons from Barlaam of Seminara. See his letter to Nicholas Sygeros, in Petrarch, *Letters on Familiar Matters*, vol. 3, 44–46 (*Fam.* XVIII, 2). On Barlaam (who died in 1348), see https://en.wikipedia.org/wiki/Barlaam_of_Seminara. My thanks to Peter Mack for alerting me to this.

39   **"It's all Greek to me":** William Shakespeare, *Julius Caesar*, act I, scene 2, line 295, https://en.wikipedia.org/wiki/Greek_to_me.

40   **Writing to thank him:** Petrarch, *Letters on Familiar Matters*, vol. 3, 44–46 (*Fam.* XVIII, 2). The Greek friend is Nicholas Sygeros.

40   **Again courting the authorities:** On his hard work: Boccaccio, *Boccaccio on Poetry*, 120 (XV, 7).

40   **"for ever lost in thought":** Boccaccio, *Boccaccio on Poetry*, 114–15 (XV, 6).

40   **Boccaccio had a reason:** Boccaccio, *Boccaccio on Poetry*, 114–15 (XV, 6).

40   **He let Leontius live with him:** Boccaccio, *Boccaccio on Poetry*, 114–15 (XV, 6). On surviving dual-language copies of his translations, and on the whole story in general, see Agostino Pertusi, *Leonzio Pilato fra Petrarca e Boccaccio* (Venice and Rome: Istituto per la Collaborazione Culturale, 1964), especially 25. Petrarch's copy of the two translations is now in the Bibliothèque Nationale, Paris: Lat. 7880. I (*Iliad*) and Lat. 7880. II (*Odyssey*).

40   **Petrarch watched from afar:** Petrarch, *Letters of Old Age*, vol. 1, 156 (*Sen.* V, 1).

41   **Petrarch gave him a copy:** Petrarch, *Letters of Old Age*, vol. 1, 100 (*Sen.* III, 6).

41   **Once in Constantinople:** Petrarch, *Letters of Old Age*, vol. 1, 100 (*Sen.* III, 6: "shaggier"), 176 (*Sen.* V, 3: "Where he haughtily").

41   **In truth, Petrarch admitted:** Petrarch, *Letters of Old Age*, vol. 1, 189 (*Sen.* VI, 1).

42   **Petrarch seems to have felt:** Petrarch, *Letters of Old Age*, vol. 1, 189–90 (*Sen.* VI, 1).

42   **Back in 1347:** Nicola Davis, "5,000-Year-Old Hunter-Gatherer Is Earliest Person to Die with the Plague," *Guardian*, June 29, 2021, https://www.theguardian.com/science/2021/jun/29/5000-year-old-hunter-gatherer-is-earliest-person-to-die-with-the-plague.

42   **A lawyer living in Piacenza:** Rosemary Horrox, trans. and ed., *The Black Death* (Manchester and New York: Manchester University Press, 1994), 24–25, quoting Gabriele de' Mussi, *Historia de morbo*, a manuscript in the University of Wrocław Library (Ms. R 262, ff. 74–77v.).

42   **As it spread:** Horrox, *The Black Death*, 22.

43   **People made efforts:** Giovanni Boccaccio, *The Decameron*, trans. G. H. McWilliam, 2nd ed. (Harmondsworth, UK: Penguin, 1995), 7 (preface).

43   **Meanwhile, thoughts often turned:** Horrox, *The Black Death*, 105–6.

43   **One of those who favored:** Horrox, *The Black Death*, 41–45, quoting Louis Heyligen. See also Edwin Mullins, *Avignon of the Popes* (Oxford, UK: Signal, 2007), 124.

43   **In Florence the situation:** G. H. McWilliam, "Translator's Introduction" to his translation of Boccaccio, *The Decameron*, xliii.

45   **All these details:** Boccaccio, *The Decameron*, 5 (preface). The preceding details of the effects of the plague on countryside and city alike are also from Boccaccio's preface.

45   **Long before Boccaccio:** Thucydides, *The Peloponnesian War*, trans. Rex Warner (Harmondsworth, UK: Penguin, 1952), 155 (book II, para. 53).

45   **Boccaccio's story was similar:** Boccaccio, *The Decameron*, 8 (preface).

45   **Boccaccio acknowledges this:** McWilliam, "Translator's Introduction," xliii–xliv.

46   **disposing of corpses:** In England, for example, records show that bodies were buried in cemeteries rather than in pits, and government business often went on in much the normal way—suggesting a surprising strength in social institutions. Christopher Dyer, *Making a Living in the Middle Ages* (New Haven and London: Yale University Press, 2009), 273.

46   **"In any public misfortune":** Alessandro Manzoni, *The Betrothed*, trans. Bruce Penman (Harmondsworth, UK: Penguin, 1972), 596.

46   **having destroyed at least a third:** Christopher S. Celenza, *Petrarch: Everywhere a Wanderer* (London: Reaktion, 2017), 100. Celenza cites sources giving figures between 30 and 60 percent.

47   **Petrarch was working in Parma:** E. H. Wilkins, *Life of Petrarch* (Chicago: Phoenix/ University of Chicago Press, 1963), 74–76.

47   **After the news reached him:** Mullins, *Avignon of the Popes*, 141.

47   **a despairing Latin verse:** Petrarch, "Ad se ipsum," quoted and trans. in Wilkins, *Life of Petrarch*, 80.

47   **A letter to his old friend:** Petrarch, *Letters on Familiar Matters*, vol. 1, 415–20, these quotations on 415, 419 (*Fam*. VIII, 7).

47   **More losses would come:** Petrarch, *Letters of Old Age*, vol. 1, 8 (*Sen*. I, 2, to Francesco [Nelli], June 8 [Padua, 1361–62]). The same letter mentions the death of "his Socrates."

48   **Writing to Boccaccio:** Petrarch, *Letters of Old Age*, vol. 1, 76 (*Sen*. III, 1: numbed), 92 (*Sen*. III, 2: "terrible fear").

48   **He also resumed:** Petrarch, *My Secret Book*, ed. and trans. Nicholas Mann (Cambridge, MA: I Tatti/Harvard University Press, 2016), 117. The work was begun in 1347 and continued through 1349, with further revisions in 1353.

48   **writing to his Socrates:** Petrarch, *Letters on Familiar Matters*, vol. 1, 415 (*Fam*. VIII, 7).

49   **"Unprovided with original learning":** Edward Gibbon, *Memoirs of My Life*, ed. Betty Radice (London: Penguin, 1990), 82.

49   **"But when you have seen vicious mobs":** Martin Luther King Jr., "Letter from Birmingham Jail," in *Why We Can't Wait* (London: Penguin, 2008), 91–92. My emphasis added on "then."

50   **Cicero drew a distinction:** Cicero, *On the Orator* [*De oratore*], 3:55, in *Ancient Rhetoric from Aristotle to Philostratus*, trans. and ed. Thomas Habinek (London: Penguin, 2017), 181. ("If we grant felicity in speaking to those who want nothing to do with virtue, rather than creating orators we give weapons to madmen.")

50   **Another rhetorician:** Quintilian, *Institutio oratoria*, trans. H. E. Butler (London: W. Heinemann; New York: G. P. Putnam's Sons, 1922), vol. 4, 355–57, 359 (XII.i.1: gift), (XII.i.7: arms). Neither this nor Cicero's *De oratore* was available in a full version in Petrarch's time.

51   **he writes to a friend:** Petrarch, *Letters of Old Age*, vol. 2, 380–91 (*Sen*. X, 4, to Donato Apenninigena [Albanzani], Padua, 1368).

51 **Petrarch's book takes the form:** Petrarch, *Remedies for Fortune Fair and Foul*, ed. and trans. Conrad H. Rawski (Bloomington and Indianapolis: Indiana University Press, 1991), vol. 1, 17 (body), 177 (elephants) (both book I). Petrarch began this work in 1354 and finished it in 1360.

52 **In the other half of the book:** Petrarch, *Remedies for Fortune Fair and Foul*, vol. 3, 153 (exile), 222 (plague) (both book II).

52 **Not all sources of misery:** Petrarch, *Remedies for Fortune Fair and Foul*, vol. 3, 10–11 (seas), 227 (prosthetics), 228 (forehead aglow) (all book II).

53 **when a friend wrote to him:** Petrarch, *Letters of Old Age*, vol. 2, 641, 633n (*Sen*. XVI, 9, to Dom Jean Birel Limousin, prior of the charterhouse north of Milan, [1354–57]).

53 **It is never any use:** Petrarch, *Remedies for Fortune Fair and Foul*, vol. 3, 37 (book II).

53 **Petrarch's whole oeuvre:** As two eminent historians of early modern humanism have recently commented, loss was a possibility that "always haunted the humanists," and the humanism of the Italian Renaissance "was born from a profound sense of loss and longing." See Anthony Grafton, *Inky Fingers* (Cambridge, MA: Harvard University Press, 2020), 9; and James Hankins, *Virtue Politics* (Cambridge, MA: Harvard University Press, 2019), 1.

54 **he looked back on past centuries:** Boccaccio, *Boccaccio on Poetry*, 8–9 (Boccaccio's preface).

54 **"My fate is to live":** Petrarch, *Africa*, IX, 451–57. Quoted in T. E. Mommsen, "Petrarch's Conception of the 'Dark Ages,'" *Speculum* 17 (1942), 226–42, this on 240. Mommsen also quotes and translates other allusions by Petrarch to a dark age, notably a description of recent centuries as times of "darkness and dense gloom," through which only a few keen-eyed geniuses could see. (Petrarch, *Apologia contra cuiusdam anonymi Galli calumnias*, quoted by Mommsen, 227.) On the "gap," see Alexander Lee, Pit Péporté, and Harry Schnitker, eds., *Renaissance Perceptions of Continuity and Discontinuity in Europe, c. 1300–c. 1550* (Leiden, Netherlands, and Boston: Brill, 2010).

CHAPTER 2. RAISING SHIPS

56 **And in such cases:** In the monastery of Bobbio in northern Italy, for example, parchment was cleaned in one case by "gently washing off the ink of Cicero's *De republica*," to make room for a section of Augustine's study of the biblical Psalms (Vat. Lat. 5757): https://spotlight.vatlib.it/palimpsests/about/vat-lat-5757-inf. On early Christian destruction in general, see Catherine Nixey, *The Darkening Age* (London: Macmillan, 2017).

57 **Benedict, the sixth-century founder:** Pope Gregory I, *The Life of Saint Benedict*, trans. Terrence Kardong (Collegeville, MN: Liturgical Press, 2019), 49.

57 **Some conservation-minded people:** *The Letters of S. Ambrose, Bishop of Milan*, anonymous trans., rev. H. Walford (Oxford, UK: James Parker, 1881), 109–10 (letter XVIII, Ambrose to Emperor Valentinian II, 384 CE).

58 **When Vesuvius erupted:** It was found in 2018. Valeria Piano, "A 'Historic(al)' Find from the Library of Herculaneum," in *Seneca the Elder and His Rediscovered* Historiae ab initio bellorum civilium [P. Herc.1067] (Berlin: De Gruyter, 2020), https://www.degruyter.com/document/doi/10.1515/9783110688665-003/html.

58 **the fascinating al-Kindi:** See Peter Adamson, *Al-Kindi* (New York: Oxford University Press, 2007), and https://en.wikipedia.org/wiki/Al-Kindi.

58 **the emperor Charlemagne ordered monks:** "From the General Letter of Charlemagne, before 800," in *Carolingian Civilization: A Reader*, ed. P. E. Dutton, 2nd ed. (Toronto: University of Toronto Press, 2009), 91.

59 **His contemporary biographer:** Einhard and Notker the Stammerer, *Two Lives of Charlemagne*, trans. Lewis Thorpe (Harmondsworth, UK: Penguin, 1969), 79 (Einhard, s. 25).

59 **Charlemagne founded boys' schools:** Einhard and Notker the Stammerer, *Two Lives of Charlemagne*, 74 (Einhard, s. 19).

59 **He kept nagging:** "A Letter of Charles on the Cultivation of Learning, 780–800," 90.

59 **Monastic scriptoria could be:** *The Rule of Benedict*, trans. Caroline White (London: Penguin, 2008), 61 (rule 38: no questions), 21 (rule 6: no jokes), 63 (rule 40: no wine grumbling), 84 (rule 57: no pride in skills). On monks being issued a book a year, see Charles Homer Haskins, *The Renaissance of the Twelfth Century* (Cambridge, MA: Harvard University Press, 1927), 34.

59 **The grammarian Gunzo of Novara:** Anna A. Grotans, *Reading in Medieval St. Gall* (Cambridge, UK: Cambridge University Press, 2011), 49.

60 **By the 1100s:** Notably Haskins, in *The Renaissance of the Twelfth Century*.

60 **made from cloth rags:** This theory has been proposed by Marco Mostert of Utrecht University; see Ross King, *The Bookseller of Florence* (London: Chatto & Windus, 2020), 154, and Martin Wainwright, "How Discarded Pants Helped to Boost Literacy," *Guardian*, July 12, 2007, https://www.theguardian.com/uk/2007/jul/12/martinwainwright.uknews4.

61 **The cathedrals provided a base:** Haskins, *The Renaissance of the Twelfth Century*, 67.

61 **Like Petrarch later:** Cary J. Nederman, *John of Salisbury* (Tempe: Arizona Center for Medieval and Renaissance Studies, 2005), 53–64. On his letters, see John of Salisbury, *Letters*, ed. W. J. Millor and S. J. and H. E. Butler; vol. 1, rev. C. N. L. Brooke (Oxford, UK: Clarendon Press, 1979–86).

62 **had made an agreement:** Petrarch, "Testament," in *Petrarch's Testament*, ed. and trans. Theodor Mommsen (Ithaca, NY: Cornell University Press, 1957), 68–93, this on 83. For the background on his will and possessions, see Mommsen's introduction, 45–50.

62 **His library went:** Mommsen, introduction, *Petrarch's Testament*, 44; Marco Santagata, *Boccaccio: Fragilità di un genio* (Milan: Mondadori, 2019), 289 (proviso about open use).

62 **The most energetic character:** David Thompson and Alan F. Nagel, eds. and trans., *The Three Crowns of Florence: Humanist Assessments of Dante, Petrarca and Boccaccio* (New York: Harper & Row, 1972), 6, citing Coluccio's letter to Roberto Guidi, count of Battifolle, August 16, 1374. On Coluccio, see also Berthold L. Ullman, *The Humanism of Coluccio Salutati* (Padua: Antenore, 1963), and Ronald G. Witt, *Hercules at the Crossroads: The Life, Works, and Thought of Coluccio Salutati* (Durham, NC: Duke University Press, 1983), especially 184–89 on his network of contacts and 183, 421 on his own library.

63 **Coluccio added twelve more:** Giannozzo Manetti, *Biographical Writings*, ed. and trans. Stefano U. Baldassari and Rolf Bagemihl (Cambridge, MA, and London: I Tatti/Harvard University Press, 2003), 101.

63 **He did not marry:** Vespasiano da Bisticci, *The Vespasiano Memoirs [Vite di uomini illustri del secolo XV]*, trans. William George and Emily Waters (Toronto: University of Toronto Press/Renaissance Society of America, 1997), 401–2. Vespasiano also mentions Niccolò making his books available to anyone who wished to use them and inviting students to come in to read and discuss books.

64   **Giannozzo Manetti wrote:** Manetti, *Biographical Writings*, 127.

64   **Poggio Bracciolini, whose lively personality:** Vespasiano, *The Vespasiano Memoirs*, 353 ("strong invective"). The punch-up was with the Greek scholar George of Trebizond. See Henry Field, *The Intellectual Struggle for Florence* (Oxford, UK: Oxford University Press, 2017), 284.

64   **At Cluny Abbey:** On Vitruvius, see Carol Herselle Krinsky, "Seventy-Eight Vitruvian Manuscripts," *Journal of the Courtauld and Warburg Institutes* 30 (1967), 36–70. On Quintilian and Cicero, see L. D. Reynolds and N. G. Wilson, *Scribes and Scholars*, 3rd ed. (Oxford, UK: Clarendon Press, 1991), 137–38. The Cicero speeches they found were *Pro Roscio* and *Pro Murena*.

65   **Then, probably in Fulda:** Poggio Bracciolini, *Two Renaissance Book-Hunters: The Letters of Poggius Bracciolini to Nicolaus de Niccolis*, trans. Phyllis Walter Goodhart Gordan (New York and London: Columbia University Press, 1974), 88 (Poggio to Niccolò, April 14 [1425]). On Lucretius's work, see also Ada Palmer, *Reading Lucretius in the Renaissance* (Cambridge, MA, and London: Harvard University Press, 2014), especially 4, where she mentions the hoarding. See also Alison Brown, *The Return of Lucretius to Renaissance Florence* (Cambridge, MA, and London: Harvard University Press, 2010).

65   **In 1423, while working:** Poggio Bracciolini, *Two Renaissance Book-Hunters*, 84 (Poggio to Niccolò, Rome, November 6, 1423).

65   **a highly humanistic amusement:** Barbara C. Bowen, ed., *One Hundred Renaissance Jokes: An Anthology* (Birmingham, UK: Summa, 1988), 5–9, this on 9.

66   **In their copying and writing:** L. D. Reynolds and N. G. Wilson, *Scribes and Scholars*, 3rd ed. (Oxford, UK: Clarendon Press, 1991), 139; A. C. de la Mare, *The Handwriting of the Italian Humanists*, vol. 1, fascicule 1 (Oxford, UK: Oxford University Press, for the Association Internationale de Bibliophilie, 1973). The latter gives examples from the handwriting of Petrarch, Boccaccio, Coluccio Salutati, Niccolò Niccoli, Poggio Bracciolini, and others.

66   **The humanists dismissed:** Apparently it was Lorenzo Valla who first used this term to describe handwriting, in the preface to his *Elegances of the Latin Language* (*Elegantiae linguae Latinae, libri sex*). See E. P. Goldschmidt, *The Printed Book of the Renaissance: Three Lectures on Type, Illustration, Ornament* (Cambridge, UK: Cambridge University Press, 1950), 2.

67   **Petrarch, during several visits:** Petrarch, *Letters on Familiar Matters / Rerum familiarum, libri I–XXIV*, trans. Aldo S. Bernardo (Albany: SUNY Press, 1975; Baltimore and London: Johns Hopkins University Press, 1982–85), vol. 1, 292 (here and there), 294 (expertise) (*Fam.* VI, 2, to Giovanni Colonna). On Gregorius's *De mirabilibus urbis Romae*, see Roberto Weiss, *The Renaissance Discovery of Classical Antiquity*, 2nd ed. (Oxford, UK: Basil Blackwell, 1988), 33–34.

67   **"Not such a hard discovery":** Matthew Kneale, *Rome: A History in Seven Sackings* (London: Atlantic, 2018), 189.

67   **Poggio wrote his own description:** Poggio Bracciolini, "The Ruins of Rome," trans. Mary Martin McLaughlin, in *The Portable Renaissance Reader*, ed. James Bruce Ross and Mary Martin McLaughlin, rev. ed. (London: Penguin, 1977), 379–84; this is Poggio's dialogue with Antonio Loschi on ruins, from the first book of his *De varietate fortunae*, or *On the Inconstancy of Fortune*, written 1431–1448. On other explorations, see, for example, his climb to read inscriptions at Porta Sanguinaria, Ferentino, in Poggio Bracciolini, *Two Renaissance Book-Hunters*, 129–30 (Poggio to Niccolò, September 15 [1428]).

67   **Two youths who lived:** Ross King, *Brunelleschi's Dome* (London: Vintage, 2008), 25.

67   **A few travelers:** See Cyriac of Ancona, *Life and Early Travels* and *Later Travels*, ed. and trans. Charles Mitchell, Edward W. Bonar, and Clive Foss (Cambridge, MA: Harvard University Press, 2003 (*Later*), 2015 (*Early*).

68   **both mean the same thing:** My thanks to Peter Mack for this point.

68   **Also interested in Roman origins:** Leon Battista Alberti, *Delineation of the City of Rome* [*Descriptio urbis Romae*], ed. Mario Carpo and Francesco Furlan, trans. Peter Hicks (Tempe: Arizona Center for Medieval and Renaissance Studies, 2007). See also Joan Gadol, *Leon Battista Alberti* (Chicago and London: University of Chicago Press, 1969), 167; Anthony Grafton, *Leon Battista Alberti* (London: Allen Lane/Penguin, 2001), 241–43.

68   **Alberti devised a method:** Flavio Biondo, *Italy Illuminated*, ed. and trans. Jeffrey A. White (Cambridge, MA, and London: I Tatti/Harvard University Press, 2005–16), this in vol. 1, 189–93, including "fish," 191 (book II, §47–49). On the ships, see also Anthony Grafton, *Leon Battista Alberti* (London: Allen Lane/Penguin, 2001), 248–49.

68   **A mosaic was detached:** Elisabetta Povoledo, "Long-Lost Mosaic from a 'Floating Palace' of Caligula Returns Home," *New York Times*, March 14, 2021, https://www.nytimes.com/2021/03/14/world/europe/caligula-mosaic-ship-italy.html. See also https://www.theguardian.com/artanddesign/2021/nov/22/priceless-roman-mosaic-coffee-table-new-york-apartment, with more information on how it came to New York.

69   **The full raising:** For information on the Nemi ships: https://en.wikipedia.org/wiki/Nemi_ships.

69   **The museum is now alive:** https://comunedinemi.rm.it/contenuti/11827/museo-navi.

69   **Flavio Biondo used it:** Flavio Biondo, *Italy Illuminated*, this in vol. 1, 5. The link to the Nemi ships is pointed out by Anthony Grafton, "The Universal Language: Splendors and Sorrows of Latin in the Modern World," in *Worlds Made by Words* (Cambridge, MA, and London: Harvard University Press, 2009), 138.

70   **Poggio described the Quintilian manuscript:** Poggio Bracciolini, *Two Renaissance Book-Hunters*, 194–95 (Poggio to Guarino Guarini, December 15, 1416).

70   **The image is slightly spoiled:** Vespasiano, *The Vespasiano Memoirs*, 352.

70   **Poggio's friend Cinzio:** Poggio Bracciolini, *Two Renaissance Book-Hunters*, 189 (Cinzio to Franciscus de Fiana, undated but apparently summer 1416).

70   **The bookseller and biographer Vespasiano:** Vespasiano da Bisticci, "Proemio della vita dell'Alessandra de' Bardi," in *Vite di uomini illustri del secolo XV*, ed. Paolo d'Ancona and Erhard Aeschlimann (Milano: Ulrico Hoepli, 1951), 543. The English translation abbreviates it, losing this point. In Italian: "In grande oscurità sono gli ignoranti in questa vita"; of writers he says, "Hanno gli scrittori alluminato il mondo, a cavatolo di tanta oscurità in quanta si trovava." The remark about ignorance as a source of evil is also from this proem.

70   **Francesco Barbaro, a Venetian scholar:** Poggio Bracciolini, *Two Renaissance Book-Hunters*, 196–203, these on 196, 198 (Franciscus Barbarus to Poggio, July 6, 1417).

71   **"I have a room":** Poggio Bracciolini, *Two Renaissance Book-Hunters*, 118 (Poggio to Niccolò Niccoli, Rome, October 21 [1427]).

71   **No wonder Poggio chose:** Poggio Bracciolini, *On Avarice* [*De Avaritia*, Basel 1538], trans. Benjamin G. Kohl and Elizabeth B. Welles, in *The Earthly Republic: Italian Humanists on Government and Society*, ed. B. G. Kohl, R. G. Witt, and E. B. Welles (Manchester, UK: Manchester University Press, 1978), 241–89, esp. 257 on avarice being beneficial.

71　**Far away to the north:** Lorenzo Bonoldi, *Isabella d'Este: A Renaissance Woman*, trans. Clark Anthony Lawrence ([Rimini]: Guaraldi/Engramma, 2015), vol. 1, 11; Weiss, *The Renaissance Discovery of Classical Antiquity*, 196–99. See also Julia Cartwright, *Isabella d'Este, Marchioness of Mantua 1474–1539* (London: John Murray, 1903).

71　**In 1984, the historian:** Joan Kelly-Gadol, "Did Women Have a Renaissance?," in *Women, History, and Theory* (Chicago: University of Chicago Press, 1984), 12–50, https://nguyenshs.weebly.com/uploads/9/3/7/3/93734528/kelly_did_women _have_a_renaissanace.pdf.

71　**Or they might flourish:** Hrotsvitha: in a classic humanistic discovery story, six of her plays were found in the Cloister of St. Emmeram in Regensburg by Conrad Celtis in 1493; he published them as *Opera Hrosvite* (Nuremberg, 1501), with illustrations by Albrecht Dürer. The manuscript is in the Bavarian State Library. See Lewis W. Spitz, *Conrad Celtis: The German Arch-Humanist* (Cambridge, MA: Harvard University Press, 1957), 42; E. H. Zeydel, "The Reception of Hrotsvitha by the German Humanists after 1493," *Journal of English and Germanic Philology* 44 (1945), 239–49; Leonard Forster, introduction to *Selections from Conrad Celtis*, ed. and trans. Leonard Forster (Cambridge, UK: Cambridge University Press, 1948), 11. See also https://en.wiki pedia.org/wiki/Hrotsvitha. More has been written about Hildegard; see, for example, Fiona Maddocks, *Hildegard of Bingen* (London: Headline, 2001).

72　**An outstanding early example:** On Christine de Pizan's early life and work, see Sarah Lawson's introduction to her translation of *The Treasure of the City of Ladies*, rev. ed. (London: Penguin, 2003), xv–xvii.

73　**In 1405, she wrote:** Christine de Pizan, *The Book of the City of Ladies*, trans. Rosalind Brown-Grant (London: Penguin, 1999), 9 (part 1, s. 2).

73　**women such as Laura Cereta:** Margaret L. King and Albert Rabil Jr., eds., *Her Immaculate Hand: Selected Works by and about the Women Humanists of Quattrocento Italy* (Asheville: Pegasus/University of North Carolina at Asheville, 2000), 81–84.

73　**Another letter writer:** Angelo Poliziano, *Letters*, ed. and trans. Shane Butler (Cambridge, MA, and London: I Tatti/Harvard University Press, 2006), vol. 1, 189–91.

73　**One of her letters:** Translated in King and Rabil, *Her Immaculate Hand*, 77. The same source gives information on her later life (48–50).

74　**The poet Vittoria Colonna:** Ramie Targoff, *Renaissance Woman: The Life of Vittoria Colonna* (New York: Farrar, Straus & Giroux, 2019), 16.

75　**The humanistic education:** See, for example, the discussion in Anthony Grafton and Lisa Jardine, *From Humanism to the Humanities: Education and the Liberal Arts in Fifteenth- and Sixteenth-Century Europe* (London: Duckworth, 1986), 23–24. On humanistic education generally in this era, see also Paul F. Grendler, *Schooling in Renaissance Italy: Literacy and Learning, 1300–1600* (Baltimore and London: Johns Hopkins University Press, 1989).

76　**Humanistic tutors liked to contrast:** This example is given by Michel de Montaigne, *Essays*, in *The Complete Works*, trans. Donald Frame (London: Everyman, 2003), 154 (book I, chap. 26).

76　**Princess Mary's teacher:** Juan Luis Vives, *In Pseudodialecticos*, trans. and ed. Charles Fantazzi (Leiden, Netherlands: Brill, 1979), 84 ("moral philosophy"), 88 ("the true disciplines").

76　**Guarino wrote in praise:** Both the Guarini letter and the dialogue (by Angelo Decembrio, *De politia litteraria*, 1462) are quoted in Anthony Grafton, *Commerce with the*

Classics: Ancient Books and Renaissance Readers (Ann Arbor: University of Michigan Press, 1997), 46 (letter), 30 (dialogue).

77   **The duke there, Federico da Montefeltro:** Julia Cartwright, *Baldassare Castiglione: His Life and Letters* (London: John Murray, 1908), vol. 1, 60–61 (treasure), 62 (copyists).

77   **The atmosphere of a slightly later generation:** Baldassare Castiglione, *The Book of the Courtier*, trans. George Bull, rev. ed. (Harmondsworth, UK: Penguin, 1976), 47 (also 63, tennis and tightrope-walking).

78   **should behave with *sprezzatura*:** On *sprezzatura* and its translation, see Peter Burke, *The Fortunes of the* Courtier (Cambridge, UK: Polity, 1995), 69–72.

78   **Castiglione claims that he wrote:** Castiglione, "Dedication," *Book of the Courtier*, 31. For the real story, see Peter Burke, *The Fortunes of the* Courtier, 22–23.

78   **One admired scholar:** Ezio Raimondi, *Codro e l'umanesimo a Bologna* (Bologna: C. Zuffi, 1987), 11–14; Carlo Malagola, *Della vita e delle opere di Antonio Urceo detto Codro: Studi e ricerche* (Bologna: Fava e Garagnani, 1878), 164.

79   **Printing, both with and without:** Endymion Wilkinson, "Woodblock Printing," in *Chinese History: A New Manual* (Cambridge, MA: Harvard University Asia Center for the Harvard-Yenching Institute, 2012), 910.

79   **Up to ten thousand:** Ross King, *The Bookseller of Florence* (London: Chatto & Windus, 2020), 142. For the numbers, he refers to Janet Ing, "The Mainz Indulgences of 1454/5: A Review of Recent Scholarship," *British Library Journal* 1 (Spring 1983), 19. The indulgences were for those who donated money for defending Cyprus against the Turks.

79   **Like most inventions:** Johannes Trithemius, *In Praise of Scribes* [*De laude scriptorium*], trans. Roland Behrendt, ed. Klaus Arnold (Lawrence, KS: Coronado, 1974), especially 53–63 (spiritual exercise) and 35 (parchment more durable). The introduction mentions his reason for printing his book (15).

80   **As Edward Gibbon wrote:** Edward Gibbon, *The History of the Decline and Fall of the Roman Empire*, abridged, ed. David Womersley (London: Penguin, 2000), 727 (chap. 68)

80   **The best use of such designs:** Martin Lowry, *The World of Aldus Manutius* (Oxford, UK: Blackwell, 1979), 119.

81   **At one extreme:** Ingrid D. Rowland, *The Culture of the High Renaissance* (Cambridge, UK: Cambridge University Press, 1998), 62.

81   **As the book historian:** E. P. Goldschmidt, *The Printed Book of the Renaissance* (Cambridge, UK: Cambridge University Press, 1950), 51.

82   **It comes with woodcuts:** Martin Lowry, *The World of Aldus Manutius* (Oxford, UK: Blackwell, 1979), 122.

82   **Small books were not new:** Martial, *Epigrams*, ed. and trans. D. R. Shackleton Bailey (Cambridge, MA, and London: Harvard University Press, 1993), vol. 1, 43 (i, ii).

82   **One of the new authors:** Pietro Bembo, *Lyric Poetry; Etna*, ed. and trans. Mary P. Chatfield (Cambridge, MA, and London: I Tatti/Harvard University Press, 2005), 194–249, this on 243. On his ascent and on Aldus's printing of the book, see Williams, *Pietro Bembo on Etna*.

82   **But the letters are clean and clear:** Gareth D. Williams, *Pietro Bembo on Etna: The Ascent of a Venetian Humanist* (Oxford, UK: Oxford University Press, 2017), 202n. For more on the semicolon: Cecelia Watson, *Semicolon* (London: Fourth Estate, 2020).

A similar symbol had been used in manuscript times, but only for representing abbreviations of common Latin words.

83 **It amounts to a demonstration:** Ernst Robert Curtius, *European Literature and the Latin Middle Ages*, trans. Willard R. Trask (Princeton, NJ: Princeton University Press, 2013), 315.

83 **Among the many who joined:** Erasmus's *Apologia adversus rapsodias calumniosarum querimoniarum Alberti Pii* (1531), translated by Margaret Mann Phillips in her *The "Adages" of Erasmus: A Study with Translations* (Cambridge, UK: Cambridge University Press, 1964), 68. Also on Erasmus's stay with Aldus, see Erasmus, "Penny-Pinching" [*Opulentia sordida*] (1531), in *The Colloquies*, trans. Craig R. Thompson (Chicago and London: University of Chicago Press, 1965), 488–99.

84 **Aldus had friends:** Aldus Manutius, *The Greek Classics*, ed. and trans. N. G. Wilson (Cambridge, MA, and London: I Tatti/Harvard University Press, 2016), 289–91.

84 **Erasmus said of Aldus:** Phillips, *The "Adages" of Erasmus*, 181.

84 **Beyond the real planet:** Thomas More, *Utopia*, trans. Clarence H. Miller (New Haven and London: Yale University Press, 2001), 95.

84 **Aldus rightly congratulated himself:** Aldus Manutius, *The Greek Classics*, ed. and trans. N. G. Wilson, 205–7 ("Nun o, nunc, iuvenes, ubique in urbe / flores spargite: vere nanque primo / Aldus venit en, Aldus ecce venit!").

84 **In one of Aldus's prefaces:** Aldus Manutius, *The Greek Classics*, 99.

85 **Erasmus compared editorial work:** R. J. Schoeck, *Erasmus of Europe* (Edinburgh: Edinburgh University Press, 1990–93), vol. 2, 158, citing a letter from Erasmus to Thomas Ruthall, March 7, 1515.

CHAPTER 3. PROVOCATEURS AND PAGANS

86 **When the emperor Constantine the Great:** For the text of the Donation, see Lorenzo Valla, *On the Donation of Constantine*, trans. G. W. Bowersock (Cambridge, MA: I Tatti/Harvard University Press, 2007), 162–83. On its historical context and how it was used, see Johannes Fried, *"Donation of Constantine" and "Constitutum Constantini": The Misinterpretation of a Fiction and Its Original Meaning* (Berlin: De Gruyter, 2007).

87 **The Donation document:** Peter Burke, *The Renaissance Sense of the Past* (London: Edward Arnold, 1969), 55. Doubt was cast especially by Nicholas of Cusa in 1432–1433.

87 **The poet Maffeo Vegio:** Maffeo Vegio to Lorenzo Valla, Pavia, August 26 [1434]: Lorenzo Valla, *Correspondence*, ed. and trans. Brendan Cook (Cambridge, MA, and London: I Tatti/Harvard University Press, 2013), 35–37. The work he was referring to was the *Repastinatio*.

88 **Bartolomeo Facio, summed him up:** Facio's first *Invective*, quoted in Maristella Lorch, introduction to Lorenzo Valla, *On Pleasure: De Voluptate*, trans. A. Kent Hieatt and Maristella Lorch (New York: Abaris, 1977), 8. Valla's other great enemy in Naples scholarly life was Antonio Beccadelli, known as Panormita.

88 **Valla acknowledged his own bumptious character:** Lorenzo Valla to Cardinal Trevisan (1443), translated in Salvatore I. Camporeale, "Lorenzo Valla's *Oratio* on the Pseudo-Donation of Constantine: Dissent and Innovation in Early Renaissance Humanism," in "Lorenzo Valla: A Symposium," *Journal of the History of Ideas* 57 (1996), 9–26, this on 9.

88 **His attack begins:** Valla, *On the Donation of Constantine*, 67.

88   **First he uses the methods:** Valla, *On the Donation of Constantine*, 11–15 (is it plausible?), 43 (documentation?).

88   **Following these blows:** Valla, *On the Donation of Constantine*, 67 (satraps), 97 (felt socks etc.).

89   **Valla knew he was on firm ground:** N. G. Wilson, *From Byzantium to Italy: Greek Studies in the Italian Renaissance* (Baltimore: Johns Hopkins University Press, 1992), 69–72. These works were commissioned by Pope Nicholas V in Rome, at a time when Valla was back in favor with the papacy.

89   **"How brilliant Valla is!":** Rudolph Langen of Munster, writing to Antony Vrye (or Liber) of Soest, February 27, 1469, quoted in P. S. Allen, *The Age of Erasmus* (Oxford, UK: Clarendon Press, 1914), 23.

89   **An alternative image:** Lorenzo Valla, *Dialectical Disputations*, ed. and trans. Brian Copenhaver and Lodi Nauta (Cambridge, MA: I Tatti/Harvard University Press, 2012). Unfortunately, a sixteenth-century editor replaced the earlier title with the dull *Dialecticae disputationes*, or *Dialectical Disputations*, which stuck; see the editors' introduction, x–xi.

89   **Valla also redug the texts:** Livy: BL Harley 2493. Facsimile: Giuseppe Billanovich, *La tradizione dal testo di Livio e le origini dell'umanesimo*, vol. 2: *Il Livio del Petrarca e del Valla: British Library, Harleian 2493* (Padua: Antenore, 1981). Valla's amendments: *Emendationes sex librorum Titi Livi*, written in 1446–1447.

89   **In his *Annotations to the New Testament*:** Lorenzo Valla, *In Latinam Novi Testamenti interpretationem ex collatione Graecorum exemplarium adnotationes*, written and revised through the 1440s. See Wilson, *From Byzantium to Italy*, 73, and L. D. Reynolds and N. G. Wilson, *Scribes and Scholars*, 3rd ed. (Oxford, UK: Clarendon Press, 1991), 144. On Valla's New Testament textual criticism, see also Jerry H. Bentley, *Humanists and Holy Writ* (Princeton, NJ: Princeton University Press, 1983), 32–69.

90   **Its main problem was not:** William J. Connell, introduction to "Lorenzo Valla: A Symposium," *Journal of the History of Ideas* 57 (1996), 1–7, this on 2. See Valla's *On Free Will*, trans. Charles Edward Trinkaus Jr., in *The Renaissance Philosophy of Man*, ed. Ernst Cassirer, P. O. Kristeller, and John Herman Randall Jr. (Chicago: University of Chicago Press, 1948), 155–82, translator's introduction, 147–54. See also Christopher S. Celenza, *The Intellectual World of the Italian Renaissance* (New York: Cambridge University Press, 2018), 216–27.

90   **Valla had written the work:** Valla, *On Pleasure: De Voluptate*, 69 (Stoic: animals), 101, 109, 131 (Epicurean: pleasures), 285–87 (Christian: heavenly ones better), 91 (Lorenzo: "My soul inclines").

91   **"What in Heaven's name":** Lorenzo Valla to Eugenius IV, November 27 [1434], in Valla, *Correspondence*, 43. See also Lorch, introduction to Valla, *On Pleasure: De Voluptate*, 27.

91   **That was one of the main reasons:** Camporeale, "Lorenzo Valla's *Oratio* on the Pseudo-Donation of Constantine: Dissent and Innovation in Early Renaissance Humanism," 9–26, this on 9.

91   **This allowed him to live:** Reynolds and Wilson, *Scribes and Scholars*, 143; G. W. Bowersock, introduction to his translation of Valla, *On the Donation of Constantine*, ix.

92   **When he died in 1457:** Jill Kraye, "Lorenzo Valla and Changing Perceptions of Renaissance Humanism," *Comparative Criticism* 23 (2001), 37–55, this 37–38 (with image of the tomb). Niebuhr told students of finding the paving slab, in a lecture on the

history of Rome at the University of Bonn in 1828–1829. The historian Francesco Cancellieri rescued it soon after that.

92 **His commentary on the New Testament:** R. J. Schoeck, *Erasmus of Europe* (Edinburgh: Edinburgh University Press, 1990–93), vol. 2, 44–45.

92 **Like Valla, he preferred:** Camporeale, "Lorenzo Valla's *Oratio* on the Pseudo-Donation of Constantine," 9–26, this on 25.

93 **They would follow him:** A notable example is Isaac Casaubon, who in *De rebus sacris et ecclesiasticis exercitationes XVI* of 1614 showed that the "hermetic" texts beloved of Renaissance Neoplatonists were not ancient Egyptian as they had thought, but written by later Christians, which explained why the ideas in them seemed so uncannily to prefigure Christianity. See Anthony Grafton, "Protestant versus Prophet: Isaac Casaubon on Hermes Trismegistus," *Journal of the Warburg and Courtauld Institutes* 46 (1983), 78–93.

93 **As he concluded this letter:** "To restore the others to their senses" and preceding quotations are from Lorenzo Valla to Joan Serra, Gaeta, August 13 [1440], in Valla, *Correspondence*, 75–97.

94 **Valla seemed to fancy himself:** Poggio Bracciolini to Bartolomeo Ghiselardi, 1454, translated in Anthony Grafton and Lisa Jardine, *From Humanism to the Humanities: Education and the Liberal Arts in Fifteenth- and Sixteenth-Century Europe* (London: Duckworth, 1986), 80. The Latin in fuller form is: "Itaque opus esset non verbis, sed fustibus, et clava Herculis ad hoc monstrum perdomandum, et discipulos suos." See Salvatore I. Camporeale, *Lorenzo Valla: Umanesimo e teologia* (Florence: Istituto Nazionale di Studi sul Rinascimento, 1972), 137. Valla was teaching in Rome during this period. See also an earlier letter from Francesco Filelfo to both Poggio and Valla, March 7, 1453, begging them to get over their quarrel, in Valla, *Correspondence*, 273.

94 **One reason Poggio had:** On all this, see *Ciceronian Controversies*, ed. JoAnn Della-Neva, trans. Brian Duvick (Cambridge, MA: I Tatti/Harvard University Press, 2007), including Angelo Poliziano to Paolo Cortesi, vowing to avoid non-Ciceronian terms, 3–5.

94 **Petrarch, who was less uncritical:** Petrarch, *Letters on Familiar Matters / Rerum familiarum, libri I–XXIV*, trans. Aldo S. Bernardo (Albany: SUNY Press, 1975; Baltimore and London: Johns Hopkins University Press, 1982–85), vol. 3, 314–16 (*Fam.* XXIV, 2, to Pulice da Vicenza, a poet, who had also been present on the occasion).

95 **While living in a hermit's retreat:** "Ciceronianus es, non Christianus." The story is told in Jerome's letter to the lady Eustochium, the daughter of his disciple Paula, 384 CE. Here as translated in Eugene F. Rice Jr., *Saint Jerome in the Renaissance* (Baltimore and London: Johns Hopkins University Press, 1985), 3. Also in Saint Jerome, *Selected Letters*, trans. F. A. Wright (London: W. Heinemann; New York: G. P. Putnam's Sons, 1933), 53–158, with the dream on 127–29.

95 **Commenting on this:** Valla, in the preface to book IV of his *Elegances*: Lorenzo Valla, "In quartum librum elegantiarum praefatio: Prefazione al quarto libro delle Eleganze," in *Prosatori latini del Quattrocento*, ed. Eugenio Garin (Turin: Einaudi, 1976–77), vol. 5, 612–23, this on 614–15. See also Rice, *Saint Jerome in the Renaissance*, 86.

96 **Longolius's problem was pointed out:** Erasmus, "The Ciceronian," trans. Betty I. Knott, ed. A. H. T. Levi, in *Collected Works*, vol. 28 (Toronto: University of Toronto Press, 1986), 430–35.

96 **The very stones of Rome:** On the background to Sandro Botticelli's *Birth of Venus* and *Primavera*, for which the artist consulted his personal humanist adviser Angelo Poliziano: Frank Zöllner, *Sandro Botticelli* (Munich: Prestel, 2009), 135, 140–41.

96 **Petrarch reassured himself:** Petrarch, "On His Own Ignorance and That of Others," in *Invectives*, ed. and trans. David Marsh (Cambridge, MA, and London: I Tatti/Harvard University Press, 2003), 333.

96 **His Fourth *Eclogue* mentions:** Virgil, *Eclogues*, IV.

97 **the poet Faltonia Betitia Proba:** In *Cento Vergilianus de laudibus Christi*. See E. Clark and D. Hatch, *The Golden Bough, the Oaken Cross: The Virgilian Cento of Faltonia Betitia Proba* (Chico, CA: Scholars Press, 1981). See also https://en.wikipedia.org /wiki/Cento_Vergilianus_de_laudibus_Christi. Twelfth-century scholars, especially in the school of Chartres, used the word *integumentum*, or "outer covering," to describe this type of classical text, meaning that the surface was a mere shawl or cloak hiding a deeper meaning: Peter Adamson, *Medieval Philosophy* (Oxford, UK: Oxford University Press, 2019), 96–97.

97 **This is why Dante:** Dante, *Inferno*, canto 4, line 39 (Virgil); canto 10, lines 13–15 (Epicurus).

97 **As Erasmus had one:** Erasmus, "The Ciceronian," 388 (Diana), 396 (museums), 383 (flamens and vestals).

97 **During the 1460s, several men:** Ingrid D. Rowland, *The Culture of the High Renaissance* (Cambridge, UK: Cambridge University Press, 1998), 13; Anthony F. D'Elia, *A Sudden Terror: The Plot to Murder the Pope in Renaissance Rome* (Cambridge, MA, and London: Harvard University Press, 2009), 95–97 (with samples of their poetry); Grafton and Jardine, *From Humanism to the Humanities*, 89–90 (plays).

98 **A report sent home:** Translated in D'Elia, *A Sudden Terror*, 88.

98 **This was plausible:** Ronald G. Musto, *Apocalypse in Rome: Cola di Rienzo and the Politics of the New Age* (Berkeley: University of California Press, 2003), 341–43.

99 **"Before boys have reached":** D'Elia, *A Sudden Terror*, 82. D'Elia is the source for most of the rest of this account of the Roman Academy and its persecution, except where otherwise noted.

99 **Disliking the humanists:** J. F. D'Amico, *Renaissance Humanism in Papal Rome: Humanists and Churchmen on the Eve of the Reformation* (Baltimore: Johns Hopkins University Press, 1983), 93.

100 **Pomponio wrote, thanking him:** Translated in D'Elia, *A Sudden Terror*, 181. Also, for Rodrigo's surprise at their eloquence: 170.

100 **He published a recipe book:** B. Platina, *De honesta voluptate et valetudine*, written in the mid-1460s but published only later. John Verriano, "At Supper with Leonardo," *Gastronomica* 8, no. 1 (2008), 75–79.

100 **Platina also wrote:** Platina, *Liber de vita Christi ac omnium pontificum aa. 1–1474* (Venice: J. Manthen and J. de Colonia, 1479).

101 **All the same, its members:** Rowland, *The Culture of the High Renaissance*, 16; D'Elia, *A Sudden Terror*, 184. A student's notes survive of a tour through the Roman ruins, conducted for a foreign visitor sometime after 1484: Roberto Weiss, *The Renaissance Discovery of Classical Antiquity*, 2nd ed. (Oxford, UK: Blackwell, 1988), 76–77.

102 **In his *Praise of the City of Florence*:** Leonardo Bruni, *Laudatio florentinae urbis*, trans. Hans Baron, in *The Humanism of Leonardo Bruni: Selected Texts*, trans. and ed. G. Griffiths, J. Hankins, and D. Thompson (Binghamton, NY: Medieval and Renaissance Texts and Studies, 1987), 116–17 (nothing out of tune), 121 (industrious and urbane).

102 **And, as he wrote elsewhere:** Leonardo Bruni, "Oration for the Funeral of Nanni Strozzi" (1428), trans. Gordon Griffiths, in *The Humanism of Leonardo Bruni*, trans. and ed. G. Griffiths, J. Hankins, and D. Thompson (Binghamton, NY: Medieval and

Renaissance Texts and Studies, 1987), 121–27, this on 126. Nanni Strozzi had died fighting for the city in 1427.

103 According to Thucydides: Thucydides, *The Peloponnesian War*, book 2, §35–46.

103 Yet in both cases the humanistic ideal: Historians have disagreed about whether the Florentine ideas of this period are best described as "civic humanism" or not. The term is associated particularly with the historian Hans Baron, who highlighted their concern with political and civic commitments more than with literary or philosophical matters for their own sake: Hans Baron, *The Crisis of the Early Italian Renaissance: Civic Humanism and Republican Liberty in an Age of Classicism and Tyranny*, rev. ed. (Princeton, NJ: Princeton University Press, 1966). On this, see also James Hankins, ed., *Renaissance Civic Humanism: Reappraisals and Reflections* (Cambridge, UK: Cambridge University Press, 2000).

103 They were particularly encouraged: J. Thiem, introduction to his edition of Lorenzo de' Medici, *Selected Poems and Prose*, trans. J. Thiem et al. (University Park: Pennsylvania State University Press, 1991), 5–6.

103 A central figure in the group: Marsilio Ficino, *Platonic Theology*, book 3, chap. 3, trans. J. L. Burroughs, *Journal of the History of Ideas* 5, no. 2 (April 1944), 227–42, this on 235.

104 Recent Pico scholars have tried: Brian P. Copenhaver details why the "dignity of man" title does not properly belong to it, in *Magic and the Dignity of Man: Pico della Mirandola and his* Oration *in Modern Memory* (Cambridge, MA, and London: Belknap Press of Harvard University Press, 2019), 28–29. On the general reception of Pico and his work, see Brian P. Copenhaver and William G. Craven, *Giovanni Pico della Mirandola: "Symbol of His Age": Modern Interpretations of a Renaissance Philosopher* (Geneva: Droz, 1981).

105 In the beginning, goes Pico's version: Pico della Mirandola, *Oration on the Dignity of Man: A New Translation and Commentary*, ed. Francesco Borghesi, Michael Papio, and Massimo Riva (Cambridge, UK: Cambridge University Press, 2012), 121, para. 29 ("shaper of yourself"), 123, paras. 31–32 (chameleon).

106 Those were in fact: Jacob Burckhardt, *The Civilization of the Renaissance in Italy* (1860), trans. S. G. C. Middlemore (Harmondsworth, UK: Penguin, 1990), especially 102–4 on Leonardo and Alberti.

106 Leon Battista Alberti seems: Leon Battista Alberti, *The Life*, in R. Watkins, "L. B. Alberti in the Mirror: An Interpretation of the *Vita* with a New Translation," *Italian Quarterly* 30, no. 117 (Summer 1989), 5–30. The account was written in 1437 or 1438; Riccardo Fubini established in 1972 that the author was Alberti himself. See Anthony Grafton, *Leon Battista Alberti* (London: Allen Lane/Penguin, 2001), 17–18.

106 Besides designing buildings: Leon Battista Alberti: *Della pittura* [*De pictura*], written in Tuscan in 1435–1436 and Latin in 1439–1441; *De re aedificatoria*, written between 1443 and 1452; *De statua*, begun circa 1450 and published in 1460.

106 He was an expert surveyor: Leon Battista Alberti, *Delineation of the City of Rome* [*Descriptio urbis Romae*], ed. Mario Carpo and Francesco Furlan, trans. Peter Hicks (Tempe: Arizona Center for Medieval and Renaissance Studies, 2007). See also Grafton, *Leon Battista Alberti*, 241–43. My thanks to Stefano Guidarini for our conversation on Alberti and Roman buildings.

106 Each of his fields: Leon Battista Alberti, *Ludi matematici* [*Ludi rerum mathematicarum*] (written 1450–1452), ed. R. Rinaldi (Milan: Guanda, 1980). See Joan Gadol, *Leon Battista Alberti* (Chicago and London: University of Chicago Press, 1969), 167.

107 Applying the same principle: All these quotations are from Alberti, *The Life*, 7–15.

107 **Vitruvian Man was:** Vitruvius, *De architectura* [*On Architecture*], with woodcut illustrations by Cesare Cesariano (Como: G. da Ponte, 1521), book 3, §1.

109 **Even designers of printing fonts:** See the font designed for Jean Grolier by Geoffroy Tory in 1529: Geoffroy Tory, *Champ fleury*, trans. George B. Ives (New York: Grolier Club, 1927).

109 **Michelangelo Buonarroti followed:** The sketch and wooden model are still kept in the Casa Buonarroti in Florence; see William E. Wallace, *Michelangelo at San Lorenzo* (Cambridge, UK: Cambridge University Press, 1994), 21, 31.

109 **Even the international symbol:** On the design of the Happy Human symbol, with Denis Barrington's original drawing of 1963 and a note by Andrew Copson, circa 2001, see British Humanist Association papers in the Bishopsgate Institute Library, London: BHA 1/8/11.

110 **Interestingly, Humanists UK has now:** https://humanists.uk. Thanks to Andrew Copson for explaining the meaning of the new symbol.

110 **But without adjustment:** Vitruvius, *De architectura*.

110 **Immanuel Kant was surely closer:** Immanuel Kant, *Idea for a Universal History with a Cosmopolitan Aim*, trans. Allen W. Wood, in Kant, *Anthropology, History, and Education*, ed. Günter Zöller and Robert B. Louden (Cambridge, UK: Cambridge University Press, 2007), 107–20, this on 113.

111 **But then he heard:** His mention of tearing up his Plato writings was made in a sermon of 1495; quoted in Donald Weinstein, *Savonarola: The Rise and Fall of a Renaissance Prophet* (New Haven and London: Yale University Press, 2011), 8. On Savonarola generally, see also Lauro Martines, *Scourge and Fire: Savonarola and Renaissance Florence* (London: Jonathan Cape, 2006).

111 **While in this world:** Girolamo Savonarola, All Souls' Day sermon of November 2, 1496, in *Selected Writings: Religion and Politics, 1490–1498*, trans. and ed. Anne Borelli and Maria Pastore Passaro (New Haven and London: Yale University Press, 2006), 46.

111 **To explain his reasons:** Weinstein, *Savonarola*, 12–13. The tract was later given the title *On Contempt for the World* [*De contemptu mundi*] by biographers, summing up its message.

111 **Having taken his monastic vows:** Weinstein, *Savonarola*, 22–23.

111 **Lorenzo at that time:** Lorenzo's death is described vividly by Poliziano in a letter of May 18, 1492: Angelo Poliziano, *Letters*, ed. and trans. Shane Butler (Cambridge, MA, and London: I Tatti/Harvard University Press, 2006), vol. 1, 239. Lorenzo's approach to Savonarola may have been Pico's idea.

112 **Yet many of the other:** Weinstein, *Savonarola*, 119 and (on Marsilio Ficino's losing enthusiasm around this time) 144. Pico remained loyal, but it did him no good: after he died in 1494, Savonarola announced from the pulpit that, according to reliable sources, Pico had not made it to heaven but only to purgatory: Savonarola's sermon of Sunday, November 23, 1494, quoted in Copenhaver, *Magic and the Dignity of Man*, 167, 184.

113 **As a witness wrote:** Letter from the orator Paolo Somenzi to Lodovico Sforza, duke of Milan, describing Carnival of February 16, 1496, translated in Savonarola, *Selected Writings*, 219.

113 **In following years, the processions:** Descriptions of 1497 bonfires in Savonarola, *Selected Writings*, 244–58.

114 **There they went:** In *A Life of Savonarola* (anonymous, although previously attributed to Fra Pacifico Burlamacchi), in Savonarola, *Selected Writings*, 257.

114 **Fra Bernardino da Siena:** Quoted in Weinstein, *Savonarola*, 72.

114 **And if the books were:** Savonarola, *Selected Writings*, 346.

114 **He would also have liked:** Savonarola's statements come mainly from a sermon of December 14, 1494, translated in Weinstein, *Savonarola*, 155–56.

115 **The Florentine authorities did not:** Weinstein, *Savonarola*, 295–96 (citing an account by Luca Landucci of the execution), 298 (the bell). The bell was supposed to be exiled for fifty years, but in fact it was brought back in 1509; it is now in the Museum of San Marco, Florence. For an account of the bell's trial, punishment, and restoration, see Daniel M. Zolli and Christopher Brown, "Bell on Trial," *Renaissance Quarterly* 72, no. 1 (Spring 2019), 54–96.

115 **The other, Niccolò Machiavelli:** Machiavelli wrote about Savonarola in several places, including *The Prince*, chap. 6, where he presents this argument. *The Prince*, trans. George Bull (Harmondsworth, UK: Penguin, 1961), 52.

116 **As for his overall philosophy:** Thomas Paine, *The Age of Reason* (London: Watts, 1938), 23.

116 **The worst shock for Rome:** André Chastel, *The Sack of Rome, 1527*, trans. Beth Archer (Princeton, NJ: Princeton University Press, 1983), 131. This is also the source, on 124, for other details of losses (including Giovio's), and 92–93, for the "Luther" graffiti (under Raphael's *Disputation of the Holy Sacrament* in the Stanze della Segnatura).

117 **Among others who lost:** K. Gouwens, introduction to his translation of Paolo Giovio. *Notable Men and Women of Our Time* (Cambridge, MA, and London: I Tatti/Harvard University Press, 2013), ix.

117 **Later, Giovio left the city:** T. C. Price Zimmermann, *Paolo Giovio: The Historian and the Crisis of Sixteenth-Century Italy* (Princeton, NJ: Princeton University Press, 1995), 86–88.

118 **The latter had even written:** Pliny the Younger to Voconius Romanus, epistle 9.7, in *Letters*, trans. Betty Radice (Harmondsworth, UK: Penguin, 1969), 237.

118 **He also published a book:** Paolo Giovio, *Elogia veris clarorum virorum imaginibus apposita* (Venice: M. Tramezinus, 1546).

118 **Sitting near him was:** Julia Conaway Bondanella and Peter Bondanella, introduction to their translation of Giorgio Vasari, *The Lives of the Artists* (Oxford, UK, and New York: Oxford University Press, 1991), vii–viii. See also Zimmermann, *Paolo Giovio*, 214.

118 **Vasari's work included:** Giorgio Vasari's *Six Tuscan Poets* (1544), in the Minneapolis Institute of Art. The other three poets are Cino da Pistoia, Guittone d'Arezzo, and Guido Cavalcanti—a friend of Dante, and an interesting figure rumored (by Boccaccio) to have been an atheist.

119 **In the *Lives*, Vasari:** Vasari, *The Lives of the Artists*, 48–49 (rebirth), 47 (historians).

CHAPTER 4. MARVELOUS NETWORK

120 **This was the starting point:** Girolamo Fracastoro, *Latin Poetry*, trans. James Gardner (Cambridge, MA, and London: I Tatti/Harvard University Press, 2013), 29 (book 1, lines 437–51).

121 **"Shun tender chitterlings":** Girolamo Fracastoro, *Fracastoro's Syphilis*, ed. and trans. Geoffrey Eatough (Liverpool: Francis Cairns, 1984), 69 (book 2, lines 133–37). Chitterlings are made from the large intestine of a hog; a chine is meat with part of the backbone. In Latin: "Tu teneros lactes, tu pandae abdomina porcae, / Porcae heu terga fuge, et lumbis ne vescere aprinis, / Venatu quamvis toties confeceris apros. / Quin

neque te crudus cucumis, non tubera captent, / Neve famem cinara, bulbisve salaci-
bus expe."

121 **"Hail great tree":** Fracastoro, *Fracastoro's Syphilis*, 107 (book 2, lines 405–12). In Latin:
"Salve magna Deum minibus sata semine sacro, / Pulchra comis, spectata novis virtuti-
bus arbos: / Spes hominum, externi decus, et nova Gloria mundi: Fortunata nimis . . . /
Ipsa tamen, si qua nostro te carmine Musae / Ferre per ora virum poterunt, hac tu
quotue parte / Nosceris, coeloque etiam cantabere nostro."

122 **Besides giving rein to:** This point is made by the more recent translator James Gardner, in the introduction to his Fracastoro, *Latin Poetry*, xiii. He drew on works such as
Ulrich von Hutten's *De morbo gallico* [*The French Disease*] (1519).

122 **Sadly, guaiacum, which induces sweating:** P. Eppenberger, F. Galassi, and F. Rühli,
"A Brief Pictorial and Historical Introduction to Guaiacum—from a Putative Cure for
Syphilis to an Actual Screening Method for Colorectal Cancer," *British Journal of
Clinical Pharmacology* 83, no. 9 (September 2017), 2118–19, https://www.ncbi.nlm
.nih.gov/pmc/articles/PMC5555855/.

123 **This is why, in his 1979 book:** Edmund D. Pellegrino, *Humanism and the Physician*
(Knoxville: University of Tennessee Press, 1979), 33.

123 **And the nineteenth-century scientist:** T. H. Huxley, "Universities: Actual and Ideal"
(University of Aberdeen, 1874), in *Science and Education*, vol. 3 of *Collected Essays*
(London: Macmillan, 1910), 189–234, this on 220.

124 **He reserved special scorn:** Petrarch, *Letters of Old Age* [*Rerum senilium*, books
I–XVIII], trans. Aldo S. Bernardo, Saul Levin, and Reta A. Bernardo (Baltimore and
London: Johns Hopkins University Press, 1992), vol. 2, 438–49, this on 444 (*Sen*. XII,
1: vegetables); vol. 1, 167–76, this on 172 (*Sen*. V, 3: "all are learned").

124 **Some thirty years after these remarks:** Geoffrey Chaucer, *Canterbury Tales*, "General Prologue," lines 443–44.

124 **They promoted their work:** Johann Winter von Andernach (J. Guintherius), preface
to his *Aliquot libelli* (Basel, 1529), sig. A2r-v, translated in Richard J. Durling, "A
Chronological Census of Renaissance Editions and Translations of Galen," *Journal of
the Warburg and Courtauld Institutes* 24, nos. 3–4 (1961), 230–305, this on 239.

125 **Pliny the Elder's *Natural History*:** Petrarch's Pliny is in the Bibliothèque Nationale,
Paris: MS Lat. 6802. The Oxford copy is in the Bodleian Library, MS Auct. T.I.27. See
Charles G. Nauert Jr., "Humanists, Scientists, and Pliny: Changing Approaches to a
Classical Author," *American Historical Review* 84 (1979), 72–85, this on 75n. The Ger-
man humanist Rodolphus Agricola also carried his Pliny with him everywhere while
traveling in Italy: Gerard Geldenhouwer, "Vita," in *Rudolf Agricola: Six Lives and Eras-
mus's Testimonies*, ed and trans. Fokke Akkerman, English trans. Rudy Bremer and
Corrie Ooms Beck (Assen, Netherlands: Royal Van Gorcum, 2012), 91–107, this on 99.

125 **For humanists, Pliny's appetite:** In particular, the earlier humanist Ermolao Barbaro
claimed in *Castigationes plinianae* (1493) that he had corrected more than five thousand errors, but he added that it was the copyists' fault. Brian W. Ogilvie, *The Science of
Describing* (Chicago and London: University of Chicago Press, 2006), 122–25.

125 **Leoniceno, however, squarely blamed:** Niccolò Leoniceno, *De Plinii et plurium aliorum medicorum in medicina erroribus . . .* (Ferrara: I. Maciochius, 1509), f. 21v. On
blaming Pliny, see also Angelo Poliziano, *Letters*, ed. and trans. Shane Butler (Cambridge, MA, and London: I Tatti/Harvard University Press, 2006), vol. 1, 103–5. On
the whole affair, see Nauert, "Humanists, Scientists, and Pliny"; Arturo Castiglioni,
"The School of Ferrara and the Controversy on Pliny," in *Science Medicine and History*:

Essays on the Evolution of Scientific Thought and Medical Practice Written in Honour of Charles Singer, ed. E. Ashworth Underwood (London: Geoffrey Cumberlege/Oxford University Press, 1953), vol. 1, 269–79; Ogilvie, *The Science of Describing*, 127–29.

125 **Like Lorenzo Valla before him:** Vivian Nutton, "The Rise of Medical Humanism: Ferrara, 1464–1555," *Renaissance Studies* 11 (1997), 2–19, this on 4.

125 **"Why did nature grant us":** Translated in Ogilvie, *The Science of Describing*, 129, with reference to Leoniceno, *De Plinii et aliorum medicorum erroribus liber . . .* (Basel: Henricus Petrus, 1529), 65–66.

126 **Leoniceno dedicated his little treatise:** Dipsas were then identified as small venomous snakes mentioned by Lucan and Cato; the New World snakes now bearing the same name are not poisonous at all. Nutton, "The Rise of Medical Humanism: Ferrara, 1464–1555," 2–19, with reference to Niccolò Leoniceno, *De dipsade et pluribus aliis serpentibus* (Bologna, 1518; written much earlier than the publication date) on 5.

126 **In Ferrara, the court physician:** On Brasavola: Nutton, "The Rise of Medical Humanism: Ferrara, 1464–1555," 12–14. On botanical gardens and collections: Paula Findlen, *Possessing Nature: Museums, Collecting and Scientific Culture in Early Modern Italy* (Berkeley: University of California Press, 1994).

127 **Galen had to use:** Susan P. Mattern, *The Prince of Medicine: Galen in the Roman Empire* (Oxford, UK: Oxford University Press, 2013), 151.

127 **Later, a long shadow:** Saint Augustine, *Concerning the City of God against the Pagans*, book 23, chap. 24.

127 **As the nineteenth-century pro-anatomy campaigner:** [T. Southwood Smith], *Use of the Dead to the Living: From the Westminster Review* (Albany, UK: Websters and Skinners, 1827), 37.

129 **The Parisian professor Jacobus Sylvius:** Charles D. O'Malley, *Andreas Vesalius of Brussels, 1514–1564* (Berkeley: University of California Press, 1964), 9 (vital spirits), 106 (Sylvius); Bernard Schultz, *Art and Anatomy in Renaissance Italy* (Ann Arbor: UMI Research Press, 1985), 25. The name Jacobus Sylvius was the Latinized form of Jacques Dubois.

129 **The real reason is simply:** https://en.wikipedia.org/wiki/Rete_mirabile.

129 **Some commentators began suggesting:** Berengario da Carpi, translated in Marco Catani and Stefano Sandrone, *Brain Renaissance: From Vesalius to Modern Neuroscience* (Oxford, UK: Oxford University Press, 2015), 154.

129 **The final blow came:** O'Malley, *Andreas Vesalius of Brussels*, 64.

130 **While still at Louvain:** Vesalius in Louvain: O'Malley, *Andreas Vesalius of Brussels*, 64 (body), 69–71 (the commentary, i.e., Vesalius, *Paraphrasis*, 1537).

130 **He went on to study:** O'Malley, *Andreas Vesalius of Brussels*, 77 (precocity), 318–20 (cutting), 81–82 (lectures). The lecture notes were made by the eighteen-year-old student Vitus Tritonius Athesinus and are in the Austrian National Library in Vienna. Vesalius describes his preferences and techniques in the *Fabrica*.

130 **It did still include:** Vesalius, *Tabulae anatomicae* (1538), which still showed Galen's *rete mirabile* in the third table: see the image online at https://iiif.wellcomecollection.org/image/L0002233.jpg/full/760%2C/0/default.jpg. The *rete mirabile* is at B. Vesalius confessed to his mistake in the *Fabrica*; see below.

130 **Vesalius became annoyed:** O'Malley, *Andreas Vesalius of Brussels*, 98–100.

131 **At last, in 1543:** Andreas Vesalius, *De humani corporis fabrica libri septem* (Basel: J. Oporinus, 1543). See also Vesalius, *The Fabric of the Human Body*, ed. and trans. Daniel H. Garrison and Malcolm H. Hast (Basel: Karger, 2014), an annotated transla-

tion of the 1543 and 1555 editions of *De humani corporis fabrica libri septem*. See the digitized version at http://www.vesaliusfabrica.com/en/original-fabrica.html. On the term *fabrica*, see O'Malley, *Andreas Vesalius of Brussels*, 139. It could also mean "form of construction," as if describing a building. See also Daniel H. Garrison, "Why Did Vesalius Title His Anatomical Atlas 'The Fabric of the Human Body'?," http://www .vesalius-fabrica.com/en/original-fabrica/inside-the-fabrica/the-name-fabrica.html.

131 **He blamed both himself:** Vesalius, *De humani corporis fabrica*, as translated in Catani and Sandrone, *Brain Renaissance: From Vesalius to Modern Neuroscience*, 152–53.

131 **This was a good warning:** Vesalius, *De humani corporis fabrica*, book 5, chap. 15. See Garrison and Hast's annotation in their translation *The Fabric of the Human Body*, vol. 2, 1069n40: Vesalius confused it with a part of the *labia minora*, the *nympha*.

131 **It took another Padua anatomist:** Realdo Colombo, *De re anatomica* (Venice: N. Bevilacqua, 1559), 243 (s. 11, lines 6–20). In Latin: "tam pulchram rem, tanta arte effectam, tantae utilitatis gratia." Colombo's book was written earlier, in the early 1540s, but not published until 1559. See Mark Stringer and Ines Becker, "Colombo and the Clitoris," *European Journal of Obstetrics and Gynecology and Reproductive Biology* 151 (2010), 130–33, and Robert J. Moes and C. D. O'Malley, "Realdo Colombo: 'On Those Things Rarely Found in Anatomy . . . ,'" *Bulletin of the History of Medicine* 34, no. 6 (1960), 508–28. The clitoris was also described by Gabriele Falloppio, who made notes about it in 1550 and published a description in *Observationes anatomicae* of 1561. Vesalius never did see the light; in a later book, he asserted that "this new and useless part" existed only in hermaphrodites, not in healthy women. Vesalius, *Anatomicarum Gabrielis Falloppii observationum examen* (1564), translated in Stringer and Becker, "Colombo and the Clitoris," 132.

131 **With a few such exceptions:** O'Malley, *Andreas Vesalius of Brussels*, 130–37.

132 **It is poignant to see:** On the influence of such considerations, see Ruth Richardson, *Death, Dissection and the Destitute* (London: Penguin, 1989).

133 **He was friends with Realdo Colombo:** Stringer and Becker, "Colombo and the Clitoris," 131.

134 **Leonardo wrote: "I dissected him":** Martin Clayton and Ron Philo, *Leonardo da Vinci: Anatomist* (London: Royal Collection, 2011), 17.

134 **He was also rather better educated:** Paula Findlen et al., *Leonardo's Library: The World of a Renaissance Reader* (Stanford, CA: Stanford Libraries, 2019), catalog of an exhibition held at the Stanford Libraries in 2019 that sought to reconstruct Leonardo's possible collection based on his lists and other mentions of books.

134 **Leonardo intended to write:** Translated in Clayton and Philo, *Leonardo da Vinci: Anatomist*, 9, with reference to his notebook RL 19037v.

134 **As Lucretius had said:** Lucretius, *On the Nature of the Universe*, trans. Ronald Melville (Oxford, UK: Oxford University Press, 2008), 89 (book 3, line 712).

CHAPTER 5. HUMAN STUFF

137 **He tried to bestow:** Lewis W. Spitz, *Conrad Celtis: The German Arch-Humanist* (Cambridge, MA: Harvard University Press, 1957), 23.

137 **"Find out the nature":** Leonard Forster, introduction to *Selections from Conrad Celtis, 1459–1508* (Cambridge, UK: Cambridge University Press, 1948), 31–33.

138 **Writing to a fellow teacher:** Rudolf Agricola to Jacob Barbireau, June 7, 1484, later published as *De formando studio*. In Rudolf Agricola, *Letters*, ed. and trans. Adrie Van

der Laan and Fokke Akkerman (Assen, Netherlands: Royal Van Gorcum; Tempe: Arizona Center for Medieval and Renaissance Studies, 2002), 203–19, this on 205–9. "Things themselves" (*res ipsas*) I took, however, from the French translation of this section: R. Agricola, *Écrits sur la dialectique et l'humanisme*, ed. Marc van der Poel (Paris: H. Champion, 1997), 264–65 ("tu dois étudier les faits mêmes [*res ipsas*]").

138 **The voracious eagerness of such:** Rabelais, *Pantagruel*, chap. 8, in *Gargantua and Pantagruel*, ed. and trans. M. A. Screech (London: Penguin, 2006), 47–49.

138 **In fact, Rabelais had mastered:** Johann von Plieningen, "Vita," in *Rudolf Agricola: Six Lives and Erasmus's Testimonies*, ed. and trans. Fokke Akkerman, English trans. Rudy Bremer and Corrie Ooms Beck (Assen, Netherlands: Royal Van Gorcum, 2012), 53–75, this on 71–73. The other details in this paragraph are from the same source, except, on his good accent, Goswinus van Halen, "Vita," in *Rudolf Agricola: Six Lives and Erasmus's Testimonies*, 77–89, this on 89. On Agricola's general effect on people: Lewis W. Spitz, *The Religious Renaissance of the German Humanists* (Cambridge, MA: Harvard University Press, 1963), 20–21. Johann von Plieningen was one of two brothers from Agricola's homeland whom he befriended in Ferrara; he called them "the Plinys" because of their names (and because he loved Pliny).

139 **his influence on others was greater:** He was best known for a work on dialectical invention: *De inventione dialectica libri tres* (Amsterdam: Alardus, 1539).

139 **he made an impression:** R. J. Schoeck, "Agricola and Erasmus: Erasmus's Inheritance of Northern Humanism," in *Rodolphus Agricola Phrisius, 1444–1485* (Proceedings of the International Conference at the University of Groningen, October 28–30, 1985), ed. F. Akkerman and A. J. Vanderjagt (Leiden, Netherlands; New York: Brill, 1988), 181–88, this on 181–82.

139 **along the lines of his advice:** Rudolf Agricola to Jacob Barbireau, June 7, 1484, later published as *De formando studio*, in Agricola, *Letters*, 203–19, this on 205–9.

140 **Erasmus and Agricola could have:** Peter Mack, *Renaissance Argument* (Leiden, Netherlands: Brill, 1993), 128.

140 **Desiderius Erasmus is remembered:** On his friendships and correspondence, see Peter G. Bietenholz and Thomas B. Deutscher, *Contemporaries of Erasmus* (Toronto: University of Toronto Press, 1985–87), which includes some two thousand names of people he knew or mentioned.

142 **"This incident destroyed all love":** Erasmus, "On Education for Children," in *Collected Works*, vol. 26: *Literary and Educational Writings*, 4: *De pueris instituendis / De recta pronunciatione*, ed. J. K. Sowards (Toronto: University of Toronto Press, 1985), 291–346, this on 326.

142 **The Deventer monks were probably:** Erasmus to Lambertus Grunnius, 1516, quoted in R. J. Schoeck, *Erasmus of Europe* (Edinburgh: Edinburgh University Press, 1990–93), vol. 1, 49.

142 **"The worst trick it ever played":** E. M. Forster, "Breaking Up" (*Spectator*, July 28, 1933), in *The Prince's Tale and Other Uncollected Writings*, ed. P. N. Furbank (London: Penguin, 1999), 273.

144 **On the basis of his experiences:** Works emerging from his English period include *On the Method of Study* (*De ratione studii*, 1511, expanded in 1512 and 1514) and *On the Abundant Style* (*De copia*, 1512, with later expansions).

144 *De civilitate morum puerilium*: Erasmus, "On Good Manners for Boys," trans. Brian McGregor, in *Collected Works*, vol. 25: *Literary and Educational Writings*, 3: *De conscribendis epistolis formula / De civilitate*, ed. J. K. Sowards (Toronto: University of

Toronto Press, 1985), 269–89, especially 276 (Spanish teeth-brushing), 277–78 (gas), 274 (cheerful brow).

145 **"Manners maketh man":** For the history of this motto, which seems to go back to William of Wykeham in the fourteenth century but was recorded by William Horman in 1519, see Mark Griffith, "The Language and Meaning of the College Motto" (2012), https://www.new.ox.ac.uk/sites/default/files/1NCN1%20%282012%29%20Griffith -Manners.pdf.

145 **Erasmus also taught the habits:** Erasmus, *On The Method of Study*, in *Collected Works*, vol. 24: *Literary and Educational Writings*, 2: *De copia / De ratione studii*, ed. Craig R. Thompson, 661–91, this on 671.

145 **He gave ample materials:** On the concept of copiousness, see especially Terence Cave, *The Cornucopian Text: Problems of Writing in the French Renaissance* (Oxford, UK: Clarendon Press, 1979).

145 **This treatise lists ways of varying:** Erasmus, *Copia*, in *Collected Works*, vol. 24: *Literary and Educational Writings*, 2: *De copia / De ratione studii*, 279–660, including 302 (Quintilian), 572–81 (causes, consequences, examples), 411 (customary), 429 (doubt), 431–32 (wheedling), 560–62 (ways of describing dying). For those unfamiliar with the comedy troupe Monty Python, this is a reference to their 1969 parrot sketch, in which John Cleese returns a dead parrot to the pet shop and repeatedly tries to convince the assistant that it really is dead. He varies his terms Erasmianly: "This parrot has ceased to be," "This is an ex-parrot," etc.

146 **His expanding, burgeoning method:** The first version, Erasmus, *Adagiorum collectanea* (1500), is now quite rare: copies are at Harvard, Sélestat, The Hague, and the Bibliothèque Nationale in Paris. The edition with 4,251 adages was that of 1533. Schoeck, *Erasmus of Europe*, vol. 1, 237–38, 241n1.

147 **"My home is wherever":** Quoted in Schoeck, *Erasmus of Europe*, vol. 2, 134.

147 **"They all know Latin":** Erasmus, epistle 391A to Johannes Sapidus, 1516, translated in Schoeck, *Erasmus of Europe*, vol. 2, 159.

147 **"It was delightful to see him":** Translated in P. S. Allen, *The Age of Erasmus* (Oxford, UK: Clarendon Press, 1914), 153.

147 **New scholarship, he thought:** Erasmus, "Letter to Dorp" (epistle 337), in *The Erasmus Reader*, ed. Erika Rummel (Toronto: University of Toronto Press, 1990), 169–94, this on 192.

148 **In his youth:** On this work, see Schoeck, *Erasmus of Europe*, vol. 1, 141.

148 **The *Annotations* were more controversial:** He found this work in the Abbaye du Parc. Schoeck, *Erasmus of Europe*, vol. 2, 44–45.

148 **Now he picked up on Valla's:** Many other such projects were under way, among them a full, multilingual "Complutensian Polyglot Bible," produced by a team of scholars at the University of Alcalá in Spain. Finished in 1517 and published in 1522, it included parallel texts in Hebrew, Greek, Syriac, and Latin. See Jerry H. Bentley, *Humanists and Holy Writ* (Princeton, NJ: Princeton University Press, 1983), 70–111. The year 1522 also saw Martin Luther's German translation of the New Testament, to be followed in 1534 by his complete Bible.

148 **He vented his annoyance:** Erasmus, "Letter to Dorp," 169–94, this on 192.

149 **"Whatever is not pleasing":** Erasmus to Albert of Brandenburg, October 19, 1519, trans. John C. Olin, in his edition of Erasmus, *Christian Humanism and the Reformation: Selected Writings, with the Life of Erasmus by Beatus Rhenanus*, rev. ed. (New York: Fordham University Press, 1975), 134–45, this on 144–45.

149 Erasmus was not of that type: Erasmus to Jodocus Jonas, May 10, 1521, in Erasmus, *Christian Humanism and the Reformation*, 150–63, this on 153.

149 He and Luther had: Erasmus attacked Luther on this point in *De libero arbitrio diatribe sive collatio* (Basel: Froben, 1524); Luther responded with *De servo arbitrio* (Wittemberg: J. Lufft, 1525).

149 Erasmus's increasing aversion: Valentina Sebastiani, *Johann Froben, Printer of Basel* (Leiden, Netherlands, and Boston: Brill, 2018), 66–67.

149 He made no secret: Erasmus to Richard Pace, July 5, 1521, in Schoeck, *Erasmus of Europe*, vol. 2, 231.

149 What he hated above all: Erasmus, *In Praise of Folly*, trans. Betty Radice (Harmondsworth, UK: Penguin, 1971), 181.

149 In his 1515 *Adages*: Erasmus, "Dulce bellum inexpertis," in Margaret Mann Phillips, *The "Adages" of Erasmus* (Cambridge, UK: Cambridge University Press, 1964), 308–53, this on 309. The title phrase is from Vegetius, *Art of War*, vol. 3, xiii (Phillips corrects Erasmus, who cites Vegetius as chap. 14). See also Erasmus, "A Complaint of Peace" [*Querela pacis*], (December 1517), trans. Betty Radice, in *Collected Works*, vol. 27: *Literary and Educational Writings*, 5 (Toronto: University of Toronto Press, 1986), 289–322.

150 Like Protagoras and Pico: All from Erasmus, "Dulce bellum inexpertis," 308–53, this on 317 (crest and beasts), 310–12 ("friendly eyes" etc.), 322 (friendship among many), 313 (damages of war), 309–10 (lawyers and theologians).

151 Later commentators observed: A good example is Stefan Zweig's biographical essay *Triumph und Tragik des Erasmus von Rotterdam*, published in Vienna in 1934 while comparable forces were being unleashed on his own world. *Erasmus* [and] *The Right to Heresy*, trans. Eden and Cedar Paul (London: Hallam/Cassell, 1951).

152 Officially, the name: It is now called Erasmus+. https://erasmus-plus.ec.europa.eu/. On the numbers who have used it: https://ec.europa.eu/commission/presscorner/detail/en/qanda_20_130. On Sofia Corradi, known as "Mamma Erasmus": https://it.wikipedia.org/wiki/Sofia_Corradi.

153 The result of these early years: Michel de Montaigne: *Essays*, in *The Complete Works*, trans. Donald Frame (London: Everyman, 2003), 913 (book 3, chap. 9). Montaigne's choice of French also reflects a general flowering of French writing in this time. He describes his father's experiment in book 1, chap. 26 (156–57).

154 His copy of Lucretius's: See M. A. Screech, *Montaigne's Annotated Copy of Lucretius: A Transcription and Study of the Manuscript, Notes and Pen-Marks* (Geneva: Droz, 1998).

155 Montaigne, like Erasmus before him: Montaigne, *Essays*, 181 (book 1, chap. 30).

155 "putting a very high price": Montaigne, *Essays*, 961 (book 3, chap. 11).

156 Having been born a Catholic: Montaigne, *Essays*, 278 (book 1, chap. 56: happy to believe), 521 (book 2, chap. 12: safe during wars).

156 "I love life and cultivate": Montaigne, *Essays*, 1041–42 (book 3, chap. 13).

156 "There is nothing so beautiful": Montaigne, *Essays*, 1039 (book 3, chap. 13).

157 "Is it possible to imagine": Montaigne, *Essays*, 399 (book 2, chap. 12: "Is it possible"), 508 (book 2, chap. 12: Protagoras).

157 Yet Montaigne trashes: Montaigne, *Essays*, 365 (book 2, chap. 10: Cicero), 362 (book 2, chap. 10: Virgil), 269 (book 1, chap. 51: rhetoric), 155 (book 1, chap. 26: "not as fine").

158 Biographies and histories are good: Montaigne, *Essays*, 367 (book 2, chap. 10: "more alive"), 362 (book 2, chap. 10: Terence).

158 **Those angles often derive:** Montaigne, *Essays*, 205 (book 1, chap. 37).

159 **He asked them, through:** Montaigne, *Essays*, 193 (book 1, chap. 31).

159 **So great was his love:** Montaigne, *Essays*, 725 (book 2, chap. 37).

159 **Montaigne writes that each:** Montaigne, *Essays*, 740 (book 3, chap. 2: "entire form" and "You can tie up").

160 **Writing a book of this sort:** Montaigne, *Essays*, 284 (book 1, chap. 56).

160 **"the *Montaignesque* element in literature":** Walter Pater, "Charles Lamb," in *Appreciations* (London: Macmillan, 1890), 105–23, this on 117.

161 **Henry Fielding's *Tom Jones*:** Henry Fielding, *Tom Jones* (Harmondsworth, UK: Penguin, 1966), 52.

161 **"fuller of human stuff":** William James to Catherine Elizabeth Havens, March 23, 1874, quoted in Robert D. Richardson, *William James* (Boston and New York: Houghton Mifflin, 2007), 152.

161 **George Eliot believed:** George Eliot, "The Natural History of German Life" (1856), in *Selected Critical Writings*, ed. Rosemary Ashton (Oxford, UK, and New York: Oxford University Press, 1992), 263.

162 **In recent times, some research:** Recent studies have come up with divergent conclusions about whether reading fiction helps us to behave more ethically. A key study found that people who have just read a passage of literary fiction make more ethical choices in a test than those who have not: David Comer Kidd and Emanuele Castano, "Reading Literary Fiction Improves Theory of Mind," *Science* 342, no. 6156 (October 18, 2013), 377–80, https://science.sciencemag.org/content/342/6156/377.abstract?sid =f192d0cc-1443-4bf1-a043-61410da39519. Others wonder whether basing moral decisions on empathy is even a good idea: Paul Bloom argues that it leads us to bond too much with our in-group at the expense of out-groups and strangers, and that a reasoned kindness might be a better guide: Paul Bloom, *Against Empathy: The Case for Rational Compassion* (London: Bodley Head, 2017).

Chapter 6. Perpetual Miracles

163 **In Lisbon, at about half past nine:** Edward Paice, *Wrath of God: The Great Lisbon Earthquake of 1755* (London: Quercus, 2008), 69, with reference to Thomas Chase's letter to his mother, Centre for Kentish Studies, Gordon Ward Collection U442; and BL Add. 38510 ff.7–14: "Narrative of His Escape from the Earthquake at Lisbon." Other details of the event come from Paice, 168–72 (numbers of casualties), and from T. D. Kendrick, *The Lisbon Earthquake* (London: Methuen, 1956).

164 **The event would later merge:** J. W. von Goethe, *From My Life: Poetry and Truth*, vols. 1–3, trans. Robert R. Heitner, in Goethe, *Collected Works*, vol. 4 (Princeton, NJ: Princeton University Press, 1994), 35.

164 **The Jesuit Gabriel Malagrida:** Russell R. Dynes, "The Lisbon Earthquake of 1755: The First Modern Disaster," in *The Lisbon Earthquake of 1755: Representations and Reactions*, ed. Theodore E. D. Braun and John B. Radner (Oxford, UK: Voltaire Foundation, 2005), 34–49, this on 42.

165 **It showed his disapproval:** This occurred between 1708 and 1711. Kendrick, *The Lisbon Earthquake*, 95–100.

165 **Augustine had urged his readers:** Saint Augustine, *Concerning the City of God against the Pagans*, trans. Henry Bettenson (London: Penguin, 2003), 475 (book 12, chap. 4).

165 **A similar idea was concisely:** Alexander Pope, *An Essay on Man*, epistle 1, line 294.

165 **Chaucer had told the story:** Geoffrey Chaucer, *Canterbury Tales*, "The Franklin's Tale," lines 885–93.

166 **He tried to imagine what:** Voltaire to Jean-Robert Tronchin, November 24, 1755, in Voltaire, *The Selected Letters*, ed. and trans. Richard A. Brooks (New York: New York University Press, 1973), 181.

166 **Being a poet:** Voltaire, "Poème sur le désastre de Lisbonne" (1756). See Theodore Besterman, *Voltaire*, 3rd ed. (Oxford, UK: Blackwell, 1976), 367–71.

166 **The problem arose again later:** Voltaire, "Good, all is" ("Bien [tout est]"), in *Philosophical Dictionary*, ed. and trans. Theodore Besterman (Harmondsworth, UK: Penguin, 1979), 72–73.

166 **Voltaire's most eloquent response:** Voltaire, *Candide*, in *Candide and Other Stories*, trans. Roger Pearson (Oxford, UK: Oxford University Press, 2006), 1–88, this on 48.

167 **It is more like:** Voltaire to Elie Bertrand, February 18, 1756, in Voltaire, *The Selected Letters*, 183.

167 **Voltaire ended *Candide*:** Voltaire, *Candide*, 1–88, this on 88.

167 **E. M. Forster distinguished:** E. M. Forster, *The Longest Journey* (Harmondsworth, UK: Penguin, 1960), 101.

168 **Their philosophy of pragmatic:** Its first recorded use was in an 1858 volume of essays by the Scottish doctor John Brown. He only partly approved of the principle, but did name it. John Brown, *Horae Subsecivae* [*Leisure Hours*] (Edinburgh: T. Constable; London: Hamilton, Adams, 1858–82), vol. 1, xix. This is the first citation in the *Oxford English Dictionary*, and is mentioned by Gordon S. Haight in his editor's note to the letter from Eliot—a letter in which she cautiously accepts credit for the term while noting that inventions are often made simultaneously by several people. She probably did not know of Brown's usage. Eliot to James Sully, January 19, 1877, in *The George Eliot Letters*, ed. G. S. Haight (London: Oxford University Press; New Haven: Yale University Press, 1954–78), vol. 4, 333–34. Sully had written a book about pessimism; he went ahead and attributed the term to her when he published it later that same year. See also James Sully, *Pessimism: A History and a Criticism* (London: S. King, 1877), 399.

168 **Discussing Eliot's meliorism:** Rosemary Ashton, "Coming to Conclusions: How George Eliot Pursued the Right Answer," *Times Literary Supplement*, November 15, 2019), 12–14, this on 14; Besterman, *Voltaire*, 397. I have been influenced in my reading of Enlightenment values by the recent work of Ritchie Robertson, who highlighted the Enlighteners' meliorist and humanist motives more than their idealizing of reason: Robertson, *The Enlightenment: The Pursuit of Happiness, 1680–1790* (London: Allen Lane, 2020).

169 **These beliefs lay behind:** P. N. Furbank, *Diderot: A Critical Biography* (London: Secker & Warburg, 1992), 128–29.

169 **Diderot also took a philosophical view:** Furbank, *Diderot*, 130.

169 **Nicolas de Condorcet was:** Nicolas de Condorcet, "The Sketch" [*Sketch for a Historical Picture of the Progress of the Human Mind*], trans. June Barraclough, in Condorcet, *Political Writings*, ed. Steven Lukes and Nadia Urbinati (Cambridge, UK: Cambridge University Press, 2012), 1–147, this on 130. On his range of applications and his ideal of progress, see Lukes and Urbinati's introduction, xviii–xix.

170 **He wrote in his 1770 work:** Baron d'Holbach, *The System of Nature*, vol. 1, adapted from original translation by H. D. Robinson, 1868 (Manchester, UK: Clinamen, 1999), 5 (mists of darkness), 189 (far from holding forth, etc.). The story of Holbach's wife is told by Michael Bush in his introduction to this edition, ix.

171 **The philosopher and historian Pierre Bayle:** Richard S. Popkin, introduction to his edition (with Craig Brush) of Pierre Bayle, *Historical and Critical Dictionary: Selections* (Indianapolis and Cambridge, UK: Hackett, 1991), xviii. The source of this story is Claude Gros de Boze, in "Eloge de M. Le Cardinal de Polignac," prefacing Polignac's *L'anti-Lucrèce* (Paris, 1749).

171 **He campaigned against the damage:** Voltaire, *Treatise on Tolerance*, trans. Brian Masters (Cambridge, UK: Cambridge University Press, 2000).

172 **"A miracle, in the full meaning":** Voltaire, *Philosophical Dictionary*, 311.

172 **"In all ages man has prayed":** Robert G. Ingersoll, "The Gods," in *Orations* (London: Freethought, 1881), 33.

173 **Spinoza had already been excommunicated:** The text of the *herem* is given in Steven Nadler, *Spinoza*, 2nd ed. (Cambridge, UK: Cambridge University Press, 2018), 139–41.

174 **It is what Condorcet called:** Condorcet, "The Sketch," 140.

174 **Earlier humanists had written:** Michel de Montaigne, *Essays*, in *The Complete Works*, trans. Donald Frame (London: Everyman, 2003), 379 (book 2, chap.11).

174 **He could not bear to watch:** Montaigne, *Essays*, 379 (chicken), 385 ("a certain respect"), 380–81 (weeping and tortures) (all book 2, chap. 11).

174 **Yet this was apparently:** Tertullian, *Of Public Shows* (*De spectaculis*), §30.

174 **But in the twelfth century:** Bernard of Cluny, *Scorn for the World: Bernard of Cluny's De contemptu mundi*, trans Ronald E. Pepin (East Lansing, MI: East Lansing Colleagues Press, 1991), 17–19.

174 **Charles Darwin said that he:** Charles Darwin, "Religious Belief" (written 1879, "copied out" 1881), in *Autobiographies*, ed. Michael Neve and Sharon Messenger (London: Penguin, 2002), 49–55, this on 49–50.

175 **"I will call no being":** John Stuart Mill, *An Examination of Sir William Hamilton's Philosophy* (London: Longman, Green, Longman, Roberts & Green, 1865), 103.

175 **The basics of an ethical system:** Anthony Ashley Cooper, Third Earl of Shaftesbury, "The Moralists, a Philosophical Rhapsody," in *Characteristics of Men, Manners, Opinions, Times*, ed. Lawrence E. Klein (Cambridge, UK: Cambridge University Press, 1999), 231–338. See also Shaftesbury's earlier *An Inquiry Concerning Virtue* (London: A. Bell, 1699).

175 **Shaftesbury's *Inquiry Concerning*:** Furbank, *Diderot*, 26.

176 **Thus, the English philosopher:** John Locke, *A Letter on Toleration*, ed. J. W. Gough and R. Klibansky (Oxford, UK: Clarendon Press, 1968), 135.

176 **The rebels thought, however:** Pierre Bayle, *Various Thoughts on the Occasion of a Comet*, trans. and ed. Robert C. Bartlett (New York: SUNY Press, 2000), 165–240 (letters 8 and 9).

176 **Bayle knew that he:** Jonathan Israel, *Radical Enlightenment: Philosophy and the Making of Modernity, 1650–1750* (Oxford, UK: Oxford University Press, 2001), 334–35.

177 **But the French authorities:** Elisabeth Labrousse, *Bayle*, trans. Denys Potts (Oxford, UK, and New York: Oxford University Press, 1983), 31.

177 **The whole experience gave him:** Ian Davidson, *Voltaire* (New York: Pegasus, 2012), 108–11 (*Letters*), 356–57 (*Dictionary*).

177 **Diderot also served time:** Furbank, *Diderot*, 48–50.

178 **Neither stopped writing, but they:** Furbank, *Diderot*, 291.

178 **In the Netherlands, too:** Israel, *Radical Enlightenment*, 286–91.

178 **The Baron d'Holbach published:** Bush, introduction to Baron d'Holbach, *The System of Nature*, vol. 1, vii.

179 **Voltaire also covered his writings:** Voltaire to Gabriel and Philibert Cramer, February 25, 1759, in Voltaire, *The Selected Letters*, 198.

179 **"These days, no book":** Voltaire to Madame du Deffand, January 6, 1764, translated in Davidson, *Voltaire*, 328.

179 **one of the key figures in charge:** Jean des Cars, *Malesherbes: Gentilhomme des lumières* (Paris: Fallois, 1994), 45.

179 **When called on to censor:** Des Cars, *Malesherbes*, 92 (grounds for banning), 93 (hiding manuscripts), 85 (Madame de Pompadour).

180 **As to the other manuscripts:** Furbank, *Diderot*, 254, 461, 472.

181 **He had another distressing experience:** Furbank, *Diderot*, 273.

181 **Malesherbes had retired:** Des Cars, *Malesherbes*, 387–91.

181 **Other Enlightenment thinkers had also:** Quoted in Joan Wallach Scott, "French Feminists and the Rights of 'Man': Olympe de Gouges's Declarations," *History Workshop Journal* 28 (1989), 1–21, this on 17. Her declaration: https://en.wikipedia.org/wiki/Declaration_of_the_Rights_of_Woman_and_of_the_Female_Citizen.

182 **Another victim, though he was:** Nicolas de Condorcet, "On the Emancipation of Women. On Giving Women the Right to Citizenship," trans. Iain McLean and Fiona Hewitt, in Condorcet, *Political Writings*, ed. Steven Lukes and Nadia Urbinati (Cambridge, UK: Cambridge University Press, 2012), 156–62.

182 **He wrote his main work:** Condorcet, "The Sketch," quotations on 147. The story of Condorcet's adventures and death is told by Lukes and Urbinati in their introduction to his *Political Writings*, xx–xxi.

182 **One final author:** Craig Nelson, *Thomas Paine* (London: Profile, 2007), 258–60; Susan Jacoby, *Freethinkers* (New York: Metropolitan Books/Henry Holt, 2004), 41.

183 **How astonishing it is:** Thomas Paine, *The Age of Reason* (London: Watts, 1938), 38 (that anything should exist), 27–28 (better suited; open air), 2 (human inventions).

184 **"I believe in the equality":** Paine, *The Age of Reason*, 1.

184 *The Age of Reason*, **with its message:** Jacoby, *Freethinkers*, 61.

184 **When Paine did die:** Paul Collins, *The Trouble with Tom: The Strange Afterlife and Times of Thomas Paine* (London: Bloomsbury, 2006).

184 **The great champion of Paine:** Joel H. Wiener, *Radicalism and Freethought in Nineteenth-Century Britain: The Life of Richard Carlile* (Westport, CT, and London: Greenwood, 1983), 46–47; G. D. H. Cole, *Richard Carlile, 1790–1843* (London: Victor Gollancz and Fabian Society, 1943), 10–11.

185 **One of his productions:** Richard Carlile, *An Address to Men of Science* (London: R. Carlile, 1821), 7. On this and the imprisonment, see Cole, *Richard Carlile*, 11, 16.

185 **But this situation also forced:** Anthony Ashley Cooper, Third Earl of Shaftesbury, "Sensus Communis: An Essay on the Freedom of Wit and Humour," in *Characteristics of Men, Manners, Opinions, Times*, 2nd ed. (1714), ed. Lawrence E. Klein (Cambridge, UK: Cambridge University Press, 1999), 34. "Esoteric" writing was originally described, as well as practiced, by John Toland in "Clidophorus; or Of the Exoteric and Esoteric Philosophy . . . ," in *Tetradymus* (London: J. Brotherton and W. Meadows [etc.]), 1720), 66. *Clidophorus* means "keybearer."

186 **Having to pretend that one:** Paine, *The Age of Reason*, 2.

187 **The twentieth-century philosopher:** Bryan Magee, *Confessions of a Philosopher* (London: Phoenix, 1998), 128.

187 **He suggests applying:** David Hume, *An Enquiry Concerning Human Understanding,*

and Other Writings, ed. Stephen Buckle (Cambridge, UK: Cambridge University Press, 2007), 101.

187 **The later science communicator:** Carl Sagan, "Encyclopaedia Galactica," episode 12 of *Cosmos: A Personal Voyage*, PBS, originally broadcast December 14, 1980. Sagan was talking about evidence for alien visits to Earth, but the phrase has been applied in more general contexts.

187 **Imagine, continues Hume:** Ernest Campbell Mossner, *The Life of David Hume*, 2nd ed. (Oxford, UK: Clarendon Press, 1980), 101.

188 **At first he intended:** Hume, *An Enquiry Concerning Human Understanding, and Other Writings*, 96–116 (section 10: "Of Miracles"). See also Mossner, *The Life of David Hume*, 286.

188 **He wrote *The Natural History of Religion*:** "Note on the Text," in David Hume, *The Natural History of Religion*, ed. A. Wayne Colver, and *Dialogues Concerning Natural Religion*, ed. John Valdimir Price (Oxford, UK: Clarendon Press, 1976), 7. See Mossner, *The Life of David Hume*, 320.

188 **One speaker says:** "Philo" speaking, in Hume, *Dialogues Concerning Natural Religion*, ed. Martin Bell (London: Penguin, 1990), 131.

188 **Despite Hume's precautions:** Mossner, *The Life of David Hume*, 162, 251–54.

188 **It could have been worse:** Aikenhead was executed in 1697. Michael Hunter, "'Aikenhead the Atheist': The Context and Consequences of Articulate Irreligion in the Late Seventeenth Century," in *Atheism from the Reformation to the Enlightenment*, ed. Michael Hunter and David Wootton (Oxford, UK: Clarendon Press, 1992), 221–54, this on 225.

189 **And yet, contrary to his alarming:** Mossner, *The Life of David Hume*, 587 (Boswell), 245 (Adam). The dinner story was told by Hume's friend Alexander Carlyle of Inveresk: A. Carlyle, *Autobiography*, ed. J. Hill Burton (London and Edinburgh: T. N. Foulis, 1910), 285–86.

189 **David Hume was living:** Hume, *Dialogues Concerning Natural Religion*, ed. Bell, 132.

189 **Having cudgeled his brains:** Hume's letter was written (but not sent) to an unnamed doctor, identified by Mossner as Dr. John Arbuthnot. On the letter, see Ernest Campbell Mossner, "Hume's Epistle to Dr. Arbuthnot, 1734: The Biographical Significance," *Huntingdon Library Quarterly* 7, no. 2 (February 1944), 135–52, 137 ("most sturdy").

190 **Hume resembled Montaigne:** David Hume, *A Treatise of Human Nature*, ed. L. A. Selby-Bigge, 2nd ed., rev. by P. H. Nidditch (Oxford, UK: Clarendon Press, 1978), 269 (book 1, part 4, §8).

190 **Restored, he does return:** Hume, *A Treatise of Human Nature*, 576 (book 3, part 3, §1: shared feeling), 470 (book 3, part 1, §2: producing morality), 577–78 (book 3, part 3, §1: producing a full moral system), 364 (book 2, part 2, §5: mirrors). Hume took his argument about morality further in *Enquiry Concerning the Principles of Morals* (1751): Hume, *Enquiries*, ed. L. A. Selby-Bigge, 2nd ed. (Oxford, UK: Clarendon Press, 1951), 167–323. Hume's friend Adam Smith argued similarly about morals and sympathy in *A Theory of Moral Sentiments* (London: A. Millar; Edinburgh: A. Kincaid and J. Bell, 1759).

191 **He wrote to a friend once:** David Hume to Anne-Robert Jacques Turgot, 1766, quoted in Mossner, *The Life of David Hume*, 286.

191 **From the outset, when he:** David Hume to Henry Home, December 1737, quoted in Mossner, *The Life of David Hume*, 112.

191 **Later, in 1757, he published:** David Hume, *Four Dissertations* (London: A. Millar, 1757). See J. C. A. Gaskin, "Hume's Suppressed Dissertations: An Authentic Text," *Hermathena* 106 (Spring 1968), 54–59, this on 55.

191 **Boswell was struck:** James Boswell, diary entry, December 28, 1764, in James Boswell, ed. F. A. Pottle, *Boswell on the Grand Tour* (London: Heinemann, 1953), vol. 1, 286.

192 **It would be only "humane":** Quoted in Mossner, *The Life of David Hume*, 587.

192 **Hume had just been diagnosed:** David Hume to William Strahan, June 12, 1776, *Letters of David Hume to William Strahan*, ed. G. Birkbeck Hill (Oxford, UK: Clarendon Press, 1888), 337.

192 **Calling on the philosopher:** James Boswell, "An account of my last interview with David Hume, esq. (Partly recorded in my Journal, partly enlarged from my memory, March 3, 1777)," in his diary, *Boswell in Extremes, 1776–1778*, ed. C. McC. Weis and F. A. Pottle (London: Heinemann, 1971), 11–15.

193 **In fact, when Boswell told:** Boswell's comment and Johnson's remark: both in Boswell's diary entry for Tuesday, September 16, 1777, *Boswell in Extremes 1776–1778*, 155.

193 **Meanwhile, in Edinburgh, Hume's friend:** "Letter from Adam Smith to William Strahan," November 9, 1776, describing Hume's last illness, included with the 1777 publication of Hume's "My Own Life" (April 18, 1776), in *The Life of David Hume, Esq; Written by Himself* (London: W. Strahan and T. Cadell, 1777), 37–62, 43–44 (dying fast), 49–50 (Good Charon).

193 **Among the works he brushed up:** Mossner, *The Life of David Hume*, 592.

194 **Strahan never did produce:** Gaskin, "Hume's Suppressed Dissertations," 54–59, this on 55–57.

194 **So come, said Charon:** "Letter from Adam Smith to William Strahan," 37–62, this on 49–50 ("please step"), 58 ("happy composure").

194 **A crowd gathered outside:** Mossner, *The Life of David Hume*, 605 (Boswell), 603 (atheist/honest man).

194 **Smith agreed, and concluded:** "Letter from Adam Smith to William Strahan," 37–62, this on 62.

Chapter 7. Sphere for All Human Beings

196 **Hume was among them:** David Hume, "Of National Characters" (1748; rev. 1754), quoted in *Race and the Enlightenment: A Reader*, ed. Emmanuel Chukwudi Eze (Cambridge, MA, and Oxford, UK: Blackwell, 1997), 33. Hume's revisions were made in 1776, and published in the posthumous edition of 1777. For Beattie's criticism, see James Beattie, *An Essay on the Nature and Immutability of Truth in Opposition to Sophistry and Scepticism*, 2nd ed. (Edinburgh: A. Kincaid and J. Bell; London: E. and C. Dilly, 1771), 508–11, this on 511.

196 **In general terms, he strongly:** Nicolas de Condorcet, "The Sketch" [*Sketch for a Historical Picture of the Progress of the Human Mind*], trans. June Barraclough, in *Political Writings*, ed. Steven Lukes and Nadia Urbinati (Cambridge, UK: Cambridge University Press, 2012), 1–147, this on 126–29.

196 **In his pedagogical treatise *Émile*:** Jean-Jacques Rousseau, *Émile or On Education*, trans. Allan Bloom (London: Penguin, 1991), 358–63, 386–87.

196 **Still, when she died:** Voltaire to Frederick the Great, October 15, 1749, in Voltaire and Frederick the Great, *Letters*, ed. and trans. Richard Aldington (London: George Routledge, 1927), 203 (letter 99).

196 In ancient Greece, for example: Plato, *Timaeus*, 42a–b, 90e (men reborn as women), 92b (shellfish).

197 Aristotle wrote Europe's: Aristotle, *The Politics*, trans. Ernest Barker, rev. R. F. Stalley (Oxford, UK, and New York: Oxford University Press, 1995), 16–17 (I, 5).

197 The philosopher Juan Ginés de Sepúlveda: At a debate on this topic, held at Valladolid, Spain, in 1550–1551. See Lewis Hanke, *All Mankind Is One: A Study of the Disputation between Bartolomé de Las Casas and Juan Ginés de Sepúlveda in 1550 on the Intellectual and Religious Capacity of the American Indians* (DeKalb: Northern Illinois University Press, 1974).

197 In a speech of 1844: Selections from Josiah C. Nott, "Two Lectures on the Natural History of the Caucasian and Negro Races" (1844), in *The Ideology of Slavery: Proslavery Thought in the Antebellum South, 1830–1860*, ed. Drew Gilpin Faust (Baton Rouge and London: Louisiana State University Press, 1981), 206–38, this on 238. Nott later went on to cowrite *Types of Mankind* (1854), which presented a similar argument for complete racial difference.

197 Augustine had influentially stated: Saint Augustine, *Concerning the City of God against the Pagans*, book 16, chap. 8.

198 This theology was confirmed: Hanke, *All Mankind Is One*, 21.

200 In 1900, the classical scholar: Jane Ellen Harrison, "Homo Sum," in *Alpha and Omega* (London: Sidgwick & Jackson, 1915), 80–115.

200 The Dante translator and novelist: Dorothy L. Sayers, "Are Women Human?," in *Unpopular Opinions* (London: Victor Gollancz, 1946), 108–9 (trousers and Aristotle).

201 But her argument was not: Sayers, "Are Women Human?," 114.

202 "We deny the right": Harriet Taylor Mill, "Enfranchisement of Women," in *The Complete Works*, ed. Jo Ellen Jacobs and Paula Harms Payne (Bloomington and Indianapolis: Indiana University Press, 1998), 51–73, this on 57.

202 Pericles telling Athenian free men: Thucydides, *The Peloponnesian War*, book 2, §46.

203 Those negativities are: Joan Wallach Scott, "French Feminists and the Rights of 'Man': Olympe de Gouges's Declarations," *History Workshop Journal* 28 (1989), 1–21, this on 17.

203 The virtue question was tackled: Mary Wollstonecraft, *A Vindication of the Rights of Woman*, in *A Vindication of the Rights of Men / A Vindication of the Rights of Woman / An Historical and Moral View of the Origin and Progress of the French Revolution* (Oxford, UK: Oxford University Press, 2008), 72 ("I shall first consider"), 119 ("human duties"), 122 (human virtues), 125 ("Confined"), 265 ("I wish to see"). On the virtue question: her argument has to contend with the fact that even the word *virtue* in its Latin origin casts maleness as the norm, because it derives from *vir*, "man"—evoking manliness or, as twenty-first-century slang sometimes has it, "manning up."

203 The key ingredient in achieving: John Stuart Mill, "The Subjection of Women" (1869), in *Collected Works*, vol. 21: *Essays on Equality, Law, and Education*, ed. John M. Robson (London: Routledge, 1984), 259–340, this on 337. Mill wrote it after Harriet's death, between 1859 and 1861; it was published in 1869.

204 Dan Goodley has argued this: Dan Goodley, *Disability and Other Human Questions* (Bingley, UK: Emerald, 2021), chap. 5 (unpaginated).

205 This was investigated in the early nineteenth century: Jeremy Bentham, *An Introduction to the Principles of Morals and Legislation*, in J. S. Mill and J. Bentham, *Utilitarianism and Other Essays*, ed. Alan Ryan (London: Penguin, 1987), 65–111, this on 80–81.

205 Instead, Bentham proposes: Jeremy Bentham, *An Introduction to the Principles of*

Morals and Legislation, ed. J. H. Burns and H. L. A. Hart (London: Athlone; Oxford, UK: Clarendon Press, 1970), 283n.

206 **In a treatise:** Jeremy Bentham, "Of Sexual Irregularities" (1814), in *Of Sexual Irregularities and Other Writings on Sexual Morality*, ed. P. Schofield, C. Pease-Watkin, and M. Quinn (Oxford, UK: Clarendon Press, 2014).

206 **In his will, he left:** On the fascinating topic of Bentham's auto-icon: Jeremy Bentham, "Auto-Icon, or, Farther Uses of the Dead to the Living: A Fragment. From the MSS. of Jeremy Bentham," unpublished manuscript [London?, 1832?]; [T. Southwood Smith], *Use of the Dead to the Living: From the Westminster Review* (Albany, UK: Websters and Skinners, 1827); T. Southwood Smith, *A Lecture Delivered over the Remains of Jeremy Bentham Esq., in the Webb Street School of Anatomy & Medicine, on the 9th of June, 1832* (London: Effingham Wilson, 1832); C. F. A. Marmoy, "The 'Auto-Icon' of Jeremy Bentham at University College, London," *Medical History* 2, no. 2 (April 1958), 77–86.

207 **Oscar Wilde was imprisoned:** Thomas Wright, *Oscar's Books* (London: Chatto & Windus, 2008), 1–2.

207 **Later he was moved:** Richard Ellmann, *Oscar Wilde* (London: Penguin, 1988), 465–66 (first station incident), 492 ("Oh beautiful world!").

207 **But as he had written:** Oscar Wilde, *De Profundis*, in *The Soul of Man and Prison Writings*, ed. I. Murray (Oxford, UK, and New York: Oxford University Press, 1990), 98.

208 **Compiling lists of notable female figures:** Giovanni Boccaccio, *Famous Women*, ed. and trans. Virginia Brown (Cambridge, MA, and London: I Tatti/Harvard University Press, 2001).

208 **Paolo Giovio's 1527 dialogue:** Paolo Giovio, *Notable Men and Women of Our Time*, ed. and trans. Kenneth Gouwens (Cambridge, MA: Harvard University Press, 2013), 367–69.

208 **Montaigne, in his better moments:** Michel de Montaigne, *Essays*, in *The Complete Works*, trans. Donald Frame (London: Everyman, 2003), 831 (book 3, chap. 5).

208 **Christine de Pizan, the pioneering humanist:** Christine de Pizan, *The Book of the City of Ladies*, trans. Rosalind Brown-Grant (London: Penguin, 1999), 57 (part 1, §27).

208 **Virginia Woolf imagined:** Virginia Woolf, *A Room of One's Own* (London: Penguin, 2004), 54–61. First published 1945, based on a paper given in 1928.

208 **"One is not born":** Simone de Beauvoir, *The Second Sex*, trans. C. Borde and S. Malovany-Chevallier (London: Jonathan Cape, 2009), 293.

209 **we simply cannot know:** John Stuart Mill, "The Subjection of Women" (1869), in *Collected Works*, vol. 21: *Essays on Equality, Law, and Education*, ed. John M. Robson (London: Routledge, 1984), 259–340, this on 276–77.

209 **Mill praised his own mentor:** John Stuart Mill, "Bentham" (1838), in *Mill on Bentham and Coleridge* (London: Chatto & Windus, 1962), 41 (questioner), 42 (subversive).

209 **He made connections:** Mill, "The Subjection of Women," 269.

209 **That failure of insight:** Mill, "The Subjection of Women," 277.

209 **The great abolitionist and autobiographer:** Frederick Douglass, "What to the Slave Is the Fourth of July?," in *The Portable Frederick Douglass*, ed. John Stauffer and Henry Louis Gates Jr. (New York: Penguin, 2016), 207. This was Douglass's Fourth of July oration to the Ladies' Anti-Slavery Society of Rochester, New York, in 1852. The cultural historian Johan Huizinga similarly asked, in an address of 1935 skewering the pseudo-scientific ideas of race then in ascendancy in Europe: "Has a race-theorist ever made the startling and shaming discovery that the race to which he deemed himself to belong is inferior?" J. Huizinga, *In the Shadow of To-morrow: A Diagnosis of the Spiritual*

Distemper of Our Time, trans. J. H. Huizinga (London and Toronto: W. Heinemann, 1936), 68–69.

210 **Born in Maryland:** Frederick Douglass, "Narrative," in *The Portable Frederick Douglass*, ed. John Stauffer and Henry Louis Gates Jr. (New York: Penguin, 2016), 15–21.

210 **Among Douglass's other works:** Frederick Douglass, "To My Old Master," in *The Portable Frederick Douglass*, ed. John Stauffer and Henry Louis Gates Jr. (New York: Penguin, 2016), 413–20, this on 418–19. This was first published in Douglass's newspaper *The North Star*, September 8, 1848.

211 **As Douglass puts it elsewhere:** Frederick Douglass, "From *My Bondage and My Freedom*" (1855), in *The Portable Frederick Douglass*, ed. John Stauffer and Henry Louis Gates Jr. (New York: Penguin, 2016), 547.

211 **"It is a terrible, an inexorable, law":** James Baldwin, "Fifth Avenue, Uptown" (1960), in *Collected Essays*, ed. Toni Morrison (New York: Library of America, 1998), 179.

211 **"a man's character greatly takes":** Douglass, "From *My Bondage and My Freedom*," 547.

211 **Douglass had a compelling voice:** John Stauffer and Henry Louis Gates Jr., introduction to *The Portable Frederick Douglass*, ed. John Stauffer and Henry Louis Gates Jr. (New York: Penguin, 2016), xxi.

211 **That new art interested him:** John Stauffer, Zoe Trodd, and Celeste-Marie Bernier, *Picturing Frederick Douglass: The Most Photographed American in the Nineteenth Century* (New York: Liveright/W. W. Norton, 2015), ix. The authors have identified 160 distinct photographs/poses.

212 **Sure enough, it did:** Douglass, "Narrative," 37.

213 **His soul was roused:** Douglass, "Narrative," 42.

213 **He favored Ciceronian constructions:** Douglass, "Narrative," 59 ("You have seen"), 58 ("You are loosed").

213 **He does not hold back:** Douglass, "Narrative," 95.

214 **The phrase features:** E. M. Forster, *Howards End* (Harmondsworth, UK: Penguin, 1987), 300 ("You shall see"), 188 (all other quotations).

215 **In his own campaigning, Douglass:** This proposal was made by Elizabeth Cady Stanton in 1848. See Siep Stuurman, *The Invention of Humanity* (Cambridge, MA, and London: Harvard University Press, 2017), 386.

215 **He wrote to a friend in 1915:** E. M. Forster to Forrest Reid, March 13, 1915, quoted in P. N. Furbank, *E. M. Forster: A Life* (London: Cardinal/Sphere, 1988), vol. 2, 14.

215 **In *Love's Coming-of-Age*:** Edward Carpenter, *Love's Coming-of-Age*, 5th ed. (London: Swan Sonnenschein; Manchester, UK: Clarke, 1906), 3 (integrating sexuality), 11–12 ("*thinning out*," "*human* element").

215 **Carpenter and Merrill welcomed visitors:** Edward Carpenter, *My Days and Dreams: Being Autobiographical Notes* (London: Allen & Unwin, 1916), 163.

216 **the idea for *Maurice* had popped:** E. M. Forster, "Terminal Note," in *Maurice* (Harmondsworth, UK: Penguin, 1972), 217.

216 **Meanwhile, Maurice also moves past:** Forster, *Maurice*, 146.

216 **He explored it:** Forster, *Howards End*, 58.

217 **he was happy to support political rights:** See a note to this effect in E. M. Forster's commonplace book, quoted in Furbank, *E. M. Forster: A Life*, vol. 1, 180.

217 **He also wearied of always having:** Furbank quotes Forster: "Weariness of the only subject that I both can and may treat—the love of men for women & vice versa." Furbank, *E. M. Forster*, vol. 1, 199.

217 **"She too is enamoured":** E. M. Forster, *A Room with a View* (Harmondsworth, UK: Penguin, 1986), 60–61.

218 **"It is race-bound and it's class-bound":** E. M. Forster, "Liberty in England" (a talk to the Congrès International des Écrivains, Paris, June 21, 1935), in *Abinger Harvest* (Harmondsworth, UK: Penguin, 1967), 75–82, this on 76.

218 **So limited was it:** Wendy Moffat, *E. M. Forster: A New Life* (London: Bloomsbury, 2011), 18.

219 **"The Master's way consists":** Kongzi, quoted by Master Zeng Can: Confucius, *The Analects*, trans. Annping Chin (New York: Penguin, 2014), 51 (*Analects*, 4:15). "Humanity" is used twice here, but translates *zhong* in the first clause, and *shu* in the second.

CHAPTER 8. UNFOLDING HUMANITY

220 **Erasmus cited an old legend:** Erasmus, "On Education for Children," in *Collected Works*, vol. 26, *Literary and Educational Writings*, 4: *De pueris instituendis / De recta pronuntiatione*, ed. J. K. Sowards (Toronto: University of Toronto Press, 1985), 291–346, this on 304–6. The bear legend is in Pliny, *Natural History*, 8:126.

221 **The Prussian philosopher:** Immanuel Kant, *Lectures on Pedagogy* (1803), trans. Robert B. Louden, in Kant, *Anthropology, History, and Education*, ed. Günter Zöller and Robert B. Louden (Cambridge, UK: Cambridge University Press, 2007), 434–85, this on 440. I've substituted the word "seeds" for "germs" in the translation, since "germs" in modern English usage has distracting connotations. As there are several key terms in this sentence, here is the original in full: "Es liegen viele Keime in der Menschheit, und nun ist es unsere Sache, die Naturanlagen proportionirlich zu entwickeln, und die Menschheit aus ihren Keimen zu entfalten, und zu machen, daß der Mensch seine Bestimmung erreiche." Kant, *Über Pädagogik*, ed. Friedrich Theodor Rink (Königsberg: F. Nicolovius, 1803), 13.

221 **One is *Bildung*:** In early notes on the subject of *Bildung*, Humboldt described it as both an inward reflection and a way of grasping the outside world. It is also something that can be passed on through the generations; an individual's culture does not disappear. Humboldt, "Theory of Bildung" (written circa 1793–1794), trans. Gillian Horton-Krüger, in *Teaching as a Reflective Practice: The German Didaktik Tradition*, ed. I. Westbury, S. Hopmann, and K. Riquarts (Mahwah, NJ, and London: Lawrence Erlbaum, 2000), 57–61, this on 58–59.

221 **The other word was *Humanismus*:** Christopher Celenza, "Humanism," in *The Classical Tradition*, ed. Anthony Grafton, Glenn W. Most, and Salvatore Settis (Cambridge, MA, and London: Belknap Press of Harvard University Press, 2013), 462. The reference is to F. I. Niethammer, *Der Streit des Philanthropismus und Humanismus in der Theorie des Erziehungs-Unterrichtsunserer Zeit* (Jena, 1808). See also A. Campana, "The Origin of the Word 'Humanist,'" *Journal of the Warburg and Courtauld Institutes* 9 (1946), 60–73.

221 **By the mid-nineteenth century:** Excerpts from Georg Voigt, *Die Wiederbelebung des classischen Alterthums*, trans. Denys Hay, in *The Renaissance Debate*, ed. Denys Hay (New York: Holt, Rinehart and Winston, 1965), 29–34, this on 30.

222 **It also comes up:** Jacob Burckhardt, *Die Kultur der Renaissance in Italien* (Basel: Schweighauser, 1860), translated as *The Civilization of the Renaissance in Italy*.

223 **While Wilhelm was a quieter:** See letters from Wilhelm to Caroline, October 1804 and November 1817, both in *Humanist without Portfolio: An Anthology of the Writings of Wilhelm von Humboldt*, trans. Marianne Cowan (Detroit: Wayne State University Press, 1983), 386, 407–8.

223 **Johann Wolfgang von Goethe said:** Johann Peter Eckermann, *Conversations with Goethe*, trans. John Oxenford, ed. J. K. Moorhead (London: J. M. Dent; New York: E. P. Dutton, 1930), 136.

223 **He was studious:** Gabriele von Bülow, *Gabriele von Bülow, Daughter of Wilhelm von Humboldt: A Memoir*, trans. Clara Nordlinger (London: Smith, Elder, 1897), 229–30.

223 **This led Wilhelm to write:** Paul R. Sweet, *Wilhelm von Humboldt: A Biography* (Columbus: Ohio State University Press, 1978–80), vol. 1, 60–61.

224 **Two years after that first:** Wilhelm von Humboldt, *The Sphere and Duties of Government* [*Ideen zu einem Versuch, die Grenzen der Wirksamkeit des Staatszubestimmen*], trans. Joseph Coulthard Jr. (London: John Chapman, 1854), 73 (fears of chaos), 90 ("sweetly and naturally"), 94 (denying right to be fully human).

225 **Human character develops best:** Humboldt, *The Sphere and Duties of Government*, 86 ("unfolded").

225 **He did try to get:** Schiller's attempts to publish parts were in *Thalia* and *Berlin Monthly Review*: see Coulthard, preface to his translation of Humboldt, *The Sphere and Duties of Government*, iii.

226 **For the earlier age groups:** Sweet, *Wilhelm von Humboldt*, vol. 2, 44.

226 **University education, Humboldt said:** Sweet, *Wilhelm von Humboldt*, vol. 2, 67.

227 **"There is only one summit":** Wilhelm to Caroline, November 30, 1808, translated in W. H. Bruford, *The German Tradition of Self-Cultivation: "Bildung" from Humboldt to Thomas Mann* (Cambridge, UK: Cambridge University Press, 1975), 25.

228 **In the secret tract:** Humboldt, *The Sphere and Duties of Government*, 33 (marriage).

228 **What fascinated him:** His journal, July 18–23, 1789: *Humanist without Portfolio*, 378–79.

229 **"The more in life one":** Wilhelm to Caroline, October 1804, translated in *Humanist without Portfolio*, 388.

230 **"It is only through the study":** Wilhelm to Caroline, October 13, 1809, translated in Sweet, *Wilhelm von Humboldt*, vol. 2, 46.

230 **One benefit of his jobs:** Sweet, *Wilhelm von Humboldt*, vol. 1, 277 (various languages); vol. 2, 108 (Native American languages).

230 **Wilhelm, by contrast, liked to claim:** Von Bülow, *Gabriele von Bülow*, 230.

230 **He hoped to write:** Wilhelm von Humboldt, *On Language: On the Diversity of Human Language Construction and Its Influence on the Mental Development of the Human Species*, ed. Michael Losonsky, trans. Peter Heath (Cambridge, UK: Cambridge University Press, 1999). See Sweet, *Wilhelm von Humboldt*, vol. 2, 460–70.

231 **"There must be something to follow":** Von Bülow, *Gabriele von Bülow*, 229–30 (spirits, languages), 247–48 ("There must be something" and "Good-bye").

232 **Harriet's arguments for women's right:** Harriet Taylor Mill, "Enfranchisement of Women," in *The Complete Works*, ed. Jo Ellen Jacobs and Paula Harms Payne (Bloomington and Indianapolis: Indiana University Press, 1998), 51–73, this on 57.

232 **"The grand, leading principle":** Humboldt, *The Sphere and Duties of Government*, 65. Quoted by John Stuart Mill as an epigraph to *On Liberty* (London: Watts, 1929).

232 **For Mill, too, the right approach:** John Stuart Mill, *On Liberty*, 68.

233 **Humboldt, too, had written:** "Variety of situations" in Humboldt is *Mannigfaltigkeit der Situationen*, a phrase reminiscent of "many-sidedness," or *Vielseitigkeit*. *Mannigfaltigkeit* is translated as "diversity" in the line featured by Mill at the opening of *On Liberty*. For the original German in both cases, see Humboldt, *Ideen zu einem Versuch, die Grenzen der Wirksamkeit des Staatszubestimmen* (Berlin: Deutsche Bibliothek, [1852]), 25 (variety of situations), 71 (diversity).

233 **as Montaigne had said:** Michel de Montaigne, *Essays*, in *The Complete Works*, trans. Donald Frame (London: Everyman, 2003), 141 (book 1, chap. 26). Cf. Mill, *On Liberty*, 24.

233 **Thus, Mill recommends:** "Absolute freedom" and "foolish" are both from Mill, *On Liberty*, 14–15.

234 **Such control could not legally:** John Stuart Mill, "Statement on Marriage," in *Collected Works*, vol. 21: *Essays on Equality, Law, and Education*, ed. John M. Robson (London: Routledge, 1984), 99, https://oll.libertyfund.org/titles/mill-the-collected-works -of-john-stuart-mill-volume-xxi-essays-on-equality-law-and-education/simple#lf0223-21 _head_034.

234 **The other delicate matter:** After Mill's death, three unpublished essays on religion, written between 1830 and 1858, were published; the last of these, "Theism" (written circa 1868–1870), raises the possibility of such a being. But in "Utility of Religion," he notes that the promise of an afterlife is a valuable consolation to people who suffer on earth; if people were happier and more fulfilled in their earthly lives, the appeal of religion would decline. Both essays are in John Stuart Mill, *Three Essays on Religion: Nature, The Utility of Religion, and Theism* (London: Longmans, Green, Reader & Dyer, 1874).

234 **Immersion in utilitarian theory:** John Stuart Mill, *Autobiography*, ed. Mark Philp (Oxford, UK: Oxford University Press, 2018), 25–28 (childhood and religion), 81 (loss of pleasure).

235 **Mill's path out of this:** Jeremy Bentham to Henry Richard Vassall, Third Baron Holland, November 13, 1808, in Bentham, *Correspondence*, vol. 7, ed. John Dinwiddy (Oxford, UK: Clarendon Press, 1988), 570. ("*Prose* is where all the lines but the last go on to the margin:—*Poetry* is where some of them fall short of it.") See also A. Julius, "More Bentham, Less Mill," in *Bentham and the Arts*, ed. Anthony Julius, Malcolm Quinn, and Philip Schofield (London: UCL Press, 2020), 178. Bentham could not have been entirely oblivious to poetry: he installed a stone tablet in his garden, inscribed as "sacred to Milton, prince of poets": see M. M. St. J. Packe, *Life of John Stuart Mill* (London: Secker & Warburg, 1954), 21. On Mill's view of poetry, see Richard Reeves, *John Stuart Mill* (London: Atlantic, 2008), 20.

235 **Now, rebelliously, John fell:** Mill, *Autobiography*, 84–86.

236 **Reading Wordsworth made Mill reflect:** John Stuart Mill, "Utilitarianism," in John Stuart Mill and Jeremy Bentham, *Utilitarianism and Other Essays*, ed. Alan Ryan (London: Penguin, 1987), 272–338, this on 285; 279–81 (different qualities of pleasure).

236 **"What pleasure comes from our faculties":** Giannozzo Manetti, *On Human Worth and Excellence* (*De dignitate et excellentia hominis*), ed. and trans. Brian Copenhaver (Cambridge, MA, and London: I Tatti/Harvard University Press, 2018), 205 (book IV).

236 **One such form is:** John Stuart Mill, "The Subjection of Women" (1869), in *Collected Works*, vol. 21: *Essays on Equality, Law, and Education*, ed. John M. Robson (London: Routledge, 1984), 259–340, this on 337.

236 **Mill always said that Harriet:** F. A. Hayek, *John Stuart Mill and Harriet Taylor:*

Their Correspondence and Subsequent Marriage (London: Routledge & Kegan Paul, 1951), 260–63. On tuberculosis, see https://plato.stanford.edu/entries/harriet-mill/.

237 **Mill continued his work:** Mill, *Autobiography*, ed. Mark Philp, 169.

238 **Also inspired by Wilhelm von Humboldt:** Matthew Arnold, *Culture and Anarchy*, ed. Jane Garnett (Oxford, UK: Oxford University Press, 2006), 9. He also describes Humboldt himself as a harmoniously developed being, "one of the most perfect souls that have ever existed" (94).

238 **Also Humboldtian is that he:** Matthew Arnold, *Culture and Anarchy*, ed. Jane Garnett (Oxford, UK: Oxford University Press, 2006), 36.

239 **Matthew Arnold had grown up:** Nicholas Murray, *A Life of Matthew Arnold* (London: Sceptre, 1997), 241.

240 **One is the statement:** Arnold, *Culture and Anarchy*, 5.

240 **The other is also a definition:** Arnold, *Culture and Anarchy*, 9.

240 **But Arnold is emphatic:** Arnold, *Culture and Anarchy*, 80.

240 **For him, real culture:** Arnold, *Culture and Anarchy*, 33.

240 **It means curiosity:** Arnold, *Culture and Anarchy*, 5.

240 **You can be cultured even:** Arnold, *Culture and Anarchy*, 6 (newspapers), 107 (reading them with a fresh mind).

240 **What must be done with:** Arnold, *Culture and Anarchy*, 54–55.

240 **The other phrase:** Jonathan Swift, "Battle of the Books," in *A Tale of a Tub and Other Works*, ed. Angus Ross and David Woolley (Oxford, UK, and New York: Oxford University Press, 1986), 104–25, this on 112.

241 **He also describes himself:** Liberal: Arnold, *Culture and Anarchy*, 32.

242 **It also had an impact:** For explorations of working-class reading habits in general, see Jonathan Rose, *The Intellectual Life of the British Working Classes* (New Haven and London: Yale University Press, 2002); Edith Hall and Henry Stead, *A People's History of Classics* (Abingdon, UK: Routledge, 2020).

242 **One early series, Bohn's:** Hall and Stead, *A People's History of Classics*, 58.

242 **Then came such outstanding:** http://www.gutenberg.org/wiki/Harvard_Classics_(Bookshelf). See Adam Kirsch, "The 'Five-Foot Shelf' Reconsidered," *Harvard Magazine* 103, no. 2 (November–December 2001).

242 **Unfortunately, Dent's own habit:** Frank Swinnerton, *The Bookman's London* (London: Allan Wingate, 1951), 47.

242 **Those employees were:** Rose, *The Intellectual Life of the British Working Classes*, 133.

242 **He gave the series:** See the account by David Campbell on the Everyman website. http://www.everymanslibrary.co.uk/history.aspx. For a list of early editions: http://scribblemonger.com/elcollect/elCatalog.pl.

242 **To help readers find:** "The Best Hundred Books, by the Best Judges," *Pall Mall Gazette "Extra,"* no. 24 (1886), 23.

243 **John Ruskin said he wanted:** "The Best Hundred Books, by the Best Judges," 9.

243 **Henry Morton Stanley, the adventurer:** "The Best Hundred Books, by the Best Judges," 21.

243 **Some feared that:** Rose, *The Intellectual Life of the British Working Classes*, 267; Ethel Carnie and Lavena Saltonstall, letters to *Cotton Factory Times*, March 20 and April 3, 10, 17, 1914. On Carnie, see https://en.wikipedia.org/wiki/Ethel_Carnie_Holdsworth.

244 **Norris, a post office worker:** Rose, *The Intellectual Life of the British Working Classes*, 277. The quotation is from George W. Norris, "The Testament of a Trade Unionist," *Highway* 39 (May 1938), 158–59.

244 **Humboldt was the most blissed-out:** Humboldt to F. G. Welcker, October 26, 1825, translated in Sweet, *Wilhelm von Humboldt*, vol. 2, 422–23.

245 **That name for it came:** Irving Babbitt, *Literature and the American College: Essays in Defense of the Humanities* (Boston and New York: Houghton Mifflin, 1908), 12. "New Humanism" was a term applied to these views by others; it should not be confused with various other movements also called "New Humanism" at various times.

245 **Such outreach projects, for Babbitt:** Babbitt, *Literature and the American College*, 8–9.

245 **When the novelist Sinclair Lewis:** Sinclair Lewis, Nobel Lecture, 1930, https://www.nobelprize.org/prizes/literature/1930/lewis/lecture/. Other responses were collected in a symposium: C. Hartley Grattan, ed., *The Critique of Humanism: A Symposium* (New York: Brewer and Warren, 1930). This was in part a reply to a collection promoting the New Humanism: Norman Foerster, ed., *Humanism and America* (New York: Farrar and Rinehart, 1930).

246 **Much later, Edward Said would observe:** Edward Said, *Humanism and Democratic Criticism* (Basingstoke, UK: Palgrave Macmillan, 2004), 21–22.

246 **"How much more fittingly":** Montaigne, *Essays*, 149 (book 1, chap. 26).

CHAPTER 9. SOME DREAM-COUNTRY

248 **Then it was the turn:** Charles Darwin, *On the Origin of Species* (London: Penguin, 1968), 459.

249 **It is a vision of majesty:** Darwin, *On the Origin of Species*, 459.

249 **It could have been even:** Janet Browne, *Charles Darwin: The Power of Place* (London: Jonathan Cape, 2002), 349. The publisher referred to here was John Murray.

249 **The *Origin* found a wide readership:** Browne, *Charles Darwin*, 88–90 (Mudie's), 186 (Mill), 189–90 (Eliot). G. H. Lewes's *Sea-Side Studies* were published in periodical form and as a book in 1858; see also Rosemary Ashton, *G. H. Lewes: A Life* (London: Pimlico, 2000), 169.

249 **A different kind of reader:** Karl Marx, *Collected Works*, vol. 41: *Letters* (London: Lawrence & Wishart, 1985), 234 ("crude English fashion"). Browne, *Charles Darwin*, 403 (*Das Kapital* sent to Darwin).

250 **Huxley's friendship with Darwin:** Adrian Desmond, *T. H. Huxley: From Devil's Disciple to Evolution's High Priest* (London: Penguin, 1998), 188 (sea squirts), 224–25 (no idea).

251 **First, he reviewed the book:** T. H. Huxley, "The Origin of Species," in *Collected Essays* (London: Macmillan, 1892–95), vol. 2, 22–79, this on 52. Originally published in *Westminster Review* 17 (1860), 541–70, and reproduced at https://mathcs.clarku.edu/huxley/CE2/OrS.html.

251 **Then he gave lectures:** Browne, *Charles Darwin*, 105.

251 **Next came the 1860 meeting:** Browne, *Charles Darwin*, 94, 118 (Darwin's excuse for not attending).

251 **A similar remark was made:** George W. E. Russell, *Collections and Recollections* (London: Thomas Nelson, [1904?]), 161–62.

251 **that was Huxley's account of it:** Ronald W. Clark, *The Huxleys* (London: Heinemann, 1968), 59, citing a letter from Huxley to Frederick Dyster.

252 **much-told tales, versions differed:** Desmond, *T. H. Huxley*, 280.

252 **Darwin was grateful to Huxley:** Browne, *Charles Darwin*, 136.

253 **In one talk to the South London:** T. H. Huxley, "A Liberal Education and Where to

Find It" (1868), in *Science and Education*, vol. 3 of *Collected Essays* (London: Macmillan, 1910), 76–110, this on 87–88 (current studies criticized), 97–98 (traces of past). Charles Dickens's remarks are in *Bleak House*, chap. 12.

253 **And elsewhere he cited Terence:** T. H. Huxley, "On Science and Art in Relation to Education" (1882), in *Science and Education*, vol. 3 of *Collected Essays* (1910), 160–88, this on 164.

253 **It was just that he:** Huxley, "A Liberal Education and Where to Find It," this on 96.

254 **Huxley, in another lecture:** T. H. Huxley, "Universities: Actual and Ideal" (1874, University of Aberdeen), in *Science and Education*, vol. 3 of *Collected Essays* (1910), 189–234, this on 212. Huxley quoted Mill's similar rectorial address at the University of St. Andrews on February 1, 1867, but changed every mention of classical studies to "science."

254 **After an 1880 talk:** Matthew Arnold, "Literature and Science," in *The Portable Matthew Arnold*, ed. Lionel Trilling (Harmondsworth, UK: Penguin, 1980), 405–29, this on 413–20.

255 **But he also realized:** Darwin noted this in *The Descent of Man*, writing that "the moral qualities are advanced, either directly or indirectly, much more through the effects of habit, the reasoning powers, instruction, religion, etc., than through natural selection." Charles Darwin, *The Descent of Man, and Selection in Relation to Sex* (London: Gibson Square, 2003), 618.

255 **It provided no *direct* basis:** Darwin, *The Descent of Man*, 612 ("habit, example" and "an all-seeing Deity"). His theory of the evolution of morality through social feeling is given mainly in part 1, chap. 4, 97–127.

256 **He had lost his Christian belief:** Charles Darwin, "Religious Belief" (written 1879, "copied out" 1881), in *Autobiographies*, ed. Michael Neve and Sharon Messenger (London: Penguin, 2002), 49–55, this on 49–50 (Hell); 54 (helping others, and "agnostic").

256 **The person who did the most:** T. H. Huxley, "Agnosticism," in *Collected Essays* (London: Macmillan, 1892–95), vol. 5, 209–62, this on 237–38.

257 **His contemporary Richard Bithell:** Richard Bithell, *The Creed of a Modern Agnostic* (London: Routledge, 1883), 10–14.

257 **More recently, another agnostic:** Bryan Magee, *Ultimate Questions* (Princeton, NJ: Princeton University Press, 2016), 26.

257 **Another noted agnostic:** Leslie Stephen, "An Agnostic's Apology," in *An Agnostic's Apology and Other Essays* (London: Smith, Elder, 1893), 1.

257 **But agnostics could carry:** Frederick James Gould, *The Life-Story of a Humanist* (London: Watts, 1923), 75.

257 **Sir Leslie Stephen was known:** Leslie Stephen, "A Bad Five Minutes in the Alps," in *Essays on Freethinking and Plainspeaking*, rev. ed. (London: Smith, Elder; Duckworth, 1907), 177–225, this on 184–85 ("At last!"), 193 ("ghastly mess"), 203 (Athanasian Creed), 221 ("something like a blessing"), 222–23 ("duty"). The piece was originally published in *Fraser's Magazine* 86 (1872), 545–61. On the question of the story's veracity: F. W. Maitland, *Life and Letters of Leslie Stephen* (London: Duckworth, 1906), 97–98, which quotes Sir George Trevelyan as saying that the story was at least partly inspired by an incident in which Trevelyan and another inexperienced climber got into difficulties after Stephen led them on a tough side-path.

260 **George Eliot held it in high regard:** George Eliot said this while walking with W. H. Myers in the Fellows' Garden at Trinity College, Cambridge, in 1873. Quoted in Gordon S. Haight, *George Eliot* (Oxford, UK: Clarendon Press, 1968), 464.

260 **Darwin also wrote of:** Darwin, *The Descent of Man, and Selection in Relation to Sex*, 97.

260 **Leslie Stephen himself seems:** A note made in 1856. Maitland, *Life and Letters of Leslie Stephen*, 144–45.

260 **His account may also have inspired:** Thomas Hardy, *A Pair of Blue Eyes* (Oxford, UK: Oxford University Press, 2005), 201. On evidence for the idea that Hardy was influenced by the Stephen piece, see John Halperin, "Stephen, Hardy, and 'A Pair of Blue Eyes,'" in *Studies in Fiction and History from Austen to Le Carré* (New York: Springer, 1988).

261 **"In brotherhood bonded close":** Thomas Hardy, "A Plaint to Man" (1909–10), in *A Selection of Poems*, ed. W. E. Williams (Harmondsworth, UK: Penguin, 1960), 95–96.

261 **In his poem "Dover Beach":** Matthew Arnold, "Dover Beach," in *The Portable Matthew Arnold*, ed. Lionel Trilling (Harmondsworth, UK: Penguin, 1980), 165–67.

262 **Apparently, he was inspired by:** Nicholas Murray, *A Life of Matthew Arnold* (London: Sceptre, 1997), 116.

262 **Elsewhere, Arnold took a more pragmatic:** Matthew Arnold, *Culture and Anarchy* (Oxford, UK: Oxford University Press, 2006), 11–12.

262 **This calls to mind:** Friedrich Nietzsche, *The Gay Science*, ed. B. Williams, trans. Josefine Nauckhoff (Cambridge, UK: Cambridge University Press, 2001), 120 (part 3, §125).

262 **The novelist and biographer J. A. Froude:** J. A. Froude, *Thomas Carlyle: A History of His Life in London, 1834–81* (London: Longman, Green, 1884), 248.

262 **He had been through:** Waldo Hilary Dunn, *James Anthony Froude: A Biography* (Oxford, UK: Clarendon Press, 1961), vol. 1, 134–38.

263 **In 1860, six clergymen contributed:** The two who were convicted were James Rowland Williams and Henry Bristow Wilson. See Josef L. Altholz, *Anatomy of a Controversy: The Debate over* Essays and Reviews *1860–1864* (Aldershot, UK: Scolar, 1994), 1.

263 **When the young Robert Louis Stevenson:** Robert Louis Stevenson to his friend Charles Baxter, quoted in Claire Harman, *Robert Louis Stevenson: A Biography* (London: Harper, 2006), 79–80.

263 **Another writer, Edmund Gosse:** Edmund Gosse, *Father and Son: A Study of Two Temperaments* (Harmondsworth, UK: Penguin, 1983), 90 ("I had no humanity"), 248, 251 (regrets).

263 **Indeed, the elder Gosse:** P. H. Gosse, *Omphalos: An Attempt to Untie the Geological Knot* (London: John Van Voorst, 1857). His son describes him as being hurt: Gosse, *Father and Son*, 105, 112.

264 **As Huxley's biographer Adrian Desmond:** Desmond, *T. H. Huxley*, 434.

264 **Some of them were swept:** Rose Macaulay, *Told by an Idiot* (London: Virago, 1983), 3, 6–7.

264 **The nineteenth century was the great era:** For a survey of the genre, see Robert Lee Wolff, *Gains and Losses: Novels of Faith and Doubt in Victorian England* (London: John Murray, 1977).

265 **On seeing just that:** Duncan Grant, "Virginia Woolf," in *The Golden Horizon*, ed. Cyril Connolly (London: Weidenfeld & Nicolson, 1953), 394.

265 ***Robert Elsmere*—the most durable:** Mrs. Humphry Ward, *Robert Elsmere* (Oxford, UK, and New York: Oxford University Press, 1987), 169 ("dirt and drains"), 179 ("live someone else's life"), 261 (troubled by Christianity), 314 ("purely human").

266 **Thus, performing a "catechism of himself":** Ward, *Robert Elsmere*, 475 ("catechism" and "the good"), 332 ("Every human soul").

267 **"I see life always as a threadlike path":** Ward, *Robert Elsmere*, 164–66.

267 **The same concern was felt:** Janet Browne, *Charles Darwin: Voyaging* (London: Pimlico, 1996), 396–97.

268 *Robert Elsmere* **is not short:** William Ewart Gladstone, "*Robert Elsmere* and the Battle of Belief," *Contemporary Review*, May 1888, http://www.victorianweb.org/history /pms/robertelsmere.html. James is quoted by Rosemary Ashton in the introduction to her edition of Ward's *Robert Elsmere*, vii. On the novel's reception, see William S. Peterson, *Victorian Heretic: Mrs. Humphry Ward's* Robert Elsmere (Leicester, UK: Leicester University Press, 1976).

268 *Robert Elsmere* **became a word-of-mouth success:** Rosemary Ashton, introduction to Ward, *Robert Elsmere*, vii.

269 **In 1819, he literally cut up:** Amphibologisms: Thomas Jefferson to John Adams, 1813, quoted in Peter Manseau's edition of *The Jefferson Bible* (Princeton, NJ: Princeton University Press, 2020), 38. Jefferson's assembled cut-up, plus the remains of the two copies used for sources, remained in separate private collections until they were found by Cyrus Adler, who acquired them for the Smithsonian Institution. The story is told by Manseau, 80–93.

269 **One such person was Matthew Arnold:** Matthew Arnold, *Literature and Dogma: An Essay Towards a Better Apprehension of the Bible* (London: Smith, Elder, 1873), xiii–xv, 383. Arnold followed that up with *God and the Bible* (London: Smith, Elder, 1875), responding to critics of the earlier book. Similar arguments for the Bible as literature were given by the Oxford don Benjamin Jowett, a contributor to the controversial *Essays and Reviews* collection: Benjamin Jowett, "On the Interpretation of Scripture," *Essays and Reviews* (London: John W. Parker, 1860), 330–433.

270 **It was reading Strauss's book:** H. W. Wardman, *Ernest Renan: A Critical Biography* (London: University of London/Athlone, 1964), 27–29.

270 **He did remain a biblical scholar:** Ernest Renan, *Memoirs*, trans. J. Lewis May (London: G. Bles, 1935), 237.

270 **The book caused a furor:** Renan, *Memoirs*, 226 (toned down), 202–3 ("reading too hard").

271 **Secretly, Renan seems to have:** The witness was Jules Lemaître. Translated in Wardman, *Ernest Renan*, 183.

271 **The American freethinker:** Robert G. Ingersoll, "Ernest Renan" (1892), in *The Works of Robert G. Ingersoll* (New York: Dresden; C. P. Farrell, 1902), vol. 11, 283–301, this on 300–301.

271 **Ingersoll himself was of a different school:** *The Best of Robert Ingersoll*, ed. Roger E. Greeley (New York: Prometheus, 1993), 14 (no interest in understanding). Robert Ingersoll to Albert H. Walker, November 3, 1882, in Robert G. Ingersoll, *The Life and Letters*, ed. Eva Ingersoll Wakefield, preface by Royston Pike (London: Watts, 1952), 98 (no interest in improving).

271 **E. M. Forster would feel:** E. M. Forster, "How I Lost My Faith," in *The Prince's Tale and Other Uncollected Writings*, ed. P. N. Furbank (London: Penguin, 1999), 318.

271 **In France, just after the Revolution:** Ruth Scurr, *Fatal Purity: Robespierre and the French Revolution* (London: Chatto & Windus, 2006), 267. See also Mona Ozouf, *Festivals and the French Revolution* (Cambridge, MA: Harvard University Press, 1988), 100–101, and https://en.wikipedia.org/wiki/Cult_of_Reason.

273 **Then there had to be saints:** Condorcet had done something similar, writing an unpublished "Anti-Superstitious Almanack," which allocated former saints' days to people who had opposed church abuses or tortures: Nicolas de Condorcet, *Almanach*

anti-superstitieux, ed. Anne-Marie Chouillet, Pierre Crépel, and Henri Duranton (Saint-Étienne, France: CNRS Éditions/Publications de Université de Saint-Étienne, 1992). See Steven Lukes and Nadia Urbinati, introduction to their edition of Condorcet, *Political Writings* (Cambridge, UK: Cambridge University Press, 2012), xvii.

274 **It had a lasting success:** On the church: https://www.nytimes.com/2016/12/25/world /americas/nearly-in-ruins-the-church-where-sages-dreamed-of-a-modern-brazil .html. On Positivism in Brazil generally, see http://positivists.org/blog/brazil.

274 **Other Positivist churches are still:** https://hibridos.cc/en/rituals/templo-positivista -de-porto-alegre/.

274 **A small congregation listened:** "A Positivist Creed," manuscript, Bod. M. C347, f. 176. Reproduced in T. R. Wright, *The Religion of Humanity: The Impact of Comtean Positivism on Victorian Britain* (Cambridge, UK: Cambridge University Press, 1986), 85.

274 **Congreve even spoke:** This from Moncure Daniel Conway's description of one such meeting on New Year's Day 1881: Moncure Daniel Conway, *Autobiography: Memories and Experiences* (London: Cassell, 1904), vol. 2, 347.

274 **One popular choice was:** Josephine Troup and Edith Swepstone each composed versions, and Henry Holmes composed a large-scale cantata. Martha S. Vogeler, "The Choir Invisible: The Poetics of Humanist Piety," in *George Eliot: A Centenary Tribute*, ed. Gordon S. Haight and Rosemary T. VanArsdel (London: Macmillan, 1982), 64–81, this on 78.

274 **"O may I join":** George Eliot, "The Choir Invisible," in *Complete Shorter Poetry*, ed. Antonie Gerard van den Broek (London: Pickering & Chatto, 2005), vol. 2, 85–86, this on 86 (lines 1–5).

274 **George Eliot herself took:** T. R. Wright, *The Religion of Humanity* (Cambridge, UK: Cambridge University Press, 1986), 87.

275 **John Stuart Mill wrote an exposé:** John Stuart Mill, *Auguste Comte and Positivism* (London: N. Trübner, 1865), 54–56.

275 **T. H. Huxley took one look:** T. H. Huxley, "On the Physical Basis of Life" (1868), *Collected Essays* (London: Macmillan, 1892–95), vol. 1, 156, https://mathcs.clarku .edu/huxley/CE1/PhysB.html.

275 **The split occurred:** Wright, *The Religion of Humanity*, 4.

275 **He preferred a slightly less:** Wright, *The Religion of Humanity*, 99 ("mumbling"), 96 ("Hail to Thee"; the collection was called *The Service of Man* [1890]), 101 (Trollope).

275 **Harrison's son Austin left:** Austin Harrison, *Frederic Harrison: Thoughts and Memories* (London: William Heinemann, 1926), 90 (Shakespeare), 83 (Gissing).

276 **Mill expressed this objection:** Mill, *Auguste Comte and Positivism*, 50 (systematizing), 60 (evolution and dogma).

276 **The memoir by Frederic's son:** Harrison, *Frederic Harrison*, 67.

277 **When the philosopher Bertrand Russell:** Bertrand Russell, "What I Believe," in *Why I Am Not a Christian* (London: Unwin, 1975), 43–69, this on 63.

Chapter 10. Doctor Hopeful

279 **As a boy, Zamenhof noticed:** L. L. Zamenhof to N. Borovko, circa 1895, in L. L. Zamenhof, *Du Famaj Leteroj* [Letters to Nikolaj Borovko and Alfred Michaux], ed. and trans. André Cherpillod (Courgenard, France: Eldono La Blanchetière, 2013), 10–11. In Esperanto with French translation and notes.

279 **While still a teenager:** L. L. Zamenhof to A. Michaux, February 21, 1905, in Zamenhof, *Du Famaj Leteroj*, 39.

280 **The Old Testament story of Babel:** Genesis 11:1–9, this in 6.

280 **It played it so well:** Dante, *De vulgari eloquentia*, ed. and trans. Steven Botterill (Cambridge, UK: Cambridge University Press. 1996), 3, 23 ("formulated") (book 1, §1 and §9).

280 **Zamenhof did consider Latin:** Marjorie Boulton, *Zamenhof: Creator of Esperanto* (London: Routledge & Kegan Paul, 1960), 11.

282 *"Malamikete de las nacjes":* Boulton's translation in prose is amended here to produce verse lines: Boulton, *Zamenhof,* 15. See also Zamenhof to N. Borovko, circa 1895, in Zamenhof, *Du Famaj Leteroj,* 17.

282 **A distressing setback:** Boulton, *Zamenhof,* 17–21.

282 **Generally known by the title:** The text of Zamenhof's *Unua Libro* in an English translation by Richard H. Geoghegan (1889), revised by Gene Keyes (2006), is online: see L. L. Zamenhof, *Doctor Esperanto's International Language,* part 1, http://www .genekeyes.com/Dr_Esperanto.html. On Dr. Hopeful, see Boulton, *Zamenhof,* 33.

283 **Immanuel Kant had observed:** Immanuel Kant, "To Perpetual Peace" (1795), in *Perpetual Peace and Other Essays,* trans. Ted Humphrey (Indianapolis and Cambridge, UK: Hackett, 1983), 125.

283 **Just as with the language problem:** Zamenhof's *The Dogmas of Hillelism* was published in the Russian Esperantist publication *Ruslanda Esperantisto* in 1906. Boulton, *Zamenhof,* 97–101.

283 **Zamenhof named the religion:** Esther Schor, *Bridge of Words: Esperanto and the Dream of a Universal Language* (New York: Metropolitan Books, 2016), 78.

283 **Not everyone in the Esperantist movement:** Boulton, *Zamenhof,* 104–5. There is some similarity between the idea of Zamenhof's shared religion and the Bahá'í faith, which also sees all religion as a unity.

284 **Zamenhof himself had been:** Zamenhof to A. Michaux, February 21, 1905, in Zamenhof, *Du Famaj Leteroj,* 33–35.

284 *First Book* **had opened:** Zamenhof, *Unua Libro,* trans. Geoghegan, rev. Keyes. The earlier translation, by Julius Steinhaus, is quoted in Boulton, *Zamenhof,* 39.

284 **In 1908, an Esperantist physician:** https://en.wikipedia.org/wiki/Neutral_Moresnet.

284 **Much later, in 1967:** https://en.wikipedia.org/wiki/Republic_of_Rose_Island.

286 **"Happiness is the only good":** Ingersoll's happiness credo appears in various formats, including in *An Oration on the Gods* (January 29, 1872) (Cairo, IL: Daily Bulletin Steam Book & Job Print, 1873), 48. The recording can be heard online at https:// youtu.be/rLLapwIoEVI.

286 **Ingersoll was an agnostic:** Susan Jacoby, *The Great Agnostic: Robert Ingersoll and American Freethought* (New Haven and London: Yale University Press, 2013), 34.

286 **When Robert was born:** Robert G. Ingersoll, *The Life and Letters.* ed. Eva Ingersoll Wakefield, preface by Royston Pike (London: Watts, 1952), 1.

286 **From his upbringing, he had:** Ingersoll, *The Life and Letters,* 13.

286 **Next, he trained as a lawyer:** Civil war: Ingersoll, *The Life and Letters,* 23–32. Hatred of war: Edward Garstin Smith, *The Life and Reminiscences of Robert G. Ingersoll* (New York: National Weekly Pub. Co.; London: Shurmer Sibthorp, 1904), 116.

286 **During his legal studies:** Ingersoll, *The Life and Letters,* 15–16.

287 **It horrified him to learn:** Ingersoll, *The Life and Letters,* 36–37.

287 **Among those who quickly gave:** Clarence Darrow, *The Story of My Life* (New York: Charles Scribner's Sons, 1932), 381. For some of Ingersoll's addresses to juries, see Ingersoll, *The Works of Robert G. Ingersoll,* vol. 10.

287 **Ingersoll did have plenty:** Ingersoll, *The Life and Letters,* 55.

287 **He used humor:** Smith, *The Life and Reminiscences of Robert G. Ingersoll*, part 2, *Reminiscences*, 32.

288 **At other moments, he could:** Ingersoll, "The Ghosts," in *The Works of Robert G. Ingersoll*, vol. 1, 272 ("spared no pains"), 326 ("Let them cover").

288 **Quintilian himself had recommended:** Quintilian, *Institutio oratoria*, trans. H. E. Butler (London: W. Heinemann; New York: G. P. Putnam's Sons, 1922), vol. 4, 411 (XII.v.5).

288 **He loved to eat:** Smith, *The Life and Reminiscences of Robert G. Ingersoll*, part 2, *Reminiscences*, 208.

288 **So well did he eat:** C. H. Cramer, *Royal Bob: The Life of Robert G. Ingersoll* (Indianapolis: Bobbs-Merrill, 1952), 102.

288 **For Ingersoll, there was nothing:** Robert G. Ingersoll, *The Best of Robert Ingersoll: Selections from His Writings and Speeches*, ed. Roger E. Greeley (New York: Prometheus, 1993), 79–80. Admiring Shakespeare: Ingersoll, *The Life and Letters*, 162–69.

289 **"Is life worth living":** Ingersoll, *The Best of Robert Ingersoll*, 55.

289 **Such mentions of his wife:** Ingersoll, *The Best of Robert Ingersoll*, 12. Photograph: Jacoby, *The Great Agnostic*, 40.

289 **"I do believe in the nobility":** Ingersoll, *The Best of Robert Ingersoll*, 83.

290 **His opponents called him:** Jacoby, *The Great Agnostic*, 2 ("Injuresoul"). Margaret Sanger remembered his being pelted when he spoke in their town of Corning, New York; her father had invited Ingersoll, but there was so much trouble they had to move the talk to a quiet spot outdoors in the woods. Margaret Sanger, *An Autobiography* (London: Victor Gollancz, 1939), 2.

290 **He even turned fruit:** Ingersoll, *The Best of Robert Ingersoll*, 56.

290 **Of his responses to these:** Ingersoll, *The Life and Letters*, 291.

290 **And as Bertrand Russell wrote:** Bertrand Russell, *Principles of Social Reconstruction* (London: Allen & Unwin, 1916), 203.

291 **he began to look around himself:** She wrote this in a letter to her own mother. Cited in Bertrand Russell, *Autobiography* (London and New York: Routledge, 1998), 12.

291 **His mother, Katharine Russell:** https://en.wikipedia.org/wiki/Katharine_Russell, _Viscountess_Amberley.

291 **Katharine's husband, John Russell:** Alan Ryan, *Bertrand Russell: A Political Life* (London: Penguin, 1988), 4.

292 **Russell said that reading:** Russell, *Autobiography*, 36.

292 **"educated at a time when easy-chairs":** Anthony Trollope, *Can You Forgive Her?* (1864–1865) (London: Penguin, 1972), 48.

292 **Yet Russell also learned:** Russell, *Autobiography*, 17. The text is Exodus 23:2.

292 **Russell considered it "undesirable":** Bertrand Russell, *Sceptical Essays* (London and New York: Routledge, 2004), 1.

292 **"If I were to suggest":** The Wikipedia article at https://en.wikipedia.org/wiki/Russell %27s_teapot quotes Russell, and discusses arguments made against the teapot analogy. The source is Russell's "Is There a God?," written for *Illustrated* magazine in 1952 but not published. A similar idea was proposed by Carl Sagan: "If I say that I have a dragon in my garage, but it is invisible, weighs nothing, cannot be felt to the touch, and breathes a heatless, undetectable fire, then what is the difference between this and my having no dragon in my garage at all?" Carl Sagan, *The Demon-Haunted World* (London: Headline, 1997), 160–61.

293 **as Thomas Paine once wrote of Voltaire:** Thomas Paine, "Rights of Man," in *Rights* *of Man, Common Sense, and Other Political Writings*, ed. Mark Philp (Oxford, UK: Oxford University Press, 1995), 145.

293 **Mathematics came into his life:** Russell, *Autobiography*, 30.

294 **He stood for election:** Russell, *Autobiography*, 156–57.

294 **During one episode:** Russell, *Autobiography*, 38.

294 **Intense emotions swept through him:** "Good hater": Beatrice Webb in her diary in 1901, quoted in Ray Monk, *Bertrand Russell* (London: Vintage, 1997–2001), vol. 1, 139. Russell in turn accused her and her husband of being cold: Russell, *Autobiography*, 76.

294 **"the loneliness of the human soul":** Russell, *Autobiography*, 149.

295 **The fact that Russell was:** For the intensity of Russell's love of mathematics and logic, see his letters to and from Gilbert Murray, quoted in Russell, *Autobiography*, 160–62. Quotation from *The Little Review* in Ronald W. Clark, *The Life of Bertrand Russell*, rev. ed. (Harmondsworth, UK: Penguin, 1978), 534.

295 **Like the long-ago Epicureans:** Russell, "What I Believe," in *Why I Am Not a Christian* (London: Unwin, 1975), 43–69, this on 47.

295 **"We ought to stand up":** Bertrand Russell, "Why I Am Not a Christian," in *Why I Am Not a Christian* (London: Unwin, 1975), 13–26, this on 26.

296 **Writing to his lover:** Russell to Ottoline Morrell, quoted in Clark, *The Life of Bertrand Russell*, 303.

296 **Even some of his own:** Another letter from Russell to Ottoline Morrell, quoted in Clark, *The Life of Bertrand Russell*, 305.

296 **The Austrian writer Stefan Zweig:** Stefan Zweig, *The World of Yesterday*, trans. Anthea Bell (London: Pushkin, 2011), 25–26.

296 **In Hungary, when the young artist:** Béla Zombory-Moldován, *The Burning of the World: A Memoir of 1914*, trans. Peter Zombory-Moldovan (New York: New York Review Books, 2014), 6.

297 **In 1916, he was fined:** Ryan, *Bertrand Russell: A Political Life*, 61–62.

297 **In 1918, police came:** Clark, *The Life of Bertrand Russell*, 420–22. Russell's article was "The German Peace Offer."

297 **Recalling his prison experience:** Bertrand Russell, "Experiences of a Pacifist in the First World War," in *Portraits from Memory, and Other Essays* (London: Allen & Unwin, 1956), 30–34, this on 33–34.

297 **Once inside, Russell:** Russell, *Autobiography*, 256 ("though they"), 257 (Strachey).

297 **While he was still incarcerated:** Russell, *Autobiography*, 326.

298 **For all his jests:** Russell, *Autobiography*, 263.

298 **He did not abandon:** Bertrand Russell, "From Logic to Politics," in *Portraits from Memory, and Other Essays* (London: Allen & Unwin, 1956), 35–39, this on 35–36.

298 **On the contrary, he felt:** Russell, *Autobiography*, 261.

298 **In a series of wartime:** Russell, *Principles of Social Reconstruction*, 18.

299 **Tagore believed in giving:** Rabindranath Tagore, "The Modification of Education" (1892), in *Education as Freedom: Tagore's Paradigm*, trans. Subhransu Maitra (New Delhi: Niyogi Books, 2014), 27–40, this on 31.

299 **Scientific literacy helped protect:** Bertrand Russell, *Education and the Good Life* (New York: Boni & Liveright, 1926), 29–30 ("what the world might be"), 142–46 (changeable ideas).

299 **Starting with some twenty pupils:** Russell, *Education and the Good Life*, 78.

300 **It was a risky experiment:** Russell, *Autobiography*, 389–90.

300 Russell also believed: Russell, *Education and the Good Life*, 213.

300 He did point out: Russell, "What I Believe," 57.

300 One story had it that a journalist: Katharine Tait, *My Father Bertrand Russell* (London: Victor Gollancz, 1976), 71. Russell's biographer Ronald Clark tells a version of the story in which it was the local vicar who came to call, but he cites a letter from the vicar's son, who remembered his parents being relaxed about the Russells' naked children, letting them play in their garden or come into their kitchen, where the vicar's wife took advantage of the opportunity to tell them Bible stories. Clark, *The Life of Bertrand Russell*, 530.

300 Juicy tales of this kind: Russell, *Autobiography*, 460.

301 The matter came to court: Horace M. Kallen, "Behind the Bertrand Russell Case," in *The Bertrand Russell Case*, ed. H. M. Kallen and John Dewey (New York: Viking, 1941), 20.

301 Russell's family ran around naked: Paul Edwards, "How Bertrand Russell Was Prevented from Teaching at City College, New York," in Russell, *Why I Am Not a Christian* (London: Unwin, 1975), 165–99, this 173.

301 But Russell's lucky stars worked: Russell, *Autobiography*, 465. For the Barnes Foundation today, see https://www.barnesfoundation.org/.

301 Whereas the First World War: Ryan, *Bertrand Russell: A Political Life*, 67.

301 Hitler's ideology represented: Russell, *Education and the Good Life*, 267.

302 First, the language: Schor, *Bridge of Words*, 180.

302 If it hoped to placate: Ulrich Lins, *Dangerous Language: Esperanto under Hitler and Stalin* (London: Palgrave Macmillan, 2016), 95, 115 (views of Hitler and others), 116–17 (ban).

302 In 1935 all teaching of Esperanto: Boulton, *Zamenhof*, 208–9.

302 Ludwik Zamenhof's youngest daughter: For example, Lidia Zamenhof, "Nia Misio," *Esperanto Revuo*, no. 12 (December 1934). See Schor, *Bridge of Words*, 186. Lidia Zamenhof also became a devotee of the Bahá'í faith, which like *Homaranismo* espouses the idea of a universal religion that all can share.

302 She tried to get a visa: Schor, *Bridge of Words*, 193–95.

303 Adam's widow and son: Boulton, *Zamenhof*, 213–14.

303 And as Robert Ingersoll said: Ingersoll's text, "Hope," is found on the phonograph record at the Ingersoll Museum, Dresden, New York, available online at https://youtu .be/rLLapwIoEVI.

Chapter 11. The Human Face

304 Gentile, who was the author: Benito Mussolini and Giovanni Gentile's "La dottrina del fascismo" ("The Doctrine of Fascism") was published in 1932 in vol. 14 of the *Enciclopedia italiana*: part 1, "Fundamental Ideas," by Gentile (though signed by Mussolini); part 2, "Social and Political Doctrines," by Mussolini. All the lines quoted here are from *Readings on Fascism and National Socialism*, Project Gutenberg e-book, ed. Alan Swallow, 2004, https://www.gutenberg.org/files/14058/14058-h/14058-h.htm. It includes both Mussolini and Gentile, "The Doctrine of Fascism," and Gentile, "The Philosophic Basis of Fascism."

306 As Gentile wrote, Fascism offered: Gentile, "The Doctrine of Fascism."

306 Leon Trotsky, the Russian revolutionary: Leon Trotsky, *Literature and Revolution*, trans. Rose Strunsky (London: Redwords, 1991), 282–83.

306 In Italy, Gentile therefore organized: Fabio Fernando Rizi, *Benedetto Croce and Ital-*

ian Fascism (Toronto: University of Toronto Press, 2003), 52. On Gentile, see also A. James Gregor, *Giovanni Gentile: Philosopher of Fascism* (New Brunswick, NJ: Transaction, 2001).

306 **A similar educational program:** Erika Mann, *School for Barbarians* (New York: Modern Age Books, 1938), 47 (incapable of imagining), 99–100 (images of war).

307 **The philosopher Hannah Arendt:** Hannah Arendt, *The Origins of Totalitarianism* (London: Penguin, 2017), 614.

307 **It was education as transformed:** Erwin Panofsky, "The History of Art as a Humanistic Discipline," in *The Meaning of the Humanities*, ed. T. M. Greene (Princeton, NJ: Princeton University Press; London: Humphrey Milford/Oxford University Press, 1938), 89–118, this on 93.

307 **His move away from traditional:** Rizi, *Benedetto Croce and Italian Fascism*, 13.

308 **The disaster left Croce:** Cecil Sprigge, *Benedetto Croce: Man and Thinker* (Cambridge, UK: Bowes & Bowes, 1952), 12–17.

308 **His friendship with Gentile:** Benedetto Croce to Giovanni Gentile, October 24, 1924, translated in Rizi, *Benedetto Croce and Italian Fascism*, 75.

308 **As he put it in a letter:** Benedetto Croce to Alessandro Casati, October 1924, translated in Rizi, *Benedetto Croce and Italian Fascism*, 76.

308 **Croce responded with what became:** B. Croce, "A Reply by Italian Authors, Professors, and Journalists to the 'Manifesto' of the Fascist Intellectuals," in *From Kant to Croce: Modern Philosophy in Italy 1800–1950*, ed. and trans. Brian Copenhaver and Rebecca Copenhaver (Toronto: University of Toronto Press, 2012), 713–16, this on 714–15; Gentile's "Manifesto of Fascist Intellectuals," 706–12.

309 **After his protest, Croce retired:** Rizi, *Benedetto Croce and Italian Fascism*, 114–20.

309 **The important thing, he wrote:** Benedetto Croce, "History as the History of Liberty" (1937), in *Philosophy—Poetry—History: An Anthology of Essays,* trans. Cecil Sprigge (London: Oxford University Press, 1966), 546–88, this on 585–86.

309 **As Stefan Zweig wrote:** Stefan Zweig, *The World of Yesterday*, trans. Anthea Bell (London: Pushkin, 2011), 389.

310 **In that same year, 1934:** Stefan Zweig, *Erasmus* [and] *The Right to Heresy*, trans. Eden and Cedar Paul (London: Hallam/Cassell, 1951), 5. See also chap. 6, "Greatness and Limitations of Humanism," 67–88.

310 **He continued writing:** Stefan Zweig, *Montaigne*, trans. Will Stone (London: Pushkin, 2015).

311 **But Zweig did despair:** The suicide letter is included in "Publisher's Postscript," in Stefan Zweig, *The World of Yesterday*, ed. Harry Zohn (Lincoln: University of Nebraska Press, 1964), 437–40.

311 **In a radio tribute:** E. M. Forster, "Some Books" (talk given on the BBC's *We Speak to India*, March 4, 1942), in *The BBC Talks*, ed. Mary Lago, Linda K. Hughes, and Elizabeth MacLeod Walls (Columbia and London: University of Missouri Press, 2008), 172.

311 **As it happens, Forster himself:** Christopher Isherwood, *Down There on a Visit* (London: Vintage, 2012), 171.

311 **"There is something truly poignant":** Roger-Pol Droit, *Humanity in the Making: Overview of the Intellectual History of UNESCO, 1945–2005* (Paris: UNESCO, 2005), 40.

311 **Making notes on Zweig's book:** Thomas Mann, *Diaries 1918–1939*, ed. Hermann Kesten, trans. Richard and Clara Winston (London: André Deutsch, 1983), 222 (entry for Sunday, August 5, 1934).

311 **But humanists' failure:** Thomas Mann, "Europe Beware," trans. H. T. Lowe-Porter,

in *Order of the Day: Political Essays and Speeches of Two Decades* (New York: Alfred A. Knopf, 1942), 69–82, this on 82.

312 **His most direct treatment:** Thomas Mann, *Mario and the Magician and Other Stories* (Harmondsworth, UK: Penguin, 1975), 113–57.

313 **The young, Naphta says:** Thomas Mann, *The Magic Mountain*, trans. H. T. Lowe-Porter (Harmondsworth, UK: Penguin, 1960), 400 (obey), 522 (future of learning).

313 **One day, lost in a mountain blizzard:** Mann, *The Magic Mountain*, 497.

314 **writers had a moral duty:** Heinrich Mann presented this view influentially in "Zola," published in the journal *Die weissen Blätter* in 1915 and reprinted in his collection of essays on French writers *Geist und Tat: Franzosen 1780–1930* (Berlin: G. Kiepenheuer, 1931). See Karin Verena Gunnemann, *Heinrich Mann's Novels and Essays: The Artist as Political Educator* (Rochester, NY: Camden House, 2002), 79.

314 **At one speech in 1930:** Thomas Mann, "An Appeal to Reason" (talk given in Berlin, October 1930), trans. H. T. Lowe-Porter, in *Order of the Day*, 46–68, this on 54–56 (heckling); Tobias Boes, *Thomas Mann's War* (Ithaca, NY, and London: Cornell University Press, 2019), 85–86.

314 **Mann saved the blackened leaves:** Thomas Mann to Hermann Hesse, December 22, 1932, *The Hesse-Mann Letters*, ed. Anni Carlsson and Volker Michels, trans. Ralph Manheim (London: Arena, 1986), 16.

314 **One thing bothered him:** Erika Mann and Klaus Mann, *Escape to Life* (Boston: Houghton Mifflin, 1939), 6–7.

315 **Thus reunited with at least some:** Thomas Mann, "Achtung, Europa!" (April 1935), in *Achtung, Europa! Aufsätze zur Zeit* (Stockholm: Bermann-Fischer, 1938), 73–93.

316 **He continued writing novels:** Boes, *Thomas Mann's War*, 148–54. For MacLeish's opinions, see "Of the Librarian's Profession," *Atlantic Monthly* (June 1940), reprinted in *Champion of a Cause*, ed. Eva M. Goldschmidt (Chicago: ALA, 1971), 43–53.

316 **As well as her study:** Erika Mann, *The Lights Go Down*, trans. Maurice Samuel (London: Secker & Warburg, 1940), 239–81. A note states that a speech on art by Hitler, quoted in the *Frankfurter Zeitung*, July 17, 1939, did indeed contain thirty-three grammatical errors.

317 **One of the greatest experts:** On Kristeller's story, see Paul Oskar Kristeller and Margaret L. King, "Iter Kristellerianum: The European Journey (1904–1939)," *Renaissance Quarterly* 47 (1994), 907–29, this on 917–25.

318 **Then there was the art historian:** Jeffrey Chipps Smith, introduction to Erwin Panofsky, *The Life and Art of Albrecht Dürer* (Princeton, NJ: Princeton University Press, 2005), xxix–xxxi.

318 **Therefore, at the age of thirteen:** Max Warburg, memorial address of December 5, 1929, quoted in E. H. Gombrich, *Aby Warburg: An Intellectual Biography*, 2nd ed. (Oxford, UK: Phaidon, 1986), 22.

319 **Toward the end of his life:** Aby Warburg, *Bilderatlas Mnemosyne*, ed. Axel Heil and Roberto Ohrt (Stuttgart and Berlin: Hatje Cantz, 2020). Two online exhibitions featuring the panels were held in 2020, at London's Warburg Institute and Berlin's Haus der Kulturen der Welt: https://warburg.sas.ac.uk/collections/warburg-institute-archive/bilderatlas-mnemosyne/mnemosyne-atlas-october-1929 and https://www.hkw.de/en/programm/projekte/2020/aby_warburg/bilderatlas_mnemosyne_start.php.

319 **In 1920, after a tour:** Fritz Saxl, "Ernst Cassirer," in *The Philosophy of Ernst Cassirer*, ed. P. A. Schilpp (La Salle, IL: Open Court, 1949), 47–48.

320 **In a feat of organization:** On the move: Fritz Saxl, "The History of Warburg's Li-

brary," in E. H. Gombrich, *Aby Warburg: An Intellectual Biography*, 2nd ed. (Oxford, UK: Phaidon, 1986), 325–38, this on 336–37. The idea owed much to the suggestion of Dr. Raymond Klibansky of Heidelberg University; it was organized by the two chief curators, Fritz Saxl and Gertrud Bing.

320 The two institutes jointly launched: *Prospectus of the Journal of the Warburg Institute*, London, 1937 ("study of Humanism"), and "Memo Regarding the Warburg Institute: How to Get It Known in England," May 30, 1934, both cited in Elizabeth McGrath, "Disseminating Warburgianism: The Role of the 'Journal of the Warburg and Courtauld Institutes,'" in *The Afterlife of the Kulturwissenschaftliche Bibliothek Warburg*, ed. U. Fleckner and P. Mack (Berlin and Boston: De Gruyter, 2015), 39–50, this on 43–44. The *Prospectus* is reproduced in illustration 2.

321 the ceramicist and sculptor: https://warburg.sas.ac.uk/about/news/warburg-institute -receive-major-gift-edmund-de-waal.

321 When the Nazis started burning books: Nikola van Merveldt, "Books Cannot Be Killed by Fire," *Library Trends* 55, no. 3 (Winter 2007), 523–35, https://milholmbc .weebly.com/uploads/3/8/0/7/38071703/bookscannotbekilledbyfire.pdf.

321 Elsewhere, microfilm photographers: Kathy Peiss, *Information Hunters* (New York: Oxford University Press, 2020), 43.

322 The literary critic Marcel Reich-Ranicki: Marcel Reich-Ranicki, *The Author of Himself: The Life*, trans. Ewald Osers (London: Weidenfeld & Nicolson, 2001), 68–70.

323 More was to come: Thomas Mann, *Listen, Germany! Twenty-five Radio Messages to the German People over BBC* (New York: Alfred A. Knopf, 1943), v–vi. See also Boes, *Thomas Mann's War*, 168–69.

323 Sometimes, in these recordings: Mann, *Listen, Germany!*, 69 (January 1942), 98 (June 1942).

323 "Mankind cannot accept the ultimate triumph": Mann, *Listen, Germany!*, 33 (April 1941).

324 As the American art historian: Frederick Hartt, *Florentine Art under Fire* (Princeton, NJ: Princeton University Press, 1949), 45.

324 Karl Marx had begun: For the alienation theory, see Karl Marx, *Economic and Philosophical Manuscripts of 1844*, ed. Dirk J. Struik, trans. Martin Milligan (New York: International Publishers, 1964), 108. First published in 1932, the book was edited together from various manuscripts written during Marx's twenties in Paris.

324 In China, home of *ren*: Frank Dikötter, *The Cultural Revolution: A People's History, 1962–1976* (London: Bloomsbury, 2017), 89–91.

325 Confucianism itself was suppressed: This happened in November 1966. See Sang Ye and Geremie R. Barmé, "Commemorating Confucius in 1966–67," *China Heritage Quarterly*, no. 20 (December 2009), http://www.chinaheritagequarterly.org/scholarship .php?searchterm=020_confucius.inc&issue=020.

325 Instead, a terrible puritanism: Dikötter, *The Cultural Revolution*, 94.

325 And there were deaths: This is a widely accepted figure given by Yang Jisheng in *The Great Chinese Famine, 1958–1962*, trans. Stacy Mosher and Guo Jian (New York: Farrar, Straus & Giroux, 2012).

325 The popular, mostly humorous novelist: Ranbir Vohra, *Lao She and the Chinese Revolution* (Cambridge, UK: East Asian Research Center, 1974), 163–65, especially 164, quoting the interview with Lao She in 1966 by a visiting couple, Roma and Stuart Gelder. They included it in their book *Memories for a Chinese Grand-Daughter* (New York: Stein & Day, 1968), 182–95.

325 **Another regime of extreme nihilism:** For the various estimates, see https://en.wikipedia
.org/wiki/Cambodian_genocide.

326 **As the writer and filmmaker Rithy Panh:** Rithy Panh and Christophe Bataille, *The Elimination*, trans. John Cullen (New York: Other Press, 2012), 142.

326 **Rithy Panh's 2013 film:** Rithy Panh and Christophe Bataille, *The Missing Picture* [*L'image manquante*], Catherine Dussart Productions, 2013.

326 **The novelist William Golding said:** William Golding, "Fable," in *The Hot Gates* (London: Faber & Faber, 1970), 87 ("anyone who moved"), 94 (spirit of the times).

327 **It is shocking to read:** The twenty-six-year-old law student Heinz Küchler, in a letter of September 6, 1941, quoted and translated in Omer Bartov, *Hitler's Army* (New York: Oxford University Press, 1991), 116. The line was also quoted in David Livingstone Smith, *Less Than Human* (New York: St. Martin's Press, 2011), 141.

327 **And, as Thomas Mann asked:** Thomas Mann to Walter von Molo, September 7, 1945, in Thomas Mann, *Letters, 1889–1955*, ed. and trans. Richard and Clara Winston (London: Secker & Warburg, 1970), vol. 2, 482.

327 **This was why the philosopher:** Theodor Adorno, "Cultural Criticism and Society" (1951), in *Prisms*, trans. Samuel and Shierry Weber (Cambridge, MA: MIT Press, 1981), 17–34, this on 34.

327 **The idea behind this oft-quoted remark:** Theodor Adorno and Max Horkheimer, *Dialectic of Enlightenment*, trans. John Cumming (London and New York: Verso, 1997). See, for example, 24, for their critique of the Enlightenment as being "as totalitarian as any system." The work was written in 1944 and expanded in 1947.

328 **In fact, some religious humanists:** Jacques Maritain, *True Humanism* (New York: Charles Scribner's Sons, 1938), 19. The book is based on lectures delivered at the University of Santander, Spain, in August 1934.

328 **In 1950, *Partisan Review* ran:** *Partisan Review*, February–May/June 1950; this from February 1950, 103.

329 **non-religious activists arranged:** "Assault of the Humanists," *Elseviers Weekblad* (1952), trans. in Hans van Deukeren et al., "From History to Practice—A History of IHEU, 1952–2002," in *International Humanist and Ethical Union, 1952–2002*, ed. Bert Gasenbeek and Babu Gogineni (Utrecht: De Tijdstroom, 2002), 16–104, this on 26.

329 **He set out his postwar anti-humanist position:** Martin Heidegger, "Letter on 'Humanism,'" in *Pathmarks*, ed. W. McNeill, trans. Frank A. Capuzzi (Cambridge, UK: Cambridge University Press, 1998), 239–76, this on 247, 260 (call of Being), 252 (not God). "Being" is not always rendered with a capital B in English translation, because in German all nouns are spelled with an initial capital letter anyway, but there is an important distinction between *Sein* ("Being") and *Seiende* ("beings") that could be lost in English without the capital to flag it.

329 **Sartre's own position:** Jean-Paul Sartre, *Existentialism and Humanism*, trans. Philip Mairet (London: Methuen, 2007), 38. The French published title was slightly different: *L'Existentialisme est un humanisme* (1946, based on Sartre's lecture of 1945). Although radically free, we are also supposed to make moral and political commitments to others.

330 **In 1966, Michel Foucault:** Michel Foucault, *The Order of Things* (London and New York: Routledge, 2002), 422 ("erased"), 420 (Enlightenment).

330 **The postcolonial thinker:** Frantz Fanon, *The Wretched of the Earth*, trans. Constance Farrington (London: Penguin, 1967), 251.

330 **Yet Fanon, too, approached:** All quotations in this paragraph are from Fanon, *The Wretched of the Earth*, 252–54.

331 **Assessing these currents of thought:** Longxi Zhang, "Humanism Yet Once More: A View from the Other Side," in *Humanism in Intercultural Perspective: Experiences and Expectations*, ed. Jörn Rüsen and Henner Laass (Bielefeld, Germany: Transcript, 2009), 225–31, this on 228.

331 **"I undertook this project":** Panh and Bataille, *The Elimination*, 268.

331 **Benedetto Croce had also stressed:** Benedetto Croce, "Progress as a State of Mind and Progress as Philosophic Concept," in *Philosophy—Poetry—History: An Anthology of Essays*, trans. Cecil Sprigge (London: Oxford University Press, 1966), 589–94, this on 589–92.

332 **In pursuit of this goal:** His Majesty's Stationery Office, "The Basic Principle of the Curriculum," in *The Norwood Report: Curriculum and Examinations in Secondary Schools* (London: His Majesty's Stationery Office, 1943), 55, http://www.educationengland .org.uk/documents/norwood/norwood1943.html.

332 **In the United States:** Harvard Committee, *General Education in a Free Society* (Cambridge, MA: Harvard University Press, 1945), 168–69, https://archive.org/details /generaleducation032440mbp/page/n5.

332 **The largest of all:** H. J. Blackham, *The Human Tradition* (London: Routledge & Kegan Paul, 1953), 50.

332 **Its Erasmian founding text stated:** *Constitution of the United Nations Educational, Scientific and Cultural Organization, signed at London, on 16 November 1945*: Preamble, https://treaties.un.org/doc/Publication/UNTS/Volume%204/volume-4-I-52 -English.pdf.

333 **Its conception was strongly humanistic:** Ronald W. Clark, *The Huxleys* (London: Heinemann, 1968), 310–12; Julian Huxley, *UNESCO: Its Purpose and Its Philosophy* [*L'Unesco: Ses buts et sa philosophie*] (London: Preparatory Commission, 1946; [facsimile edition] London: Euston Grove, 2010).

333 **As he wrote in his memoirs:** Julian Huxley, *Memories* (Harmondsworth, UK: Penguin, 1972, 1978), vol. 2, 30–31.

333 **Unfortunately, the effect could not:** Huxley, *Memories*, vol. 2, 22.

333 **Then there was the matter of wording:** United Nations, *Universal Declaration of Human Rights*, article 1, https://www.un.org/en/universal-declaration-human-rights/. On the process, see M. A. Glendon, *A World Made New: Eleanor Roosevelt and the Universal Declaration of Human Rights* (New York: Random House, 2001), especially 68, 90, for these particular discussions. See also Lynn Hunt, *Inventing Human Rights: A History* (New York and London: W. W. Norton, 2007).

334 **The first draft originally spoke:** Sumner Twiss, "Confucian Ethics, Concept-Clusters, and Human Rights," in *Polishing the Chinese Mirror: Essays in Honor of Henry Rosemont, Jr.*, ed. M. Chandler and R. Littlejohn (New York: Global Scholarly Publications, 2007), 50–67, this on 60.

334 **The result of all these negotiations:** Geraldine Van Bueren, "I Am Because You Are," *Times Literary Supplement*, Human Rights Special Feature, December 21–28, 2018, 5–6.

335 **Those words, said Mann:** Mann, *Listen, Germany!*, 71 (January 1942).

335 **Often, he followed in the steps:** Damiano Fedele, "Cesare Fasola, il partigiano che salvò la Primavera di Botticelli," *Il Fiesolano*, April 25, 2020, https://www.ilfiesolano

.it/persone/cesare-fasola-il-partigiano-che-salvo-la-primavera-di-botticelli/. See also Eric Linklater, *The Art of Adventure* (London: Macmillan, 1947), 260–63.

336 **He and Hartt were among the first:** Hartt, *Florentine Art under Fire*, 18–19. The Montegufoni works are described and listed in Osbert Sitwell, *Laughter in the Next Room* (London: Macmillan, 1949), 350–64.

336 **One of the Allied visitors:** Linklater, *The Art of Adventure*, 266–67.

336 **This at least was the case:** David Hapgood and David Richardson, *Monte Cassino* (New York: Congdon & Weed, 1984), 13.

336 **A member of the crew for this second bombing:** Walter M. Miller Jr., *A Canticle for Leibowitz* (Philadelphia: Lippincott, 1959; London: Orbit, 2019), 26. See William H. Roberson and Robert L. Battenfeld, *Walter M. Miller, Jr.: A Bio-Bibliography* (Westport, CT: Greenwood Press, 1992), 1–2.

337 **Similar destruction almost happened:** http://www.friendsofchartres.org/about /chartres/colonelwelborngriffith/ and https://valor.militarytimes.com/hero/6100%7C title=Militarytimes. See also https://www.washingtonexaminer.com/the-american -hero-who-saved-chartres-cathedral.

338 **As Jean-Paul Sartre put it:** Jean-Paul Sartre, "The End of the War," in *The Aftermath of War (Situations 3)*, trans. C. Turner (London: Seagull, 2008), 65–75, this on 65.

338 **"There lies before us":** Bertrand Russell, "Man's Peril" (December 23, 1954), in *Portraits from Memory, and Other Essays* (London: Allen & Unwin, 1956), 215–20, this on 220.

339 **He repeated it in another:** The Pugwash manifesto is online at https://pugwash .org/1955/07/09/statement-manifesto/.

339 **After one such occasion:** Russell, *Autobiography* (London and New York: Routledge, 1998), 609.

339 **Russell worked for many other causes:** Bertrand Russell, *Authority and the Individual (The Reith Lectures, 1948–49)* (London: Allen & Unwin, 1949), 93.

339 **Around the same time, Julian Huxley:** https://en.wikipedia.org/wiki/International _Union_for_Conservation_of_Nature.

339 **One part of nature almost:** Russell, *Autobiography*, 511–12; 537. On the crash, see https://en.wikipedia.org/wiki/Bukken_Bruse_disaster.

340 **In an autobiographical talk:** Bertrand Russell, "Hopes: Realized and Disappointed," in *Portraits from Memory, and Other Essays* (London: Allen & Unwin, 1956), 45–49, this on 47.

341 **"I may have thought":** Russell, *Autobiography*, 728.

CHAPTER 12. THE PLACE TO BE HAPPY

342 **During the crisis of the 1930s:** Edwin H. Wilson, *The Genesis of a Humanist Manifesto*, ed. Teresa Maciocha (Amherst, NY: Humanist Press [American Humanist Association], 1995), 23 (Raymond B. Bragg, letter of February 17, 1970, "humanist blast"), 63 (Buschman), 83 (Schiller).

343 **Although the manifesto called:** The 1933 manifesto is online at https://en.wikipedia .org/wiki/Humanist_Manifesto_I.

343 ***The Bristol Press* in Connecticut:** Wilson, *The Genesis of a Humanist Manifesto*, 108–9.

344 **In the postwar years:** A good overview of international humanist societies and their origins, in the UK and internationally, can be found in Jim Herrick, *Humanism: An Introduction*, 2nd ed. (London: Rationalist Press Association, 2009), 123–58. For a history

of humanist organizations in the UK, see Callum Brown, David Nash, and Charlie Lynch, *The Humanist Movement in Modern Britain: A History of Ethicists, Rationalists and Humanists* (London: Bloomsbury, 2022).

344 **The most flamboyant:** J. B. H. Wadia, *M. N. Roy the Man: An Incomplete Royana* (London: Sangam, 1983), 10.

344 **But he became disillusioned:** M. N. Roy, *New Humanism: A Manifesto* (Delhi: Ajanta, 1981), 41.

344 **As Bertrand Russell remarked:** Bertrand Russell, "The Triumph of Stupidity" (May 10, 1933), in *Mortals and Others* (London and New York: Routledge, 2009), 203.

344 **Roy's manifesto prominently featured:** Roy, *New Humanism*, 43.

345 **According to an entertaining account:** Hans van Deukeren et al., "From History to Practice—A History of IHEU, 1952–2002," in *International Humanist and Ethical Union, 1952–2002*, ed. Bert Gasenbeek and Babu Gogineni (Utrecht: De Tijdstroom, 2002), 16–104, this on 21.

345 **The latest version, issued by Humanists International in 2022:** The "Declaration of Modern Humanism," ratified at the Humanists International General Assembly, Glasgow, United Kingdom, 2022, is in the Appendix of this book, and online: https://humanists.international/policy/declaration-of-modern-humanism/. The 1952 "Amsterdam Declaration," ratified at the World Humanist Congress of 1952, is online: https://humanists.international/policy/amsterdam-declaration-1952/. Between these two, there were revised Amsterdam Declarations in 1975 and 2002.

347 **"We aim for our fullest":** American Humanist Association, "Humanist Manifesto III, a Successor to the Humanist Manifesto of 1933," 2003, https://americanhumanist.org/what-is-humanism/manifesto3/. For AHA's history: https://americanhumanist.org/about/our-history.

347 **The Black American humanist:** Debbie Goddard, quoted in "Celebrating the Diverse Spirituality and Religion of African-Americans," *Huffington Post*, February 17, 2004, https://www.huffpost.com/entry/diverse-african-american-religion_n_4762315.

348 **Goddard decided to work toward:** https://en.wikipedia.org/wiki/Debbie_Goddard, citing Brandon Withrow, "What It's Like to Be Black and Atheist," *Daily Beast*, November 19, 2016, https://www.thedailybeast.com/what-its-like-to-be-black-and-atheist. On the complexities of atheism and/or humanism in Black communities, see also https://en.wikipedia.org/wiki/Atheism_in_the_African_diaspora.

348 **In return, as a 2001 declaration:** AAH, "An African-American Humanist Declaration," in Anthony B. Pinn, ed., *By These Hands: A Documentary History of African American Humanism* (New York and London: New York University Press, 2001), 319–26, this on 326.

348 **humanists of color:** U.S.: https://www.blackhumanists.org/about-the-bha. UK: https://en.wikipedia.org/wiki/Association_of_Black_Humanists.

348 **The poem was certainly shocking:** James Kirkup's "The Love That Dares to Speak Its Name" can be found at https://www.pinknews.co.uk/2008/01/10/the-gay-poem-that-broke-blasphemy-laws/.

349 **The previous one had been:** https://en.wikipedia.org/wiki/John_William_Gott.

349 **After the case, he would:** https://www.channel4.com/news/archbishop-admits-church-failed-terribly-over-abuse-revelations.

349 **The poet himself avoided:** Tania Branigan, "I Am Being Used, Claims Blasphemy Trial Poet," *Guardian*, July 11, 2002, https://www.theguardian.com/uk/2002/jul/11/books.booksnews.

349 But no literary testimony was heard: "Blasphemy at the Old Bailey," *Everyman*, BBC, 1977.

349 He would later recall: Quoted in John Mortimer, *Murderers and Other Friends* (London: Penguin, 1995), 87.

350 The implication, as John Mortimer wrote: Mortimer, *Murderers and Other Friends*, 88.

350 Meanwhile, with all the publicity: "Blasphemy at the Old Bailey."

350 Therefore, gay humanists decided: http://www.lgbthumanists.org.uk/history/.

350 In honor of its origin: My thanks to Andrew Copson for telling me this.

350 In the United States: https://en.wikipedia.org/wiki/Blasphemy_law_in_the_United _States.

350 An international "End Blasphemy Laws Now" campaign: End Blasphemy Laws Now: https://end-blasphemy-laws.org/. Secular Rescue: David Robson, "The 'Underground Railroad' to Save Atheists," *Atlantic*, January 18, 2018, https://www.theatlantic.com /international/archive/2018/01/the-underground-railroad-to-save-atheists/550229 /. Secular Rescue's website is here: www.secular-rescue.org; see also https://www.center forinquiry.net/newsroom/center_for_inquiry_launches_secular_rescue_to_save_lives _of_threatened_acti/.

351 All this lies at the most dramatic end: For example, for the campaigns of Humanists UK, see their list at https://humanists.uk/campaigns/.

351 In Britain, Humanists UK has some: https://humanists.uk/campaigns/secularism /constitutional-reform/bishops-in-the-lords/.

351 Both there and in the House of Commons: On the problem of reserving a seat: https://www.secularism.org.uk/news/2020/01/calls-for-parliamentary-prayers -review-after-mp-compelled-to-attend. For the form of prayers: https://www.parliament .uk/about/how/business/prayers/.

351 The option to choose: G. W. Foote, *Reminiscences of Charles Bradlaugh* (London: Progressive, 1891), 35. On Bradlaugh, see also Charles Bradlaugh, *The True Story of My Parliamentary Struggle* (London: Freethought, 1882); Bryan Niblett, *Dare to Stand Alone: The Story of Charles Bradlaugh* (Oxford, UK: Kramedart, 2010); David Tribe, *President Charles Bradlaugh, M.P.* (London: Elek, 1971); John Robertson, *Charles Bradlaugh* (London: Watts, 1920).

353 Thomas Jefferson, for example: Thomas Jefferson, *Notes on the State of Virginia* (1787) (Baltimore: W. Pechin, 1800), 160.

353 Some of the most conspicuous: https://en.wikipedia.org/wiki/Pledge_of_Allegiance.

353 "In God We Trust": https://en.wikipedia.org/wiki/In_God_We_Trust.

353 A quietly determined activist: Vashti Cromwell McCollum, *One Woman's Fight* (Garden City, NY: Doubleday, 1951; rev. ed. Boston: Beacon Press, 1961; Madison, WI: Freedom From Religion Foundation, 1993), 86 (cabbage), 85 ("ATHIST"), 101 ("May your rotten soul"), 104 ("Well, it's a cinch"). See also Jay Rosenstein's documentary, in which McCollum and her sons are interviewed: *God Is Not on Trial Here Today* (*McCollum v. Board of Education*), Jay Rosenstein Productions, 2010: http://jayrosenstein.com/pages /lord.html. It can be found online at https://youtu.be/EeSHLnrgaqY. See also https:// en.wikipedia.org/wiki/Vashti_McCollum and her obituary, http://www.nytimes.com /2006/08/26/obituaries/26mccullum.html.

354 In the UK, a similar outcry: Margaret Knight, *Morals without Religion, and Other Essays* (London: Dennis Dobson, 1955), 22–23 ("She looks"), 16–17 (Russell, and speaking openly). On opposition within the BBC, see Callum G. Brown, *The Battle for Christian Britain* (Cambridge, UK: Cambridge University Press, 2019), 139–40.

354 **This was why both British and American:** Bishopsgate Institute Library, London: BHA papers. BHA 1/17/148, on the bus campaign, including a BHA report, "Atheist Bus Campaign: Why Did It Work?" BHA 1/17/149, correspondence and messages concerning the campaign, 2008–2009. See also https://humanism.org.uk/campaigns /successful-campaigns/atheist-bus-campaign/.

356 **"I would not, by word":** Zora Neale Hurston, *Dust Tracks on a Road*, reprinted in *Folklore, Memoirs, and Other Writings* (New York: Library of America, 1995), 764.

356 **Julian Huxley wrote:** Julian Huxley, *Religion without Revelation* (London: Ernest Benn, 1927), 358.

357 **"If a man knows the theory":** Anton Chekhov to Alexei Suvorin, May 15, 1889, translated in *Anton Chekhov's Life and Thought: Selected Letters and Commentary*, trans. Michael Henry Heim, ed. Simon Karlinsky (Evanston, IL: Northwestern University Press, 1997), 145. The song is by Mikhail Glinka, a setting to music of words by Pushkin. You can hear Galina Vishnevskaya singing it here: https://www.youtube.com /watch?v=ymfoXrdWVQM&ab_channel=GalinaVishnevskaya-Topic.

357 **In 1968, the doyen:** H. J. Blackham, *Humanism* (Harmondsworth, UK: Pelican, 1968), 159.

358 **Geoffrey Scott, author of the influential:** Geoffrey Scott, *The Architecture of Humanism* (London: Constable, 1914), 211–15 (bodily sense), 235 ("for physical conditions").

358 **These goals drove:** Jane Jacobs, *The Death and Life of Great American Cities* (New York: Random House, 1961, 1989), 50, 55, 83.

359 **The work of Jacobs influenced:** Annie Matan and Peter Newman, *People Cities: The Life and Legacy of Jan Gehl* (Washington, DC, and Covelo, CA: Island Press, 2016), 14–15 (including reproduction of a picture of him in an Ascoli Piceno newspaper, captioned "Sembra ma non è un 'beatnik'"), 18 ("act of vandalism"; this project was in 1969). See also Jan Gehl, *Cities for People* (Washington, DC: Island Press, 2010), which includes pictures of people dwarfed or squeezed aside by cars and roads.

359 **"He said—and no one":** Leonid Sergeyevich Madyarov speaking, in Vasily Grossman, *Life and Fate*, trans. Robert Chandler (London: Vintage, 2006), 267.

360 **As another character:** From the testament of Ikonnikov-Morzh, in Grossman, *Life and Fate*, 393.

361 **When he began *Life and Fate*:** On the story of its rescue: Robert Chandler, introduction to Grossman, *Life and Fate*, xvii–xix; Robert Chandler, introduction to "Late Stories," in Vasily Grossman, *The Road*, trans. Robert and Elizabeth Chandler with Olga Mukovnikova (London: Maclehose/Quercus, 2011), 197. See also https://en.wikipedia .org/wiki/Life_and_Fate.

362 **It was immediately hailed:** The comparison with Chekhov's stories is made by Robert Chandler in the introduction to his translation of Grossman's *Life and Fate*, xii–xiii.

362 **Every time a person dies:** Grossman, *Life and Fate*, 539 ("the stars"), 201 (machine, Fascism).

363 **Jaron Lanier, himself a pioneer:** Jaron Lanier, *You Are Not a Gadget: A Manifesto* (London: Allen Lane/Penguin, 2010), 32.

363 **To see this demeaning thought:** George Eliot, "Shadows of the Coming Race," *Impressions of Theophrastus Such* (Edinburgh and London: W. Blackwood, 1879), 299–309, this on 307.

363 **These days some think that:** https://www.theguardian.com/environment/2016/aug/31/domestic-chicken-anthropocene-humanity-influenced-epoch. See also Jeremy Davies, *The Birth of the Anthropocene* (Oakland: University of California Press, 2016). On the idea that the concept gives us too much importance, see Peter Brannen, "The Anthropocene Is a Joke," *Atlantic*, August 13, 2019, https://www.theatlantic.com/science/archive/2019/08/arrogance-anthropocene/595795/.

364 **Contemplating this, some human beings:** http://www.vhemt.org/. See also https://www.theguardian.com/lifeandstyle/2020/jan/10/i-campaign-for-the-extinction-of-the-human-race-les-knight. Posthumanism: The term was first defined in 1977 by the literary theorist Ihab Hassan, who said, "We need to understand that five hundred years of humanism may be coming to an end, as humanism transforms itself into something that we must helplessly call posthumanism." Ihab Hassan, "Prometheus as Performer: toward a Posthumanist Culture? A University Masque in Five Scenes," *Georgia Review* 31, no. 4 (Winter 1977), 830–50, this on 843. See also David Roden, *Posthuman Life: Philosophy at the Edge of the Human* (London and New York: Routledge, 2015).

364 **Posthumanism has a benign air:** For similar remarks, see James Lovelock and Bryan Appleyard, *Novacene* (London: Penguin, 2020), 56.

364 **It is not all that remote:** David C. Barker and David H. Bearce, "End-Times Theology, the Shadow of the Future, and Public Resistance to Addressing Global Climate Change," *Political Research Quarterly* 66, no. 2 (June 2013), 267–79.

364 **In a 2016 survey:** https://climatecommunication.yale.edu/publications/global-warming-god-end-times/.

365 **In the stage after that:** Ray Kurzweil, *The Singularity Is Near: When Humans Transcend Biology* (London: Duckworth, 2005), 15. On transhumanism, see also https://humanityplus.org/philosophy/transhumanist-declaration/ and Max More and Natasha Vita-More, eds., *The Transhumanist Reader* (Oxford, UK: Wiley, 2013).

365 **The story begins:** Arthur C. Clarke, *Childhood's End* (London: Pan, 1956), 122.

365 **A few people resist:** Clarke, *Childhood's End*, 159.

366 **Such an ending for humanity:** Clarke, *Childhood's End*, 178.

366 **He goes where Dante went:** "Trasumanar significar *per verba* / non si poria." Dante, *Paradiso*, trans. Robin Kirkpatrick (London: Penguin, 2007), 6–7 (canto 1, lines 70–71). On these lines, see Prue Shaw, *Reading Dante* (New York and London: Liveright/W. W. Norton, 2015), 245–46.

367 **"One is responsible to life":** James Baldwin, "Down at the Cross," in *Collected Essays*, ed. Toni Morrison (New York: Library of America, 1998), 339 (part of *The Fire Next Time*, 1963; originally published in *The New Yorker*, November 17, 1962).

367 **"Humanism is a frail craft":** Tzvetan Todorov, *Duties and Delights: The Life of a Go-Between. Interviews with Catherine Portevin*, trans. Gila Walker (London, New York, and Calcutta: Seagull Books, 2008), 264.

368 **"Happiness is the only good":** Robert Ingersoll's happiness credo, from *An Oration on the Gods* (January 29, 1872) (Cairo, IL: Daily Bulletin Steam Book & Job Print, 1873), 48. Also in the 1899 recorded version, found online at https://youtu.be/rLLapwIoEVI.

List of Illustrations

Page 83: Opening lines of Pietro Bembo, *De Aetna*, Venice: Aldus Manutius, 1496. (The Picture Art Collection / Alamy Stock Photo)

Page 85: Desiderius Erasmus, *Erasmi Roterodami adagiorum chiliades tres*, Venice: Aldus Manutius, 1508. (Bridgeman Images)

Page 87: Lorenzo Valla. Engraving by Johann Theodor de Bry, from Jean-Jacques Boissard's *Bibliotheca chalcographica*, Frankfurt, 1650. (© Florilegius / Bridgeman Images)

Page 101: Platina and Pope Sixtus IV with the Vatican Library collection, by Melozzo da Forlì. (Alinari / Bridgeman Images)

Page 108 (top left): Vitruvius, *De architectura*, 1521, illustration by Cesare Cesariano. (The Stapleton Collection / Bridgeman Images)

Page 108 (top right): Geoffroy Tory, *Champ fleury*, 1529, showing letter from the font Tory designed for Jean Grolier. (© British Library Board. All Rights Reserved / Bridgeman Images)

Page 108 (center right): Francesco di Giorgio Martini, *Trattato di architettura civile e militare*, circa 1470, from the Biblioteca Nazionale, Florence, showing church design corresponding to the human figure. (The Picture Art Collection / Alamy Stock Photos)

Page 108 (bottom right): The humanist "Happy Human" symbol, in the slightly rounded variant. (Humanists UK)

Page 108 (bottom left): Leonardo da Vinci, *Vitruvian Man*, circa 1490, from the Gallerie dell'Accademia, Venice. (The Stapleton Collection / Bridgeman Images)

Page 112: Girolamo Savonarola. Line engraving by H. Hondius. (Wellcome Collection)

Page 113: Savonarola preaching in the pulpit of the cathedral of Florence, from his tract *Compendio di revelatione*, Florence: Pietro Pacini da Pescia, 1496, fol. i r. (Universal History Archive / UIG / Bridgeman Images)

Page 122: Girolamo Fracastoro. Line engraving by N. de Larmessin, 1682. (Wellcome Collection)

Page 128 (top): Anatomical theater at Padua, diorama. (Wellcome Collection. Attribution 4.0 International [CC BY 4.0])

Page 128 (bottom): The motto "Here death delights in helping life," from the anatomical theater at Padua. (Sarah Bakewell)

Page 129: A man seated in a chair in a landscape, holding an open book, directing a dissection that is taking place in the foreground, circa 1493. (Wellcome Collection)

Page 130: Vesalius's copy of Galen on respiration, with signature "And. Vesalius" on the title page. *Libri V jam primum in latinam linguam conversi / Jano Cornario medico interprete. De causis respirationis, liber I. De utilitate respirationis, liber I. De difficultate respirationis libri III*, Basel, 1536. (Wellcome Collection. Attribution 4.0 International [CC BY 4.0])

Page 131: Andreas Vesalius. Woodcut, 1543, after J. S. van Calcar (?). (Wellcome Collection)

Page 133: Andreas Vesalius, *De humani corporis fabrica libri septem*, p. 164, Basel, 1543. (Wellcome Collection)

Page 139: Rodolphus Agricola. Portrait by Lucas Cranach the Elder, Alte Pinakothek, Munich. (Bridgeman Images)

Page 141: Desiderius Erasmus. Portrait drawing, circa 1795, after H. Holbein. (Wellcome Collection)

Page 150: Two fifteenth-century armored knights. Lithograph from Paul Lacroix, *Les arts au Moyen Âge et à l'époque de la Renaissance*, Paris: Firmin Didot, 1873. (Bridgeman Images)

Page 154: Michel de Montaigne. Portrait by unknown artist, seventeenth century. (Bridgeman Images)

Page 155: Michel de Montaigne, *Essais*, Paris: Abel L'Angelier, 1588, copy with author's amendments ("Bordeaux Copy"), from Bibliothèque Municipal de Bordeaux, via Gustave Lanson, *Histoire illustré de la littérature française*, Paris and London: Hachette, 1923, vol. 1. (Lebrecht Authors / Bridgeman Images)

Page 164: Earthquake at Lisbon, 1755. (GRANGER—Historical Picture Archive)

Page 166: Voltaire writing, after a sketch by D. N. Chodowiecki. Vignette from German edition of Voltaire's *Candide*, 1778. (The Picture Art Collection / Alamy Stock Photo)

Page 176: Comet of 1680–1681. Print by Jan Luyken, Amsterdam, 1698. (Artokoloro / Alamy Stock Photo)

Page 180: Lamoignon de Malesherbes. Engraved portrait. (Ivy Close Images / Alamy Stock Photo)

Page 186: David Hume. Engraving based on a portrait by Allan Ramsay in the National Gallery of Scotland. Photographer: Oxford Science Archive / Heritage Images. (The Print Collector / Alamy Stock Photo)

Page 201: Amelia Bloomer wearing bloomers, from *The Illustrated London News*, September 27, 1851. (Look and Learn / Illustrated Papers Collection / Bridgeman Images)

Page 205: Jeremy Bentham. Etching by G. W. Appleton after R. M. Sully. (Wellcome Collection)

Page 212: Frederick Douglass. Daguerreotype portrait, circa 1855. (GRANGER—Historical Picture Archive)

Page 216: Edward Carpenter and George Merrill. (Prismatic Pictures / Bridgeman Images)

Page 224: Wilhelm von Humboldt. Engraved portrait. (© SZ Photo / Scherl / Bridgeman Images)

Page 233 (top): Harriet Taylor Mill, portrait by unknown artist, circa 1834, in the National Portrait Gallery, London. (GRANGER—Historical Picture Archive / Alamy Stock Photo)

Page 233 (bottom): John Stuart Mill, circa 1865. (GRANGER—Historical Picture Archive)

Page 237: "Mill's Logic; or, Franchise for Females," cartoon showing John Stuart Mill with Lydia Ernestine Becker and others, by John Tenniel, from *Punch*, March 30, 1867. (Photo 12 / Alamy Stock Photo)

Page 241: Matthew Arnold. Illustration captioned "Sweetness and Light," showing him as a trapeze artist moving between poetry and philosophy. Drawing by Frederick Waddy, 1873, for *Cartoon Portraits and Biographical Sketches of Men of the Day*. (© Look and Learn / Bridgeman Images)

Page 252: Thomas Henry Huxley. Cartoon showing him giving School Board Lecture, with a poster labeled "Genus Homo: Learned Baby." Lithograph, 1871. (Wellcome Collection)

Index

Note: Italicized page numbers indicate material in photographs or illustrations.